TOTAL WAR 2006

Simon Pearson was born in Aberdeen in 1961. He joined the RAF as a navigator in 1980 and flew in Germany for five years on Buccaneers and Tornados before returning to the UK for a tour as an instructor.

Following an exchange with the Luftwaffe on Alpha Jets near Munich he attended the German Staff College in Hamburg and won the Clausewitz Medal. He then served as a flight commander on 12 Squadron Tornados at Lossiemouth. On his final tour he was Military Assistant to the Assistant Chief of Defence Staff for Policy in the Ministry of Defence. He is married with three sons.

Total War 2006

Simon Pearson

CORONET BOOKS

Hodder & Stoughton

First published in Great Britain in 1999
by Hodder and Stoughton
First published in paperback in 2000
by Hodder and Stoughton
A division of Hodder Headline

A Coronet Paperback

10 9 8

A CIP catalogue record for this book
is available from the British Library

ISBN 0 340 74856 7

Typeset by Hewer Text Ltd, Edinburgh
Printed and bound in Great Britain by
Clays Ltd, St Ives plc

Hodder and Stoughton
A division of Hodder Headline
338 Euston Road
London NW1 3BH

To the lost children

Contents

Part Two – The War of 2006

List of Maps and Illustrations

Acknowledgements

This book has been made possible only through the gentle encouragement of many people. To those not named here, and you know who you are, I extend my personal thanks.

The book began in 1993 as an academic exercise to find a way of predicting the effectiveness of air power in any scale or type of warfare. It developed into a personal aim to reach a wider audience on the limitations of air power following the post-1991 Gulf War euphoria where I felt that many wrong lessons were being learned.

For taking the time to kick around ideas with me and encourage some of my more heretical theories on air power I am thankful to the staff at the German Armed Forces Staff College in Hamburg and Lieutenant Colonel Erik Gulseth of the Royal Norwegian air forces. I also extend my thanks to the mass of academics engaged in historical and air power research; the senior gurus at the United States Air Warfare College at Maxwell, Alabama, in particular Colonel Richard Sfranski (Ret'd); Professor Philip Sabin at King's College, London, and to Air Vice-Marshal Tony Mason (RAF Ret'd) for his encouragement to write a book in the first place.

The research required for this book has been enormous. Aside from the Internet there are a few organisations that stand out head and shoulders above the rest in terms of open-source quality information. These are the Jane's Information Group, whose journals, in particular *Jane's Defence Weekly* and the lesser known *Jane's Intelligence Review*, are simply superb; the International Institute of Strategic Studies and the website of the Conflict Studies Research Centre at Sandhurst.

For their enthusiasm, unwavering vision, guidance and wise counsel in keeping the project on track, my deepest thanks to my agent Mark Lucas and to my editor Roland Philipps and their ever-patient assistants Sally Hughes and

Roseanne Boyle. Thanks also to Stuart Larking and Cliff Webb (cover and maps) and to Ian Paton, the copy editor, who had the painful task of extracting English from military jargon.

I am indebted to my very talented brother William for, among other things, his love, encouragement and patience with me over the years and for giving me my first laptop computer. And to my mother, Isabel, who taught me to write, thank you.

My deepest thanks goes to the Royal Air Force, in which I count myself privileged to have served, and with whom I have been extremely lucky in having had such an enjoyable and varied career.

Last but not least, and without whose unconditional support, time, love and understanding none of this would have been possible, I give my biggest thanks to my family: my wife Nikki and my sons Joseph, Mark and William.

Prologue

'World events in the 21st Century will likely unfold in ways
that none of us will predict, just as the events of this century
stunned and shocked even the most savvy of global political
pundits . . .'

John H. Dalton, US Navy Secretary,
October 1998, in RUSI Journal

'What man is wise enough to understand this? Who has
been instructed by the Lord and can explain it? Why has the
land been laid waste like a desert that no one can cross?'

Jeremiah, 9, xii

San Diego – The Second Pearl Harbor
28 August 2006

The United States Navy was now poised and ready to sail, the
weeks of intensive preparation finally at an end. The plans for
the second phase of the Pentagon's great air offensive against
the Islamic Alliance were almost complete. In the western
Mediterranean there was already an enhanced Sixth Fleet
Carrier Battle Group comprising three Nimitz-class carriers
that had joined the lighter European carriers in readiness for
the air assault. In the Pacific theatre all was quiet. Every jet
would be needed in the Middle East. The Pentagon had
gathered the four aircraft carriers of the US Pacific Fifth Fleet
in San Diego. The three newest Nimitz-class ships, *John C.
Stennis* (CVN-74), *Harry S. Truman* (CVN-75) and *Ronald
Reagan* (CVN-76), were joined by the aged *John F. Kennedy*
(CV-67) in San Diego harbour. With their accompanying
Aegis-class area anti-air ships and myriad escorting destroyers

and frigates, this was a formidable armada. The plan was simple and followed the second principle of war – concentration of force. The fleet was to sail directly across the Pacific to the Indian Ocean via the Straits of Malacca to join *Nimitz* (CVN-68) and *America* (CV-66) in the greatest gathering of naval air power since the Battle of Midway. Six carrier air wings could dominate one million square miles of sea and air space. After gathering in the Indian Ocean the fleet would turn north-west into the Arabian Sea and thereafter into the Red Sea, the Gulf of Oman. It might be able to force a passage through Hormuz into the Persian Gulf – close enough to give the Islamic Alliance nations a real taste of the dominance of air power. The naval forces would attack in concert with the USAF long-range assets to ensure swift submission of the Islamic forces gathering on Israel's borders. Air power had always performed brilliantly against military traffic jams and there was no reason to suppose that this time it would be any less successful. The architects of navy global power projection congratulated themselves on their foresight. They had always argued that airbases within reach of desired targets would not always be available to USAF tactical assets. This argument had been vindicated after the rather hasty withdrawal from Saudi Arabia following the establishment of an Islamic-dominated monarchy. And although there were bases available in Kuwait, Qatar and Bahrain, they were extremely vulnerable to Scud and artillery attack. Kuwait, Qatar and Bahrain, the only Arab states that had not undergone a New Islamic Revolution, had become islands of American military presence. Now naval aviation had a point to prove. These were the air forces that would destroy the multitudes gathering on Israel's borders. The smugness of the visionaries was, however, short-lived. This great gathering had been anticipated by the enemy.

Four nuclear submarines of the Russian Northern Fleet left Archangel in June, at the height of the Baltic crisis. There was a single 30,000-ton Typhoon monster and three refurbished 15,000-ton Severodvinsk SSGNs. Each carried twenty-four NPO Mashinostroeniya Yakhont Mach 2.5 anti-ship missiles. These missiles were nine metres long, weighed 3,900 kgs and were powered by a solid rocket motor which, on burn-out, was replaced by a liquid-fuelled ramjet. Their maximum range was 200 nautical miles. They would climb to 50,000 feet, identify a target at 120 miles, then dive to a fifteen-foot terminal height. Called ONYX by Nato, they were the very best Russia had produced, with chaff-discriminating synthetic aperture active radar homing from twenty-five miles, as well as the best in home-on-jam technology.

The submarines were tracked from space through the Barents Sea as far as Novaya Zemlya. Once under the Arctic ice they disappeared. Moving at walking pace, it had taken them one month to creep undetected through the Bering Straits off Alaska. Thereafter the group turned south-west to stay in the deep trenches off the Kamchatka Peninsula before heading out into the Pacific Ocean. Their course to San Diego was dictated by the weather. They looked for the autumn storms and systems caused by 'El Niño', which formed in the mid-Pacific and lashed the western coast of the American continent. Only with the weather systems did they move. This was the only way to hide from the array of satellite sensors that were able to read newsprint from orbit. On 15 August the group settled on the continental shelf next to Santa Rosa Island. The Typhoon then moved on its own, first to San Clemente Island – a mere sixty miles from San Diego. On 21 August, using Hurricane Ruby as cover, she crawled to ten miles off San Diego itself. The trap was set, the crews made last-minute preparations, the captains smoked nervously, waiting for the single word which would tell them that there would be action that day. On 28 August it came. 'Humble' – it was the only transmission the group received in three months at sea.

At dawn on 28 August, like the original dreadnoughts, the four US carriers sailed out in line astern to a hero's send-off. They then turned in place to receive their aircraft, which had been packed on the flight lines under maximum guard at Miramar, Torrejon and Long Beach airbases. It was as the last S-3 Viking anti-submarine aircraft was landing that the first waves of cruise missiles were spotted inbound from the north-west some 150 miles distant. In all, seventy-two ONYXs were fired in two salvos five minutes apart. In the six minutes available from warning to first predicted impact, the US Navy's reaction was predictably good. The AAW Cruisers quickly took command, and soon the air was full of white plumes – the Standard Plus 4 missiles launched to counter the incoming wave of destruction. Some sixty-three ONYXs were either knocked down or failed to find targets. There was no time to launch F-18Fs or the newer Joint Strike Fighters, which were sitting on the decks armed but without fuel. Of the nine ONYXs that got through the missile screen, all but three sustained some sort of damage from the multi-barrel Phalanx gatling weapons or the newer PDLs – Point Defence Lasers. Five ships sustained minor damage from single hits, one destroyer, the *Charlie Brown*, suffered major damage with two hits amidships, and a single Spruance-class frigate, the *Alaska*, was abandoned after fires took hold and swept through her following massive secondary explosions after two hits.

The admirals were both elated and in the mood for revenge. The carriers steamed back south as the task force changed shape to put as many ships between its prize assets, the carriers (indeed, its raison d'être), and the threat direction. The three Severodvinsks dived and split at 45 knots. Their position at firing would be known all over the US within minutes. The carriers prepared their anti-submarine aircraft for an onslaught in return.

The Typhoon sensed them all turning south. Its patient waiting was over. In its former intercontinental ballistic missile tubes were twenty midget submarines. Each had an Islamic crew of two specialist divers – their commitment to the cause unquestioned, their martyrdom never in doubt. These small submarines, capable of 55 knots submerged, were each packed with penetrator noses and a delayed fuse controlling 5,000 lbs of high explosive. One by one the hatches opened and were flooded. The midgets slipped out and formed an unseen arc. The four carriers and their escorts were moving fast, but their course would take them directly over the Typhoon. At 1907 hours, in sight of the skyline of San Diego, the *John C. Stennis* was rocked by three massive explosions from within its bowels. The midgets had come in unseen from the front quarter. By 1915 all four carriers had had their keels ripped apart. Three million gallons of aviation fuel mixed with several thousand various warheads on each carrier made for a spectacular, if macabre, display. Forty-eight hours later only *Ronald Reagan* was still afloat, but it was without power and listing heavily to starboard. Only forty aircraft out of nearly three hundred managed to launch to safety from their dying 'mothers'. The Islamic martyrs were hailed as heroes across the Alliance. Over three thousand US Navy personnel were killed. Crowds gathered in mourning on San Diego's beaches.

Introduction

> 'Academics are so combative and pugnacious because the stakes in their fights are always so low. Historians, God bless them, are among the worst of the lot. They fail to appreciate that their retrodictive renderings are constructed from the fabric of ultimately inconsequential and grossly incomplete records.'
>
> Henry Kissinger

Today is 11 November 2009, just over three years since the war ended. The world is still adjusting to those climactic events. There have been few celebrations. The purpose of this book is to document for future generations the events of the past decade – I have attempted to set down, as clearly and logically as possible, the events which led up to the War of 2006 and, of course, the war itself. What is certain is that history needs to be written down. It is only by learning what has happened in the past that we will have an understanding and insight into the choices the future hold for us. As for the victor . . . I'll let the reader be the judge of that.

The Peace Dividend – New World Disorder

In 1991 the fall of the Berlin Wall and the collapse of the communist Soviet Union ushered in a period of change and a period of hope. The end of the Cold War deprived Western military and political strategy of its comfortable and unifying focus: a good, solid, definable threat from Soviet communism. The 'Peace Dividend' was what the West rewarded itself with for having won the Cold War. In reality it meant disarmament in a less stable world. Nato entered an era of redefinition and would not become confident of its role until 2005. Although the end of the Cold War made the prospect of a total war remote, through the removal of superpower restraints it also increased the likelihood of smaller wars breaking out. During the Cold War the Eastern power bloc had acted like a cultural freezer. Every aspect of society that was good, bad or indifferent, from faith through to racial hatred, was packed and frozen if it did not contribute to the welfare of the state. The demise of communism saw the great freezer unplugged; the contents thawed and began to rot. Across eastern Europe tensions which had been held suspended for so long let rip in continuous civil wars, punctuated by uneasy peaces, from Armenia to Bosnia. Yet in the West, with the imminent threat of hordes of Russian tanks rolling across German plains removed, Nato began to disarm. Western governments and their military forces stood at a crossroads. They were faced with choosing between preparing for an unthinkable worst-case scenario based on the Cold War, or simply remaining capable of fighting as part of a US-dominated alliance.

The removal of the 'Threat', as it was universally known, enabled governments to cut their armed forces willy-nilly, see what was left, and around the tattered remains build a semblance of defence policy. The critics charged that management consultants were paid vast sums to popularise the cuts and they did not disappoint. 'Options for Change' was the name of the first round of swingeing cuts in Britain; 'Front Line First' was another loud Conservative banner. It was sold by the generals themselves as 'cutting the fat', 'smaller but better', and so on. The sceptics remained unmoved. It appeared to the neutral observer that *ad hoc* processes were put in place merely to save money rather than produce armed forces that were capable of being suitable instruments of policy. The 'Treasury Culture' under European socialism was such that money spent on defence was regarded by the mandarins as money wasted. The realpolitik was that the shape and size of Europe's armed forces had since the formation of Nato been dictated by the threat of a Soviet charge to the Rhine. This was no longer the case and, in an increasingly uncertain but apparently less apocalyptic threat scenario, the removal of the 'Threat' forced the military and policy-making hierarchies to adjust the size of the armed forces to fit the new circumstances. Without exception force reduction, or 'downsizing', became the order of the day. As the men and machines dwindled in number the worldwide commitments of the forces in 'little war' increased. This was real efficiency – doing more with less. Playing a significant role on the world stage meant committing troops to the crises that erupted everywhere. A new generation of the armed forces of Nato, the 'peacekeepers', was born. It was exactly for the 'wider peacekeeping' scenarios that the smaller, more mobile, more flexible and affordable forces were suited, it was claimed. The critics described them variously as merely an adjunct of superior American forces at best, and at worst as the armed wing of Oxfam.

Not surprisingly it was the USA that was the first to recognise the warning signs of a new emerging threat and put dollars back into defence. By 2004 the entire European defence budget had fallen to less than two-thirds of the US budget and, because of duplication of effort in hierarchies and infrastructure, was producing less than one-third of the equivalent product. Fifteen years of peace dividend and disorder from 1991 to 2006 enabled the US to emerge as militarily more dominant and technically more advantaged than at any time in history. She was without equal, almost unchallengeable.

PART ONE – THE SECOND AGE OF REVOLUTION

'Tell us what the former things were, so that we may consider them and know their final outcome. Or declare to us the things to come, tell us what the future holds, so that we may know you are gods.'

Isaiah, 41, xxii–xxiii

Chapter One – 2001

Stirrings

The Algerian Army's support had always been critical to the survival of the regime that had declared the Islamic Salvation Front's (FIS's) overwhelming victory in the 1991 elections invalid. The ultimate aim of the FIS was to transform Algeria into an Islamic state. This intention, like that of the Islamic Party in Turkey, worried both the military and the West. The FIS view, which had the support of most of the population outside the army, was that the time had come to end years of socialist incompetence and religious and social repression. From December 1991 there followed more than a decade of terror and murder by the fundamentalists. Initially, as both the new regime and the army had hoped, the violence and terror of the extremists served to alienate many influential figures in the middle ground, including journalists and academics, as well as causing rifts over the methods used and the leadership within the FIS itself and among other smaller Muslim extremists. Ten years of terror and a hundred thousand deaths later even the army eventually realised that it was in an unwinnable and increasingly untenable situation. By early 2001 the Islamic insurgency had gained enormous momentum and was beginning to attract support from elements within the armed forces. The civil war was bleeding Algeria to death. Also, as the numbers of guerrillas increased to fifty thousands, the ability of the insurgents to strike when and where they liked also increased. They were ineffectually opposed by an army comprised mainly of conscripts who had much sympathy with the Islamic ideals (and therefore desertion increased to alarming proportions). With time, the loyalty of the army to the ruling élite wavered. The dissenters

were led by a core of disillusioned middle-ranking officers.
The average Algerian was poor and embittered by the legacy
the French had left. They saw evidence of widespread corruption and collusion, and the increasing wealth of the government and its close advisers. The government, it seemed, was
prepared to do little to improve the lot of the average citizen,
and was concerned only with remaining in power to preserve
the wealth of a chosen few. The direct effects on the Algerian
Army and its swing towards Islam would have far-reaching
consequences not only for Algeria but for all Islamic nations.

Racial Unrest

The French economy continued to be burdened by maintaining state-owned industries, an outsized bureaucracy and a
generous welfare and benefit system. With unemployment
high and rising, the French people began increasingly to
question the additional burden and social unrest in the cities
caused by the presence of a large minority of North African
immigrant groups. Meanwhile the minority groups themselves were suffering from unemployment levels of nearly
50 per cent, and took to the streets both in support of the
increasing unrest in Algeria and to demand equality as French
citizens.

The venting of frustration and anger at their lot by the
North African ethnic minority, especially the 'French-born'
generation, took the form of a rapidly escalating number of
demonstrations and riots in the poorer suburbs and ghettoes
of Paris, Toulouse and Marseilles. The French police attempted to crack down hard on the spreading urban violence
but found that the unfortunate death of the occasional pro-
tester only served to spark off larger and more violent
demonstrations. The attempted repression of the disaffected
minority using such direct methods caused the 'Algerian'
leaders to become more organised. Under the aegis of the
newly formed FFE ('Front for Freedom and Equality'), they
began to diversify their campaign for equality and an end to

racism and continued French support for the unpopular
Algerian government by attacking France's transportation
system using ever more sophisticated methods. Graduating
from petrol bombs thrown at buses and lorries, the FFE
brought the pride of France's railways, the 300 km/h TGV,
to a standstill and only a few tens of metres from disaster
when they blew apart two small sections of track on the Paris/
Lyons route. The whole country felt the effects when the three
main unions, led by the communist CGT, staged a series of
national one-day strikes protesting that it was no longer safe
for them to work. The FFE was penetrated by Muslim
extremists, who came complete with thorough training in
Islamic ideals (most were recruited via the FIS in Algeria) and
urban terrorist warfare and an abundant supply of arms (the
former from Syria and the latter from Iran) in order to take on
the security forces. As happened in Northern Ireland and
Germany, rioting was used as cover for snipers to hit the
security forces. The French people were infuriated by the
government's apparent inability to control or even dampen
the rioting, and were then stunned by the death of three
members of the Gendarmerie in Toulouse on a single night.
The government called in counter-terrorism experts from the
UK, and after extensive consultation while the streets burned
decided that internment was the only policy that would work.
The mass arrests of suspected leaders did nothing to quell the
violence. The difference between France in 2001 and 2002
and Northern Ireland thirty years previously was that French
intelligence was poor. While the British special intelligence
units had found it relatively easy to penetrate the hierarchies
of the IRA and UVF, the clear ethnic divide between the white
majority of the French security forces and the black Algerian
minorities made life very difficult. Indeed, it is estimated that
at least half of the ethnic informers recruited provided good
intelligence to the FFE and misleading information to the
security effort. Internment only fuelled the fires of discontent
further, and the violence and rioting spread so rapidly that
hardly a town in central and southern France remained
unaffected. The French government watched events in Algeria
closely, and throughout the summer of discontent inclined

increasingly towards eliminating the terrorist elements at source in Algeria. Contingency plans were rapidly drawn up to assist the Algerian government with military forces if they were asked to do so.

The First Domino

On 1 September 2001, when the attacks by the FLA spread to the rich minority French business community in Algiers and thirteen French citizens were massacred, Paris became alarmed. Noting the increasing disaffection of the army's middle leadership, the French government persuaded the Algerian regime to 'invite' France to provide direct military assistance to the Algerian Army and advise on protection for the frightened French nationals. Two battalions of the French Foreign Legion were promptly dispatched to Algiers in a gesture of support.

The effect of this action, as far as the Algerian government was concerned (and later the French for that matter), was catastrophic. Led by a group of disaffected colonels who were not receiving direct financial benefit from the ruling élite, the greater part of the army did not need much persuading to believe that the French troops were proof that a return to colonial domination was being considered by the ruling élite in Algiers and that it was imminent. On the tenth anniversary of the 1991 elections the FIS leader demanded one final push and, being an ex-officer himself, called on his former comrades to compromise and give Algeria her inevitable destiny. The army mutinied. Every officer of two-star rank and above was arrested and two were shot while resisting. There were isolated units whose loyalty to their senior commanders caused brief firefights, but as soon as the streets began to throng with thousands of people embracing the mutineers in their bold move most units quickly changed sides when faced with the inevitable. The two Foreign Legion battalions held their ground, divided as they were between their temporary barracks and defensive positions around the small French community. An over-zealous commander of an Algerian armoured brigade began an unauthorised assault on the barracks. The first two attacks were repelled, but not before seven tanks had been knocked out and a dozen legionnaires killed and more wounded in the firefights. It was a black day for France when the commander of the barracks, his troops running low on ammunition and especially anti-tank weapons, offered conditional surrender. The stand-off at the barracks and the state of siege in the French suburb lasted for forty-eight hours until the Algerian military commanders intervened. They accepted the conditional surrender of the barracks and offered favourable treatment of the other battalion. This was a shrewd move in that they did not want to spill any more French blood and risk incurring a huge military reaction by France. The French High Command, realising the limitations of employing air power effectively in an urban area, especially with all the attendant risks of collateral damage, and in the full knowledge that nothing short of a full-scale amphibious invasion would restore the situation, advised the remaining battalion to accept the terms offered.

At the same time the Algerian military leadership announced that they would hold their position of power only until free and fair elections had taken place. And this time they would ensure that the result was respected by all parties. In a clever propaganda move the announcement was made via CNN, and the 'Junta' was flanked by the smiling faces of both the leaders of the previously outlawed Islamic opposition and members of what had been the ineffectual token opposition of moderates under the previous regime. Once assurances had been issued with respect to the rights and safety of the French community, and control over looters and all elements of the armed forces and police had been established, the Foreign Legion troops were invited to leave with their dignity just about intact. There was very little else they could have done. They were given safe passage to the harbour area and then crammed a week later on to two large ferries that had been sent from Marseilles.

The Irish Problem

Perhaps surprisingly looking back on it, the biggest failure of the successive Labour governments was Northern Ireland. Instant Devolution at the end of the millennium and the preciptous release of all political prisoners was followed by an arms decommissioning that, for all the fanfare, probably realised no more than around twenty five per cent of the guns, grenades and bullets available to the antagonists. The 'Irish Problem made a rapid transformation from being apparently centred on politics to what had all along been the underlying reality – racial hatred and control through Mafia-style organisations. Regardless of any political peace process or settlement, the authority on the streets was held by those whose livelihoods and positions were based on control over their communities through intimidation, beatings, the occasional execution and racketeering. The continued use of guns within the community in protection rackets and robberies underpinned a major source of income for both sides. Peace and disarmament were an anathema to these men. They were not about to relinquish control of the people through the gun for the sake of political ideals on either side of the border, and their influence, in ensuring the myth of decommissioning and obstruction of verification, was unmistakable. As a precondition to any further secret talks with the Government about real decommissioning and under continued surveillance, harrassment and infiltration from British Military Intelligence the Republicans began to demand a right to retain a 'small percentage' of arms for self-protection. The Unionist hard men, not unnaturally, demanded the same. Neither side was represented by the Real and Provisional IRA and the UVF and emergent Orange Volunteers, was prepared to give up their reserved right to resort to arms on the unsatisfactory outcome of any negotiation. With the real men of power freed from prisons, the extremists on both sides of the divide were able to harden their positions, back away from compromise and make more unrealistic demands.

By late 2001 it was clear to all sides that a solution acceptable to both sides was not on the horizon. Ultimately the real Ulster problem was the rule of opposing gangster factions against the rule of law, and had little to do with a united Ireland. The British government remained entrenched in its position, secretly insisting on full decommissioning, something the people of Ulster were told they had but something that the day-to-day evidence of events in the province clearly contradicted. From the winter of 2000 the number of 'incidents' of shootings and beatings increased at a steady rate. In the secret war British Intelligence had scored a series of spectacular successes against the Real IRA. The Republicans, their patience exhausted and fear of the enemy within threatening to send the fanatics out of control, issued a public ultimatum demanding a halt to interference. The British government and its security forces were given until the New Year to effectively cave in or 'face the consequences'. On the other side the Orange Volunteers emerged as the major armed faction of the Loyalists. Their reaction to the IRA ultimatum was to redouble their acquisitions of guns, grenades, rocket-launchers and Semtex.

The storm broke on Christmas Eve 2001 with a massive car bomb causing substantial damage to the centre of Belfast, but thankfully few casualties. This was a serious disappointment to the security forces, which had recognised all the warning signs of an impending attack but were unable to ensure the replacing of the 'ring of steel' around central Belfast in time. The following day the Loyalists answered the announcement by the IRA of a return to armed struggle with an even larger bomb that blew apart the centre of Dublin. The worst fears of both British and Irish governments were realised. The war had finally, as it had often threatened to, spread to the South and back across the Irish Sea to Liverpool, Manchester and London. The Orange Volunteers and UVF stated that they were on the offensive and not inclined to sit back and be reactive to 'Republican terrorism' in the North. Dublin apart, perhaps the biggest shock was the assassination in Chicago and New York of the two leaders of the Irish-American communities. Through a press statement the Loyalists vowed to fight fire with fire and to stamp out the huge financial support the Republican cause generated in the US. The Irish problem had spread from Ulster to all of Ireland and mainland UK, and thence across the Atlantic.

Chapter Two – 2002

An Islamic Landslide

In the months that followed the September Revolution, as it became clear that the Islamic Party would win a landslide victory, there was an exodus of French expatriates and former government officials out of Algiers. The pride of the French people had been greatly wounded by the ignominious exit of the Foreign Legion battalions in what they thought had been an ill-considered débâcle on the part of the military and dubious interference on the part of the government.

In March 2002 the Algerian elections duly took place with a host of international monitors invited to ensure fairness. Knowing the strength of their hand, and the subsequent measure of control they would be able to exert over any fundamentalist regime, the army could afford to be generous, magnanimous and even democratic – for a while at least. The world was not surprised when the FIS won, gaining more than 70 per cent of the votes cast. In April 2002, after just one short month in office, the promised referendum took place. The Algerian people voted overwhelmingly to change the constitution from an attempt at an élitist Western-style democracy to a theocracy based on Islamic law along the lines of the Iranian model. Islamic fundamentalists took great comfort from the success of their brothers in Algeria, and the power of the people, not seen since the overthrow of the Shah of Iran, was duly noted in extremist headquarters across the Arab world.

The effects of the Algerian Revolution in France would be twofold. In the short term the French government, keen to reassert its foreign-policy credentials, redoubled its efforts to gain international credibility for and leadership of a WEU-

based European defence force. The longer-term effect was
that from mid-2002 the new Algerian government engaged in
active support of the rights of the 'oppressed' ethnic minorities in France. The fruits of this effort would not, however,
become fully apparent until much later. The only good thing
to happen to France in 2002 was her retention of the soccer
World Cup when she beat Brazil 1–0 in the final in Tokyo.
The winning goal was scored by Nicolas Anelka.

Labour – But Only Just

In spite of its failure in Northern Ireland the Blair Labour
government was returned to power with a twenty-four seat
overall majority in the May 2002 elections. The adoption of
the Euro was at first a popular move with both business and
industry. A strong foreign policy and uncompromising attitudes to the perpetrators of terror both at home and, in
concert with the US, abroad showed that the ideals of a
centre-right party, even though it was still 'Labour', were
still popular with enough voters to ensure a second term in
office. The Conservative Party was still in relative disarray
and was in the process of redefining its identity after the
election of a new leader in January.

The Decline of an Army

Probably the most accurate assessment of the USSR was the
statement that the Soviet Union as was in 1989 was not a state
which had an impressive war machine but that the state itself
was a war machine. Every aspect of the communist economy
was geared towards a heavy industrial base that built and
sustained a massive military machine. The sheer effort and
expense required to maintain the machine on a war footing
eventually proved too much in a world dominated by Western
economies and an equally determined succession of US Re-

publican Presidents. Gorbachev was the man who foresaw the
implosion, but he was not thanked for his vision. In the
following decade, with few exceptions, the economy, industrial base and military forces went into free-fall decline. By
early 2001 the Russian armed forces had reached a state of
disintegration and collapse. The navy was receiving only 18
per cent of the required oil and lubricants even for its ever-
reducing fleets. The major surface combatants had started to
seize up in port and priority was given to maintaining the
ballistic missile-armed Typhoon-class submarine fleet, and
thereafter the super-quiet Delta-class attack submarines. Figures now available show that fully 70 per cent of the surface
and submarine fleets rusted and rotted in port to an irrepar-
able state between 1992 and 2002.

The air force tumbled into a dire state with enough cash
being made available to purchase only 5 per cent of the
required spare parts and 8 per cent of its aviation fuel. This
meant that its pilots flew on average for only fifteen hours per
year and that the air force was receiving only twenty of a
stated requirement of two hundred new combat aircraft each
year. By mid-2000 there were so many crashes of Mig-31
Foxhounds (a complex and unforgiving interceptor aircraft
even for the best of pilots, having a tendency to depart from
controlled flight if slightly mishandled at high altitudes) that
the fleet was simply grounded and scrapped in early 2001.
Officers' pay in all forces was nine months in arrears and the
suicide rate climbed to an all-time high – an average of four
deaths per day. Worse, officers and soldiers saw their primary
duty not as service to the mother country but to keep their
families housed, clothed and above all fed. Some 90 per cent
of servicemen moonlighted to supplement income. Their skills
were also in great demand by the increasingly powerful Mafia
– former paratroop officers were able to command monthly
salaries of US$2,000 working to organise and enforce 'pro-
tection' among other less palatable money-raising activities

The army was forced to rationalise. Strength was cut from
sixty divisions of less than half-strength to thirty divisions of
moderate strength (only nine of these would be tank divisions), with only one or two full-strength divisions in each of

the eight military districts. This was down from 220 armoured divisions (88 tank divisions) in 1988 at the end of the Cold War. Even the élite airborne forces were not left untouched, their strength halving from 68,000 to 33,000 in 2001. As early as the mid-1990s there had been an increasing number of disturbing reports filtering through to the West that conscripts stationed in remote locations in the harsh eastern border areas were starving to death during the winter months. There were other reports of soldiers with rickets and scurvy among the many other diseases and ailments associated with lack of nourishment and poor diet.

In his address to the Duma in October 1996 Colonel General Boris Gromov warned that 'the army is sick and tired of lies and empty promises. The combat readiness of the army has been undermined to the point where it is a threat to national security.' This statement could be, and was, read two ways. Defence Minister Rodionov added in November of the same year that any further lowering of combat readiness could produce 'unpredictable and catastrophic consequences'. He did not specify who or what for.

In the late 1990s it was thought that the Russian armed forces would not be able to turn professional before 2005. Long-term plans were drawn up for a gradual transition away from a conscript army. These plans were, however, overtaken by events. Despite sweeping cutbacks in 1997, the Russians were still trying to maintain 1,700,000 men under arms on a defence budget of $20 billion compared to the UK's forces of 170,000 on a budget of $30 billion – and even that was considered tight. By June 2002 the pressure for change had become irresistible. The new Russian President declared that Russia's armed forces would be restructured to reflect the needs of the modern world. Russia, despite her internal problems, still wished to continue to play a major role in European and world affairs, and felt that a professional force would restore the pride of the nation. However, events in Russia herself and elsewhere in the region would conspire to ensure that conflict became inevitable. The death of the President in early 2002 and the turmoil caused by the 'professionalisation' of the army that followed were both signifi-

cant events. Russia was focused on the demobilisation of tens
of thousands of soldiers, sailors and airmen. It was largely the
failure of the corrupt system to deal with a sudden mass of
unemployed soldiers, let alone even make it appear that it
cared about their fate, that led to the growing discontent of
'the people'. And it would be to the army that the people
turned to for help. The army genuinely cared about those
former members of its ranks, and it was this mass military
disillusionment, which was shared by the vast majority who
were not embroiled in the corruption that was bleeding the
state to death, that was a major contributor to a Second
Revolution in the autumn of 2003.

While Russia was sorting out her internal problems she
was, for two years, simply not in a position to flex her
muscles. The Russian armed forces, with the help of vast
sums of aid from the US and Europe, began the painful
process of 'downsizing' in June 2002 with a cap of initially
one million men, further reduced to 850,000 the following
month on the advice of Western consultants. Indeed, the
West, in particular the UK, had been involved for some time
in actively helping the Russians cope with cuts imposed in the
late 1990s. The West foresaw the increased social and financial burdens on Russia and remained keen to keep the nation
both 'engaged and on-side'. In theory, a significantly smaller
Russian military was equated with a reduced threat to both
the stability of Russia from disaffected army units and a
reduced threat to Nato's eastern border. That this would
actually have exactly the opposite effect in the longer term
was not even considered at the time. One year later the
Russian armed forces would emerge stronger, more cohesive
and with their own agenda that would change the face of
European history.

A President Neutralised

The US strategy of containing Iraq had evolved out of a police
action sanctioned by the UN into one of freedom of action

over Iraq by US and to a lesser extent British air units, who continued to nibble away at Saddam Hussein's air defence networks.

The US had fired punishment cruise missiles at Iraq on two occasions in both 2001 and 2002, and on three other occasions were talked out of doing so by their more pragmatic but steadfast British allies. The attacks, carried out with little or no warning, were more an expression of US displeasure at what had become a decade of non-cooperation with the UN inspectors as well as the fact that evidence from many sources indicated that Iraq continued to cheat all along. Militarily the raids achieved little. Politically they served only to immunise the world against their utility and purpose and were viewed in most parts as American aggression – whether the raids were justified or not in terms of international law came to be rather beside the point. And the point was that the world was beginning to grow weary of what it saw as single superpower petulance. Also, by this time the US was keen to temporarily disengage from Iraq as stirrings of more unsavoury activity were manifesting themselves in Korea. However, in late June 2002, she decided that regardless of world opinion Iraq should be left in no doubt that the global reach of US aerospace power would never be more than a few hours away.

Before sanctions were lifted the Democratic President authorised one last big raid so that Iraq would not forget who was in charge. In a seven-day campaign the US and UK flew over a thousand sorties against 'strategic targets' throughout Iraq and, unwittingly, achieved what they had always hoped to do by other means – the effective elimination of Saddam Hussein. There was one target that the US and UK intelligence services had known about for four years but had never attacked, and this was a top-secret biological weapons research laboratory located under a nursery school in northern Baghdad. The site was attacked on a Friday to ensure that there would be no collateral toddlers in the rooms above. By coincidence and not design the Iraqi President was visiting the facility to award the research scientists medals for their work when the single Tomahawk missile with penetrator warhead struck. The Iraqi President, much as in Hitler's miraculous escape in 1944, was not killed but was badly injured and remained in a coma. The Arab world, for all its misgivings about Saddam Hussein's regime, was outraged at what was described as an act of state terrorism. France, Russia and China were equally appalled. The direct consequences of this action were that Saddam's son took up the reins of power and announced that he would take over as President until his beloved father recovered. He promised open dialogue and co-operation with the West but vowed that no American or Briton would ever set foot on Iraqi soil again. World sympathy for what appeared to be an assassination attempt against a president gave the apologists just the opportunity they had been seeking to insist on the lifting of sanctions.

Sanctions against Iraq were finally lifted in late 2002. France and Russia were instrumental in this decision, much to the annoyance of the US and to a lesser extent the UK. The French defence industry, which had supplied Iraq with vast quantities of military hardware in the 1980s, was keen to be part of the process to begin rebuilding the Iraqi armed forces, which had been shattered in 1991. France reasoned that someone would supply Iraq and the rearmament might as well benefit her, especially with the entire defence industry staring bankruptcy in the face. Her main competitors in this area would be China and Russia, which also supported the French line that 'enough was enough'. France was keen to secure a monopoly over future Iraqi oil contracts for further exploration and exploitation of one of the world's largest oil reserves. Russia, strapped for cash as ever, was keen to unfreeze the billions of dollars, with interest, she had been owed for more than a decade and a half. The French television station Canal 5 also played a significant role in the shifting of world opinion towards toleration of Iraq. Allowed free rein in Iraq during the summers of 2001 and 2002, the station focused on the humanitarian disaster that was being inflicted on the Iraqi people. The Americans and British argued cogently and forcefully that this suffering was entirely due to the misdemeanours of the Iraqi regime. Iraq's apologists, mainly in the Arab world, insisted that the sanctions affected the people and not the regime. The vested interests remained silent, but raw television of cruise missile attacks alongside suffering civilians planted a lie in the minds of the liberals to the effect that one led to the other and therefore both should stop.

Whatever the truth, the pictures beamed across Europe and the US of children starving and dying from simple ailments due to the lack of medical supplies and adequate facilities were difficult to stomach. While the governments of Britain and the US remained unmoved, their media and the rest of the world's media became increasingly vocal in their support for relaxation of the stranglehold that had been applied for the past ten years, which was increasingly choking the Iraqi people. The new millennium had ushered in a feeling in the West that this was the beginning of an era of renewal, tolerance, second chances and goodwill to all men, even Iraqis. And the cruise missile that rendered America's nemesis unconscious was the final straw. So against a background of media hype, sanctions against Baghdad were lifted, albeit unilaterally at first by Saudi Arabia and Turkey (irritated at US interference with the independence-seeking Kurds) in late June 2002, closely followed by Russia and China in July and France in August. And for the following two years Iraq, led by Saddam's very able son, concentrated on becoming the model neighbour while, without the presence of US or UK inspectors, she was able to continue undisturbed in making her own preparations, under Saddam Hussein's finest palace for action against Israel.

The Army Takes Charge

Morocco, like Algeria, still suffered from the legacies of five hundred years of European domination. King Hassan II, who came to power in 1961, ruled via a House of Representatives from the early 1970s. Most Moroccans, while they remained at times fiercely loyal to their King, could not help but conclude that the administration was inefficient and corrupt. The King, as head of government and Defender of the Faith, was the single unifying factor that stopped Morocco from splitting apart for many years died in mid-1999. As king the former Crown Prince Sidi Mohammed proved both to be less popular and to have less of a unifying influence than his father. The raised expectations of political reform were not realised.

Islam was encouraged by Hassan but not by his son. Extremists were persecuted. The old King's protracted failing health and subsequent death had fuelled rifts between the rival power groups. During the 1980s and 1990s the government had embarked on ambitious building programmes to modernise the infrastructure of the country. The improvements included new hotels, motorways, schools and universities and hospitals. However, this programme did nothing to tackle the real Moroccan problem – that of the huge gulf that existed between the rich ruling class and the utter poverty of the rest. There were general strikes, instigated by graduates and undergraduates protesting at the high levels of unemployment and the lack of real investment in the social infrastructure and economy. They argued that Moroccan 'progress' was hollow. While there might be new hospitals there were few trained doctors and endless shortages of medicine; new universities without good lecturers or libraries; and new roads for the cars of the rich. The prospects for 'the rest' were poor and the future did not look bright.

Initially the power of fundamental Islam in the country was undermined by the very fact that most of the extremists were of Algerian origin. The rising flood of illegal immigrants fleeing either the authorities or the terrorists of the Algerian civil war themselves put an extra strain on both the government and the poorer urban slums. Also Algeria had been traditionally regarded as the only real (however unlikely) external threat to Morocco. The Islamic extremists, however, persisted, and their ideas gained currency, especially among the younger generation. The authorities, not wishing to see Morocco become embroiled as Algeria was, were forced to increase the arrests of known Islamic activists, and tension steadily rose between the security forces and an unsettled and disgruntled underclass.

By mid-2002 a culmination of events made the pressure for

change irresistible. The new King, Mohammed VI was stricken with cancer and his confinement to hospital meant that the country was being more directly governed by those most suspected of incompetence and corruption. The situation with respect to the glaring differences between rich and poor and rising unemployment had got steadily worse. The people had followed with great interest the upheaval that had taken place next door in Algeria, and looked on with envy at the overthrow of the rich and the mood of disciplined optimism that was exuding from the fledgling Islamic state. The Moroccan students and intelligentsia, encouraged by a sympathetic media, intensified their protests against the government, and a wave of general strikes followed. When the army attempted to remove barricades set up by protesters to halt all traffic, outbreaks of violence and rioting ensued. And as a backdrop to the deterioration of public order there was an extremely weak economy and a currency that was crashing against the Euro and the US dollar.

For the government the timing of the unrest could not have been worse. In order to secure an IMF loan as a temporary bail-out measure, the government was forced to adopt an austerity package and plan to cut public spending. With the threat from a belligerent Algeria gone – the new regime in Algeria was going through a honeymoon phase of friendship and forgiveness with all its near neighbours (except France, of course) – the first target for cuts was the armed forces. The number of men in the services, an inflated 210,000 (of which 187,000 were army), was viewed as expensive and unnecessarily large considering that their major threat had disappeared, as had happened in Europe, and their primary role would be keeping the Polisario behind the sand berm in the western Sahara. As soon as swingeing cuts were announced, proposing to reduce the number of soldiers alone by some 70,000, the army announced that it would not accept the government's decision. This should have been no surprise since the professional soldiers had little or no prospects of pay, pension or employment outside the military. Nevertheless, in a show of determination the House of Representatives announced that it would be sacking two-thirds of the army's generals.

The army stood firm and responded by occupying both government chambers and Morocco's national television and radio stations. What followed was a virtual carbon copy of the previous year's events in Algeria.

Swearing allegiance to the ailing King, and after paying hefty bribes to the 1,500-strong Royal Guard, the army incarcerated the ruling élite and announced that it would run the country in the best interests of all the people. The people were invited to take to the streets to show their support for the army's actions. They needed no prompting, and for two days the streets thronged with those who saw an end to all the years of bureaucracy and incompetence. There was optimism that any form of government would be better than that which had gone before.

However, things did not turn out as rosily as they had in Algeria. As the first anniversary of the military takeover approached, the discontent among the people grew from disillusionment to open rebellion as it became clear that the army had little intention of handing over power to any other form of government. The ruling junta was faced with the same problems and temptations that the previous regime had faced. Indeed, the junta made a worse job of it. They also saw the need to reduce public spending and the massive external debt, but were not prepared to contemplate any changes to the military structure. Military spending was actually increased with the purchase of M-60A3 tanks and 155mm artillery pieces from US surplus stocks. To pay for such extravagance other areas of public spending – health, education and social security – were cut. And all the while the less scrupulous officers simply lined their pockets and were not averse to flaunting their new wealth and status. One corrupt self-interested regime had been replaced by another, complete with fleets of private black Mercedes, and the gap between rich and poor yawned even wider. But there were two important and critical differences between the military regime and its predecessor. These were a short period of rapidly deteriorating relations with Spain, and a more repressive attitude towards Islam.

As soon as the US tanks had been delivered, the ruling

junta, virtually without notice, carried out the first item on its foreign policy agenda with startling haste. This was the occupation of the disputed Spanish enclaves of Cueta and Melilla. These two Spanish possessions on the northern Moroccan coast had been the source of diplomatic wrangling between the two countries for some time. Both were ancient port cities with populations of around sixty thousand, and had remained under Spanish rule for several hundred years. Their status was to Morocco what Gibraltar was to Spain. Both were historically significant: Cueta, lying opposite Gibraltar, was the first North African city to be conquered by the Portuguese in 1512 and marked the beginning of four hundred years of European expansion and domination of North Africa; Melilla, lying a hundred miles or so east along the coast, was where the first shots had been fired in the Spanish Civil War in the late 1930s. Spain had antagonised Morocco from the late 1990s by declaring Moroccan claims of sovereignty over the territories invalid and pushing legislation through the Spanish parliament that would give the cities a form of autonomous self-government. While the old regime was in power there was little that the military could practically do to alter this diplomatic slight. But with the restraint of politicians removed, the army felt that swift occupation of the cities with military units would force Spain into serious negotiations with a view to the long-term future of the cities under Moroccan rule.

Backed by the rest of Europe, Spain's reaction was both rapid and uncompromising. The UN Security Council condemned Morocco, and at Spanish insistence imposed immediate economic sanctions. The right-wing opposition in Madrid called for military action to be taken to return to the *status quo ante* and deter such blatant aggression in the future. They insisted on air strikes and the planning of an amphibious task force landing Falklands-style to satisfy Spanish pride. As it turned out both the Spanish and Moroccan governments would be losers, but while antagonism was simmering the world's attention turned next to Turkey, where the military had also had enough.

A Triumph for Secularism

The real power in Turkish politics lay for many years with the army. After threats of a military takeover if the government continued to appease fundamental extremists, the Islamic Virtue Party, which had replaced the banned Welfare Party, was in turn banned in July 2002 for being 'too Islamic'. This move was very unpopular in many of the poorer rural areas of Turkey, and there was a brief attempt to reinstate it through popular uprising and direct resistance to the power of the army. The Islamic activists, watching the success of their brothers in Algeria with envy, chose the wrong moment. Their action and dissent would set Turkey inexorably on the road to conflict with the neighbouring Arab states. The unrest was brutally crushed in the early summer of 2002 after repeated warnings by the army leaders; the army seized power in a bloodless coup to ensure that Turkey's future lay with the West.

The politicians were temporarily sidelined as the army reiterated Ecevit's programme ideals of the late 1990s, which stated that Turkey would remain 'the vanguard of democracy and secularism in the Middle East'. The army, through a series of increasingly harsh anti-Muslim purges to evict activists coupled with serial indoctrination within its own ranks, had ensured a secular future through the power of the gun. The Turkish Army did not want even a whiff of what had happened in Algeria to happen in Turkey. The ruling junta stated that it was not prepared to allow Turkey to fall into the hands of those extremists who were hell-bent on a return to a medieval system of government. The Turkish Army remained as alert and prepared as it was secular, and installed itself as ruler of all Turkey 'for a short period of time' during which 'peace and stability' would be brought to the nation.

Turkey was regarded as positively European by some members of the Arab League, as simply decadent and corrupt by others. This view was reinforced when the army drastically reduced Islamic religious education programmes in schools and colleges and turned the tables on the EU by insisting that it would only relinquish control to a secular democratic authority once it had received cast-iron guarantees of EU membership. Meanwhile, in the political arena, the Turkish alliance with Israel was strengthened. This was viewed with great distaste and dismay in the East and proved beyond doubt to the rest of the Arab world that the Turks were first and foremost Turks, not Arabs and hardly Islamic.

Germany Steps Right

During its economic heyday and rise to almost unparalleled wealth compared to the rest of Europe during the 1980s and 1990s, Germany had been the envy of Europe. Her manufacturers produced goods of the highest quality and in return the employees gained significant concessions. The German trade unions, superbly set up and organised along lines that had been suggested by Britain after World War II, became powerful protectors of their workers' rights. By the mid-1990s German workers enjoyed the highest average wages, had the most holidays, the shortest working week, and the most generous health and pension benefits in Europe. IG Metall, Germany's and Europe's largest and most powerful union, insisted in late 1998 that with German exports at record levels it was time to pass on the benefits of growth and profits to the workers. Their demands included an even shorter working week, pay rises three times the rate of inflation, and a reduction in the age of retirement. November 1998 proved to be the high-water mark of the German economy. The economists in the larger companies had long since foreseen what they regarded as the unhealthy trend in worker power and subsequent poor competitiveness and loss of profits for their bosses. The larger companies were forced to begin relocating to factories outside Germany, and more often than not outside Europe. The smaller companies, crippled by high business taxes and over-generous health, pension and insurance contributions, found that increasingly they were no longer competitive either in the domestic or export markets, and simply went under.

There were three major contributing factors to the mini economic crash and subsequent social disorder of late 2002 and the change of German government and identity the following year. After it happened, the mini-collapse of the German economy and disastrous crash of the health and social security system seemed obvious and inevitable to everyone. The reunification of East and West Germany was the first obvious contributing cause. It was a political triumph but an economic black hole. The additional burden of twenty-eight million people to an already creaking system was not the most healthy injection, although it would take more than a decade for the full effect to be realised. By pouring money into the East and investing in infrastructure and business, successive governments convinced themselves that the eastern states would one day be as economically independent and powerful as their western counterparts. This was simple folly. The $100 billion annual investment in the East gave growth rates of between 5 and 10 per cent, but much of this was in the construction industries as the East was rebuilt after forty-five years of communist neglect and poor taste. By 2002, although the East accounted for one-third of Germany's population, she only managed to produce 10 per cent of the GDP. Unemployment in the East started at between 15 and 20 per cent and rose to 30 per cent by early 2002, taking the total number of unemployed to well over five million. The return on much of the investment was, on the whole, an increase in the number of companies that were either deeply in debt with little sign of recovery (although the banks and the government, having invested so much, were always prepared to give the benefit of the doubt) or that simply went bust. There were serious shortages of the skills required in the booming computer-based sectors which no amount of investment could rectify in such a short period of time. The second contributing factor was the rise of unemployment in the West. The failure of businesses and the exportation of manufacturing sectors to the US and Asia only exacerbated this problem. The average German was simply not prepared to work harder for a lower return and blamed the third contributor, the influx of foreigners into the country, for bleeding the system dry. Germany's loose immigration policy and generous benefit system was enough for her to act as a magnet for refugees from the warring Balkans as well as from all over eastern Europe, along with an increasing number of ethnic Turks and Kurds. And Germany was geographically the first port of call, a kind of demographic front line, for any person migrating east to west to start a new life – and there were hundreds of thousands of them.

The net effect of these factors was that an uncompetitive and unemployed (and largely unemployable) workforce plunged Germany into two winters of industrial and social discontent in 2001 and 2002. The opposition right-wing CDU claimed that Germany was suffering from 'an overdose of foreigners' as small ethnic-minority service-based businesses flourished where German businesses failed. The first cracks appeared in September 2001 with the collapse of one of Germany's largest health and pension insurance companies. This enabled three other major health insurers, all of whom had been existing on borrowed time for some years, to call in the receivers. The shock waves were felt through every strata of German society as ordinary Germans took to the streets after watching their planned comfortable retirements and healthcare schemes disappear. The demonstrations against the government for not acting quickly enough or in the interests of the average citizen were enough to encourage the extremists to go on the offensive.

This came as little surprise to those who had followed the trends among Germany's youth since reunification. The generation of Germans under the age of twenty-five saw a sharp increase in the number of those who held extreme right-wing beliefs. The hooligan culture and all its trappings of bomber jackets, boots, camouflage trousers and Nazi salutes became more organised and more vocal. This was especially true in the discontented East, where the ideals of the young right meant that many teenagers risked becoming social outcasts. In an attempt to curb the number of racist attacks, the socialist government introduced a 'suss' law in early 2002, giving the police extended powers to arrest and question any person or group of persons deemed to be acting suspiciously. This move appeared to have the opposite effect to what had been intended. The police were increasingly accused of harassment of ethnic minorities while being apathetic or turning a blind eye to the activities of the extreme right. The German Interior Intelligence Service confirmed the government's worst fears with an estimate that around a quarter of its young policemen were also members of right-wing groups, while a much larger proportion sympathised with their aims and activities. Fear of the future and economic gloom precipitated a public backlash on the large minority of Turkish (5 per cent of the population) and other eastern European and Muslim 'Gastarbeiters'. Using nationalistic slogans such as 'Foreigners Go Home! Keep Germany for the Germans!', attacks by elements of the hooligan neo-Nazi right became so vicious and frequent that the ethnic minorities began to arm themselves for self-protection.

In the first week of October 2002 the German right swept to power in the elections, but things would get worse before they got better. The time had come to draw a line under all things of the past (an oblique reference to the Holocaust) and for Germany to claim an active and rightful place among the forces of good in the world.

A President Impeached

October 2002 was quite a month. President Clinton's successor was impeached with a rapidity that astonished the world. Discontent from within his own party in early September over the awarding of lucrative defence contracts to those who had paid the most into the President's personal campaign funds quickly turned into accusations of misappropriation of funds. The Senate demanded and got an immediate inquiry, and with two of the President's closest advisers caving in under intense questioning the scandal expanded to include not only grace-and-favour payments but also money-laundering. It was just four weeks from the first whispers to full impeachment. The Clinton sagas of the late 1990s had given the US people a low tolerance of the abuse of public office. What made the situation all the worse for the Democrats was that the Vice-President was also heavily implicated. Both Congress and the Senate agreed that the Vice-President would be immune from prosecution in return for full co-operation, and that the United States would let the people decide by calling a mid-term election in early November 2002. In an effort to win votes in the five short weeks of campaigning, the out-going Vice-President gained the grudging approval of Congress and the Senate for the withdrawal of all interests but the US strategic surveillance assets from the Balkans. The US military had long been unhappy with what it viewed as an over-commitment to European problems, and especially with the US elements of the Nato force on the ground in Kosovo, which was unique in that it was the only place in the world where US troops were not commanded by a US general. Also, the Pentagon had begun to receive unwelcome intelligence information from the Far East that forced it to consider shifting its focus from central Europe to a greater threat emerging from North Korea.

American Disengagement

The chance for a purely European-led force as had long been advocated by the French (keen to show their real strengths and leadership after the Algerian débâcle) came much more quickly than expected and, as had become almost a norm, had as much to do with US domestic politics as US foreign policy. The underlying antagonisms that had been rumbling in the Balkans refused to go away. In Bosnia, in spite of the best efforts of SFOR, both sides used the period of enforced stability to arm their citizens to the teeth in anticipation of a deciding conflict. As the levels of violence rose and the prospect of war increased, Nato reacted by reinforcing SFOR. The cost to the Nato nations that provided troops spiralled with time. In the US there had for some time been calls to withdraw US troops from the messy European affair. There was a sense that if the warring parties did not want peace, then why not just let them get on with it.

The Kosovo Settlement was revised in 2001 and the tiny province was divided into a Serb north, policed by Russian and Ukrainian 'peacekeepers', and an Albanian south policed by an EU-led force – EuroFor K. The Russians and Ukrainians started turning a blind eye to Serb preparations to begin direct military action against a resurgent KLA that had grown weary after seven years of stalled talks on total independence for the province.

The French and German governments, sensing the US's waning commitment to what seemed to be a never-ending struggle, had proposed in the spring of 2002 that the time had come for the Europeans to take responsibility for affairs in their own back yard, and that the first such test of a 'Euro-Force' might be the imposition of a purely European solution in the Balkans. The French view had for some time been that the presence of US troops on the ground, as well as its past actions and pronouncements, were stumbling blocks to any settlement. They, like the Russians, continued to be disappointed by the US view that the Serbs were always the 'bad guys'. Convinced that an even-handed approach towards Belgrade would give the Serbs an avenue to acceptance of a moderate and fair peace plan for the whole of the Balkans, rather than any American solution that would inevitably involve loss of face, France proposed that the US ground forces should withdraw and be replaced by a French-led WEU force. The British balked at the 'WEU' aspect and initially blocked the proposal. It was only when the French agreed to the force coming under a 'European Nato' command that the British reluctantly accepted the inevitability of an American withdrawal. There would still be European Nato air force units based in Italy and Hungary, but there was no sense in pretending that they were as capable as the departing US fighter-bombers. The US agreed to continue to provide strategic reconnaissance and surveillance simply because no other members of Nato had the assets, but the British were distinctly unhappy and uneasy about being in an unstable situation without a direct US presence.

At the end of the Kosovo crisis Montenegro took advantage of a severely weakened Serbia to declare her full independence and invited Nato troops to advise and retrain her armed forces with a view to engagement in the Partnership for Peace programme, and ultimately, her President declared, full Nato membership. Practically there was little that Serbia could do other than bide her time and await an opportunity to exact revenge.

In late October 2002 nearly thirty thousand additional (mostly European) troops deployed as EuroFor B to replace the Americans in Bosnia, and EuroFor M in Montenegro. There were also significant troop levels in Macedonia and Albania securing the lines of communication to Kosovo. It was indeed a grand plan. The Russians did not like it and the Serbs were severely disgruntled but defeated. The Americans were pleased to be out of it and the Democrats gained ground in the pre-election run-up. The French were triumphant, the Germans cautious and the British plain worried. With respect to foreign policy and the rest of the world, the one constant that remained the preserve of British governments, regardless of their colour, was unwavering support for the US policy. The standing joke of what the British thought was epitomised by some more pragmatic senior officers in the MoD who produced a standard retort, when asked for their view or opinion on any subject, of 'I'm not sure, I'll have to ask the White House and get back to you on that'.

Belgrade decided to play its final card once US troops were well away from any potential action. The US withdrew her forces from Bosnia in the autumn of 2002 and handed over to the EuroFor Command led by France, which had provided by far the largest contingent of troops. This was the first chance that Europe had to prove its own collective strength, will and determination outside an American command and decision-making umbrella – and what a disaster it would turn out to be.

In the first week of November the US elected a Republican President. She would turn out to be the Margaret Thatcher of the early twenty-first century.

The US Strikes

By August 2002, thanks primarily to the information gleaned from two senior military defectors, the US intelligence service had incontrovertible evidence that North Korea was in possession of some four ten-kiloton nuclear warheads (about half the yield of that used on Hiroshima). Moreover, she was rapidly overcoming the technical problems associated with getting them to function on the tip of the Tae-po Dong medium-range ballistic missiles. Worse still, she was able to manufacture enough weapons-grade uranium to produce a further two weapons per year. The possible implications for South Korea and Japan were frightening. The scenario of a nuclear attack on Seoul, Tokyo and any two other major Japanese cities was now a reality. Beijing sat uncomfortably within range of the unstable regime's nuclear arsenal, and even the Russians in Vladivostock began to look south with a little consternation. Another possible scenario was that the four weapons might be used to melt a hole some twenty-five kilometers wide in the South Korean defence line south of the Demilitarised Zone (DMZ – the stretch of land four kilometers wide that marked the internal Korean border). A mere forty kilometres south of the DMZ lay Seoul, which would be at the mercy of tens of thousands of North Korean troops and massed armour which, it was presumed, would be able to sweep aside any dazed defenders that remained in the 'hole'. If one had no moral objection to the use of nuclear weapons, then this was an elegant solution, and one which would give the North her best chance of overrunning the South before significant reserves were able to arrive. This scenario was the one that worried US and South Korean military planners the most.

The summer harvest in North Korea in 2001 had been barely adequate, but by early autumn 2002 it was becoming clear that the year's crop would be a bumper failure. The regime, at its head a dead man – the immortalised Kim Il Sung – had been teetering along at starvation level for five years. North Korea had received food aid from 1997 onwards from the US. This had limited the starvation to the remote mountain regions. The intransigence of Kim Jhong Il in talks during the following three years ensured that the US 'punished' him (in reality the people suffered) by reducing grain shipments. Moreover, China, which had been supplementing the US grain imports to the North, had suffered catastrophic flooding and was unwilling to give to the prickly regime what she could no longer give to her own people. The series of harvest failures meant that by November 2002 the whole country was seriously hungry, and by December was not only starving but also cold and desperate. The first cracks in the worshipping of their leader almost as a deity appeared earlier that summer with ordinary citizens, emboldened by seemingly endless hunger and deprivation, staging riots, even in the capital, Pyongyang, itself. The riots were brutally repressed, but even the army generals were becoming uneasy: the men were not happy; people they knew were dying, not just the peasants in the hills. Kim Jhong Il, son, Prime Minister and commander-in-chief of the armed forces, was indirectly threatened by his senior army commanders. Kim did what most dictators do when faced with internal strife. He executed a handful of those he considered to be the central troublemakers and used the state media to create an expectation of imminent attack from the 'enemies of the people'.

It was his mini-purge that convinced several senior military generals to attempt defection. Only two managed it successfully before all external contacts with the rest of the world were closed. These two men were, to all those interested in the security and peace of the north-west Pacific, harbingers of doom. The information they disclosed enabled a rapid and focused intelligence effort to verify their claims of the capabilities and ambition of the Stalinist regime. Although, for their own reasons, they did not tell the whole story.

During the second week of November the new Republican President and her advisers had come to a firm decision. It was a decision that would set precedents and have long-term effects in ushering in an era of proactive American world strategy rather than the normal reactive stance. The acceptance of the President's proposals merely underlined to the

Americans the *de facto* situation that she was the world's only superpower and was, in pure military terms, unchallengeable. It took only seven days of closed-session top-secret meetings with the premiers of Japan, China, Russia and South Korea to convince the American President that she had *carte blanche* approval for the policing action about to be undertaken. And, of course, this was only being done in the interests of world security.

The four B-2s left Guam, each armed with eight Super JDAMs, at 1200 hours on 8 December 2002. Later that evening they opened their bomb doors over the four remote silo installations which had been identified as the 'nuclear ones'. The mission had been brought forward twenty-four hours when the two Dark Star reconnaissance UAVs (Unmanned Air Vehicles) had detected increased activity around the silos. The Dark Star was a large, long-range, very stealthy drone which was packed with sensors and real-time data links that enabled commanders to have an instant view of what an enemy was up to. The Dark Stars had been flying missions at 85,000 feet undetected over North Korea for some two weeks. The interpretation of 'preparations being made for launch' at all four sites enabled the President and the Joint Chiefs to come to a rapid decision. The Super JDAMs had twice as much high explosive as normal JDAMs as well as penetrator warheads, and were tailor-made for bunker-busting and similar target sets. The bombers made two passes each, dropping four bombs on each run to maximise the chances of knocking out the nuclear weapons. As they left, the first Tomahawk TLAMs arrived in the target area. This was belt and braces. For if the B-2s had missed a single weapon, then Tokyo or Seoul might be waking up to a 'bucket of sunshine' breakfast. The guided missile cruisers and attack submarines of the US Pacific Fifth Fleet had worked frantically during the twenty-four hours of preparation time given to ensure the Tomahawks were armed with the desired mix of warhead. This was one-third penetrators for the silos and control bunkers; these were the latest SLAMs that had been rushed into production and service. The other two-thirds were evenly divided between unitary high explosive for the bar-

racks and support areas and area denial scatter mines which
would render the launch areas and their environs 'no go' areas
for three or four days. In all, approximately seventy-two
cruise missiles were used.

The operation was a spectacular success. Post-mission
reconnaissance showed that the silos and bunkers targeted
had suffered some 95 per cent damage, the supporting facilities around 80 per cent. Only three of the Tomahawks had
not reached the target area. It remained unknown whether
they had been hit in the hail of triple-A fire which had erupted
after the first pass of JDAMs had struck, or whether they had
simply malfunctioned and flown into the ground.

War in the East

North Korea had had half a century to plan its attack on the
South. The speed of the North Korean reaction to the US
strike was stunning. Only after the war did it become clear
that the North had been within hours of launching a surprise
attack with minimal preparation. The attack was to have been
preceded by a nuclear attack on Seoul, Pusan and on the two
powerful US mechanised infantry brigades which formed the
backbone of the second defensive line north of Seoul. The
regular reconnaissance overflights by satellites and Global
Hawk UAVs had revealed that despite preparations for the
launch of the Tae-po Dongs there was nothing to suggest that
the two-million-strong army of North Korea was massing for
an assault across the DMZ. In fact the opposite had been the
case, with much less troop activity than normal noted.

The reason why troop movements were reduced was because thousands of NKPA troops had literally disappeared –
underground. The fifty years of preparation for this day had
not been wasted by the North. They knew that if they were
foolish enough to step out of their trenches and advance
slowly across the five to twenty kilometres of no-man's-land
before reaching the South's first prepared defensive line,
which was anchored in terrain that clearly favoured the

defender, they would be inviting disaster in the form of a Korean Somme. Endless scenario variations run through US military computer models had confirmed this.

The North Koreans had to minimise the fire-power and technological advantages possessed by the South and the US if they expected to make any headway. They felt that if they could come to grips with the South in hand-to-hand combat their numbers, ideology and fanaticism would be more telling than the South's other technological and training superiorities. The fifty years of preparation had been spent building tunnels under the DMZ and into and behind the Hollingsworth Line. By late 2002 only seven tunnels had been discovered and dynamited. The US suspected that there may have been between twelve and twenty tunnels in total, but were shocked to learn after the war that there were no fewer than fifty-three tunnels. Each had been painstakingly and literally carved by hand, inch by inch until the inches had grown into feet and the feet into miles. The tunnelling had to be done this way because on discovery of the first tunnels the US and South Korea had placed hundreds of seismic and acoustic listening devices. When the third and fourth tunnels were discovered and blown, the North changed the digging techniques and dug deeper. Raw labour was something a state that had to maintain full employment was not short of. By late 2002 the tunnel network was massive, almost unimaginable. There were larger tunnels with railways for supplies at the rear, feeder tunnels giving personnel access and ensuring ventilation linking the network, and finally assault tunnels each big enough to take armoured vehicles and trucks, with the largest tunnels able to accommodate vehicles two abreast. The South Koreans were sitting on the equivalent of a human ants' nest.

At 0200 hours on 11 December 2002 it was as if someone had poked the nest in several places with a large stick. Out of the tunnels and into a white and freezing night with a snowstorm blowing across central Korea poured thousands of angry North Korean soldiers. This was it. No several days of warning and preparation. No massive artillery barrage. No chemical attack, just up and out of the tunnels and directly to the assigned targets.

The special forces assault teams had marched through the tunnels all of the previous day, their boots fitted with felt outers to mask the noise. The listening sensors had picked up this increased activity but only with sufficient time to order the front-line units to maximum readiness. The tunnel assault was concentrated on the twenty-five-kilometre stretch of the defensive line which lay across the closest approach to Seoul – forty kilometres to the south of the DMZ. This infantry assault was aimed primarily at Dongducheon, the first major city across the border on a direct route to Seoul.

The North fired two hundred Nodongs (Scud-type SSMs) at three target groups. These were the assembly areas of the two US brigades, the principal airfields and, for pure terror, Seoul itself. Nothing was more capable of harassing the mobilisation and movement of reserves to critical areas than a flood of civilian refugees jamming all roads out of Seoul against the flow of military traffic. To make matters worse commando teams inserted weeks before from mini-submarines managed to blow the bridges on the outskirts of Seoul as well as use explosives to induce landslides to block the roads.

The attacks themselves varied in their success. The thousands of special forces that had emerged from the tunnels caused mayhem along the defensive line. Their primary targets were the artillery bunkers and lines and the mutually supporting machinegun and anti-tank missile nests. All along the front fierce hand-to-hand fighting took place. Around each position the snow was splattered with blood, flesh and frozen corpses, and black soot which marked the discharge and impact points of mortars, Rocket Propelled Grenades (RPGs) and hand grenades. There were areas where whole companies of the assault pioneers were mown down in the open as the weather and battlefield smoke lifted temporarily to reveal inviting targets to undetected defenders with clear fields of fire.

On the flanks the attackers had done what the planners had feared most. They had traversed the DMZ through the very worst terrain, steep wooded hills and gullies, correctly deemed impassable by any mechanised force. But this was a motivated light infantry force. They moved in single files across a broad

front through the barbed wire and minefields, the point squad
of each assault file hoping they would be the one that found
the clear path. The losses to anti-personnel mines, many of the
casualties left maimed and bleeding marking the progress of
columns through the minefields, would have been enough to
stop a less fanatical attacker. In the woods and on the steep
and thickly bushed slopes, however, the sowing of effective
minefields had proved an intractable problem. The columns
emerged through the minefields and, in the poor visibility,
made worse by the light patter of smoke artillery rounds, they
regrouped to assault the defences through measured infiltration.

The defenders fought tenaciously but they were outnum-
bered, air support in such atrocious conditions was all but
impossible, and they, the most forward-stationed troops,
listened with growing consternation to the sounds of battle
to their rear. As the amount of artillery and mortar fire
support fell away, they realised that these positions were
either being overrun or put out of action.

Years of covert insertion and direct special forces surveillance by North Korean commandos ensured that virtually
every South Korean artillery position was known and surveyed. As the initial wave of troops out of the tunnels became
embroiled in hand-to-hand fighting, the subsequent wave
moved south towards the artillery positions. Many of these
moved rapidly in 4 × 4 off-road vehicles to attack the South's
artillery positions, following up the barrage which had started
some two hours after the first soldiers emerged from the
tunnels.

The fear that grips units which feel they are surrounded or
being overrun is normally enough to induce panic, the abandoning of positions and weapons and headlong retreat. The
defenders knew well the stark alternatives they faced. They
could either hold out until the defences stabilised or expect
death to come from direct enemy assault or later as prisoners
of war – the NKPA was not going to fight this one by the rules
of the Geneva Convention.

All along the defensive line small islands of organised
resistance began to emerge. In Dongducheon there were

scenes reminiscent of Stalingrad as the defenders stubbornly held on to the centre of the city in the worst of weather. The defenders clung tenaciously to an ever-decreasing perimeter where success for the NKPA was measured in yards and buildings captured rather than miles advanced. Out to the east along the Imjin River line and in the hills north-east of Dongducheon there were several breakthroughs, but again the defenders did not flee south; instead they established defensive hedgehogs. At the core of each was a handful of Hyundi K-1 tanks. The attackers had found it difficult to get close enough to the hull-down tanks to take RPG shots, and when they did the tanks were robust enough to continue to fight even after they had absorbed one or two hits.

The mass armour assault had rolled across the start line some twelve hours after the first infantry attacks had gone in from the tunnels and flanks. The progress of this force across the DMZ was deliberate and slow. It was led at walking pace by mine- and obstacle-clearing T-62s. The lead tanks ran into major problems every time they came within sight and range of the K-1s. At one to two kilometres the K-1s could not miss their targets. The fire-control system on the K-1s was some twenty years better than their opponents'. The K-1 commanders knocked out the leading obstacle- and mine-clearers first, forcing those following into the uncleared minefields. Wherever the North's ancient tanks were engaged by the defenders there quickly appeared a major jam of armoured vehicles, at the head of each jam a morass of smoking and disabled tanks. On either side, as commanders were ordered to bypass these points of resistance, the trail out of the DMZ was marked by tank after tank with blown tracks as the attackers had attempted to find a clear path using sheer numbers. In their quest for surprise the armour had not been able to concentrate in the hours preceding the infantry assaults for fear of losing that surprise element and becoming vulnerable to air and artillery attack.

The Nodongs fired at the US brigade areas were tipped with chemical warheads. These had the more persistent nerve agent Tabun, which would kill within two minutes. The North had chosen Tabun for this area because its persistence is some two to three days. They had calculated that by the time their advance had reached this area it would be clear, while during the forty-eight to seventy-two hours of contamination all reserves that the US or the South wanted to move through the area had to be fully protected. The US brigades suffered some 287 casualties from the initial nerve attack, but the shock was such as to force it into immediate action. Some of the casualties included wives and children occupying military quarters near the base areas. This was significant because it made the Americans less inclined to show mercy later on when the counteroffensive got under way.

The US had been prudent enough before the B-2 attacks to put the 25th Infantry Division in Hawaii and US forces in Japan on stand-by. Also made ready were the US Marines' 4th and 5th Brigades and the remaining infantry brigade and supporting elements to complete the 2nd Infantry Division. The infantry units were airlifted into the theatre a mere twenty-four hours after the initial attack and married up with pre-positioned equipment. In terms of relative combat power the US ground forces alone in the theatre at the end of Day 3 were equivalent to some 20 per cent of the total North Korean attacking force.

By 1400 hours on 12 December the weather had cleared sufficiently for air power to begin pounding the attacking forces. The leading elements of the flanking forces had also been forced to break from the heavy terrain in the push for Seoul. As long as they had remained in the heavily wooded areas it was difficult both to identify and target the infantry-heavy forces. Out in the open, however, on the frozen plains and rice paddies, the collective heat signature of swarms of sweating infantrymen against an ice-cold background was enough for the defenders to cause havoc. The AH-1 Cobra and AH-64 gunships were able to stand off and scythe down the massed attackers with chain guns and unguided rockets. The further south the NKPA penetrated the more vulnerable it became to air attack. Its attached air defences were on the slow side of mobile, and many of the older Soviet systems, such as the ZSU-23/4s, SA-4s and SA-6s, suffered the same fate as the tanks they were escorting. Even those that penetrated south did not last much longer than thirty minutes after switching on their radars before being pinpointed and struck either by artillery or High-Speed Anti-Radiation Missiles (HARM – used to knock out active radars associated with threat SAM and AAA systems). The attackers' hand-held SA-7s, SA-15/16s and their Chinese equivalents performed very poorly against fast-moving targets and against any aircraft able to spot a launch and counter it with a flare. Without any effective air defence the attack, as soon as it lost its momentum, was doomed.

As the defensive line north of Seoul stabilised it quickly became clear that the second phase of the offensive was running out of steam. The badly battered armoured spearheads had been unable to push through the gaps in the defensive line in sufficient numbers to constitute an overwhelming threat to the second line of defence. On 19 December the NKPA command called off all offensive action and ordered those troops it could still communicate with to dig in. Again history was to repeat itself. With the skies clearing over the battle zone, the USAF and USN fighters were able to establish immediate air control by their mere presence.

The poor weather had prevented the North Korean Air Force (NKAF) generals from launching any ground support missions during the first thirty-six hours and, as soon as they were able, the air force generals showed a distinct disinclination to commit any aircraft to what would be one-way missions. They at least were aware of the first rule of modern air war, which is that you do not attempt to fight a superior enemy on his home territory. And conventional air war was the American speciality. The USAF strategic air assets had not been inactive during this period. The blankets of cloud that covered most of Korea were too dense to allow any form of laser-guided bomb attacks on the NKAF, but the B-2s, worth their weight in gold, were able to fly unmolested over the North's airbases and hit the hardened shelters with JDAMs. The rapid destruction of some twenty concrete shelters and their contents forced the NKAF to disperse to camouflaged sites around each airbase and to attempt to prepare for operations from some of the many highway strips. The

NKAF's jets were forced to sit under camouflage netting around each base while personnel watched the systematic destruction of their concrete shelters and holes bored in their runways from an unseen and unreachable enemy above. Initially interceptors were scrambled in a vain attempt to find the B-2s, but the fruitless efforts were halted when more jets were lost attempting to land back at their bases in white-out conditions. The anti-aircraft artillery regiments poured swathes of random fire into the air at the onset of each attack, ceasing only when the barrels became too hot and began to warp. Kim Jhong Il had other ideas and would not accept the inactivity recommended by his air force generals. On his direct orders a massed strike was attempted as soon as the weather had improved from appalling to marginal.

The NKAF managed to get three packages of its more capable jets airborne from runways that were beginning to resemble strips of tarmac undergoing major disorganised roadworks – without any bollards. The remaining 250 or so MiG-17s and MiG-19s were retained for base defence against the expected counter air operations. Their short range and age dictated that they were capable of little else.

When the air battle commander in the E-3 confirmed that the NKAF was finally getting airborne and forming into attack packages, the allied fighters were launched. The allied force assembled to counter the expected attack was impressive. In total there were twelve F-18E Hornets and twelve F-14 Tomcats from the carrier USS *Independence*, twenty-four F-15Cs from the 47th Tactical Fighter Wing at Pusan, thirty F-16Cs and twenty-four F-4Es from the South Korean Air Force, and thirty-two F-15Js of the Japanese Self-Defence Forces.

The NKAF fighters approached the border on a direct route to Seoul, flying in high subsonic gaggles of between two and five aircraft in loose formation, their radars on, at between 15,000 and 20,000 feet. The initial fight was a turkey-shoot. The Tomcats and Eagles, flying south-to-north racetracks, sorted* the approaching MiGs with ease. Both types of

---

* 'Sorted' is military speak for the analysis of incoming enemy aircraft – how many, how high, what formation, what spacing, what speed, etc.

aircraft, like the British Typhoon, were capable of tracking
and designating multiple targets. The US jets accelerated to
near Mach 2 and in succession fired their missiles at the
apparently oblivious attackers. The Tomcats were able to
launch their active-homing Phoenix missiles at a range of
some sixty-five miles then close to forty miles where they and
the F-15s launched their AMRAAMs. The Phoenixes and
AMRAAMs were fire-and-forget. They would be launched to
a point in space where they would switch on their own radars
and home individually on to the designated targets. Of the
sixteen Phoenixes fired by the first four Tomcats seven found
targets. The thirty-two AMRAAMs knocked out a further
twenty MiGs. For the nine NKAF pilots of the fighter package
that survived, the experience of aircraft exploding and dis-
integrating all around them under what felt like a hail of
supersonic arrows was too much. They turned tail and exited
at high speed to the north. The bomber packages of some fifty
aircraft each suffered a similar fate at the hands of the second
and third Tomcat/Eagle four-ships. The bombers and their
escorts also did not feel a pressing need to continue south
towards certain death, and ran for home. The remaining US
aircraft were ordered north to pursue as far as the border.

The air battle from first to last missile launch lasted fourteen minutes. The score stood at 89–0. For the sixty remaining
NKAF jets the ordeal wasn't over. In their haste to reach
safety they crossed the border still disorganised and at high
speed outside their own safe lanes. The individual air defence
batteries guarding military sites and installations were acting
on default 'free fire' orders as soon as the B-2 and cruise
missile attacks had started. This enabled them to open fire on
anything that flew within the airspace they were protecting.
As the area between Pyongyang and the border was packed
with such military sites, it was inevitable that any aircraft
outside the NKAF's safe lanes would stumble into such a
zone. This was exactly what some fifty of the sixty or so
remaining NKAF jets did. The air defence guns and SAMs let
rip for all they were worth against targets that were not
manoeuvring, were not using their very rudimentary self-
protective chaff and flares, and were mostly unaware that

they were being targeted. The SA-2s and SA-6s claimed some seventeen aircraft and the guns a further five. In little over thirty-five minutes any offensive potential that the NKAF might have had was reduced to over a hundred smoking holes in the ground.

European Engagement

Ironically, it was the US that was the key player in providing the 'cast iron' guarantees of security long demanded by Israel. The peace process, which had stumbled so badly in 2001, was given new momentum by the Republican troubleshooter sent by the President to explore the possibilities for a long-term solution in early 2002. 'Special Envoy' Reiman was another in a series of envoys sent in by the US. The special envoys, answerable only to the President, had become the diplomatic norm for the US in conducting sensitive negotiations between antagonistic nations and bodies. Reiman was the architect of the Third Camp David Agreement of September 2002 which bound the US to providing a direct and unequivocal military response to aid Israel if attacked by Syria, in addition to extra funding for the purchase of a further two Arrow 3 Anti-Tactical Ballistic Missile (ATBM) batteries by the IDF. The Syrians agreed not to interfere with water in the Mt Hermon catchment area and the Israelis agreed to a phased withdrawal of their military forces to the pre-1967 borderline. The Israeli nightmare of Syrian forces massing on the shores of the Sea of Galilee was also neatly avoided by declaring the whole Golan Heights disputed area a demilitarised zone.

The zone was unique in that for the first time the UN devolved responsibility for the task purely to the Western European Union (WEU) with the stipulation that the forces in the zones were to be commensurate with the expected task. According to its critics the WEU had for many years not even merited the title of paper tiger. France, and to a lesser extent Germany, frustrated by American dominance of all Nato operations, had been particularly proactive in the formation of a 'Eurokorps' which would, in theory, be controlled by WEU military staffs. The WEU had nothing like the infrastructure of Nato, but the political will ensured that a joint German and French headquarters was set up in Strasbourg.

By mid-2002 the WEU considered itself tailor-made for this type of international policing where the presence of American troops was unwelcome and United Nation troops were regarded as ineffective. Nato, or more specifically the US and Britain, paid lip-service to the aspirations of the WEU as being militarily viable but privately considered the WEU's military activities with some disdain, viewing the whole set-up as being an unnecessary duplication of Nato's efforts.

During the negotiations for Camp David 3 it emerged that neither the Israelis nor the Syrians wanted the traditional UN token, and often ineffective, 'hundred dollars a day' light infantry force provided by nations that needed UN money to pay for their armies. In the past such forces had proved no deterrent to belligerent action by the antagonists and, in times of tension, were either overrun and neutralised or simply bypassed and politically discounted. With due respect to Reiman, the Syrians were insistent that the US, whose sympathies were suspect, had zero involvement or control over the deployed forces.

The UN insistence on force effectiveness meant that the providing nations had to supply the equivalent of a full brigade of heavy troops. The stipulation was for two tank battalions, a mechanised infantry battalion, armoured engineers and an artillery regiment, plus the required signals and logistic support. Not surprisingly, therefore, the senior commanders of the WEU fell over themselves to provide the required forces in an undisguised effort to justify their existence to and independence from both the US and Nato. The prospect of inserting a neutral force into the Golan Heights was seen as an excellent opportunity to train and prove their crack troops and staffs in a multinational environment under exacting conditions at relatively low cost. The WEU lobbyists were extremely active in their approach to the UN and the UN, pleased that an instant solution to the impasse was at hand, agreed to give responsibility for the policing of the

DMZ to the WEU. The British would have nothing to do with the new fervour for European operations, considering them already overstretched in the Balkans where, in the absence of the Americans, the heat was slowly but surely being turned up. For the French military these were heady days indeed. In mid-December 2002, as the Americans prepared ground troops for dispatch to Korea, the first WEU force embarked on ships and set sail for the Middle East.

In the short term all sides were satisfied: Israel had secured *de facto* the same guarantees that the US had with her Nato allies with bonus protection against ATBM attack, through the provision of the extra Arrow 2 battery, on her cities, while the Syrians regained control of half of the occupied Golan area. Israeli Cabinet hawks, ever mistrustful, remained extremely sceptical about Syria's motives and promises.

Missile Crisis

With the US military engaged in Korea and preparing for air and ground offensives, and the various EuroFors becoming increasingly bogged down in the Balkans and Israel, the Turkish military government judged that the time was right to destroy the Greek-Cypriot S-300 'Patriotski' SAM batteries.

The Greek Cypriot President, Glafcos Clerides, had begun a policy of buying Russian arms in the mid-1990s. The Turks were unperturbed when Clerides ordered T-80 tanks. He had tried to buy American, British and German tanks in turn but each nation had refused the request. The French had offered the Leclerc MBT but Clerides was unwilling to wait a minimum of three years or to pay three times the price of a T-80. In 1997 Clerides agreed to purchase thirty-six Russian S-300 PMU-1 SAMs, better known under the Nato code-name SA-10d Grumble, to give Cyprus a 'strategic air defence capability'. The whole package, however, included the very best of Russian technology in the form of the surveillance and tracking radars that would be able to actively monitor virtually all Turkish aircraft movements over southern Turkey.

The deal was frozen in late 1998 and the missiles were deployed on Crete and fully operational by late 1999. The fear in Cyprus and Greece over the 'temporary' seizure of power by the Turkish military caused the planned deployment to Cyprus to be rapidly reinstated in July 2002 as a pre-emptive 'defensive' measure. The entire package was dismantled and delivered to Cyprus at the end of May. The Russians made it clear that they had an interest in the missile issue, aside from the fact that Russian advisers and in-theatre training were very much in evidence on Crete. To ensure that the Turks would not interfere as they had threatened, Greece agreed to a Russian suggestion that the Atlantic Squadron of Russia's much-depleted Northern Fleet would be used to transport the missiles and radars while the Greek Navy transported the personnel. By mid-July the systems were up and running, arrayed on the slopes of Mt Trodos, and the Greek Cypriot Patriotski batteries began tracking all aircraft movements, not only on Cyprus but also over a large portion of southern Turkey. The pride of the Greek Cypriot government in their new deterrent was short-lived. The Turks had begun practising air attacks on mock-up sites in Israel using high-angle dive profiles as early as mid-1998. They also purchased 120 AGM-142 Popeye air-to-surface TV guided missiles from Israel which could be used in stand-off attacks. The training with the latter, of Vietnam War vintage, including twelve live firings, did not go well with no fewer than eight missiles missing their intended targets by over a hundred metres. This, coupled with the Greek Cypriot response of ordering shorter-range SA-8s and mobile anti-aircraft guns to enhance the protection of their 'strategic' SAMs, made the prospects of an air attack uncertain at best. The Turkish Air Force felt that an air strike would be highly risky and, without a mass of jamming and electronic support aircraft such as that available to the US, would invite disaster and embarrassment.

The Turks came up with a neat and virtually risk-free solution. The practice air attacks were widely publicised, as was the build-up of troop strength on the island from 30,000 to 50,000. With the Greek Cypriots looking nervously skywards and at events on the partition line in fear of an invasion from the northern half of the island, the Turks inserted three small commando teams which would act as artillery spotters and designators. They had procured a large number of 155mm Copperhead artillery rounds and laser designators, discarded by the US Army. The commando teams, once in position, were able to mark the radar and communication buildings as well as the launchers themselves with their hand-held designators. In a precision artillery strike lasting just twenty-five minutes some sixty rounds of mixed-impact and low-airburst fused laser-guided 155mm shells picked off their targets one by one. Their mission complete, the commandos were able to exit the target area with ease and return to heroes' welcomes. Cyprus's multimillion-dollar investment was left in ruined mounds of rubble and dust. The world was naturally outraged, but practically there was very little that could be done. The Turks pleaded self-defence and expressed regret. Russia, in spite of her threats of reprisal and action, was not really in a position to punish Turkey in any way, shape or form. And with a rapidity that was almost rude, two years later she was welcomed back into close alliance with the USA. The Turks signed agreements enabling the USAF almost unlimited access to its airbases in return for F-15s, the final batch of F-16s and pilot training in the US. The question of Turkey's European Union membership was not, however, up for discussion.

Chapter Three – 2003

A Model Air Campaign

Once North Korea had been denuded of any serious air defence capability, the mission emphasis changed to the systematic destruction of her remaining aircraft, which hardly ever rose to protest. The first two weeks of the new year saw the effort concentrated evenly between completing the destruction of the North's military and civilian communications networks and the taking out of ammunition and POL dumps.

Also, after the initial shocking barrage, the number of Scuds being fired had been reduced to a trickle, and the USAF and US Army had flown in several batteries of the latest Patriot PAC3 missiles with enhanced anti-missile capabilities. These accounted for some forty-one Scuds, although almost all the successes were against single missiles. Those Scuds fired in close sequential salvos of more than three had a good chance of seeing one penetrate to somewhere near the intended target. The level of damage the Scuds were causing was minimal, both in Seoul and against the targeted airbases.

With control of the air won, the real 'fun' for the 'mud-movers' began. The armoured and mechanised units of the NKPA were exposed, massed and without any form of defence against air attack. The Joint Surveillance Target Attack Radar System (JSTARS) aircraft had quickly identified the attacking columns as they formed behind and across the DMZ, and directed the attack packages via data links to fast Forward Air Controllers (FACs) – two-seat Hornets loitering above the strike areas acting as airborne traffic controllers. They were also able to pass this information to B-1 Lancers and B-52s flying round the clock from bases in Japan and

Guam, which proceeded to rain high-explosive ironmongery on the targets presented. The onslaught by the SKAF, the USAF and USN combined was relentless. The Americans had finally learned from the Gulf War, during which they had failed to eliminate the Iraqi Republican Guard, that the power base of any military dictator is his 'personal' army, and he will only be removed if his army is 'removed'.

The carnage wrought was reminiscent of 1967, when the Israeli Air Force destroyed the Egyptian Army in the Mitla and Gheddi passes, or more recently of 1991, as the Iraqis tried to get out of Kuwait City. The damage done to the American servicemen and their dependants in the Scud attacks during the opening hours of the war ensured that this time there would be less mercy shown. With the situation on the ground static, the air attacks sapped the strength of the North. As the allied ground forces were reinforced and strengthened by six mechanised or armoured divisions (five US and one mixed US/UK/Japan), plans were prepared for a counter-attack to regain lost territory and to complete the annihilation of the NKPA. The NKPA infantry units posed a more tricky problem than their unfortunate armoured counterparts. They were able to melt back into defensive positions in the dense terrain, where it was difficult for the air and artillery units to find and hit them with any measure of success. Without any meaningful resupply, however, they were forced to abandon their positions in search of food to the rear. The B-1Bs and B-52s were again called in for carpet bombing missions, each carrying a load of some fifty 750lb bombs. These were especially effective in terms of pure destruction and terror and further sapped the morale of a cowering NKPA.

The air attacks continued for twelve weeks through some very indifferent weather while the allies prepared for a counter-assault and Pyongyang ignored the repeated calls for unconditional surrender. By mid-March, the air forces had completed the demolition of the NKPA armoured, mechanised and truck-borne units to a depth of forty miles north of the DMZ. The US and South Korean forces were ready for a counteroffensive.

The New Belfast

The strident tones emanating from the new German government in Berlin and a widening of its predecessor's perceived anti-immigrant policies led to a winter of discontent in Germany. The winter of 2002 saw the first outbreaks of street warfare in Munich, home to the largest minority communities. The single event which caused the sore of nationalism to break into a running wound was the gunning down of six skinheads who were attacking a hostel with petrol bombs on 5 January 2003. This set off a wave of reprisal and counter-reprisal across the country. The seething discontent turned Munich into the Belfast of the new millennium. There were four groups, all in conflict with each other to a greater or lesser degree. These were the police, and in increasing numbers the army sent in to aid the civil authorities, the extreme right, the Turkish minority, and the Kurdish and other Muslim groups. There followed six months of shootings, bombing – including the wrecking of Munich's historical Platz by a huge Semtex-packed lorry bomb causing the death of over forty people – and running battles. These, like the Northern Irish riots of the 1970s, were often used as cover for snipers on both sides to pick off security forces or identified troublemakers.

The Munich bomb jolted the German political system and the right into action. A motion of no-confidence in the government was narrowly defeated. The CDU/CSU/Republican alliance had swept to power late the previous autumn with a landslide victory over the left on a wave of promises about jobs, stability, economic investment, and a promise to 'do something' about restoring an acceptable social order which put the interests of ethnic Germans first. The implementation of the 'Ethnic German' policy would be a major blow to both the left and the nine million non-ethnic Germans. The Turks, by far the largest group of '*Gastarbeiters*', were understandably angry at this populist policy which would refuse citizenship even to fourth-generation German Turks. The policy would at the same time endorse the continuation of granting citizenship to the flood of ethnic-minority Germans who were still coming in from all parts of economically crippled eastern Europe, even though these diverse groups had migrated many centuries before. That this policy would be the first to be implemented by the new right-wing government in Berlin set the whole of Europe on a course of worry about Germany's dark history and the stated intention finally to draw a line under the activities of previous generations.

Eastward Expansion

In 1999 Poland, Hungary and the Czech Republic became full members of Nato. In 2001 they were followed by Finland and Romania, in 2002 by Slovenia, and in 2003 by Lithuania, Latvia and Estonia. The latter were given associate member status, mainly thanks to the persistence of the Germans and against the will of the Americans who, with some foresight as it turned out, viewed them as a non-contributing liability whose uncertain status would only lead to trouble.

There were several events and factors which led up to the 2006 'Baltic War' and the Russian decision to side with the Islamic Alliance. The granting of associate member status to the Baltic states, Estonia, Latvia and Lithuania, irritated Russia greatly, and she tore up the Founding Act of May 1997 in which she had agreed to Nato enlargement. Russia had indeed been sidestepped by Nato. In 1998 Boris Yeltsin had described the Baltic States as the 'red line' which, if crossed by Nato, would cause tension that European stability might not be able to withstand. In the same year the Russians had clearly declared that the Baltic region was a zone of Russian national interest. The 1997 Concept of National Security declared: 'The prospect of Nato expansion to the East is unacceptable to Russia since it represents a threat to [our] national security.' Furthermore, in 1998 the then Deputy Foreign Minister wrote in the Russian government newspaper: '. . . we have clearly told Nato that it should not admit any one of the former Soviet republics. If, in spite of our warnings, this occurs, stability in Europe will be put under threat and we will immediately have to re-examine our attitude to Nato.'

By fudging the issue with 'associate member' status it was unclear whether the 'red line' had been crossed or not. The Baltic states were jubilant. They had firmly opined for a decade that their future security lay as members of Nato. A decade of political and diplomatic effort had been aimed at securing the sacred cow of membership with little or no thought given to extreme Russian reactions the day after this was achieved.

Russia felt deceived and out-manoeuvred by the West with respect to the eastward march of Nato's borders, and viewed the resurgent Germans with more than a little distaste. Additionally, Russia had been continually denied any status within Nato which gave her significant decision-making powers, even though important elements of her new professional army were deployed in northern Kosovo.

The Baltic states were regarded as 'different' by Russia. They were being offered associate membership with a view to full membership in 2006, while all Russia received was vague promises of 'close consultation'. Russia's repeated offers of security guarantees to the Baltic states in return for them staying militarily outside Nato were ignored. Worse still, Nato began actively to court the Ukraine to consider associate membership. The eastward expansion of Nato was considered by Russia to be the biggest threat to her national interests. The Russian mentality also presumed that there was a hidden agenda, orchestrated by the United States, to continue to undermine the stability of the Russian Federation through economic and information warfare, as well as CIA support for the controlling Mafia underclass. The ruling élite was well aware that the Americans would be able to minimise Russian influence on the world stage by encouraging all those aspects that contributed to prolonging a tottering, stagnant Russia focused on internal strife and hardship. From a giant and ailing economy flowed a multitude of undesirable consequences – growing discontent by the people and the military, a geometric increase in crime (especially organised crime), alcoholism, suicide rates, state debt and erosion of the industrial technological base were all aspects of a deteriorating situation which the proud Russians would not allow to go on indefinitely. A continuing weak and strife-riven centre resulted in the growth of sub-nationalist and ethnic tensions as well as beginning to undermine traditional Russian values, culture, language and the Orthodox faith.

In spite of the angry rhetoric about the Baltic states with respect to Nato, there was initially practically little Russia could do. To soften the blow, she was offered direct financial assistance by the EU, money she desperately needed, to consider the future of the Kaliningrad Salient. A move that was financed by Germany for political, practical and historical reasons.

Terrible Swift Sword

On 19 March 2003 the maximum effort in the Korean campaign was switched to ten days of intensified bombardment of defensive positions in preparation for what was to become Operation Terrible Swift Sword.

The counteroffensive began at 0200 hours on 1 April 2003. Eight South Korean armoured divisions and five US divisions launched a two-pincer thrust through Kaesong and T'Osan aiming to link up between Kumchon and Pyongsan.

On 2 April 2003 the 1st and 2nd US Marine Divisions made a daring night landing along the beaches at Haeju directly into North Korea. The site was some forty miles north-west of MacArthur's landing at Inchon some fifty years earlier. Here in the shallow waters the US Navy suffered its only major setbacks of the war. One frigate was sunk by a North Korean submarine and another was crippled, although casualties on both were light. The South Korean Navy also lost a corvette to a torpedo attack and a second corvette, a mine-hunter and a destroyer were all very badly damaged by mines in the approach sweep to the beaches at Haeju. Indeed,

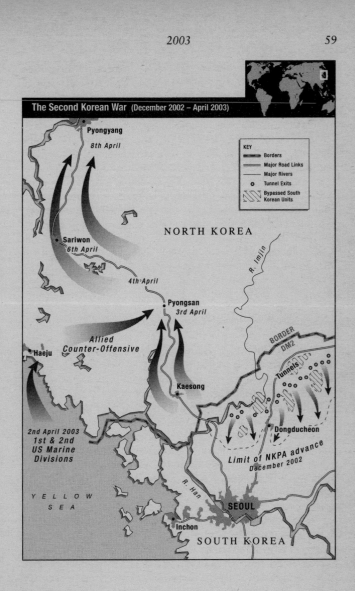

The Second Korean War (December 2002 – April 2003)

KEY
- Borders
- Major Road Links
- Major Rivers
- ○ Tunnel Exits
- Bypassed South Korean Units

Pyongyang
8th April

NORTH KOREA

Sariwon
6th April

4th April

Pyongsan
3rd April

R. Imjin

*Allied
Counter-Offensive*

BORDER
DMZ

Haeju

Tunnels

Kaesong

2nd April 2003
1st & 2nd
US Marine
Divisions

Dongducheon

Limit of NKPA advance
December 2002

YELLOW
SEA

R. Han

SEOUL

Inchon

SOUTH KOREA

the war at sea was, as expected, also a very one-sided affair.
The surface units had no answer to the combined strengths of
US carrier air power and hunter-killer submarines. With three
carrier air wings off the west coast and two off the east coast,
by the turn of the year the North's surface fleet was rapidly
reduced to scattered remnants which fled north along the
coast in an attempt to hide in the many bays and inlets. The
North's large sub surface fleet was more problematical. The
small submarines were particularly difficult to detect, especially in the shallower waters.

Each of the US Marine divisions, equivalent in fire-power
to some ten NKPA divisions, moved aggressively inland and
cut the main arteries between the capital and the bulk of the
NKPA forces. The focus of their strike was the transport
infrastructure running into and out of Pyongsan. Once Pyongsan was isolated the major resupply route to all NKPA forces
south of it would be definitively cut. There was no intention of
becoming embroiled in a fight for the town itself which would
have involved heavy street fighting and a consequent number
of body-bags. The result was as spectacular as in the first
Korean War. News of the landings spread rapidly through the
NKPA ranks and it was not long before the troops, already
demoralised, were in a state of simmering panic. On the right
flank the Combined Division (all US except for token British
and Japanese battalions) was given a holding role. The
counteroffensive across the left flank was initially tentative
and traditional in nature, as it aimed to take certain objectives
according to a timetabled plan. As soon as it was clear that the
North's men were not going to resist at all it became a race.
Commanders down to brigade level were given autonomy of
command and control not seen since Patton's Third Army
raced across France in 1944.

The 1st US Marine Division reached Pyongsan at dusk on 3
April, arriving only two hours before the US 2nd Armoured
Division, which arrived on the eastern outskirts having come
via T'Osan a full twelve hours before the first South Korean
army units came up from the south.

On 4 April the allied units spent twenty-four hours con-
solidating their gains and allowed the logistic chain to catch

up with the blitzkrieg-like advance. The NKPA broke and
disintegrated. Resistance to the heavy armour had been
minimal and the few small pockets that did resist were bypassed. But for North Korea it was all over. The men of the
North's army, no longer a functioning entity, began a headlong retreat north to what they hoped was safety, throwing
away their weapons as they went. On 8 April the allied
armour reached the southern outskirts of the capital, Pyongyang.

In a last show of defiance mini-showers of Nodong 2
missiles, some with nerve agent warheads, were fired at Seoul.
Many were intercepted by Patriot 3 Anti-Tactical Ballistic
Missile batteries. Nevertheless there were significant civilian
casualties in Seoul. On 1 April the Chinese launched a limited
attack across the northern border in what Beijing variously
described as 'a border straightening exercise' and as a counter
to American global imperialism. They were, after taking
surprisingly heavy casualties, able to occupy the areas of
the border that had been in dispute for decades in the central
highlands and pushed to almost ten kilometres south of the
Yalu River in the west. With the Taiwan crisis not going well,
the army halted its advance to attend to more pressing needs
at home.

On 9 April Kim Jhong Il disappeared and all resistance
collapsed. The military commanders of what was once a two-
million-strong army volunteered unconditional surrender.
This was immediately accepted, but because they were out
of touch with most of their army, and had been for some time,
it was a further three weeks before the final shot was fired and
the last of the isolated pockets were persuaded to lay down
their arms. In excess of 200,000 men of the North's armed
forces are thought to have perished. Even today it is not
possible to put an exact figure on the North's losses. The
South lost a total of 7,300 men with twice that number
wounded, and the US lost only 1,200.

Today Korea is united. The people of the North are in the
process of being re-educated.

A Black Project Triumph

The Asian and South American economic crashes of 2003 produced a rash of side effects that contributed to the reshaping of the twenty-first-century world. These included, by early 2004, the emergence of economically more powerful, leaner and robust tiger economies in the Far East which would go from strength to strength during the first decade. However, for China the summer of 2002 marked the beginning of what seemed to be a terminal decline, a decline that was not halted by the contrasting spectacular success of Hong Kong. The Chinese system had been threatening to implode for some time. The economic crisis which was almost identical to that of 1998 sounded the death knell of the Chinese system.

The Chinese economy had been running in serious debit for over a decade, and there had been many rumours of rioting and unrest, especially in the poor rural areas, which had been leaked to the West. The high-single-figure growth in the economy was not, as had been popularly assumed, due to deregulation of markets or inflow of foreign investment. The whole system was supported by the government's continual investment of the state banks' financial capital into loss-making, creaking state-owned industries. This was money invested in industries that employed the vast majority of urban Chinese workers which did not show any return on the capital investment. It was only a matter of time, therefore, before the state banks ran out of money; arguably they had all been technically bankrupt from around mid-1998. Luckily for the Chinese government the people were addicted savers. What the people were not fully aware of until the crash of 7 January 2003 was the extent to which their savings had been and were being used by the government to finance its massive external debt and the propping up of wasteful state industries.

The collapse of confidence in Asia started in China as the government attempted to forestall actual state bankruptcy by announcing plans to lay off an incredible twenty-five million state employees. The Western investment houses had seen the writing on the wall and forced the crunch to come by uni-laterally withdrawing $25 billion from China between New Year and 7 January alone. The Asian countries surrounding China had far more at stake and accounted for around 70 per cent of all foreign investment in China. It was in their interests to prop the ailing Chinese economy up for as long as possible and simply hope for the best. As the crisis in Asia unfolded, rumours abounded about the misuse of trillions of dollars of private savings by the government. There was a rush by the populace to the banks in an attempt to withdraw what they had saved (or thought they had) in order to turn it into hard US dollar or Euro cash. Stock markets in the Far East lost 50 per cent of their value overnight, and even the robust Dow Jones lost nearly 14 per cent on 8 January.

The rioting that followed the refusal of the banks (on the orders of central government) to hand over any cash spread rapidly throughout the land and was severely dealt with by local army units. Details of the number of deaths and injuries remain scant to this day. We can only be sure that the expression of dissatisfaction by the people, as well as veiled threats by the army made to the Party (since the army was also full of officers and men who saved for retirement), were enough to cause a shiver of fear to pass through the edifice that was the Communist Party upper echelons. In the second week of January the rural poor joined the urban soon-to-be-unemployed and the pro-democracy students in rioting all over China on a massive scale. The army's less than one hundred per cent enthusiasm for the brutal repression of people who were demonstrating on an issue with which most of its personnel sympathised was enough to force radical change on the Chinese leadership. Also, before the attempted reforms of the previous regime, much of Chinese manufactur-ing and private enterprise was controlled by the local military commanders, who acted as local warlords and were able to cream off profits. The military had become increasingly antagonistic when the government committed itself to reform which would entail divesting it of all its interests and control over private enterprise. They were keen to back a new leader who hinted at the return of the system of privilege and waste.

Into the breach stepped Deng Xhion, an aggressive leader, a stripling at only forty-nine, who was out to make his mark and who well understood the need to distract the Chinese people from economic hardship that had gripped the country for the previous two years. The most obvious distraction was Taiwan, and Xhion judged that the time for action against Taiwan would be while Europe was embroiled in the Balkans and the US heavily engaged in Korea. Previously, when China had threatened, the US had dispatched a couple of carrier battle groups to Taiwan to show solidarity and deter the Chinese from stepping over the brink. With the entire US Pacific Fleet engaged in air operations over Korea, China judged that the US could hardly detach a significant portion of her air assets to deal with their rightful reclamation of Taiwan.

In mid-February the Chinese began making plans in earnest to finally attempt their much-practised and often-threatened amphibious invasion of Taiwan. The US had watched the build-up of forces from space with incredulity. The Chinese had over the previous four years been steadily building an arsenal of tactical ballistic missiles across the Taiwan Strait. By 2003 there were no fewer than eight hundred Type M-9 and M-11 missiles targeted at the 'errant province' of twenty-three million Taiwanese. This deployment was more of a political move to force the issue of sovereignty rather than to enhance any real military capability. The Chinese strategy was to increase the pressure on the US and Taiwan through the presence of so many missiles that the US would include Taiwan as part of the US–Japanese pacific tactical missile defence shield plan, which would be tantamount to acknowledging Taiwan's *de facto* independence. If this happened China could justifiably cry foul and carry out her threat to invade. The Chinese government, economically crippled as it was, was also at the end of its tether with the rest of the world, especially countries of the West, which were using Taiwan's application to join various world bodies such as the WTO (by threatening to approve the applications) as a lever to forcing through increased democratic reform on the mainland. The US and Taiwan had, in spite of Chinese posturing with missiles, avoided the wider TMD issue. Taiwan herself refrained from declaring independence in the full knowledge that doing so would invite a direct response, and that the longer she stayed *de facto* independent the greater her chance would be of eventual political separation from the Chinese agenda.

Thus with China's long-term plans thwarted, the US and Taiwan playing their cards very close to their chests, and the US military distracted and engaged in Korea, the new Chinese leader decided to use what he perceived to be a window of unparalleled opportunity. The Chinese view of the war in Korea had changed from approval at the removal of the nuclear threat to one of veiled antagonism. Beijing called on the US and South Korea to respect the sovereign right of the North to exist. She had foreseen the end state, which would be a united Korea, with a strong US military and possibly also a Japanese presence along her border. At the same time, therefore, Chinese troops began building up their strength along the Yalu River area for their own invasion of North Korea. In Washington the President warned China in the clearest possible terms of the consequences of aggression against Taiwan and detached a small battle group headed by two guided missile cruisers to the east of Taiwan. Beijing was only encouraged by this limited response and read it as a mixture of weakness and a lack of determination by the US to defend Taiwan.

Accordingly the Chinese sent a vanguard of some sixteen destroyers and frigates and a dozen Kilo- and Ming-class submarines to effect a blockade of Taipei in the hope of provoking the Taiwanese into firing the first shots. (The entire Chinese Navy was essentially a large coastal force, comprising some twenty destroyers, forty frigates, around two hundred fast attack craft and sixty submarines. In technology terms it was some two decades behind the might of the US Navy.) The skies over the Taiwan Straits were patrolled by the cream of the Chinese Air Force which consisted of virtually the entire inventory of Su-27 Flankers (225 aircraft organised into ten regiments). Having ignored several airspace infringements in the last week of March, the Taiwanese fired a salvo of SAMs at a cluster of Flankers that were approaching Taipei directly at high speed, downing two of them. For the Chinese this 'aggression' was sufficient excuse for escalation, and there followed a sea battle some 150 miles north-east of Taipei with exchanges of SSMs between the two fleets. The Taiwanese Air Force was reluctant to challenge the presumed dominance of the patrolling Flanker horde and was retained for point air defence. In the sea battle the Chinese lost two frigates, a destroyer and one submarine, with six others damaged to a greater or lesser extent by Harpoon missile hits, in exchange for two Taiwanese destroyers and four missile craft sunk and a similar number damaged. China decreed that the moment had come for Taiwan to meet its destiny and the invasion fleet sailed on 31 March from ports across southern and eastern China in what was planned to be an attempt at an amphibious landing in the classic Normandy manner.

The US had done much in an attempt to defuse and resolve the crisis by diplomatic means and had been scrupulous in ensuring that the USN kept its distance from the Battle of the East China Sea, as it was subsequently called. Once it became clear that an invasion was under way, the US President decided to take direct action. The details of what followed are still, five years later, held in top-secret classified vaults under the Pentagon, but we can guess at the sequence of events. On the morning of 1 April, with the invasion fleet gathering, news started to emerge from GCHQ Cheltenham intercepts of Chinese military radio traffic. The reports stated that in the space of a few minutes between 0804 and 0809 two of the largest Chinese troopships and four anti-air war destroyers had been 'hit' and were sinking with thousands of sailors and soldiers jumping into the shark-infested seas. Four hours later, at 1217, a second report stated that a further troopship, two destroyers and two frigates had suffered similar backbreaking attacks.

The Chinese military flew into a panic and assumed, as the rest of the world did, that either Taiwan's tiny force of six submarines had scored spectacular successes or that US SSNs had directly intervened – which the US vehemently denied. There was some unease at this assessment on the part of the armchair experts as the details of the stricken ships' positions emerged. Also, there was no sign of any submarine activity and not a single report of SSM attacks.

We can still only hypothesise that these were the first and second operational sorties by the prototype Aurora hypersonic bomber. The Aurora, now understood to be called the Black Horse, was a super-stealthy development of the SR-71 Blackbird. The difference was that Black Horse was powered by twin ramjets capable of speeds between Mach 7 and Mach 10. The only clues to its existence were the occasional sightings of doughnut-ringed vapour trails that formed in the upper atmosphere during deceleration through the stratosphere. The single Black Horse was almost certainly launched from Area 51 in the heart of the Nellis Range area in Nevada. From there it would have flown the great circle route up over Alaska and the Aleutian Islands and down over Kamchatka and Korea, going into lower space as it did so and descending to 120,000 feet and decelerating to around Mach 4 for the release of its weapons. Total flight time from take-off to weapons release would have been a little under two hours. The weapons were probably uranium-tipped tungsten darts that did not have any kind of warhead. With impact velocities in excess of Mach 5 the sheer kinetic energy was enough to cause catastrophic damage to any target, and anyway the sensor and warhead fusing problems created by the speed of such a projectile had still not been fully solved. Once the real-time target data had been fed via satellite the autopilot calculated the optimum approach to a multiple target set and fired the weapons (probably a load of six but possibly eight) automatically.

Again, what happened on the second trip home is a matter for conjecture, especially since the Black Horse would not be seen again and its existence publicly acknowledged until early 2007. It seems probable that the craft encountered difficulty during the re-entry over the north-eastern Pacific and broke up, vaporising some two hundred miles off the coast of Vancouver. This theory would explain the unusual daytime 'comet' spotted by Alaskan and Canadian fishermen, as well as the delay into service of the subsequent four Black Horses until late 2006 – the loss of the only prototype is always a major setback, but even more so when all telemetry and evidence that might have given clues as to the causes of the failure have vanished.

The Chinese Central Command was left with no choice. The invasion had to be called off. China railed against the West, Taiwan and the US in particular, but was met with a wall of silence; in reality, short of a nuclear exchange, there was little China could do to respond. For the Americans, despite the loss of Black Horse, this was a real strategic victory in ambiguous warfare.

Domestically, the failed invasion had historic ramifications. And to make matters worse the Chinese Army did not distinguish itself in North Korea. The UN had imposed immediate and all-inclusive commercial and economic sanctions on China at the very beginning of her belligerence and was not disposed to lift them in a hurry. The Chinese economy, heavily dependent on imports of raw materials and especially petroleum, went into meltdown in late April and early May. The army was stunned by the loss of thousands of its men at sea and laid the blame squarely at the door of an embarrassed navy, which remained without adequate explanation or excuse for the losses. The top seven admirals in the navy, and five senior army generals, were tried by 'People's Courts' and shot for incompetence, but this only served to anger the armed forces further. Revolution was in the air.

A European Failure

With the departure of the Americans the multiple antagonists in the Balkans, much like naughty children, immediately set about testing the strength of the resolve of the new Euro-Russian 'authority' to establish where their behavioural boundaries lay. Throughout the winter months, without the centrality and authority that had been part of the US presence, the number of 'incidents' increased alarmingly. The US reconnaissance and intelligence-gathering system continued to provide excellent indicators of Serb, Croat, Muslim, Montenegrin and Kosovan intentions, and the Pentagon, via Nato's headquarters in Brussels, worked overtime providing 'advice' on what it saw as the best course of action in response to events. Unfortunately, without the 'first among equals' being present, the actual responses by the EuroForces were sluggish, indecisive, sometimes uncoordinated and often too late. This, combined with mixed and disparate diplomatic signals about the consequences of non-compliance with the EuroForce agenda, served only to weaken the impact and authority of the military forces while encouraging the potential combatants to prepare to take matters into their own hands. Indeed, without the strong and relatively independent hand of the US overseeing decision-making, the European effort quickly degraded into a struggle of private agendas between the French, Russians and Germans while the British attempted to broker compromise. The private view of regional governments was that conflict was inevitable. As a result the arming and rearming of both the disaffected and threatened increased: the Russians provided Serbia with the best equipment they could offer, including S-300 SAMs; the Austrians and Hungarians provided arms for the Croats, financed by Germany; the Muslim world did the same via Albania for the KLA and Bosnian Muslims. It was only five months from the departure of the last American soldier (on the last day in office by the Democratic administration) to the reignition of war.

The Serbs remained deeply unhappy not only with the loss of Montenegro but also with the loss of two-thirds of Kosovo. The departure of the Americans gave them an opportunity that was too good to pass up. The Serb aim was to make it too painful, in terms of casualties, for the peacekeeping forces to remain anywhere in the Balkans. Additionally, by avoiding attacking the Russian and French forces, they hoped to increase divisions and mutual suspicion among the providing nations.

Small 'civilianised' elements of the Serb Army, as well as special forces and a host of patriotic sympathisers, initiated a guerrilla war against all non-Slav and non-French forces in the region. The sheer volume, geographic spread and tenacity of attacks on the peacekeeping forces astounded the West. The first hit-and-run attacks occurred in southern Kosovo and within twenty-four hours the number of incidents had increased to a flood. Soldiers were gunned down, convoys ambushed, barracks mortared or bombed in Kosovo, Montenegro, Bosnia, Albania, Macedonia, Croatia and even Greece. The Serb leadership naturally disavowed the attacks. Within one week the number of casualties inflicted on the peacekeepers exceeded four hundred. Across Europe, as the first body-bags arrived home, governments flew into a state of panic while opposition parties demanded a withdrawal of peacekeepers from where there was no peace to keep. The fragile peaces in Bosnia, Kosovo and Montenegro were shattered as militia groups and civilians, all armed to the teeth, carried out increasingly overt attacks on each other's populations.

Nato's Military Council went into emergency session and emerged in full condemnation of the Serbs. The UN, after a warning by Nato, ordered all members of aid agencies and any other westerners in Serbia that were involved in the post-Kosovo rebuilding programme to leave the country within twenty-four hours. The in-theatre disarray of the peacekeepers and poor weather encouraged the Serb Army to attempt limited raids out of northern Kosovo. They fared very badly against British and German forces on the few occasions when they attempted to force a passage. The British Brigade, with its Challenger 2s and handful of Apache helicopter gunships, stopped the Serbs in their tracks in the few defensive encounter battles that took place when the Serbs tried to force the issue. Possibly the deciding incident which convinced Nato to take strong and immediate action was Sky television footage of Russians in northern Kosovo refusing point blank to interfere with the military movements of their 'fellow Slavs', let alone open fire, and indulging in waving them through with encouragement. This coincided with a Greek threat to invade Macedonia to deal with Kosovar terrorists and a counter-threat by Turkey to come to the direct aid of the same.

In the early hours of 3 March the three aircraft carriers, six guided missile cruisers and a host of other escorts of the reinforced 6th Fleet sailed into the Adriatic and, in conjunction with land-based units flying from Italy, began an air campaign that was to last sixty days. The plan, carried out by in excess of 1,500 Nato combat aircraft, in sharp contrast to the slow start of the 1999 campaign, was one of pure punishment. The majority of the strikes, led by waves of cruise missiles, were aimed at causing as much destruction as possible of the reconstructed Serb war machine and military infrastructure. It was the Serb Army that represented the centre of gravity of Serb power and it was the army that would be hit directly. In the operational area the lessons of 1999 had been learned and a fleet of over two hundred attack helicopters swarmed under the weather and directly hammered Serb Army units and advancing columns. The Serb Air Force resisted only as long as it took for the entire inventory of aircraft to be destroyed on the ground.

This time around there were no half-measures and on 1 May a Nato ground force of five US (three shipped directly from Korea), two French and German divisions and a British division invaded Serbia from the north out of Hungary. As the weather cleared they swept all Serb Army opposition before them and reached Belgrade in just six days. Russian threats at direct intervention were politely and firmly ignored, and even the Russians had to admit privately that there was actually little they could practically do. On 8 May there was a military coup and the Serb President disappeared.

The Serb Army commanders accepted an unconditional cease fire and on cessation of the air campaign the US President embarked on a charm offensive to Moscow to persuade the Russians that it might be in the best interests of all concerned if it were Russian troops that were given the role of policing all of an errant Serbia proper in the aftermath of the Nato onslaught. Russia, keen to lead on the international stage, put aside her immediate outrage and sent three crack air-mobile divisions directly to Belgrade. The Serb guerrilla offensive across the region, without supply and denied high-level guidance and backing, faltered but never faded completely.

By early summer the second rebuilding of Serbia with American money began. This time it included an education programme similar to that under way in Korea and the setting up of an interim civil administration before free and fair elections that would take place one year later.

For the French, German and British governments the failure of the European-led initiative both in the Balkans as a whole and to contain an errant Serbia was among the last nails in the coffin of the dreams of a federal European state. The conclusion across Europe was that any act of foreign policy that required military force had become unthinkable without the direct involvement of the USA.

A Change in China

Back in China during May the shortage of food and complete loss of value of any kind of monetary currency meant that rioting and civil disobedience spread rapidly across the whole of the country. On 4 June 2003, the day of the fourteenth anniversary of the Tiananmen Square massacre, crowds gathered in Beijing, Shanghai and all major cities. There were millions thronging the streets in a day of national protest and a general strike. The army was ordered to disperse the protesters. The first tanks to fire upon the crowds in Peking were themselves knocked out by tanks whose soldiers sympathised with the protesters. The army view was that the ruling regime had betrayed the nation and the people – not only militarily. More importantly for the wage packets and stomachs of the 1.2 billion Chinese, the government had knowingly led China into insolvency, catastrophic currency devaluation and economic chaos. The execution of those held responsible for the failure of the Taiwan expedition was enough to convince most of the army that the government was not acting in their best interests either. The generals, seeing a chance to extend their period in power and therefore a chance to plunder state coffers, turned the revolution on its head and ordered their men not to resist the crowds. Extra BBC, Sky and CNN television crews were flown in on Chinese military aircraft to record the scenes of protesters and soldiers embracing and marching together to occupy government buildings and offices and to arrest officials. Curiously the army also ensured that the scenes of massacre by the 'forces of tyranny', as they described the few dissenting army units still loyal to the government, were not suppressed and were shown nationwide and worldwide. This enabled the rest of the army to be portrayed as liberators and protectors of the people and gain much popular support, thus helping them to enlist the support of the air force in neutralising the 'rebel' army units. Following three weeks of protest and demonstration in every village and every town where reporters from the West were invited, the army had incarcerated all the major figures of the old regime and set up a new Chinese Ruling Council which consisted of its own chosen men. In the mêlée Deng Xhion disappeared. Free(ish) elections followed the lifting of sanctions (achieved surprisingly rapidly following acquiescence to the US insistence on formal recognition of Taiwan and renunciation of all historical claims), and China became a pseudo-democracy. Taiwan was recognised as an independent state on 1 January 2004, fifty-five years after her struggle for independence had begun. During the Chinese elections the representatives of the various parties were genuine enough, but all ends of the political spectrum were dominated by a Military Council which carried a very big stick.

The 'China Crisis' following so closely on the heels of success in Korea was a landmark in global politics. It confirmed what had been suspected by the world, and known by the Americans, all along. This was that the USA was, whether rightly or wrongly, the self-appointed world policeman, and that she would act where and when she saw fit, in her own interests and only by coincidence in concert with others, with or without allies or approval. Moreover, the US military was deemed to be unchallengeable. Today, China is a relatively poor but stable democracy, very much in the mould that India was in the 1990s, but with the army always in the shadows in an 'oversight' role. Trade and investment are increasing steadily as confidence, so suddenly lost in 2002, has grown over five years of peace since the revolution.

The Second Domino

Unlike in Algeria, where the acceptance of an Islamic government was inevitable, the Moroccan Army took the opposite view. The 'Reform and Renewal Islamic Party' had been tolerated by the King as part of the political process. All known and suspected Islamic activists were rounded up under newly introduced anti-subversive laws and the more extreme religious preachers were, on occasion, dragged off to prison directly from the mosques. Islam was no different to any religion when faced with adversity and persecution. It thrived, and rapidly became the focus for anti-junta activity and discontent. The people had an expectation that as in Algeria an Islamic state would follow military rule; it soon became clear that the army had an entirely different agenda. The situation worsened in late November 2002. Although there was a wave of nationalistic fervour when Cueta and Melilla were occupied in July, this soon vaporised as economic sanctions bit. On the announcement of further public spending cuts, and with the distinct possibility of rationing looming, the people, led by the universities' undergraduates and a mass of unemployed graduates, took to the streets in a series of general strikes. The army, without any political restraint, attempted to clear the streets by force. When young and poorly trained and led conscripts feel threatened by hostile mobs there is normally a predictable outcome, and it came as no surprise to observers that the situation deteriorated into a series of running battles, with the army units becoming increasingly willing to open fire on protesters. It took just three weeks of a complete breakdown of the social and economic order for the army to realise that the Cueta/Melilla move was a blunder of Crimean proportions.

The King, still commanding great respect from his hospital

bed, entreated the leader of the Royal Guard to effect a compromise with the leading protesters who had rallied the support of virtually all the working and middle classes as food disappeared from the shelves. He would not sit by and watch his country ruined by the personal ambitions and agendas of greedy generals. The army was given an honourable opt-out to defuse the situation and agreed to the formation of a 'reasonable' Islamic-based government with the King remaining head of state and Defender of the Faith. On the first anniversary of the military takeover, 24 July 2003, Morocco established an Islamic monarchy and sanctions were lifted pending negotiations on the future of the Spanish territories.

An American Precedent

By 2003 several ballistic missile programmes had matured to the point where the US felt compelled to take unilateral action. And the events in Korea, China and the Balkans had served to confirm America's absolute supremacy in purely military terms and political dominance of the world stage. In Iraq's case the US would be able to kill two birds with this particular stone, namely the destruction of the threat from Iraq and a warning shot across the bows of other nations. The 'other nations' were an ever-growing number who qualified through the possession of weapons of mass destruction (nuclear, biological or chemical), the capability to deliver them well beyond their own borders via medium-range ballistic missiles (MRBMs), and were perceived to have an anti-American inclination. The historical ripples of the North Korean propensity (before she was brought to heel) to sell advanced missile technology to whoever paid hard cash were being felt uneasily in the West. The original Scud series was developed across the Third World; the Scud B had a range of some 500 km, the Scud C 700 km and the Scud D 900 km. From later Scud models the North Koreans developed the Nodong 1 and 2 with ranges of 1,000 km and 1,500 km respectively. Pakistan, India, Iran and Iraq were able to substantially advance their own programmes based on No-dong technology. While India and Pakistan's arsenals remained pointed at each other, the Iranian and Iraqi missiles were clearly for use further afield.

The North Korean Tae-po Dong programme was dual track. The Tae-po Dong 1, which had a range of around 1,750 km, was purely military. The Tae-po Dong 2 represented an attempt to develop a true ICBM and a satellite launch capability. From the North Korean Tae-po Dong 1 and Nodong series the Iranians developed the Shahabs. The Iraqis were not far behind, and rumours of a new missile dubbed the Al Hussein IV emerged as early as 2001. It was based on the Tae-po Dong design and from anywhere inside Iraq would be able to reach all of Israel, Ankara and Cyprus. Thanks to the lifting of sanctions Iraq was able to develop this relatively rapidly.

Back in 1996 Mossad agents had firm evidence that Iraq was in the process of building two small nuclear implosion devices. The yield of such weapons would be comparable to the Hiroshima bomb, and all that was missing was the expertise to fit the warheads to the extended-range Scud C missiles and ensure a high-confidence firing sequence as well as the few kilograms of enriched uranium required to fill the warheads. The lifting of sanctions made obtaining both of these missing elements eventually possible. It remains unclear where the enriched uranium came from. The major suspects were Russia, the Ukraine and China, none of whom would feel threatened by a nuclear Iraq and all of whom had much to gain elsewhere by introducing a further element of instability to an area where they shared mutual borders with those countries that also bordered Iraq. The Chinese had single-handedly solved Pakistan's long technological struggle for a nuclear capability in 1997 by supplying both Nodongs and the enriched U-235 for the warheads. Whoever it was who helped them, Iraq had paid them an astronomical sum in order to complete her dream of being able to single-handedly 'burn half of Israel' – a slogan repeated throughout Iraq from 1991. Aware of what the US had done in Korea in the winter of 2002, the Iraqis kept their achievements top secret. However, again the human link in the chain of knowledge was to prove the weak link. A young Austrian scientist, Dr Joachim Kreusler, who had been working on the Iraqi special weapons project from the lifting of sanctions, was unable to contain his moral conscience in spite of the footballer's salary he was earning and the promised bonus for success. Ostensibly on holiday in Vienna, he walked into the US embassy on a late August morning in 2003 and told the Americans that their worst fears were on the verge of being realised. The marriage of an MRBM with a credible nuclear warhead was taking place just outside Baghdad.

The US had long since given up any pretence of neutrality in the Middle East. Unpublished papers from Capitol Hill and the Pentagon reveal that on the lifting of sanctions the US had resolved to take unilateral action 'in the long-term interests of the free world' – whether the 'free world' liked or approved of US methods or not. The missile programmes around the world had all been monitored extremely carefully by the US. Prior to 2003, there had been but two practical US responses to the proliferation of ballistic missiles. The first was to use force, as she had done in Korea; dictators understood applied force. The second, fuelled by dismay at the continuing failure of its own THAADS (Theatre High-Altitude Air Defence System), was to fund two-thirds of the $2 billion Israeli Anti-Tactical Ballistic Missile (ATBM) Arrow 2. The young Austrian scientist had brought the first tried and tested method back into immediate and sharp focus.

The US President called the Joint Chiefs and senior advisers to an emergency session. The decision was made to act alone and without warning against this threat to world peace. Iraq could not be allowed to have nuclear-tipped ballistic missiles. The policy statement was as simple as that. The Cabinet doves correctly warned of the world outrage that would follow such an apparently unprovoked and unannounced attack. The President agreed to 'inform the English', from whose soil the attack would be launched, and silenced the doubters by simply announcing that the USA 'was not involved in a popularity contest' – which was just as well.

Two B-2s flying from Lakenheath in eastern England were

launched twenty-four hours later, each flying directly to Iraq without fear of detection. Both aircraft carried four GBU-24 deep-penetrator weapons. The target was some five storeys below ground.

The palace, Saddam Hussein's finest, which was atop the underground storage bunker where the warheads were having the finishing touches applied, was wrecked. Eighteen Iraqis were killed. The Iraqi nuclear arsenal was eliminated in an instant. Iraq, indeed the whole Arab world, was outraged at the 'premeditated rape of national sovereignty'. Of US allies only the UK and France's new right-wing regime came out in unqualified support. Iraq warned the US that revenge would be swift and terrible. The US, unperturbed, had now confirmed the precedents set in the Second Korean War and the Taiwan crisis: she would act without reference if she felt that it was in the interests of the long-term safety of the American people. And, the President added in his address to the nation, 'history will one day thank us for what we have done.' Of that we cannot be certain. What is certain is that despite the hue and cry revenge was not immediate. This was the first step, however, a catalyst in the process that was to unite the Arab world into a powerful global alliance that was more than the Arab League had ever been. The demonstrations provoked across the Arab world in outrage at 'unprovoked American aggression' were massive. In Saudi Arabia and the United Arab Emirates in particular the streets were packed with protesters demanding an end to the American presence in their lands. Israel looked on and nodded sage approval of the American action.

The Second Revolution

Following the death of the Russian President in early 2002 there followed a power struggle in Russia that culminated in the Second Russian Revolution, led by the army generals in Moscow. Boris Yeltsin's successor had been a weak man, dominated by corrupt civil servants and an all-powerful mafia. It was probably the thought of the $50 billion, which the EU had agreed to pay for examining the process of independence for the Kaliningrad Salient, falling into the hands of the mafia 'crooks and criminals' which so appalled what was to become the Kremlin 'junta'. While nothing of long-term value could be achieved for Russian society by such a sum, many of the immediate debt problems would be solved: soldiers' back pay, unpaid pensions, contracts military, industrial and agricultural which had not been honoured. Everyone, it seemed, owed someone else something. Printing roubles only caused inflation. The useful national currencies had become US dollars and Euros, which slowly replaced the German mark. The feeling at the secret meeting of the military council was that something had to be done. If the money were to be effectively handed over to the godfathers it would simply disappear, as so much of 'democratic' Russia's wealth had already done.

The Russian military had been ruthless in its cuts during the professionalisation process to ensure an efficient and self-loyal core. This was in sharp contrast to many sections of society and industry which continued down what seemed to be an endless spiral of slow decay. The military, however, and the industry that supplied it, saw a renaissance fuelled by exports. Cash from Russian exports of high-tech fighters and surface-to-air missile systems to Asia, the Middle East and anyone with sufficient cash was used by the armed forces to supplement the government revenue required to keep them at a minimum acceptable standard. Every tank or aircraft sold meant that one could be supplied to the military. The Russian salesmen became ferociously competitive. Large bribes, on a scale not seen since the sale of F-104 Starfighters to the air forces of Europe in the 1970s, were the order of the day. The world's new economic tigers, revitalised after the slumps of 1998 and early 2002, were conveniently grouped together, such that keeping up with one's neighbour in terms of military size and sophistication was seen as not just a necessity but a definite patriotic duty. The advantages of buying Russian instead of Western were rather like those of buying a Volkswagen instead of a BMW. The Russian equipment came with all the extras already fitted at no extra cost, were rugged and reliable, and only cost half as much. As the Germans were always so fond of saying about their own Volkswagens, with Russian military equipment of the early twenty-first century 'one knows exactly what one has got'. The tigers could not get enough of the new sleek 'Black Eagle' T-100 tanks complete with a 140mm smooth-bore main gun and the world's best reactive armour. The Russian route was the fast track to military respectability. As well as supplying the Asian tigers, Russia was able to re-establish her position of major arms exporter to the Middle East. Egypt, Syria, Iran, Libya and Iraq were able to purchase the best available to the Russian forces. These included Su-27s and some Su-32 fighters, T-100s and scores of SA-10s (Russian Patriot SAMs) and SA-12s, Tunguskas (a Russian version of the German Gepard and Roland combined) and advanced missile technology which would improve the accuracy of Scuds by a whole order of magnitude.

In spite of the upturn in the military-industrial base, the economy was still creaking along, its growth stunted by corruption. The investment capital, which had begun to flow from Western acceptance of real political freedom and economic growth, was being wasted. The ruling mafia underclass was using both profits and project dollars* to finance its dachas, sports cars and whorehouses. And the army was not about to allow Russia to take a back seat in European and world affairs with a revitalised Germany beginning to throw her weight and unencumbered opinions around, and with Nato's 'capture' of the Baltic states in the early spring, following as it did with almost disrespectful haste the death of the Russian President. And of course the Russians were dismayed at the unending series of 'police actions' being carried out by her once-equal superpower opponent the USA without, it appeared, any restraint.

The Second Russian Revolution began on 25 October 2003 (eighty-six years to the day since the Bolsheviks had assumed

---

*'Project dollars' means money donated by the international community to be spent on projects to revitalise the economy or industry.

power). It was less bloody and more popular than the first. The so-called 'new model' army simply moved out of its barracks and into the streets proclaiming its loyalty to the incumbent President and its distaste for the rulers of the underworld. Platoons of T-100 Black Eagles led companies of BTR and BMP 2000s into the business and residential districts of all Russia's major cities. The army had been biding its time, and with its sister service the KGB had compiled exhaustive lists of mafia bosses, workers and sympathisers. The district bosses were identified and executed – most of them with a bullet to the nape of the neck.

The lesser lights of the organised crime gangs were pardoned in exchange for denouncing their bosses. Once the buzz spread throughout the districts, queues began to form at regimental command posts of loyal citizens eager to denounce their neighbours. In traditional Russian style the families of the executed were paraded before being deported to Siberian labour camps. This sent waves of euphoric nostalgia through those in the crowds old enough to remember the discipline of the communist state and its military machine. The general public came out into the streets to celebrate this temporary 'return to the old days and old ways'. The Russians had genuinely missed the sense of military control pervading their lives and now welcomed it back to replace the uncertainty, fear and distrust that were the trade tools of the mafioso. In the Russian psyche there appeared to be a deep-rooted desire for non-independence and collective incompetence – a trait first noticed by Tolstoy when he tried to get his peasants to work their own plots of land.

The army rapidly organised elections which ensured that their own men were given places high up the President's party's list. Those that they trusted were in power. These same men were the real controllers of Russia's economy and harboured expansionist desires, especially towards the Baltic, that were not out of step with the desires of the high-calibre officers in command of the New Model Army.

The system of government was seen by the West as a 'military democracy'. It was a purely Russian solution which could only have happened in Russia. The people needed strong leadership; now they had it. They felt able to stand proud on the world stage. Certainly a little bit of 'democracy' had been lost, but having tasted both communism and mafia democracy the Russians were not unnaturally wary of Western ideas on government.

There would no longer be any mutiny now that the army was well paid, without conscripts and politically aware. The military being 'paid' to 'protect' its own industrial base was the biggest racket of them all. With the country and system of government once again stable, the people expected the new Russia to reassert itself on the world stage, to be respected as a major player as the old Soviet Union had been. The turmoil to the south, across Africa and the Middle East, which would end up with the emergence of an Islamic super power coalition, combined with the arrogance of Nato, would give Russia the ideal opportunity to flex her muscles. She would be provided with an excuse to do so by Nato and the Baltic states themselves.

Unease in the Baltic

Complicating Baltic politics was the Kaliningrad Salient, known in the West as the Oblast. This was an area of former East Prussia which the Russians had annexed in 1945. It was separated from Russia and Byelorussia by Lithuania and Poland. It was about the same size and economic significance as East Anglia, with a population of 900,000, of whom some 80 per cent were ethnic Russians. For the Russians it was a permanent reminder of the 'Great Patriotic War' of 1941–5, and a disproportionate number of troops were stationed there during the six decades that followed. For Russia it was her foothold in the Baltic and gained importance as Nato expanded eastwards to include Poland as a full member and the Baltic states as associate members. In early 2003, on the accession to Nato of the Baltic states, the EU agreed to help Russia ease its vast foreign and crippling internal debts with a single payment of US $50 billion. In return the Russians agreed in principle to enter negotiations that were aimed at allowing this former part of East Prussia to become an independent neutral state, a fourth Baltic republic. In spite of the large ethnic Russian population the 'Governors' of the Oblast had become increasingly vocal in their calls for independence. The Baltic Republican Party, formed when Gorbachev was in power in Russia, was the major political party. Its number-one manifesto item was the issue of sovereignty. The people of the Oblast had great sympathy with this. They were, they felt, different from Greater Russia in many respects; they had rapidly developed a Western-style business culture with private enterprises springing up at a rapid rate. This was both helped and encouraged by Germany, Poland and to a lesser extent Lithuania, all of which had invested sums of money, disproportionate to that spent in Russia, to further develop the region. As the Oblast's economic strength grew, so did her resentment at having to hand a large percentage of the profits back to Moscow, which in turn showed little interest in reinvesting in the Oblast. It was not surprising therefore that the Oblast, having tasted both prosperity and democracy, increasingly inclined towards the West.

The Russian Baltic Fleet would, however, continue to use Kaliningrad as its main port and it would become a sovereign Russian base on a ninety-nine year lease. The Russians committed themselves to a ten-year withdrawal plan. At the height of the Cold War there had been more troops, tanks and aircraft in the salient than the whole of the UK's combined armed forces. By 2003 the Russian presence had dwindled to a single mechanised infantry division of some 15,000 men, 500 tanks and 30 helicopters. Following the Second Revolution in October, the situation changed dramatically. The anti-Nato voice in Russia's new military-controlled government grew louder and more hostile. The government announced that Russia would no longer put up with being pushed around by Nato, and her isolation in the east was no longer acceptable. The stance taken by the Baltic republics only exacerbated the situation. Once inside Nato they naturally assumed that they were free to do what they felt best in their own long-term interests without any further reference or deference to Russia. In Estonia the first acts of the new Nato-aligned government were to withdraw voting rights from the 400,000 resident Russians – granted in 2001 – and to abolish the teaching of the Russian language in schools and its use in business. Russian was replaced by English. The third action was one that cut straight to the core of the Russian leadership's concerns, and it was that old nemesis oil.

All oil exploration rights were sold by the Estonians to the highest bidder. In the event the country was split between Shell, Amoco and Exxon. Russia could not hope to compete financially with any single one of these powerful multinationals. To rub salt into the wound Estonia invited the now 'unemployed' Russian oil and gas workers, numbering some 20,000, to leave. Only two months after Estonia had done this Latvia, emboldened by Russia's apparent inability to react, announced her intention to embrace a similar lucrative policy.

Thus the final contributor to the Russian decision to invade the Baltic states in 2006 and to throw in her lot with the Islamic Alliance was an economic one. The world's largest oil company in terms of reserves was the Russian Yuksi Company. It was the third-largest in terms of extraction behind Exxon and Shell. Russia's other massive corporation was Gazprom, which accounted for 95 per cent of Russian gas production and controlled the world's largest reserves of natural gas. As if the economic strength of these two companies wasn't enough, between them they also controlled Russia's largest banks, Menatep and Most. These banks in turn had significant controlling interests in the Russian media, namely the ORT, TV6 and NTV television stations. The political power wielded by these companies was massive. Their combination of media, financial and economic strength gave them unhealthy political influence. They were able to finance candidates and their campaigns as well as promote them in the media while denigrating opponents. The two men at the head of the extraction companies were the pinnacle of the ruling élite. It was the production of oil and gas which underpinned the finance of the whole of the Russian state. The return they expected from those they had levered into positions of power was simply a large say in the formulation and execution of Russian foreign policy. The interlinking of oil and gas reserves with foreign policy was not a new phenomenon. The previous sixty years had seen the West adopt an increasing readiness to take direct action many times in the Middle East while remaining ambivalent to other conflicts around the world. Oil, and to a lesser extent gas, was the single commodity that made politicians and in turn their respective military machines take notice.

And so it was with Russia. Except that in 2002 the Yuksi and Gazprom geologists had discovered clear indicators of vast deposits of oil and natural gas under the shales of northern Latvia and central Estonia. The size of these reserves was estimated as being roughly equivalent to all that under the North Sea. The discovery was kept highly secret. It remains unknown whether the Estonians and Latvians had an inkling of the mine of black gold they were sitting on, but the discovery of the reserves marked the beginning of the undeclared policies in those two countries to de-Russianise. The licences granted in the 1990s to the Russian companies were revoked and the campaigns of harassment and eviction began; most of them directed against the employees of the oil and gas giants who made up the greater part of the Russian expatriate community. The controllers of Yuksi and Gazprom were unimpressed by the turn of events in the Baltic and began their own media and direct but discreet political lobby campaigns for 'something' to be done. And it was. But patience was needed.

A New Kind of Monarchy

For Saudi Arabia the American attack on Iraq's nuclear capability was to be a defining moment in its history. The Saudi people had become increasingly antagonistic towards the large US military presence in the country, while the new King attempted to tread a fine line between containing Iraq and appeasing a growing section of the population that was dissatisfied with the state of the nation. Even after the bombing of Saddam Hussein and the lifting of sanctions against Iraq, the US argued for continued military presence while the stability of the new regime was being ascertained. Secretly she let the royal family know that the US might find it difficult to supply spare parts for all the sophisticated US-built weaponry in the Saudi armoury. Grudgingly the King agreed, but the token reduction of US troops in the kingdom did nothing to mollify the regime's mainly Islamic critics who wanted a radical policy of forgive and forget and foreigners out.

The roots of dissatisfaction were many and varied and had as much to do with the cultural and intellectual revival of Islam in the kingdom as unemployment and perceived domination by 'infidel' outside influences. The security of Saudi Arabia and her massive oil reserves was pivotal in defining policy in the West towards the whole of the Middle East. Saudi Arabia herself wished to play a central role but accepted that she would always be disadvantaged with respect to Iraq, Iran and Egypt by her relatively small indigenous population. Of twenty million people in the kingdom in 2003 just over half were Saudi. The rest, which accounted for two-thirds of the actual labour force, were made up of non-Western nationals in unskilled and manual work (mostly other Muslims and Asians) and Westerners who were crucial to the functioning of the economy, working in the petroleum, construction, business and health sectors. The discontent on the part of young and devout Saudis focused on what they described as the endless acquiescence of the ruling élite to American military interests and the staining of Islam through the presence of so many foreigners and their goods. With unemployment among the native population running at over 50 per cent by 2003 they had much time to consider the finer points of Islam and to assess the royal family's role in upholding those values. Also, with the price of oil more than halving from its 1994 levels, the real income of the average citizen more than halved in turn, bringing about a phenomenon unknown to the Saudi people since they had stepped out of their nomadic way of life – economic hardship.

Shortly after the millennium there emerged a powerful

cleric who named himself after the eighteenth-century Muslim reformer Muhammad ibn 'Abd al-Wahab. He called for a return to government through Islamic law. His grassroots support was vast, and the ruling Sudeiri brothers dared not arrest him for fear of open revolt.

What al-Wahab's influence did manage to secure, however, was the subtle replacement in Saudi society of secular values such as justice, nationalism and socialism with Islamic ideals. More importantly perhaps the army, and to a much lesser extent the National Guard, were comprehensively infiltrated, although that is probably the wrong word in this sense, by Islamic fundamentalists. Also, there was simmering resentment between the few who had the direct patronage of the royal family and the many who did not. The spontaneous demonstrations in all echelons of society that followed the US attacks on Iraq gave al-Wahab his chance. To tens of thousands of pilgrims in Mecca he called for the immediate eviction of all evil influences in the country. Furthermore he called for all true Muslims to show their feelings by taking to the streets until the 'infidels' had been banished from the land.

The King, who was a devout Muslim and the head of the National Guard (which, at 60,000 strong, was almost as large as the army), was also an economic pragmatist. He well recognised that throwing out all foreigners would be tantamount to destroying the Saudi economy, dependent as it was on Westerners in particular to function at all. The rhetoric from Mecca continued unabated; the ideal of the purification of all Saudi Arabia was irresistible to the more devout sections of the population. And al-Wahab argued somewhat perniciously that the kingdom could solve its unemployment problems overnight since there was no reason why any Saudi man could not do the job of the highly paid 'infidels', and probably better. To the horror of the King the numbers on the streets grew daily, and the Islamic underground emerged to organise tens of bus-loads of protesters to demonstrate outside military facilities where there were US and UK personnel.

During the second week of December the clamour had still

not died down as the King had hoped and his advisers expected. The people had taken hold of the idea and were not about to let it go. The King hesitated to use force to break up the demonstrations with which, deep down, he had much sympathy. His hope was to ride out the storm and use the memory of the demonstrations and resentment as a lever to curb foreign military activity in the country.

Encouraged by the apparent royal paralysis, al-Wahab's pronouncements grew more daring and critical with each day. He called on the people to demonstrate their solidarity with the Faith by protesting against all things and people that were not of the kingdom. It was with this single message that the situation began to deteriorate. The demonstrators thronged outside the compounds of the Western workers and effectively closed down the banks and commerce centres, the petroleum and chemicals industries and the hospitals by blockading the Westerners in. By now the King was aghast. Every hour that ticked by meant millions of dollars of lost oil revenue. Soon his hand would be forced; it was already too late to attempt to arrest al-Wahab for anti-state activity since virtually the whole nation was captivated by his ranting. And the unrest was not confined to Saudi Arabia. In the neighbouring United Arab Emirates the people also took to the streets; while the end result would be different to that in Saudi Arabia, the effect would be the same.

It was perhaps inevitable that eventually the chanting and shouting would turn to violence. In every society there are undesirable elements and these young men were responsible for the intervention of the Guard. They began by hurling first bricks and then petrol bombs at the compounds and embassies, then spread their activities to the hijacking and wrecking of as many sparkling 4 × 4 vehicles (the status symbol that so clearly separated the haves from the have-nots in Saudi society) as they could find. This was pure lawlessness and enabled the King to order the National Guard to attempt to break up the demonstrations by force under Article 12 of the Constitution. A young lieutenant in Medina, in charge of a platoon of LAVs and a dozen equally young and frightened soldiers, was faced by an angry mob that refused to disperse in one of the confined market squares. He ordered his troops to open fire over the heads of the crowd. Unfortunately the high-velocity bullets and 25mm cannon shells ricocheted around the square, hitting not only several of the crowd, who fell screaming with blood pouring from wounds, but also three of the soldiers. Certain that they were under fire from revolutionary elements, the officer ordered his men to return fire against any identified gunmen. The inexperienced soldiers must have spotted several of the 'gunmen' who had wounded their colleagues, who were lying next to the vehicles, since they poured a devastating hail of fire around all parts of the square. The mob, assuming it was being gunned down, at first recoiled but then turned in fury on the soldiers. In the mayhem, confusion and panic that followed eighteen soldiers and seventy-seven civilians were killed and scores more civilians wounded.

Al-Wahab wasted no time in misinterpreting this unfortunate incident as evidence that the National Guard was anti-Islamic. The fervour of the people now appeared to be unstoppable and the rioting increased. He made his boldest proclamation to date by reminding the people of Article 7 of the Constitution, which stated that the government in Saudi Arabia derived its power from the Holy Koran and not from the King (conveniently ignoring Article 6 on allegiance to the King in time of trouble). With foreign nationals being encouraged to leave by the plane-load the ruling family divided.

One of the brothers, known privately as the Black Sheep, entered into secret negotiations with al-Wahab to call for peace and the establishment of a new regime which would be an Islamic monarchy. And this is what was achieved, but only after the Black Sheep had bribed the King's personal bodyguard, two companies of Pakistani troops, to turn their guns on the King in exchange for safe passages to Karachi and a life of wealth and luxury.

With the King dead the loyalties of the army and National Guard became uncertain, but al-Wahab championed the Black Sheep and called for unity under him as the new Crown Prince and defender of the faith under Islamic law. Al-Wahab had forced the people to chose between their faith and the royal family and the higher calling had won. Left with little choice, since any action against al-Wahab and the Black Sheep would be construed as anti-Islamic, the other royal brothers fell in behind the new Crown Prince in an attempt to hold on to what influence they could muster in exchange for their loyalty.

The Black Sheep wasted no time in giving all foreign troops until the end of the year to leave the country. This first edict found great sympathy with all Saudis and especially the military, who were tired and frustrated by what they perceived as more than a decade of American military highhandedness and insensitivity in the kingdom. For the US the Saudi revolution was a disaster, but it did have some positive aspects. The countries neighbouring Saudi Arabia were left with a clear choice in terms of their future directions: they could either embrace more fully the ideals of Islam and government under the Sha'ria or place themselves entirely in the 'Western' camp and continue as before but accept that their existence could only be guaranteed by the presence of 'Western' forces. The UAE, surprisingly given its wealth but not so given its position sandwiched between and exposed to both Saudi Arabia and Iran, chose the former and like Saudi Arabia became an Islamic monarchy embracing the ideals of an Islamic society. Kuwait, Bahrain and Qatar were all small enough to fear being consumed by their more powerful neighbours no matter what they did and cleverly opted to invite the US forces that were being pushed out of Saudi Arabia to 'temporarily' establish a vastly increased presence in each of their countries. Thus by the end of the year there was a clear divide in the Middle East and a new perception of the nations. Saudi Arabia and the UAE were now firmly in the camp of Islam, alongside Iran and Iraq, and viewed the US as the great enemy. Kuwait, Qatar and Bahrain on the other hand had become much like Calais was to the English in the fifteenth century: bastions of a former era with huge garrisons of foreign troops to guarantee their safety and survival. The Islamic world condemned the three small states as being no more than vassals of the US. While this may have been true the men and tribal families in control were more interested in their own survival than higher ideals, and there was only one nation on earth which was powerful enough and had the political will to guarantee this, and that was 'the Great Satan', as Islamic extremists called the USA.

Chapter Four – 2004

The Birth of a Nation

The family struggles that had replaced the unifying reign of King Hussein of Jordan in 1999 had grown steadily worse, thanks mainly to the increasing influence and clout of the Palestinian majority that now made up three-quarters of the Jordanian populace. The ruling Hashemites were very much in the minority and sons of the old King, aided and abetted by their powerful mothers, actively courted the various Palestinian leaders in order to gain real influence in the country. The new King was a wise man with vision and had anticipated the depth of the Palestinian problem. The late King had been able through measured patronage and the sheer weight of his office to maintain a balance between competing ethnic, political, tribal and religious interests. In order to achieve this, however, he had to effectively filibuster through the pressure for serious reform during his last decade in power, from the time the Islamists became the largest single political party. The essentially Bedouin army underpinned the Hashemite dynasty, but through the millennium, as the Hashemites became an increasingly smaller proportion of the population, the Islamists began openly to accuse the young King of rule through corruption and tribal favouritism.

In the early summer of 2004, following a series of secret meetings with the Palestinian authorities both within and outside Jordan, and with the full backing of all other Arabic interested parties, he declared Jordan to be a Palestinian Islamic monarchy whose territory included the West Bank and Gaza, subsuming the independent state of Palestine into a greater Jordan. The new state would represent all interests fully. Even the Hashemites had to accept that the small loss of their power and influence in the new institutions was better than their complete marginalisation. In one fell swoop Trans-Jordan was reborn and was immediately more anti-Israeli and less inclined to compromise than any previous regime. This bold move, which was welcomed by the whole Arab world, met with silence from the West and outright rejection from Israel and Turkey alone, embracing as it did the ideals of Hamas, Hezbollah and Islamic Jihad. It enabled the wayward 'terrorist' elements of the previously divided Palestinian state to reconcile themselves with the authorities. The political unity provided by the new King in 2004 was sufficient to embolden the activities of all those engaged in anti-Israeli activities.

The first move of the new government came in mid-July and was a royal decree that enabled the local authorities to drill for water to relieve the suffering of the people. By late July drilling into the main aquifer that ran under the West Bank had begun in earnest.

Water Crises*

> 'Judah mourns, her cities languish; they wail for the land and a cry goes up from Jerusalem. The nobles send their servants for water; they go to the cisterns but find no water. They return with their jars unfilled; dismayed and despairing they cover their heads. The ground is cracked because there is no rain in the land; the farmers are dismayed and cover their heads'
>
> Jeremiah, 14, ii–iv

In 1991 the Secretary-General of the United Nations, Boutros Boutros Ghali, stated that 'the next war in the Middle East

---

* The factual basis for this section is taken from 'The Oldest Threat: Water in the Middle East', Jane's Intelligence Review, Al, J., Ventnev, February 1998. 'Water and Conflict', International Security, Vol. 18, No. 1, Harvard and MIT, Peter H. Gleick, September 1993. 'The Strategic Importance of Water', Parameters, Kent Hughes Butts, Spring 1997 Edition.

will be over water not politics'. In this he was half right. The seeds of the 'next war' were indeed over water, but little did he suspect that the conflicts over water would be the precursor to a war that would encompass the whole of the Middle East and not be just a localised Arab–Israeli spat. In 1970 Shimon Peres encapsulated the Israeli view of the long-term Arab policy towards Israel. Somewhat prophetically he wrote: 'The Arabs do not seek just one particular portion of Israel's land, sources of water, oil wells; they are not interested only in political advantage or economic domination. The Arab purpose is all-absorptive – the destruction of Israel and the annihilation or banishment of her inhabitants.'*

This was the view, often unstated, which dominated Israeli politics and underpinned Israel's attitude towards her near and distant neighbours. The Israelis were in no doubt that the final settlement of Israel's future would come through military battle. They were well aware that as long as her neighbours were only beaten militarily, and not crushed as entities, they would, with each succeeding generation, make another more determined attempt to achieve their goal. The series of wars in 1956, 1967, 1973 and 1982 had found the Israelis being less convincing in victory with the progression of time. For twenty years from 1982 the Israelis watched the fighting quality of her own troops decline in both absolute and relative terms. This was blamed on the secularism, or irreligiousness, of her youth, a generation that subscribed to the powerful temptations and arguably degrading moral values of Westernisation. The collectivism that found its expression in the kibbutz was replaced with the freedom of the individual to live his or her life as he or she saw fit without regard to the greater or long-term good let alone sacrifice for such outmoded ideas. *Dulce et decorum est pro patria mon*† was not on the agenda of young Israel. At the same time the collective competence, cohesion and relative quality of equipment and arsenals of her potential adversaries increased.

---

* Shimon Peres, *David's Sling* (Random House, New York, 1970), pp. 9–12.
† 'It is sweet and fitting to die for your country.'

The focus of Arab and world discontent (and US disapproval) throughout the decade before the war was threefold: Israel was perceived to be intransigent on settlers' rights; the view of the Jewish settler apparently had primacy over every other consideration in Israeli politics. Israel remained unwilling to give up meaningful control of land to the fragmented Palestinian state and continued her harsh treatment of the Palestinian people, regarding them a group that harboured terrorists in every home. Israel most visibly expressed her stance of hostile indifference to the Palestinians through a single issue. This single issue, which united the Arab world in its antagonism towards Israel, alongside the activities of Mossad, was water. In the minds of all the Middle East antagonists fresh water, and the control of it, eclipsed in importance petroleum (the West's fixation) or disagreements even about tracts of land.

Israel and her neighbours had been engaged in three separate water disputes for almost forty years. These centred on the Jordan river basin and the West Bank ground aquifers and the supply to the Palestinians in Gaza. In each case the tensions existed because of Israel's 'selfish water management programmes'.

It was in Gaza that the problem was first turned into a crisis. Most of the water available in the Gaza Strip was piped directly from Israel. This gave Israel enormous control over the lives and the population packed into Gaza. Gaza had been rationed from 2003 to an average consumption of 10 cubic metres per family per day for all purposes. This compared unfavourably to the West Bank areas which had 35 cubic metres and was in stark contrast to Israeli consumption of 115 cubic metres (California's average consumption was some 220 cubic metres). What made matters worse was that Gaza's own small water supply, used to supplement that piped from Israel, was decreasing markedly in quality. The few underground aquifers that fed Gaza were not being replenished as fast as even the miserly usage in 2003 would allow. Overuse had caused the water to become increasingly saline as sea water crept in through the lowered underground water table, and poor sanitation meant that human effluent and other wastage also began to creep in. As Gaza began to dry up, the incidence of disease, infant mortality and, with them, discontent grew apace. The Israelis suggested that Gaza should look to Egypt and the Nile to solve her water problems.

The West Bank is an upland area that catches rainfall off the Mediterranean which then percolates through the limestone and into the subterranean aquifers. Some 80 per cent of the water drawn from this source (and 35 per cent of Israel's total supply) was distributed to Israel and West Bank settlers' with the remainder given to the Palestinians. The withdrawal of major elements of the Israeli Defence Forces from the West Bank in 2001 meant that in theory there was much-reduced physical control above ground on the water management activities of the Palestinian authorities. Before the withdrawal, Jerusalem had controlled all drilling activities and water extraction. The Palestinians argued that possession of water and land were inseparable. If they owned the ground above they were within their rights to drill into the aquifers to extract the water below. And this was exactly what they proceeded to do. With the blessing of the new King of Trans-Jordan, the Palestinians carefully orchestrated a media campaign during the late summer of 2004 which highlighted the contrasts between the 'rich Israelis' enjoying their swimming pools in leafy suburbs and the 'poor Palestinians' queuing at wells for buckets half filled with what appeared to be ditch-water. With the world's press showing concern at the inequality, the Trans-Jordan government passed laws setting up and empowering 'independent' water companies to drill for water wherever they saw fit.

The effects in Israel began to be felt immediately. The Israelis were vociferous in their condemnation of the 'willy-nilly and irresponsible' approach adopted by the Palestinians, and their stance hardened when it became apparent that not only was the amount of water available to Israel beginning to decrease at a steady and alarming rate, but that the water was being polluted by the Palestinians. Worse still the water filters were being clogged with limestone run off as a direct result of the drilling.

During the 1967 Six Day War Israel captured significant portions of Jordan and Syria, which enabled her to become the occupier and upstream state for most of the Jordan basin; a position that left Jordan in a particularly vulnerable situation vis-à-vis fresh water. The Israelis had been drawing water from the Golan to supplement their own resources since initial occupation in 1967. The Golan Heights issue was not one of artillery observation or any other military consideration. It was simply one of control over water. And there was no room for compromise. If the Israelis gave up the Golan then Syria would immediately attempt to control the Golan's water. The consequences of such action would be twofold. As well as denying Israel water, Syria would have a significant economic and political lever of control over Jordan, which was utterly dependent on the River Jordan and its feeders for her water. Secondly the Dead Sea, whose level was already drying up at the rate of 50 cm per year by 2000, would dry up at more than twice that rate. The possibility of compromise on the issue of water was stuck between a rock and a hard place. Yitzhak Rabin, before he was assassinated, stated that giving the Golan to Syria in return for peace was an issue that it was impossible to consider without cast-iron guarantees. He went on to say that to the Israeli people water was even more important than peace. It should be remembered that one of the underlying causes of the 1967 war was the Arab League's attempt in the early 1960s to divert the headwaters of the Jordan away from Israel. Rabin was only echoing Premier Levi Eshkol's statement in 1965 that 'water is a question of life for Israel', and therefore if this was ever threatened 'Israel would act to ensure that the waters continue to flow'.

The End of the Peace Process

'Look, their brave men cry aloud in the streets; the envoys of peace weep bitterly. The highways are deserted, no travellers are on the roads. The treaty is broken, its witnesses are despised, no-one is respected. The land mourns and wastes away.'

Isaiah, 33, vii–ix

From the time of her occupation of the West Bank in 1967 Israel pursued a relentless programme of settlement building in what was originally Jordanian, but which became Palestinian, territory. The decades of 'Peace Process' proved, in the end, to be no more than what both parties already knew in their hearts – an illusion. The illusion was perpetuated mainly to satisfy US domestic opinion, which in turn allowed successive administrations to continue their massive financial backing which was designed to ensure Israel's survival. Real peace never had a chance thanks to the extremists in both Israeli and Palestinian camps, and it was only a matter of time before this ultimate truth was accepted by the antagonists.

Thus on top of the gathering storm over the water crisis, in the five years leading to the war the Israeli government hardened its controversial and antagonistic settlement policy with respect to its Arab neighbours. By 2004, in spite of US pressure, Jewish settlement on the West Bank continued; the possession of East Jerusalem, taken from Jordan in 1967, became 'non-negotiable' as long as Israel's enemies continued to support terrorist groups openly dedicated to the destruction of Israel. The Palestinian declaration of independence in the early millennium included East Jerusalem as the new state's capital. In addition, although the WEU force was ensconced as a steel barrier (the WEU's description, it should be noted, not Israel's) across the Golan Heights, Israel steadfastly refused even to discuss giving up the southern Lebanon security zone as long as settlements in northern Israel continued to come under sporadic rocket and artillery attack.

Accordingly, the Arab states surrounding Israel became increasingly miffed and, with the exception of Egypt, redoubled their active support for militant groups such as Islamic Jihad, Hamas and Hezbollah.

Conventionally, Israel's enemies posed little threat to her, so Israel remained relatively content with the status quo, even at the expense of the increasing discomfort of the citizens in the border towns. Despite its disapproval of Israel's actions, the US's bottom line was always to support Israel, thanks to the powerful and influential Jewish lobby within the US government.

The agreements reached by Arafat and Netanyahu in the late 1990s were viewed with severe distaste by Hamas and the newly formed West Bank Action Group (WBAG). The WBAG was formed around Israeli settlers who felt that their future could no longer be entrusted to any Israeli government that continued with a policy of appeasement. They had many sympathisers both within and without Israeli military and extreme right-wing government circles, and in no time their hidden arsenals matched those of Hamas.

The Israeli government began the process of handing over control of the West Bank to the Palestinian Authority (PA). And that was as far as things got – a mere beginning. One of the hidden conditions of the first handover, the Thirteen Percent Deal, was that the PA set up a 'police state' on the West Bank. For Hamas, who had always uneasily coexisted with Yasser Arafat, the implementation of this policy was not unnaturally viewed as doing the enemy's work for him. In mid-2001 the PA police crackdowns on Hamas activities, which included incarceration of nearly two hundred suspected terrorists (list supplied by Mossad) and both the spiritual leader and the military chief of staff of Hamas, spilled over into open war between the two sides. The carrot for such drastic action by the PA was the agreement in principle by the Israelis to progressively hand over more and more West Bank land if (a big if) the Thirteen Percent Deal was concluded to the satisfaction of the Israelis. Sceptics have since argued that the hidden agenda of the Israeli government was to allow the PA nothing more than the day-to-day running of a string of disconnected and disgruntled dependent territories. Regardless of what was agreed on paper, on the ground in the West Bank the Palestinian extremists argued convincingly that as long as Israeli soldiers were near by then all its territories would always be subject to Israeli surveillance, as well as the threat of overwhelming Israeli force, and would therefore remain ultimately always under Israeli control.

It was in Hebron that the mask of peace first disappeared. Hebron, perhaps best of all, represented the magnitude of the problem facing any controlling authority. It was a town of 150,000 Palestinians and 500 Jewish settlers. The PA had to guarantee the safety of the tiny Jewish community under the deal and found that, like the Israeli military authorities before them, the only way to do this was to enforce a curfew on up to 50,000 Palestinians who lived in or adjacent to the 'Jewish area'. To Hamas, the main perpetrator of continued grenade, suicide bomb and random shooting attacks, and therefore the root cause of the curfews, the arrest of two of their top three leaders was too much.

Complicating events was the decision by an ailing Yasser Arafat to declare unilateral independence for Palestine. Practically this meant little change to the situation in the West Bank but politically, because Palestine was immediately recognised as a sovereign state by the whole Arab world, anything the Israelis subsequently did in the West Bank was viewed as a violation of Palestine's sovereign status.

On the ground the situation deteriorated. Yitzhak Rabin, the first real peacemaking Israeli Prime Minister, who was assassinated in 1995 by Jewish extremists, had correctly predicted that the Palestinians would be more effective in controlling the 'terrorist' groups because they were not answerable, as Israel was, to the West's supreme courts and human rights groups. With intelligence supplied by Mossad the PA purges were more brutal among their own people than the Israeli equivalents had ever been. In the West Bank Hamas, backed by Syria and Iran, divested itself of all pretence at covert action and intensified its attacks both on the PA police and Israeli settlers and security forces. There were multiple attempts made on the lives of Arafat's successor. In Israel the WBAG claimed responsibility for a series of attacks on Labour politicians and supporters that left two dead and several wounded. And all the while settlement building and consolidation continued. It was only when Israel decided that enough was enough on the water problem the following summer that the real battle lines were drawn. Israel became increasingly isolated; the sympathy and understanding she had once had from world opinion faded as her intransigence increased. The water situation in the West Bank and Gaza hit crisis point towards the end of the hottest summer on record in 2004. By mid-August, with the water flow available to the Israelis diminishing daily, contingency plans, prepared in anticipation of just such an event, were put into action. The Israeli Army and water specialists moved in rapidly to restore the *status quo ante*. All drilling was stopped and, with the overall flow reduced and the Israelis taking out the same levels of water as before the Palestinians' action, the latter suffered serious shortages whose effects were felt immediately all over the West Bank and Gaza.

In Gaza, Jericho, Hebron and Ramallah large-scale rioting over the water shortage broke out and quickly developed into armed attacks on the vulnerable, but heavily armed, Israeli settlers. These were on a scale and of a viciousness unprecedented even in Israel. The settlers, their very existence threatened and long since armed to the teeth, opened fire with automatic weapons on the violent mobs. The PA 'Blue Police' (so called because of their dispersed-pattern blue camouflage uniforms), some nine thousand strong, trained and armed in street fighting, needed no urging to join in in sympathy with their fellow countrymen. Hamas, Islamic Jihad and Hezbollah likewise rejoiced in the escalation and immediately fell in beside the 'treacherous' Blue Police to fight the common enemy.

The Israeli Army advanced into the West Bank cities and Gaza in several armoured columns. These were attacked as soon as they entered the urban areas by elements of Hamas and Hezbollah, emerging from their homes and secret bases to join the fighting, armed with RPG-7 anti-tank weapons. Several of the leading Israeli armoured personnel carriers were knocked out or disabled in the initial thrust. The advances were only restored when the Israeli infantry dismounted, and with Merkava 3 tanks and Apache gunships in support began to sweep the flanks of the roads, clearing house after house as they progressed. Some 200 of the 650 settlers in Kiryat Arba, isolated on the northern outskirts of Hebron, were killed in the gun battles. The Israelis also suffered the loss of sixty-three soldiers when two CH-53 helicopters, attempting to land in the area as part of an air-mobile assault force tasked with the initial relief of the besieged settlers, were brought down by a mass of small arms and shoulder-fired SAMs.

The view of the Arab world and most of the rest of the world was that Israel had illegally used her military might to occupy the Palestinian state (or part of the new state of Trans-Jordan, depending on whether the government in question had recognised Trans-Jordan as a legal political entity). The Arabs claimed that the provocation caused by mere drilling was insufficient to justify the extremeness of the Israeli reaction. Israel had indeed occupied Palestine/Trans-Jordan (the Jordanian Army was conspicuous by its absence and careful not to be overhasty in entering into a tangle with the power of the Israeli Army), but had grown weary of endless attacks on her citizens from the terrorist groups that had grown in strength under the protection and, in spite of their differences and skirmishes, unofficial approval of the PA. Ultimately, whatever was at stake, the heart of the Palestinian people, regardless of the colour of their uniform or factional loyalty, lay in fighting Israel together as a united people and not each other. And, although there had been crackdowns in the past by the PA against Hezbollah and Hamas, and although these had been harsher in some respects than anything the Israelis had done, when viewed with a longer-term historical perspective both sides were able to understand the necessity of such actions. On the north-western front in the Golan and southern Lebanon the Islamic 'terror' groups, as Israel called them, received massive backing in terms of cash, arms, equipment and training from a mischievous Syria, whose young and fanatical Muslim leader (the successor of Assad) was not going to let such a golden opportunity to antagonise Israel slip by. Not only did the isolated Israeli forts and settlements in the north come under heavy and sustained attack from an enemy that melted into the countryside, but also attacks began to take place on EuroFor G across the Golan and on Israeli settlers in the area.

Israel was not impressed and in early September advanced in force, backed up by air strikes and heavy artillery strikes on suspected terrorist areas, into the Lebanon as far as Sidon and Jezzine in a mini-version of the 1986 Operation Peace for Galilee, and into the Golan Heights, simply brushing aside the protests of the EuroFor G commanders. One of the first rules of peacekeeping is that there is no point in putting or retaining peacekeepers anywhere where there is no peace to keep. In Europe the pressure in the contributing nations grew to withdraw EuroFor G as losses of men climbed from a handful to nearly forty in September – it was suspected but never proved that Israeli special forces had also been responsible for attacks on EuroFor G in order to precipitate withdrawal. It soon became academic when within hours of each other Israel, Syria and Trans-Jordan declared the formal peace process to be dead. Both sides cited the unacceptable behaviour and aggression of the other in taking this unprecedented and precipitous step and so, in spite of intense US lobbying to hold out, EuroFor G was withdrawn from the Golan Heights and UNIFIL from southern Lebanon. The feeling in Europe towards the Middle Eastern antagonists had very much become: if they want to fight it out, then let them – there is little to gain, and a great deal to lose at home politically, by keeping our soldiers there to act as little more than live target practice for the belligerents. Once more the Israeli and Syrian armies were face to face in some strength across southern Lebanon, and in the Golan Heights and all along Israel's eastern and northern borders and in Gaza, hatred, resentment and anger burned. The future did not look rosy.

A 'Satanic Alliance'

The water 'management' programmes conducted by the Israelis were lightweight compared to those of Turkey. Turkey's programme, to the delight and full support of Israel, was aimed simply at denying Syria and Iraq access to their claimed historical water rights. The mighty Euphrates and Tigris rivers, which had been the cradle of civilisation many thousands of years previously, rise in Turkey and flow through Syria and Iraq, emptying into the Persian Gulf. Syria had long argued that as the river spent one-third of its course in each country, each should be entitled to a third part use of its water. Turkey pointed to double standards by the Syrians.

The Orontes, a small but significant river, rises and runs for a mere twenty-five of its two hundred miles in Syria before flowing into the Mediterranean via Turkey. However, once the Syrians had completed two dams across it by 2001, only 2 per cent of its potential flow actually reached Turkey. The Turks therefore had other ideas for the rivers rising in their territory, and during the 1990s began a massive programme of damming across the upper Euphrates and Tigris basins.

The aim of the programme, involving an area half the size of the UK, was to turn south-eastern Turkey into a European bread basket. The South-East Anatolia Project, known as GAP (*Guneydogu Anadolu Projesi*), involved the building of some twenty-two dams and the undertaking of nineteen hydroelectric projects and twenty-five large irrigation projects. The electricity provided and the subsequent irrigation made possible would recreate part of the original 'Fertile Crescent' and enable the population to grow from some three million to ten million by 2006. The Turks defended their actions vigorously, especially when there was talk of a 'water war' on completion of the gigantic Attaturk Dam – the fourth-largest in the world. Turkey, for many years lagging behind both Iraq and Syria in the amount of land irrigated and irrigation techniques, described Syria's irrigation methods as wasteful and 'Sumerian' (i.e. four thousand years old). Turkey argued in response to the alarmists in Damascus and Baghdad that her dams would serve to regulate, not control, the flow of the Euphrates and to a lesser extent the Tigris. International experts were called in to confirm the efficiency of Turkey's projects, which they duly did, and Turkey proceeded to gain international approval for her 'control' of the Euphrates.

Also, Turkey was able to proceed with some confidence and without fear of conventional attack. Her borders with Syria and Iraq were hilly, and with their miles of razor wire, barbed wire, anti-tank blocks, ditches and minefields, resembling the old inner German border, were easily defendable against conventional attack with her superior army and air forces. By contrast the Syrian and Iraqi northern borders comprised miles of flat open terrain with little natural ad-

vantage for the defenders – pure tank country. As early as the
late 1990s, however, Turkish irrigation had already begun to
reduce the quality of water flowing downstream. Increasing
amounts of nitrates, other chemicals and salts had begun to
seriously affect the soil quality and therefore crop yields in
Syria and Iraq. Both countries became increasingly agitated at
their vulnerability to Turkey's strategic control over the Tigris
and Euphrates water. Moreover, neither was in any position
to apply military, economic or political leverage to modify the
decisions and behaviour of the region's strongest military
state. Attempts to knock out the dams would be futile. Dams
are extremely robust targets and Syria would require dozens
of 617 Dambuster squadrons, let alone the Guy Gibsons to
lead them, to make any impact. And even if they did, a
massive flood downstream would be more catastrophic than
anything achieved against the Mohne and Eder dams in
World War II and as such would be tantamount to scoring
a massive own goal should the topsoil also be lost. Syria,
which drew 80 per cent of her water from the Euphrates, was
not intent on sitting idly by and watching her agricultural base
be slowly destroyed.

The water issue was, in Arab eyes, the one that cemented
the 'Satanic Alliance', as its detractors called it, between Israel
and Turkey. Syria continued her financial and military support for the various extremist groups dedicated to the destruction of Israel, and more damagingly provided a safe haven
and training ground for the separatist Kurdistan Workers
Party, better known as the PKK. Turkey refused to sign any
water-sharing agreement with Syria as long as Syria backed
the PKK, whether overtly or covertly.

The Shadow of Franco

In Spain the temporary loss of Cueta and Melilla in 2003
proved to be a severe embarrassment to the ruling socialist
government which had been back in power since just after the
millennium. The opposition had argued that Spanish marines

should be detached to the cities as 'political insurance' as soon as it became apparent from American strategic information sources that something was afoot. The government, perhaps wisely, neither wanted to repeat the French débâcle in Algiers nor unnecessarily provoke the military regime in Rabat. In the event the government did send a frigate to Cueta, but there was little it could do to stop Moroccan armour from rumbling through the streets other than 'threaten them with a cocktail party', as the opposition pointed out. The failure to take direct action as well as the over-hasty acceptance of the lifting of sanctions against Morocco and the failure to achieve an unconditional Moroccan withdrawal made an already unpopular government fall to rock bottom in the approval ratings.

The Spanish people looked with envy at the strength of the new German government and the independence of the uncompromising new French government while looking over their shoulders with increasing apprehension at the Islamic takeovers going on in their back yard. In times of increasing tension the voters of any nation naturally become more nationalistic and inclined to the political right, with its traditional strengths of increased defence spending and robust foreign policies. There was also a view that increased defence spending actually reduced unemployment and, with Spain's official rate running at close to 25 per cent, any straw that could be clutched as a possible solution to internal problems was grabbed without too much research. The turning point was the death of twenty-two Spanish infantrymen in the Golan Heights. The opposition, with perfect hindsight, recalled its warnings about Spain getting involved in an operation that did not have the immediate and massive backing of the US military – surely the disastrous Balkans episode had proved them right. The Spanish were no different in their natural sympathy for the political right, its assumed militarism and strong foreign policy in tense times. The threat of the spread of Scud-type missiles tipped with chemical or biological weapons to a potentially hostile neighbour was enough to ensure a record turnout at the Spanish elections in November 2004 and the bringing to power in a landslide victory of the most right-wing government Spain had seen since the days of Franco. The Popular Party and its newer but more extreme offshoot, the Franco Party, formed a coalition that promised a tough new stance on immigrants and an active foreign policy of engagement from a position of strength in the new Nato. The government vowed that Cueta and Melilla would be returned to Spanish rule. The Spanish people, like the French, were also concerned by the immigrant community in their southern cities, as well as the presence of Islamic activists, and the government embarked on a dual policy of closed doors and deportation alongside economic austerity.

The Gaullists Return

The legacies of both Algeria and de Gaulle were pivotal in shaping the France that emerged in the twenty-first century. The insistence of the French socialist government on holding on to the 'European Dream', and her part as a major leader in it, was the root cause of its own downfall. An equal cause was Algeria itself. The French people, like those in Spain, felt threatened by the growing menace to the south. The military disasters in Algeria, Serbia and more recently in the Golan sat uncomfortably alongside a continuing failure to curb the immigrant violence and terrorism, let alone tackle a bleak economic outlook. The socialist coalition collapsed in a heap of ignominy. The reaction towards all non-white Caucasian foreigners was expressed in the November 2004 elections by the bringing to power of the far right. The French had had enough of being a military laughing-stock, and the Gaullists, Republicans and National Front ousted the leftists in the general election. The already draconian powers of arrest and search that had been given to the police and Gendarmerie were extended to allow the local security authorities to impose curfews on areas of immigrant settlement. The successors of de Gaulle promised French independence through military strength, including the use of the army in internal affairs, as well as the deportation of all workers without permits, a refusal to admit any asylum seekers, and the closure of her airports to all trade and business emanating from North Africa.

As for Nato, France was alone in going in the opposite direction to the rest of Europe; thanks to the long shadow cast by de Gaulle she was not going to acquiesce, regardless of her political colour, in falling in line with any form of American power politics. She had long been antagonistic towards American domination of Nato, and the Algerian and Serbian crises, while denting national pride, served to ensure that France would be even more determined to deal with future crises on her own terms and without external political hindrances; doing anything else would have been tantamount to accepting that the pursuit of 'European solutions to European problems' had been a policy of total failure and that the Americans had been right all along – which it had and they were! France was not prepared even to contemplate this and officially viewed the Algerian, Serb and Golan events as mere setbacks on the learning curve which any force acting independently of the US political and military umbrella inevitably had to accept. The socialist cause in France had lost out with its backing of the crumbling European ideal and the dashed hopes of French leadership of a European state.

Chapter Five – 2005

The North Takes Control

Italy alone remained relatively unchanged in overall character during the decade leading up to the war, but the political trends identified in the late 1990s solidified into two separate entities at opposite ends of the political spectrum. Up to 2004, confusion, scandal and corruption in Italy reigned, which was business as usual for the majority of Italians, as she averaged one new government every year. Nevertheless, Italy was more than able to sustain her economic growth and competitiveness. Again, as in the rest of Europe, it was in the elections that took place in early 2005 that the centre right firmly grasped the reins of power. This was due more to the closeness and worrisome nature of events unfolding on the other side of the Mediterranean than any other single factor. Italy had continued to achieve a delicate balancing act between her commitments to Nato and playing a full part in exploring the possibilities of a WEU-based European Army. The major political trend observed was the increasing dominance of the Northern League over the political aspirations of the rich industrial north, and the strengthened grip of the communists over the Mezzogiorno. Italy was essentially two states within a state but, in spite of their fundamental political differences, the right and left were astute enough and nationalistic enough to recognise that Italy's future security, strength and influence were to be founded on a united and coherent foreign policy. Following the elections, Italy emerged as a far more coherent political entity. She accepted that the ideals of a European state were fundamentally flawed, and with her economy larger and more efficient than the UK's and catching up rapidly with that of France she embraced the emerging

European ideal of independent economic strength militarily
protected by a unified and purposeful Nato under the firm
leadership of the USA.

A Conservative Win

The UK's economy remained brittle under successive Labour
governments. However, the late entry into the European
Monetary System, even though it happened before the end
of the first term of office of the Blair government, caused
temporary damage to the City as a world financial centre. The
financial institutions that had begun to migrate to Frankfurt
to take advantage of being co-located with the Central
European Bank had serious second thoughts. This was a
serious blow to a British economy that relied hugely on
business and financial services as a major export earner to
counter the continuing decline of manufacturing industries.
Moreover, the competitive edge that British businesses had
held over their European counterparts was seriously eroded
by the full adoption of the Social Chapter and similar Brus-
sels-based edicts on working practices, pay rates and business
taxes. The British people, like the Germans, had had enough
of the impersonal power, politics and alleged corruption of
Brussels to call increasingly for a total rejection of the idea of a
federal Europe. British businesses and industry began to cry
foul at the imposition of higher taxes and associated employee
benefits that came from Brussels and which were beginning to
stifle the spirit of enterprise.

The Irish problem festered all the while with a greater
intensity than at any time in the previous thirty years of
sectarian strife. In the eighteen months following the return
to gun law, the waves of killings, bombings, violence, intimidation and reprisal increased dramatically. The Labour
government, even with 22,000 troops in Ulster, admitted
failure and, to the outrage of the Loyalists and those on
the opposition right, agreed to the setting up of an independent European Commission of Arbitration to decide the

future of Ulster. By the end of 2003, although things were not going well in the Balkans, the WEU persuaded the Labour government to accept a transfer of policing duties from the British Army to an independent European force – EuroFor U (European Force in Ulster).

The final nail in the coffin of British socialism was the conduct of ministers and the endless allegations of sleaze. As in John Major's government, it seemed that it was only the Prime Minister himself who emerged with his integrity unquestioned and pride intact. By late 2004 the government found its position untenable. The narrow majority with which the Labour government had been re-elected in 2002 had disappeared in by-elections, such that the Conservatives were able to force a no-confidence vote in February thanks to the Ulster Loyalists, and an election in May 2005. The Conservatives, under a new, young, good-looking, single, dynamic leader, came to power not so much on waves of anti-European sentiment as irritation and fatigue with European solutions and ideals. The British people were appalled at the performance of the European peacekeeping troops that had replaced the British Army in Northern Ireland and which were attempting to aide Eire's police. To the British and the Loyalists it appeared that the whole of Europe was unsympathetic to the Loyalist cause and actively sympathetic to the ideals of a united Ireland and therefore the IRA.

The people were also tired of sitting back and watching what appeared to be a clandestine attempt by bureaucrats in Brussels to ruin everything British, especially industry and farming, while continuing to refute all allegations of corruption, waste and nest-feathering. Weakness with respect to Europe was something the British would not tolerate. The new Conservative government was dominated by a right-wing, nationalist, anti-federalist, pro-US majority. It promised to take a firm stance on all matters relating to British interests and restore the erosion of British influence that it blamed on successive Labour governments. The UK stood, the new Prime Minister declared, ready to play her full part on the world stage, as part of a strong Nato under clear American leadership. Britain revelled in a wave of Thatcher nostalgia.

New Germany

By 2005 it was the complete change in the outlook of Germany, the first to jump from the sinking ship of Euro-federalism, which not only set the political trend for the rest of Europe, France excepted, but also contributed the most to ensuring that Russia would be wary and antagonistic when conflict loomed. Edicts coming from Berlin rather than the unthreatening and rural Bonn made the whole of Europe subconsciously sit up and take notice. Germany was transformed from a nation of considerate liberals whose every pronouncement on foreign policy was set against an undercurrent of Holocaust guilt into the large, black-coloured menace that sits firmly at the centre of the Diplomacy game board.

Perhaps the most radical of all the policies that underlined the new twenty-first-century German agenda were the promises to re-examine Germany's contributions to Brussels and her role in Europe, as well as the adoption of a 'more robust and proactive' foreign policy. Germany had for many years been by far the largest net contributor to the EU. One of the first acts of the new government was to suspend all funds for Brussels until Germany was satisfied with the accountability of the European Commission. The leader of the CDU stated that Germany would only resume her payments once she was happy with the outcome of an independent inquiry into all the activities of the Brussels machine. In the meantime the government abandoned conscription and embarked on the pursuit of a foreign policy that embraced US ideals on the future role of Nato. It was almost sixty years since the end of World War II, and the new government made it clear that the time had come for Germany to play a foreign policy role that was in line with her industrial and economic strength (although it was struggling, it was not in a complete state of collapse) and military potential. By late 2003 the more hawkish elements in the government were confident enough of Germany's position and future to reopen the once taboo debates on the former East Prussia and Kaliningrad, much to the consternation of

the Poles and Russians. And all the while the strife raged,
especially in Bavaria and the East, as the Turks, Kurds and
other Muslim groups and right-wing extremists armed themselves with more and heavier weapons. The long-term effects
of the seeds of hatred and revenge that were being scattered,
as well as the perceived oppression by the state of minority
communities, set the latter up to be well disposed towards
calls for sabotage and open and armed revolt when offered the
chance in 2006. But Germany, new and powerful Germany,
was making waves in the east and west. By early 2004
Germany, as a force to be reckoned with on the international
stage, was back with a vengeance. She rejected the ideals and,
as she saw it, pointless duplication of the WEU with respect to
Nato and threw her lot firmly in with the US/UK agenda.

The End of a Dream

To summarise the state of Europe on the outbreak of war in
2006 is difficult. As a whole the citizens of western Europe
had seen fit to elect right-wing governments. The reasons for
their doing so were many and varied as outlined above, but
there were consistent themes. These were, firstly, an increasing disillusionment with Brussels and all its apparatus which
culminated in a distinct lack of enthusiasm for European
federalism and a concurrent fear of the loss of national
identity and independent political, financial and economic
processes. The unique heritage of each European state made
them less inclined towards and unsuitable for any sort of
United States-style model, especially when the people in each
country concluded that they would be losing out – across
Europe there were none, with the possible exceptions of the
Belgians and to a lesser extent the French, who perceived
themselves as net gainers in the European experiment. And
the governments that backed the European dream, mostly
socialist and mostly struggling with internal economics and
racially based social problems, fell from favour along with the
dream.

The 'Golden Age of European Socialism' made a slow and unobtrusive beginning during the 1990s, flourished through the new hope of the millennium and came to an abrupt end in 2005. At the turn of the century virtually every government in Europe was either mildly left-wing or had the left of centre as the brokers of power in coalition. The vision of the European leaders going into the millennium was one of a bright and federal future. The hoped for success of the Euro was seen as the cornerstone on which greater integration could be built. The political pace was set by France and Germany. The UK did its best to catch up and maintain influence with a rapid policy revision and its almost embarrassingly hasty adoption of the Euro in mid-2001. But the French and Germans, followed closely by Spain, Italy and Belgium, were already making detailed plans in other areas, notably taxation, foreign policy and military co-operation. And while the rhetoric of the united Europe visionaries grew in volume, the major problems with the idea became increasingly apparent, as did the flaws in the practicalities of the propositions put forward.

Without exception the economies of the EU stuttered and staggered under the weight of the clumsy attempts to impose economic and social uniformity on a body of nations made up of so many disparate parts. Fundamental to the rejection of the European dream were the ugly realities of nationalism, pride and racism. Whatever the view of their ruling governments, the average citizens found the idea of being dictated to by Brussels, as increasing power in determination of policy and standards was transferred there, as distasteful. Try as they might, it proved impossible to disassociate being ruled from Brussels from being ruled by 'beer-swilling Belgian apparatchiks' (as one unidentified cynic observed) 'in cahoots with faceless politicians who were on an express gravy train'.

The problem firstly was, as the people saw it, one of accountability. The bottom line was that the administrators in Brussels appeared to be answerable only to their own ineffective regulating bodies (which were often privately browbeaten into submission and therefore unable to air their worries and grievances publicly) and not to national govern-

ments. Secondly they appeared to be indifferent to the plight
of farmers and small businesses across Europe where the
number of failures in both sectors began to reach catastrophic
proportions. Rumours of massive fraud, waste, cronyism and
subsequent attempted cover-ups did much to undermine the
European Commission. While the political leaders in the
member states continued publicly to express their support
for increased integration for fear of being left behind, or more
importantly left out of the decision-making process, they
began increasingly to have private doubts and reservations
about the continuing viability of signing up to Europe when
their public was becoming more and more vocal in expressing
its dissatisfaction with the whole process. It was a case of
waiting to see who would be the first to jump, or at least make
a stand.

The effect of the German action was cataclysmic for the
Euro-visionaries; without the funding of the largest net contributor it would only be a matter of time before the Brussels-
based European structures failed to function. For the federalists it was disastrous. All confidence was lost in the Euro and
its value fell 35 per cent in the week before Christmas. Berlin
remained unmoved. Germany had over five and a half million
unemployed and was not inclined any longer to continue to
finance other countries' disastrously inefficient industries or
medieval agricultural systems at the expense of a single German job. The German population was elated with such a
nationalistic and selfish stance, but this was the new Germany, and her identity was being formed with each passing
day.

Resurgent nationalism did, however, have an unfortunate
domestic downside. Nationalism has always been closely
linked with racism and xenophobia. Culturally speaking
the political right in Europe had always identified itself with
and found most sympathy from the ethnic white Caucasians.
Across Europe the sub-political extremes of the right, now
more organised and co-ordinated than at any time since 1938,
took exception to the opposition to such ideals voiced by
minority religious and ethnic groups and increased their racial
harassment. In the UK it was the Asian minorities which were

targeted, and as we have seen already in France and Spain the targets were ethnic North Africans, while in Italy and Germany it was every minority that was not of the purest ethnic origin. By late 2005 street violence and running battles between the rival groups were endemic; within a year the violence would be much worse. The European dream was over.

The Threatening Bear

To complete the pan-European canvas it is now necessary to cover briefly the final shaping and hardening of Russian attitudes to understand why, when they learned of the Islamic plan to wrong-foot Nato, the Russians threw in their lot with the Islamic Alliance in 2006 without hesitation. In the short to medium term, the new government concluded that through a limited military excursion at worst they could expect to gain significant concessions, if not outright control of the oil reserves from the Baltic states. Ever Machiavellian, they realised that the pretext for an invasion had to be rock solid, and as early as 2003 the special forces and the new KGB began their own clandestine campaign against hapless Russian employees in the Baltic. Of course, knowing where and when attacks on Russian citizens were going to take place they ensured that their own television crews were there to film unedited highlights of the attacks and broadcast them back to an increasingly outraged mother Russia. Something had to be done, screamed the media. Something was already being done.

Under the new military government relations with the West deteriorated rapidly. The first official Russian moves in the Baltic came in December 2004. Russia's new strong government, in a bid to show Nato that she meant business, did an about-face on the Oblast Agreement. The military presence in the Oblast was trebled with the arrival by sea of a full armoured division and a. lighter airborne division and a regiment of Su-27 Flanker fighters. Of course, Russia accepted the EU cash and the principle of negotiation over the future status of the Oblast, but she was going to be no walk-over. A strong military presence, sitting in a position to interfere with any future Nato lines of communication with her new members, was tangible evidence of a credible foreign policy backed by force. Russia had decided to use the Oblast as a bargaining chip in its bid for influence in Nato. Nato turned this around. An occupied Oblast was very much like Tobruk had been to Rommel – a thorn in his side – and made even initial discussion to consider Russian associate member-ship status of Nato conditional on Russian withdrawal. Up with this the Kremlin would not put.

The year 2005 was one of simmering Russian resentment. By late 2005 Russia had become both isolationist and antag-onistic and deeply suspicious towards Germany. These factors allowed her to listen with impartiality, patience and not some little interest to the secret proposal of the Islamic Alliance in November. Additionally, Russia's own standing had been significantly enhanced by the not unexpected expansion of her own empire to the west and south.

An Historic Document

The immediacy and reality of emerging and potential threats from the south and east (Islam and Russia) reinvigorated a western European mind-set of proud nationalism and a strong and united defence under the US–Nato aegis. This collective view, not unnatural when once again faced with a definable and tangible threat which had been missing since the fall of the Berlin Wall, and which had seen its definitive expression during the halcyon days of Reagan and Thatcher, was very much back in vogue and still very much the property of the political right. By mid-2005 the manual tools of active foreign policy – the armed forces of Europe under a Nato that had survived its mid-life crisis to emerge with flying colours – were sharper and more readily available for use than at any time since 1939. Spain, Germany, Italy and France had all finally rid themselves of the essentially Napoleonic hangover of conscript armies. While this had proved to be a painful transition while extra funds were allocated to cope with the increased levels of instant unemployment, the senior officers were delighted. Once they had fully accepted the reality that in modern hi-tech warfare any number of poorly trained conscripts are an acute liability rather than any sort of national defence asset, many wondered why it had not been done years earlier (the British observed the correspondence with a wry smile). The politicians also finally understood that the idea of political plus points from the identity gained by citizens in uniform, and the subsequent source of sympathy or pride from those who had served, was pure fallacy.

The US was also elated with the new European mood and continued to court the military isolationists in France. The US had long been of the private opinion that conscripts were a complete waste of rations, especially when the training, as in Germany, was so limited. The US was even more pleased by the constitutional changes in France, Germany, Italy and Spain that allowed increased involvement in military action outside their respective borders. Although France had returned to her position of 1966 and retained a natural suspicion of all things American-led, the US remained confident that she would be there in any larger crisis, and indeed the French military, through shrewd procurement and the need to work alongside other European nations in fulfilling her dream of leading a WEU force, remained compatible with the rest of Nato. So although her pride ensured political isolation from the inner sanctum of military decision-making in Nato, pragmatism and inter-operability were key features of the new professional French forces, and their time would come.

As early as 2002 the US had begun to argue fiercely that a twenty-first-century Nato was no longer about defending tracts of land from Warsaw to the Portuguese beaches. Nato should become a collective of militarily responsible nations (under her leadership) that were prepared to defend not only the land but also the interests of the West and its cherished democracies. By 'defending interests' was meant becoming proactive in the pursuit and persecution of rogue nations that were acquiring the means to threaten Nato from well beyond its borders. She had long chastised the Germans in particular for holding on to a field army and armed forces that were dominated by hundreds of main battle tanks that sat waiting for the non-existent Russian hordes to roll into Poland.

The major sub-themes running through the American attempt to steamroller a new outlook on Europe were central to the fundamental differences in outlook between both sides of the Atlantic. These were most obviously encapsulated in the respective policies and attitudes towards the Middle East, in particular Israel. The US viewed Israel as the major regional power and tended to give her the benefit of the doubt during crises. The backing for Israel was underpinned by the powerful Jewish lobby in US domestic politics and manifested in billions of dollars handed out in grants for both military equipment and the settlement of immigrants. To the US, Israel was a natural military counterbalance to the countries that surrounded it, which, with the exception of pre-revolutionary Egypt, it viewed as threatening to the American sacred cows of stability, weapons of mass destruction proliferation, the free flow of oil, and the spread of democracy. Although Europe sympathised with the 'sacred cows', the fundamental European starting point was deep suspicion of anything the Israelis said or did, an inclination to side with the Palestinian cause (but not its attendant terrorism), and an unchanging view that the continued Israeli occupation of all land taken in the 1967 war was illegal. Indeed, up until 2002 US pronouncements on how she saw world order being maintained simply alienated the European federalists, in particular France.

By mid-2005, however, the US argument was that if Nato was to become a force to be reckoned with – one that assured the West's global interests – then it would require a little more freedom of action than it had enjoyed in the past. The US suggested a small amendment to Nato's Article V. This was that the phrase '. . . an armed attack against one or more Nato nation in Europe or North America shall be considered an attack against them all' be amended to read '. . . Nato nation or interests in any part of the world be . . .' Europe had little real choice. Faced with emerging threats to the east and south, and acknowledging the recent failure of purely European military ventures as well as the reality that protection was only guaranteed under a US umbrella, the change was agreed and the global outlook of the new Nato set in concrete on 31 August. Practically the US was suggesting that if it was obvious to the West that any Nato action pending was in everyone's best interests, then a UN Security Council mandate would not necessarily always be required. The US was not looking for a *carte blanche* to act outside international law; she was merely attempting to enable the European part of the Nato alliance to play a part in a US-led (or dominated) collective foreign policy. This would be a Nato as opposed to a singular US or federal European foreign policy, and the new wording neatly sidestepped the ever-present threat of the Russian or Chinese UN veto.

And the US, by the early years of the millennium, was in a position of supreme and unchallenged military and economic strength sufficient to demand such a relatively radical departure from what had been half a century of cosy internal self-defence. It was now the unchallenged leader of the world's most powerful alliance. The new Europe that emerged by the end of 2005 was one that was, with the exception of France, militarily united behind the US and the power of a confident and resurgent Nato, albeit economically fragmented once again. This situation suited the right-wing governments, resurgent nationalism, the emergence of two clear military 'threats' to the east and south and the governments' new vision of a more pure form of capitalism and the survival of the fittest, down to the ground.

An Empire Rebuilt

In October 2005 Belarus (also known as Byelorussia or White Russia), both impressed by and envious of the stability and confidence emanating from her large neighbour – the equivalent of a Russian 'feel good factor' – and perhaps apprehensive about the power of a competent Russian Army, chose to apply for closer ties. Only one month later, following a referendum, she reabsorbed herself into 'Federal Russia' after a decade and a half of failed so-called socialist reform. Most observers of Russian policy, especially given what was to happen later in the Baltic, agreed that this was pre-empting the inevitable in the most painless way possible. The move by Belarus caused acute discomfort in both Latvia and Lithuania, which each shared a common border with Belarus. Kazakhstan, ever fearful of an unstable China, followed suit in March. The Russian half of its population had never been happy with the chaos and bylaws of Islamic theocracy – most of the Muslim population, after seventy years of communism, felt that the Islamic government was oppressive by comparison. Thus when the opportunity arose in the form of a veiled threat from Russia, where 'protection' was the major theme, the planted 'subversives' went to work. They had been installed in numbers in Karaganda and Alma Ata by the Russians to instigate popular uprisings, and found such overwhelming support that there were very few 'government sympathisers' left to round up those who weren't actually clerics.

It was thought at one stage that the Ukraine might become part of the EU and even be offered associate membership of Nato. The Ukraine, however, watched closely the progress of Hungary and Poland and, much like France, secretly had no desire to be part of an organisation that was so dominated by one nation – the USA. And the Ukraine was deeply unhappy about the fate of its fellow Slavs in Serbia at the hands of Nato. Also, she was still scarred by the German occupation between 1941 and 1944. Her people could not forget that having welcomed the Germans as liberators from the Soviet yoke they were subsequently trampled all over. The occupation forces, in particular the SS and various regional gauleiters, had been severe in their repression of the Ukrainians and treated them as they had treated all the Soviet peoples, as *Untersmensch*. The Ukraine, like her powerful northern neighbour, continued to harbour deep suspicion over the resurgent and militarily and politically powerful Germany,

regardless of how many '*Unterstrichs*' the Germans drew over
their past. This single factor did much to move Ukrainian
national sympathies away from the West and back towards
Russia.

From Nato's point of view the Ukraine would always be
difficult to embrace thanks to her historic closeness to Russia
and to Russian attitudes to 'nation poaching'. While Russian
expressions over Nato's expansion into the Baltic states
amounted to anger, belligerence and posturing, her response
to any claims by the West of a polite embrace of the Ukraine was
a stony and serious 'over my dead body' style of diplomacy.
Following the Russian Revolution and the subsequent accession of Belarus and Kazakhstan to Greater Russia, the Ukraine,
like Bulgaria and Moldova, was alone, along with the small and
strife-torn Caucasus republics, with no major partners or
sponsors. And the mutual benefits, even if only in the short
term, of belonging to some form of geopolitical alliance were
clear to all. Her history and culture dictated an inevitable return
to the Russian fold, but as a more equal partner in the empire.
Without a referendum the Ukrainian government voted with
an 80 per cent majority to apply formally for accession to the
Greater Russian Federation. Russia was delirious. To mark the
resurgence of a militarily strong Russia and celebrate the
victory over government by corruption, the military leaders
persuaded their political 'masters' to rename 'St Petersburg'
'Leningrad' and 'Volgograd' reverted to 'Stalingrad'.

The fresh snows across Europe in the new year of 2006
were brought on an icy blast from the east. Russia had been
very active since the Second Revolution in her encouragement
of instability in her Baltic neighbours. Once again she stood
strong and confident. The time to take action was drawing
near.

The Tehran Raid

The final steps to war were about to be taken, again in the
name of self-defence and, though this was left unsaid, self-

Above: British Challenger 2 engages dug-in Serb armour during advance to Belgrade. (4 May 2003)

Right: American AH-64 Apache fires rocket salvo at retreating Serb Army soft-skinned vehicle column, 50 miles north of Belgrade. (5 May 2003)

Above: Israeli Merkava 2 tank column advances through Hebron at the height of the water crisis. (17 August 2004)

Left: 'The Raid' Capt. Tal's Israeli F-15I Thunder releases a stick of 500lb Mk82 bombs in a high-angle dive attack against Iranian Shahab nuclear missiles. (25 September 2005)

Opposite page

Above: 3rd Shock Army motor-rifle troops advance across northern Estonia. (23 April 2006)

Below: Estonian ZSU23/2 AAA gun, pictured shortly before it's demise, engages Russian helicopter gunships just east of the barracks at Jarve. (23 April 2006)

Above: Tallinn aftermath. The Siberian troops were ruthless in their suppressio of resistance in the Estonia capital. (25 April 2006)

Left: Lazarus in the cockp of his F-18E Super Horne before launching above th Baltic in the fading light. (25 April 2006)

Opposite page

Above: A pair of Russian SU-35 Flankers led by Bor Yeremenko of the 72nd Intercept Squadron just west of Leningrad bristlin with missiles before their tangle with Hardy and Lazarus. (25 April 2006)

Below: Lazarus launches heat-seeking, air-to-air - missile on fleeing Russian fighter. (25 April 2006)

Above: Russian Spetnatz Special Forces patrol in Latvia. (Late April 2006)

Left: The opposition. British S.A.S. patrol lies in wait to ambush Russian forces in the secret war in Latvia. (Late April 2006)

Opposite page

Above: 'Patton's Sprint' US Marine M1 Abrams deploy temporarily off road on meeting minor resistance in the race to Kaunus. (28 April 2006)

Below: 'Moodkee Wallah', Maj. Charles Davies's Scimitar Squadron (3rd King's Own Hussars) in position on the edge of Riga airport. (29 April 2006)

Left: Short's Starstreak HVM engages Russian Flankers during low-level bombing attack on Riga. Shortly after this photo was taken they were destroyed by Rossovski's Havocs. (30 April 2006)

Below: T-72s and Hind gunships of 2nd Guards Division probe NATO defences east of Riga. (30 April 2006)

interest. The third issue that catapulted Israel into war with her neighbours was that of weapons of mass destruction. The Israeli action the previous summer was really a public statement to the effect that she was ready for war; that war was now inevitable and was the only course of action that was open and that she would consider. The water and settlers problems paled into insignificance when Israel put the seal on her new but unstated stance. It was Israel that fired the first shots not only into Palestine in 2004 but one year later into Iran.

Israel, ready for the fight, was aware that there would be a backlash around the world over her actions and decided that now was the time to solve the problem that had been vexing her for some time – in for a penny, in for a pound, the War Cabinet had decided. In October 2005 matters came to a head. But the precedent for action had been set by the US in her attack on Iraq. The target and motivation were provided by the same problem that had begun to nag the West, and seriously worry Israel, by the late 1990s – ballistic missiles. Iran developed her own prototype version of an atomic bomb as early as July 2001. However, she was only able to refine what was originally a device similar to the 'Fatman', which had destroyed Hiroshima, into a reliable Medium Range Ballistic Missile (MRBM) version some four years later, and astounded the world with the declaration that she was a nuclear power and expected to be treated as such. Iran had announced in August 2005 that she was about to test a nuclear device in the remote high desert of central eastern Iran. This she duly did with much consternation caused around the world, then announcing that she had six such devices. Iran had also perfected the Shahab-4 MRBM, and by the end of August CIA and Mossad field operatives confirmed that she had successfully integrated the nuclear warheads with the 2,300km-range Shahab 4. Iran made moves to counter international fears over her intentions with the weapons and surprisingly and quickly acceded to a Security Council request to sign a 'no first use' affidavit at the earliest opportunity. Israel had watched the growing menace in Iran and noted that the Shahab 3s paraded in Tehran over the previous six years had been daubed with slogans in both English and Farsi that read: 'Israel should be wiped off the map' and 'the USA can do nothing'. Israel decided that she knew Iran's real intentions and decided to act. The day chosen for action was 25 September, Iran's national day and the day of the annual massive military parade through Tehran. Israeli military intelligence was certain that Iran would only wait as long as Yom Kippur, two weeks away, to give Israel an altogether different Passover surprise.

The Israeli Air Force had received twenty-five F-15Is between early 2000 and mid-2002. The F-15I, which the Israelis called 'Thunder', was capable of very long-range precision attack. They had not hesitated in the past to undertake such long and daring missions; in 1986 Israeli F-16s had flown to Osirik and destroyed the almost complete French-built nuclear reactor inside Iraq. Twenty-four Thunders took off from Israel and headed north-west out over the Mediterranean towards Cyprus. Ahead of them, flying at a mere 500 feet over the calm waves, were four KC-135 air-to-air refuelling tankers. The force remained low to avoid detection by Syrian coastal radar. Once over Turkey they were met by eight F-16s, which would escort them as far as the border. The force comprised two attack packages of four bombers, two fighters and two air defence suppression (SEAD) aircraft, as well as a complete spare package ready to fill in, in case of any hitches. The Thunders turned east and refuelled high over the southern Turkish plateau, well out of sight of prying eyes. Once off the tankers the force turned south-east and down into the deep valleys of the Taurus mountains before heading just south of east to Tehran. The first eight bypassed Tehran to the north and headed for the Shahab production facility at Kruh. The second eight arrived over Tehran at extremely low altitude as the parade was beginning its march. The two fighters and HARM carriers zoomed to 35,000 feet and waited for all hell to break loose. They were aware that the skies around Tehran would be full of Iranian military jets, preparing for the ceremonial fly-past. This was a good thing, since none of them would be armed with live missiles for such an event. The Iranians were confident that they would be able to detect any Israeli raid from the west, assuming the attackers had to transit through Jordanian, Syrian and Iraqi airspace. An attack via Turkey was not even considered.

At the head of the parade would be two whole divisions of the Revolutionary Guard, some 25,000 men; theirs was always the place of honour. The first vehicles behind them would be the twelve Shahab-4 Transporter Erector Launchers (TELs), each four times the size of a standard articulated lorry. In a show of unprecedented bravado and machismo the commander of the newly formed Iranian Strategic Nuclear Missile Force had insisted that the four leading TELs be loaded with the available nuclear warheads. He hoped that to allow the Iranian leadership the privilege of personally getting so close to the pinnacle of the country's military pride and technological achievement would ensure him a large pension, comfortable retirement and a place in Islamic history.

The four bombers climbed to 10,000 feet as soon as it became evident that the alarm bells were not ringing in the air defence and missile stations. The Tehran area radar controllers had their hands full directing the military traffic around the cramped skies. The parade jets had all been assigned identification squawks which highlighted their positions on the ground controllers' radar screens. This served only to make it less likely that the F-15Is would be spotted among the mass of other aircraft milling about in holding patterns before forming up for the fly-past. Captain Ben Ibrahim Tal, leader of the Israeli bombers, takes up the story:

From 10,000 feet we could see the whole of the parade route. The crowds were streaming to the main avenue to get a good look at what was going to be the most impressive parade in Iranian history. Way above us it was difficult to pick out the fighters and SEAD, but we knew they were there. Out to the east we could see several groups of aircraft flying unconcerned lazy circles, waiting for their cue to begin the fly-past. They naturally assumed that we were just another formation waiting for the fly-past to begin. It was precisely midday; the first of the massed ranks of Revolutionary Guard infantry were passing the VIP dais, taking the salute of a proud government. Marching in 1,000-men blocks these were easy to see. We made the switches live and traced the route to where the infantry ended and the vehicle parade began. And there they were, twelve monster artics, each easily distinguished with the double boosters strapped either side of the main body.

And in we went. Upside down, 15 degrees dive, acquire target, roll right way up, check to 10 degrees, speed fine, tracking fine, 3,500 feet, pause and pickle. Six rapid thuds told me our Mk82 500lb bombs were on the way down to shred the rockets which disappeared under the nose as we pulled hard to 6G to regain height. Assuming you found the target, high-angle dive with dumb weapons was the most consistently accurate method of delivery. When detonated at a height of 75 feet the shrapnel footprint would be sufficient to destroy the missiles and minimise civilian casualties. My wingman followed ten seconds behind. Numbers three and four had a different attack profile; shallow dive followed by an ultra-low-level release. They were both carrying six cluster bombs, each with 150 sub-munitions that spat jets of white-hot metal through all but the thickest armour on contact.

Looking back as we climbed there were no spectacular fireballs, just a mass of smoke. We then watched as the number three, just a black dot from where we were, swept in over the grey smoke, down to 60 feet between the buildings before release. The combination of airburst and cluster bomblets would ensure that the pride of Iran was destroyed and the threat to Israel removed, for the time being at least.

One minute later we were together at 10,000 feet and the four escorts came down to join us. As they did two Iranian aircraft flights drifted across our noses. This was too good an opportunity to miss. I watched the fighter leader close with the first four, who were oblivious to the wreckage below. From about 800 metres astern and slightly offset both he and his wingman fired a single Python heat-seeking missile at the rear pair of F-14 Tomcats. Both struck home into the jet pipes of the Tomcats; each one then rolled outside the formation and down, like a mirror image, both trailing black clouds of smoke. The two leading Tomcats seemed not to have noticed and seconds later the F-15Is were astern at 200 metres. From this range they could hardly miss, and both let fly with their M-61 Vulcan rotary cannons. Firing at a rate of 6,000 rounds per minute the Tomcats on the receiving end hardly had a chance. The left-hand one exploded into a bright fireball, the right-hand one, sensing something amiss, began a hard right turn as the first 20mm rounds struck. The shells chewed his back end off and sent him spinning on to the northern outskirts of the city below. That was a bonus, but it was time to exit stage left and we did so at Mach 1.2, diving back into the Talegan and Shah-Rud valleys which had shielded our approach.

We were able to relax slightly only when we had touched down at Yudekan, a rudimentary airstrip nestling between the mountains on the south-eastern extremity of Turkey. A thirty-minute fuel stop followed. If the Iranians had aircraft bombed up on stand-by they would be able to hit us in the open here. They would, however, have first to get through the F-16 CAP the Turks had put up – we could see them contrailing high above at around 25,000 feet. As we taxied out for the return trip to Israel we saw the other eight Thunders coming in to land. They had been all the way out to Kruh, high on the eastern Iranian plateau, and destroyed the Shahab missile construction and testing facility. It had been a good day's work.

The world did not agree with Captain Tal's assessment. The raid had been covered by CNN and both Sky World and BBC World news television stations, which were present as honoured guests of the Tehran government to give world coverage to what was supposed to be Iran's proudest moment. The number of Iranians killed in the raids was actually less than one hundred, with a further hundred treated for burns in Tehran. As the pictures were shown unedited around the world, even the US found it difficult not to sympathise with the invective streaming out of Tehran and the other Arab capitals. The Israelis were pleased that they did not have to conduct a covert battle damage assessment; the results of the raid were plain for all to see. In a speech to the nation and the world, the Israeli Prime Minister mimicked the famous words spoken by the US President four years earlier to justify the attack on North Korea's nuclear missile silos: 'Today Israel has acted in the interests of world security. We will not hesitate to act now or in the future against states or state-sponsored groups that threaten the very fabric of our society and step outside acceptable behaviour in the eyes of the civilised world. The world will one day thank us for what we have done.'

The Final Dominoes

The wave of protest that coursed through the Arab world following the Israeli attack on Tehran had two major effects that would make the clash of cultures between Islam and Russia on the one side and Israel and the West on the other inevitable. From the time of the Algerian Revolution the secular governments in Egypt and Tunisia had been increasingly isolated in their continued leaning towards the West and rejection of the Sha'ria as a basis for government. The ideals of the Islamic fundamentalists contrasted sharply with official neutrality, if not appeasement, towards Israel and the all-powerful arm of American aerospace power.

In Egypt in particular the US attack on Iraq that caused the incapacitation of Saddam Hussein and Israeli actions in Trans-Jordan/Palestine and then Iran served only to harden the attitudes of the people against what the fundamentalists described as the common foe. It was no surprise that support for the Islamic revolutionaries in both countries made great strides with each action. The Egyptian Army had been used to dispersing demonstrators that had flocked to the streets in sympathy with the Saudi Revolution. The increase in support for the revival of Islam through the actions of the US and Israel enabled the Islamic opposition parties to halt all terror actions against tourists and present themselves as a reasonable and inevitable alternative to secular government by

presidential decree. As their support grew, the opposition
were increasingly bold in their outspoken criticism and pure
haranguing of what they portrayed as a weak and 'Western-
crony' ruling regime. The clumsy and ineffectual attempts by
the authorities to stamp out dissent only encouraged the
opposition all the more, especially as soon as it became clear
that the Islamic penetration, some would say revival, of the
armed forces caused the authorities to have less and less trust
in their ultimate power base. The combined appeal of Islam
and dreams of commanding an élite Republican Guard
proved to be overwhelming incentives for more than a handful of senior generals. During the mass protests in Cairo and
Alexandria the Islamic revolutionaries, inspired by the support of the people and nudged by the secret agreement of
senior army officials, demanded that Egypt must choose
between East and West and called for the formation of what
they referred to as 'the government of our destiny'. With the
army and police force refusing to act on presidential orders to
disperse the crowds on 4 October, the entire Egyptian government resigned with honour, as the army did not hesitate to
point out, before they could be incarcerated as enemies of
Islam.

In Tunisia the process was slower but far more peaceful and
pragmatic. The government simply called a referendum and
adopted the Sha'ria wholeheartedly as its basis of rule. Little
changed practically in Tunisia, but the extremists were satisfied. By the end of October 2005 Islamic governments
stretched in an unbroken line from Morocco's Atlantic coast
across four thousand miles to Pakistan's Indian Ocean ports.
Syria and Libya remained the least changed of all Arab
nations. The blood successors of Assad and Gaddafi simply
declared their nations to be truly Islamic which embraced the
Sha'ria. In actual fact the grip on power of the leaders was
such that they remained simply military dictatorships, but
that did not make them any less committed to the greater
ideals of Islam and the ultimate aim of extinguishing Israel.
For the first time since Suleiman the Magnificent in the
fifteenth century, Europe was surrounded by the crescent
of Islam. The only Arab states that did not fall were Oman,

Kuwait, Qatar and Bahrain. These became military 'islands', each with more than just a permanent brigade of US marines to deter their increasingly hostile neighbours.

The Awakening

The single most important event that enabled all Islam to challenge the West was the appearance of a leader under whom all of Islam was able to unite. There is little doubt that 'Saladin', as he called himself, after the conqueror of the Crusaders, was seen by every Islamic state as a short-term opportunity for gain. The rifts between Iran and Iraq, as well as the natural suspicions about each other's motives among all the other nations of what was to become the Islamic Alliance, were too deep and ingrained for the unification to be viewed as anything other than a temporary window of opportunity. This was a rare aberration of history which was unlikely ever to be repeated, and therefore had to be seized before it passed.

And Saladin gave them hope, vision and a concrete plan through which Islam would attempt to gain equal status through a clash of civilisations as envisaged by the philosopher Samuel Huntington in the early 1990s. Saladin's real name was Hans Niebelung. He was born in 1961 in Bavaria on the shores of the Ammersee, where his father married a Kurdish restaurant owner. He graduated from the European School of Business at Reutlingen near Stuttgart in 1984, before studying at Harvard and becoming a Doctor of Philosophy in 1987. That he was a genius is not in doubt. The CIA attempted to recruit him during his time in Boston, and it was probably his disgust at their arrogant and clumsy approach which set him on his anti-American course. A devout Muslim, he spoke English, French, Spanish, Arabic and Hebrew fluently. He was appalled at America's 'video dependent' society and the social depravity whose origins he traced directly to Hollywood. He became convinced that as America conquered and littered the world with McDonald's,

Marlboro and Coca-Cola, while draining the Second and Third Worlds of their resources, somebody had to stand up and say 'stop'.

At a very young age he became the senior professor for Middle Eastern studies in Berlin. Between 2000 and 2005 he held various professorships throughout the Arab world. These included Algiers in 2002 during the revolution, Tehran in 2003, Mecca in 2004 during the revolution, Cairo in early 2005, before he was finally induced back to Tehran to become Chancellor of Tehran University that summer. His credentials as an intellectual and inspiring revolutionary theologian were impeccable. There was hardly a revolution that he did not play some part in, and by late 2005 he had cultivated a mass of contacts and friendships in both Islamic governments and high military circles across the Arab world. He had ridden on the crest of the revival of Islam and had grown in stature with the changes in each country rather than just 'arriving' on the scene. His message of unification and hope was what Islam had been waiting for for centuries. In spite of his origins he was a devout Muslim and claimed, through his mother's heritage (having publicly disowned his father's side), to be a true Arab. As such he was an acceptable neutral to the whole of Islam. By 2005 his writings and public speeches were printed and distributed throughout the Islamic crescent. He was not seen as a new prophet, yet his words were revered. The more extreme and vitriolic he became the more he was applauded.

In early 2005 he called for the unification of all Islam at the Second Islamic World Conference. While this call fermented, the events of the year ensured that unification would become a reality before the winter began. Saladin's dream was to achieve a real equal status for Islam in world affairs. The East was determined to act in the face of what appeared to be a reinforcement of cultural imperialism. The emergence of a new Nato in 2005 was a cause of great concern in eastern capitals. The East had hoped that outrage at US actions around the world from the millennium would continue to bring the East more influence and relative power while Europe dithered. The political and military changes that were

brought about by Europe's lurch to the right, and the prospect
of increased domination of the world by US-led power, were
too much for the East to contemplate. The Eastern view of the
UN, IMF and World Bank was that they were run by the USA
for the benefit of the USA, and occasionally her allies, and to
the detriment of the Second and Third Worlds. There would
have to be a struggle that would equalise or neutralise that
controlling influence. Following the Israeli strike on Tehran a
single broadcast among many proved to be the defining
moment of what was to come. On 6 November in Cairo
the leaders of the Arab nations held an emergency meeting
under the aegis of the World Islamic Council. Saladin, whose
works were widely read and respected, was invited from
Tehran to give a speech on his 'Islamic Vision'. He did not
disappoint. He spoke slowly and deliberately:

> The 'Israel' problem is one that true Arab countries can only
> resolve with patience, force and unity. Israel has gone one step
> beyond what the Arab world can or will bear. We have waited
> three hundred years for this moment. Once we were ascen-
> dant, but since the death of Suleiman the Magnificent our
> culture has been choked by the arrogance, ignorance, brutal-
> ity, suspicion and superstition of the Ottomans, the Jews and
> the Christian West. It is the duty now of every Muslim to
> sacrifice their personal enmities and antagonisms for a higher
> calling. This is a greater cause, a greater good, that will rid the
> world of the Zionist terror and its evil alliances. We will, in the
> final battle, be triumphant. We will lose sons and daughters
> and husbands and wives and fathers and mothers fighting for
> the cause. But not a single death will be wasted, and each will
> be guaranteed an eternal resting place. They will be remem-
> bered always in our prayers with gratitude and in history as
> those who gave their lives in establishing a new world order.
> Let us from this moment then be brothers in arms.

The rest of his speech was a mixture of similar rhetoric
exhorting the value and power of a united Islam. He received
a twenty-minute standing ovation. The vision had been immediately grasped by those present, and the delegates retired

for lunch engrossed in excited chatter about the new future. The practical outcome of the afternoon meeting was the formal foundation of the Islamic Alliance. The Islamic nations formed their own version of Nato, called the Holy Islamic Alliance, which was directed by a Ruling Council. Naturally Saladin was asked to become President of the Council, and therefore the most powerful figure in the world of Islam. The 'Great Theocracy' had become a reality.

Within two weeks of the decision to form a politico-military power block to oppose Israel and the US, a unified political and military council structure had been agreed. Saladin was invited to preside over both councils and unanimously voted into office to perform a task he had dreamed of for many years. In just over a month from the fall of the last secular Arab government in Egypt, the Islamic Alliance had acquired a focus that would provide the means to formulate a collective foreign policy and military strategy. The councils lost no time in agreeing a plan of action. The plan was, of course, Saladin's, and he alone would ensure that it was adhered to. In the aftermath of Iran's shame and ignominious defeat at the hands of a few Israeli jets sprang a phoenix of hope, purpose and not a little euphoria. Iraqis were reported to be hugging Iranians and Saudis – something unthinkable only a few years previously.

Israel was now isolated on the world stage. Only Turkey stood by her as a clear and friendly ally. The neutrals in the West were no longer able to sit on the fence, but the collective silence of the more powerful nations over the Israeli action (which they secretly welcomed and approved) was interpreted by the Islamic world as collusion. There were many calls for economic sanctions against Israel from the rest of the world, which were dampened only by the public threat of an American veto and private reminders of credits and favours owed to the US. But even the US made it clear to the government of Israel that her patience was not endless. Despite intensive lobbying from powerful American Jews, Congress voted narrowly in favour of a steady reduction in financial aid to Israel – most of which, it knew, was spent on arms anyway. Across Europe Israel's behaviour over recent months was privately viewed as variously intolerable, selfish, aggressive, even imperialist, but only the socialist opposition parties dared voice any meaningful condemnation. Israel remained unrepentant. The Israeli government saw the writing on the wall. On 22 October Israel began preparing for war. Her anticipation was underlined by the formation of the Islamic Alliance three weeks later. Indeed, from the day of the raid on Tehran in late September, Israel began to prepare for mobilisation. Turkey did likewise. While both Israel and Turkey had powerful standing armies, neither was prepared to be caught off guard by a surprise attack from their temporarily united and unanimously hostile neighbours. Full mobilisation at this stage was neither warranted nor justified. The speeches of Saladin might just be empty rhetoric, and it would be damaging both to the economies of the two countries and to the effectiveness of the troops if the large numbers of reservists and fresh conscripts had to be held at a high state of readiness for any length of time. Full mobilisation was a costly and last-ditch measure. By late 2005 Israel had become a military hedgehog, curled up, waiting for the inevitable attack.

PART TWO –
THE WAR OF 2006

'*When you hear of wars and rumours of wars, do not be alarmed. Such things must happen, but the end is still to come. Nation will rise against nation, and kingdom against kingdom. There will be earthquakes in various places and famines. These are the beginning of the birth-pains.*'

Mark, 13, vii–viii

Chapter Six – The Baltic War

Havoc over Estonia

Sergeant Igor Rossovski, a gunner with the 22nd Assault Helicopter Regiment, equipped with the latest variation of Havoc attack helicopter, the H model, took part in operations over Estonia. This is an extract from his book, *Havoc!*, published in September 2008.

At 2000 we were given orders to support the main attack on Jarve which stood some twenty miles from the border. We had no idea what sort of resistance, if any, the Estonians would put up, but we didn't expect any real bother. There was a large army base on the eastern edge of the town and our intelligence men told us that this would probably be the centre of any resistance by the tiny Estonian Army as it was the base for around one-third of the whole army.

The tanks had advanced across the border just after midnight and drove through the simple high fence that divided our countries. The flight of four Havoc-Hs we were leading was supposed to operate in two pairs to act as the eyes and ears of the leading tanks and reconnaissance unit. The weather was absolutely awful, with dense driving snow restricting visibility to tens of yards. We got airborne anyway, but even with all the latest technology couldn't see a bloody thing. It was all my pilot could do to decide that our contribution would be futile and then find the helibase and land again. We did all this at walking speed. With the mission postponed none of us slept that night. The delay was an irritating rolling one, with our take-off times being put back only an hour at a time. Outside the crewroom we were occasionally able to make out the rumble and crack of distant gunfire carried on the wind.

The weather had cleared sufficiently at first light for us to
get airborne, the driving snow replaced by a very low cloud
base and occasional snow showers. We flew due west following the route the tanks had taken, astride the parallel highway
and railway. On the ground the impressions left by the tanks'
tracks in the snow were still easily visible. On the highway
itself columns of armoured infantry carriers were moving
slowly eastbound two abreast. The customs post was burnt
out and slightly blackened. In the distance we saw several
columns of smoke, easily visible against the winter backdrop.
A couple of minutes later, as we swept low to the south of a
small hamlet, we were surprised to see three tanks and a
couple of armoured personnel carriers still smouldering. Obviously the Estonians were putting up some sort of a fight.
There were some buildings burning in the village and others
were clearly pockmarked with heavy-calibre machinegun fire
or had larger holes and were partly demolished where HE
shells had been fired direct. In the streets were several black
and brown bundles which I realised were dead bodies, though
whether Russian or Estonian I didn't know at the time.

We continued west for a further five minutes and established contact with the forward air controller (FAC) as the two
Russian Orthodox church spires in Jarve became visible. The
leading tanks had covered some twenty-two miles in the dark
and were clustered around 4 km east of the town. Eight
hundred metres beyond them and still fiercely ablaze was
an armoured recce vehicle and a tank with nothing apparently
wrong with it except a body in the snow beside it. The FAC
said that they had been attacked by a wave of anti-tank
missiles which needed rooting out. Although several had been
fired we later found out that the inexperienced defenders had
fired the Milans at maximum range. After losing the tanks we
had earlier seen, the leading elements had been more prepared
to spray any resistance with maximum suppressive fire, using
the 12.5mm anti-aircraft machineguns to put the firers off
their aim. The two tank companies and supporting infantry
had halted to await our arrival. Calling artillery support on to
the town, even its edges, was not going to be approved. Direct
support from aircraft was also discounted in urban areas.

There still existed a great deal of mistrust between the army and air force ground support units stemming all the way back to the Chechnya débâcle. The air force, when they eventually arrived, usually missed the target and occasionally even bombed our own forward troops. Even our commanders had realised the presentational problems caused by inadvertently killing civilians through stray shells or wildly thrown bombs.

The leading tank company commander came on the net and asked us to move ahead of the tanks and APCs that were about to charge at full tilt towards what looked like a military training area adjacent to Jarve barracks. Meanwhile we could see another column of armour moving off to the south-west. Jarve was being bypassed until the resistance had been dealt with. My pilot, leading the flight of four, acknowledged and called the other three Havocs into loose line abreast. The lead tanker shouted across the radio net 'Go go go!' and we could see clouds of diesel fumes as the Black Eagles were revved to the limit and slammed into gear to begin the charge. Once it was clear the tanks were on the move the nose of the Havoc dipped as my pilot increased the collective and made the transition from hover to slow forward flight.

Around 2 km short of the barracks area a point of light caught my attention. As I looked right the first point of light grew and began to curve towards us. It was followed by a rapid stream of more lights chasing it through the sky. Tracer rounds! 'Contact right, duck!' I yelled as the pilot stuffed the nose forward and we dropped like a stone from 500 metres altitude to just a couple. The tracer rounds flew past at seemingly crazy angles as we turned to face our attackers. At over 4 Gs it was all I could do to keep my helmet-mounted sight in the vicinity of the target. The weapons switches were already 'live' so I fired a short burst from around 1,800 metres. From inside the armoured cockpit the rotary 23mm cannon sounds like someone gunning a motorbike. My pilot, ever supportive of my gunnery skills, observed the strikes.

'Nowhere fucking near, well short and left.' We straightened up and closed the range. The tracers were still coming in bursts, arcing towards us all the time but never quite catching us as the gunner, probably with limited training and using optical sights to aim with, consistently failed to take enough lead.

'Bravo is engaging,' came the call from our number two. With that the small mound ahead where the AA gun was emplaced erupted in a shower of earth, smoke and debris. The number two had let him have a whole 57mm rocket pod. We jinked left and right as we approached the position to avoid the cloud of bits. Emerging on the other side, we almost flew directly over another two gun positions. I saw the face of one of the men in the gun emplacement. He looked as startled as I felt as we passed within 30 metres of his trench. On the twin AA gun another man was furiously working the elevation and azimuth wheels to swing his gun to bear on us.

At this range I could hardly miss. I looked at the middle of the position through the helmet sight and immediately got a contrast lock. With the aiming pipper on the man sitting behind the swinging gun, I pressed the trigger. Two short bursts and the position exploded in a shower of sparks as the rotary cannon's HE shells found targets. I admit that I grimaced as the soldier I'd been aiming at seemed to burst in a shower of crimson blood as the 23mm shells scythed diagonally through his upper body, leaving the lower half of a torso on the gun. His two companions just dropped in crumpled heaps.

'Too slow, comrades,' came the remark from behind me. My pilot, who had seen this sort of thing before on his first tour in Afghanistan, was actually enjoying himself. The second position, a further 100 metres north, got the same treatment. The first burst missed. To make sure with the second I held the trigger for a moment longer than we'd been trained to do. As it too disintegrated the voice from behind was on at me again. 'You don't have to write your name in the snow. Good shooting, anyhow.'

We continued to turn through 270 degrees hard right and pulled up into a low hover above the leading tanks now some 1,500 metres from the barracks and going at full tilt.

'Suspect missile position identified' – it was the FAC – 'large building with orange slate roof, fifty metres left gap in wall, covered small black building.' He'd obviously got a thermal hot spot in his sights. I followed his description and saw the position he meant.

'Visual,' I replied.

'You are clear to engage with friendlies 1,400 metres short.'

'Visual both. Alpha engaging.' I selected the Koronet guided missile. We had eight strapped to the sides in addition to four full 57mm rocket pods. The missile left the rails almost in slow motion, it seemed. All I had to do was keep the laser spot on the target area. The red flare of the orange motor bobbed up and down through my sights as the missile's computer continually corrected its flight path to keep it in the centre of laser energy. Five seconds after trigger press, and wham! The small black outhouse erupted into a column of grey and brown smoke.

'Target hit. Target destroyed.' The FAC confirmed what I already knew. Then all hell broke loose below us. There must've been a dozen or so Milans 'fired from concealed positions along the edge of the barracks. I later learned that this barracks was the training centre for the newly acquired Milan missiles, unlucky for those tanks below. Three tanks were hit immediately. One exploded in a ball of fire, giving its crew no chance of escape. Another was hit in the rear as it manoeuvred to avoid a direct hit. It skewed sideways, shedding a broken track as it did so and grinding to a halt. With the back end pouring smoke the crew bailed out and lay in the snow. We didn't have time to watch any more. My pilot ordered suppressive fire to be put down on the defensive line. This was going to be a serious fight now – it was obvious that the Estonians weren't going to just give up after a token show of resistance.

I selected the rocket pods and ripple-fired all four in sequence at two buildings from where we could see small flashes of gunfire emerging. The other three Havocs and the tanks on overwatch had the same idea. The whole line of low buildings disappeared in a hail of high explosive. The fight was over almost as quickly as it had begun. To the south the other pair of Havocs were right on the edge of the missile line, their guns firing almost continuously, chewing up some final resistance or fleeing Estonians unseen to us.

With the barracks and training area secure we had to return east to rearm and refuel. We flew one more sortie that morning against the last pocket of resistance in Jarve. The Estonians had managed to disable a tank and an APC with close range RPG fire. We were called in to demolish two multistorey buildings, which we didn't quite manage, although we left them in need of a serious facelift by the time we departed, again expending most of our ammunition in the process. The rest of Jarve was under control of our forces by midday.

The following morning [24 April] our operating base was moved to Jarve itself as the ground forces paused before the assault on Tallinn. The spearhead units had pushed on at top speed to the outskirts of the capital, covering the 200 km from their start line in just forty-eight hours against minimal resistance. We heard that the Estonian government had vowed to fight to the last man and the last bullet in the capital. They might have made a different choice had they known what was coming. We knew that our commanders didn't want to waste any time; we also heard that Nato was assembling an armada and we needed to take as much territory as possible with which to bargain.

Late on the 23rd my pilot returned from the forward headquarters muttering, 'Oh dear oh dear oh dear.' He had been to the commanders' brief for the assault on Tallinn. Our job would be to fly further west to the naval base at Paldiski to destroy the half-dozen fast attack craft that were the Estonian Navy, but this wasn't the source of his worry. We pressed him and it emerged that the major armoured units would bypass Tallinn and swing south to the Latvian border, but Tallinn itself would be left to the Siberians. Two whole divisions of them were ordered to take Tallinn, house by house, street by street if necessary. I agreed, with some misgivings.

A Deal Is Struck

The spring of 2006 saw the emergence of a Russia that was more akin to the old Soviet Union than anything in the

preceding fifteen years. The Russian Federation, now including Belarus, the Ukraine and Kazakhstan, was hard-
nosed and indifferent verging on hostile towards Nato. The
Islamic Alliance had watched events in northern Europe
unfold with great interest. It was clear to the most unbiased
observer that Russia was planning to do something. The
Islamic Alliance military planners visited Moscow over
Christmas 2005 for exploratory talks aimed at identifying
areas of mutual military and geostrategic interest. Following
a series of visits, they came away in mid-January with a
plan and a deal. Russia would benefit to the tune of some
$200 billion in cash and credits over a four-year period. In
return she would agree to pin down as much of Nato's
military hardware as possible and this would be achieved by
a 'policing action' in the Baltic. If she was able to regain
some measure of long-term direct control over Estonia and
its oil and reserves, that would be a major bonus and
would, at the same time, fulfil the leadership's economic
and military desires.

For many military men in the West there was, curiously
enough, a feeling of bright expectation and confidence. The
'Threat' was back, and with a vengeance. Much of Nato's
senior leadership had been battalion- or regimental-level
commanders when the 'Threat' collapsed with the fall of
the Berlin Wall and the unification of Germany.

This did not stop a barrage of questions being raised in the
House of Commons in Britain. The so-called experts had long
assured their governments that Nato would have at least two
and probably nearer five years of warning time of a renewed
Russian threat. The debates in London were fierce. The
Conservatives had increased defence spending dramatically
in their first year in office and would brook no criticism from
a Labour opposition that had managed eight years of downsizing and redundancy programmes. 'Continuing the sound
policies of eighteen years of Conservatism,' came the retort.
Everybody, it seemed, was blaming everyone else. They had
barely two months of warning, and even then there were
many sceptics who had become used to the idea of enduring
peace in Europe and saw the idea of a Russian 'land grab', in

spite of the evidence, as unthinkable; until it actually happened, that is.

The buoyant mood in Nato's senior headquarters reflected a return to the old days. It was almost nostalgic to have a good, solid Russian threat reappearing on Nato's eastern flank; the defence community would again have a rock of justification for force levels rather than depending on worldwide peacemaking operations. And there was not just one 'Threat' but two, with united Islam emergent to the south and east. The new right-wing governments and military hierarchies now needed little justification for the massive increase in defence spending that they had initiated on coming to power. The generals knew that in the long term this meant, assuming Russia remained aggressive, that defence spending would also have to go on increasing year on year as it had done throughout the decade from 1980 to 1990. More money meant that many of the procurement projects, so long stalled or delayed through lack of cash, would be reinvigorated and enhanced. At first it was 'kiddies in a sweet shop' time. After just two short months the pervading optimism had all but disappeared. It appeared that the Russians were going to start whether Nato was ready or not.

The First Hints

As early as 4 March 2006 US routine satellite surveillance began to pick up the first signs of unusual military activity in and around the barrack areas of Smolensk and Minsk. By 7 March increased coverage confirmed that the Russians were up to something and the Allied Rapid Reaction Corps (ARRC) was secretly put on twenty-four hours' notice to move. On 20 March the first troop movements towards the Poland/Belarus border were noted. These were military convoys along the Minsk to Brest expressway. Immediately the whole of Nato's reconnaissance and surveillance effort was focused on western Belarus. It soon became apparent that there were several divisions moving by road or the parallel rail link out of their barracks in western Russia towards the Polish border. The Russians, as expected, knew that they would be unable to hide such a mass movement and announced that joint military exercises would be taking place between the forces of Russia and Belarus.

As soon as the movement was confirmed the major ground elements of the ARRC were given orders to deploy to eastern Poland. This was a sizable, balanced and comprehensive force that included everything from reconnaissance and engineer elements to artillery, air defence, electronic warfare and combat support units.

The Oblast Is Reinforced

The move to the Poland/Belarus border was not the only one made by the new Russian Army. In order to secure a maximum Nato reaction and provoke distraction and uncertainty about Russia's long-term intentions, as well as gauge Nato's resolve, Russia also decided to reinforce the Kaliningrad Oblast. This would demonstrate both Russia's own resolve and the efficiency and rapid mobility of the new force. It would also show that the art of operational manoeuvre had not been lost by the Russians and would seriously menace the ARRCs and the whole Polish left flank and supply routes. The Russian intention was also to kill two birds with one stone and use the deployment to Kaliningrad to spoil the pro-independence celebrations in the Oblast, impose martial law and keep Nato guessing as to the real Russian intent.

In conjunction with the moves by ground forces in the Oblast, the 1st Air-Mobile Brigade, some three thousand crack troops, was flown from its barracks in Grodno in eastern Belarus over Lithuania to the airfield at Chernya-khovsk. For the twenty-four hours that the corridor was open the first 'squadron' of six Lithuanian F-16As, recently purchased second hand from Belgium, remained on the ground.

The only other aircraft capable of challenging this clear

violation of Lithuania's airspace were Polish. Nato had deferred deploying Reaction Force Air units to poorly equipped forward bases in Poland until it felt confident of the real Russian intent and capable of sustaining extensive air operations from those bases. However, what was unclear was the status of the airspace of an 'associate member' of Nato, and whether a fight over this was worth it in terms of risking wider conflict. The Polish general staff was quick to point out to the more hawkish Nato planners that the 'bear' was now in their back yard and Poland did not want to prod it.

The mood in Russia was buoyant as extensive media coverage of Exercise 'Iron Fist' showed the again-proud Red Army crashing into action. Nato expressed its severe displeasure at not being given the requisite thirty days' notice for an exercise involving in excess of twelve thousand men, and at the crass violation of Lithuanian sovereign airspace. By dusk the next day all was quiet, a curfew was in place throughout the Oblast and martial law had been imposed. In the intervening forty hours Russian tanks, troops and armoured personnel carriers had smashed their way through towns, fields, villages and back gardens. It was Nato's turn to be concerned; the Russian bear had shown its teeth.

The unease was all the more real because of the change in quality of the troops the Russians now commanded following the ending of conscription. It was no longer possible to be complacent about relative combat power since the new Russian Army was very much an unknown quantity. It did not have the Cold War disadvantages of being a polyglot of poorly trained conscripts drawn from the dregs of society and from all areas of the former USSR, where Russian was very much a second language. The army was now professional in every respect, filled with 'real' Russians who were motivated, cohesive and well equipped. Morale was reported to be at an all-time high, and the sum capability of the new army was assessed as being an order of magnitude better than its much larger predecessor.

Nato Moves East

Meanwhile, back on the Polish border, Nato was alarmed, and it was Poland's turn to be fearful. Reform in the Polish Army following her accession to Nato had been slow. Modernisation of equipment, with the singular exception of the Polish Air Force (PAF) purchase of Gripens, remained virtually at a standstill thanks to a lack of funding and difficulty in reforming the central military bureaucracy. By 2006 only half of the army was both 'Nato compatible' and somewhere near the required 80 per cent strength. Despite Russian assurances that she was merely carrying out the first set of Army Group-level exercises, the West decided to act.

Nato's response was to prepare to move a further four divisions, three of which were German Panzer and Panzergrenadier to double the commitment to Poland. The Poles, who had more experience than most of Germans marching through their country, politely rejected the plan and asked for a 'no Germans' alternative. Nato stood its ground while the affronted Germans fumed silently. A further delay of a week followed, and a compromise was finally reached whereby the Dutch would send their 2nd Armoured Division to the eastern border and the Germans a single reduced-strength Panzer division. The French were politely invited to assist with their 1st Armoured for the western end of the Oblast front. The scenario had been foreseen, war-gamed and planned. Now these contingency plans were put into action. The German, Dutch, American and French divisions moved from Augsburg, Kassel, Dortmund, Berlin and Strasbourg by train through Germany and Poland. The civilian rail networks in Germany and Poland ground to a halt as priority was given to long and slow military freights. These Nato units, which formed a defensive arc from Gdansk to Warsaw and Brest, represented the best of all of the 'army heavies' that were available and willing in central Europe; the operation was code-named 'Eastern Forge'.

On 12 April, two days after the manoeuvres in the Oblast had begun, the Russians began their exercise along the

Poland/Belarus border. Europe was in the grip of war fever as the media turned the deployment by Nato's heavies into a race against an inevitable Russian attack. In the week or so that followed, Nato's defensive line in eastern and northern Poland solidified with a reconnaissance screen near the border. The infantry dug in to receive the expected tank thrusts with ATGMs; tucked in behind them were the armoured formations ready, with their attack helicopters, to act as a counter-attack force cum fire brigade to plug gaps and prevent breakthroughs.

While the world waited with bated breath to see whether and when the Russians would jump, Nato became more assured of its position with each passing day. When the Russians had not attacked Poland by the 19th there was an increasing sense of relief, a belief that Russia had missed her chance, if indeed she ever intended to attack, and a certain amount of back-slapping in SHAPE. The Pentagon, or more accurately the astute Tungsten Lady as the new US President was nicknamed, began to smell a rat. And her intuition was rewarded.

The tension in Latvia had been escalating steadily throughout the late winter and early spring and had become something of a sub-news event compared to events to the south. The Russian orchestration of events had been masterly. In early March there had been several assassinations of leaders of the Russian community in Estonia. Additionally, Russian businesses and residential areas were bombed and Russian nationals harassed. The Free Estonia Group claimed responsibility for these attacks. The actual missions were carried out by the new KGB and Spetznatz cells on orders that came directly from Moscow.

Russia naturally expressed her outrage in response to these incidents, demanding state protection for her nationals and threatening to provide the protection herself if the Estonian government was unable to supply it. Despite Estonia's assurances the attacks continued. In an attempt to stave off direct Russian action, the governments of Estonia, Latvia and, after some hesitation, Lithuania continued to refuse Nato's request for its own 'armed monitors' to be put in place in these two countries, especially since half of Nato had rumbled in to Poland. The monitors' mission would be to attempt to discourage those behind the unrest and bring expertise in combating widespread terrorism to the small and inexperienced Baltic armies. Secret reporting had revealed to Nato the extent of the Russian manipulation of events, and Nato remained determined to counter the destabilising influence of the Russian secret and special forces. The polite rebuttals of Nato's suggestions, justified in both parliaments as actions that would only serve to antagonise the angry Russian bear, changed into flat refusals when Nato upped the ante and attempted to implement its larger-scale contingency plans. These included the sending of brigade-sized units to exercise with the Baltic forces. Russia intensified the war of words as the Nato forces moved through Poland, accusing Nato of belligerence and unnecessary aggressive action with the build-up of forces in Poland. As for the situation in the Baltic, in particular Estonia, Russia declared that she would brook no interference from the forces of Nato imperialism within her sphere of influence, and Nato had to understand that the patience of the average Russian citizen was wearing very thin. Russia had had just about enough of what she called 'aggressive apartheid' in Estonia.

Third Shock Army

With the focus of intelligence effort on the Polish/Belarus border and on events and possible Russian intentions in the Oblast, little attention was paid to the military activities in Leningrad. Third Shock Army, the most feared of all Russian formations, was still an élite among the élite. It had first call on the brightest graduates from the Frunze Military Academy and the stars of the general staff. The senior commanders of the Russian Army, many of whom had served in Third Shock formations, ensured that the favouritism continued at all levels of command. The 1st British Corps had faced Third Shock in the old Cold War days where the two would have contested the hinge of the entire North German Plain flank. It was a responsibility that was not envied by the Allied corps on either side of the Brits.

From the beginning of the planning phase for the Baltic operation there was little surprise when Third Shock had been identified as the formation that would have the honour of leading the attack. While all attention was directed towards Poland, Third Shock began a trickle night-time deployment through Leningrad to either side of Lake Peipus on the border with Estonia. This movement went unnoticed in the West until it was too late, for Estonia anyway. Nato was not to be put off and the US in particular was not going to allow Russia to throw her weight around without having to consider the consequences.

Contingency plans for a worst case initiated in mid-March at the insistence of the US President were now coming to fruition. A second operation, code-named Baltic Forge, which consisted of an amphibious and air-mobile battle group, had been readied. Even if the Baltic states did not see the writing on the wall, the most powerful voices in Nato were not going to allow Russia to set precedents for aggression while the rest of Europe dithered. It took just over a month for the amphibious and air-mobile groups to prepare and assemble. These forces would, in time, be strengthened by the addition of the US Marines Atlantic Amphibious Group and the whole of the US 82nd Airborne Division. The amphibious force began to assemble on RoRo (roll-on roll-off) ferries and hired (or commandeered) cargo ships in Southampton, Rotterdam and Bremerhaven. The air-mobile and air landing units formed up around the military air hubs in the UK at Fairford, Mildenhall, Lyneham and Brize Norton. By 20 April the force was finally ready to move, having taken just over four weeks and a massive logistic effort. The scenes in the UK in particular were reminiscent of those back in 1982 when the South Atlantic task force had been assembled. This operation, in which the transport planes of the US's MAC (Military Airlift Command) dominated the airways of western Europe, was a whole lot bigger. The timing of the operation was perfect. On 23 April two

American carrier battle groups and the Marine Amphibious Group sailed up the English Channel ready to escort the NRF (Nato Reaction Force) to a destination as yet unknown, but given the Russian invasion of Estonia the previous day, somewhere in the Baltic was a good bet.

The Russian media followed events in Germany and Poland with a keen interest. The endless stream of broadcasts hyped the situation by on the one hand appealing for peace and stability while on the other warning Poland that the Germans had never really given up their desire for a greater Germany. This was, it was claimed, the dream of the German government, which, given events over the past three years in Germany, Russia described as being as near to fascist as anything previously seen in the preceding fifty years. Russia claimed that the Germans had been secretly looking at ways of restoring 'Greater Germany' with those parts of Poland, Lithuania and the Oblast that were once parts of East Prussia, arguably the birthplace of the modern German state. Once the Poles allowed the Germans in, warned Russian state television, there would be no getting them out; Germany was still fixated with '*lebensraum*' (living space) – as the build-up of second-echelon forces on Poland's western border 'clearly proved'. As the entrenching of Polish and Nato units on the Oblast and Belarus borders was completed, the Russian exercises came to end. The Russian High Command were now ready to sidestep right and focus on their real intent of tying Nato down in the Baltic.

In Estonia events took a turn for the worse. The Russian ambassador's wife and eldest son were wounded in a deliberately abortive 'assassination' attempt. This was seen by Moscow as the last straw. It was in fact Moscow's own final action in what had been a carefully orchestrated campaign to provide a pretext for invasion. Nato had finally picked up the clues as to Russia's real intent only a week previously. Two Siberian Motor Rifle Divisions were spotted by routine satellite reconnaissance and SIGINT while in transit between Leningrad and the northern end of Lake Peipus. In and around Narva at the northern end of the lake there were already two tank corps of what was to become Third Shock's northern pincer, each comprising two tank and one motor rifle division. The arrival of the Siberians, who had since World War II maintained a fearsome reputation in their apparent disregard for life through their participation in campaigns in Afghanistan, Georgia and Chechnya, meant that action was probably imminent. Nato redoubled its effort to complete preparations for the declaration of readiness for the NRF. Squadrons of Typhoon fighters and Tornado GR4 fighter-bombers, held on between twenty-four and seventy-two hours' notice to move since the beginning of the build-ups on the Poland/Belarus border, were ordered to deploy, along with a host of other nations' fighters and bombers, to forward bases in Denmark and northern Germany.

Russia Invades

At midnight on 22 April Radio Moscow and all Russian television stations blacked out normal programmes and in their stead patriotic songs and stirring marching music were played to an eagerly waiting public. Such changes to programming had only occurred in the past on the deaths of presidents or during state funerals. At 0700 Moscow time a stern-faced announcer, dressed in full army ceremonial uniform resplendent with his 'Hero of the Soviet Union' star, interrupted the military musical diet. He announced that at midnight Russian forces had begun a limited police action across the border into Estonia to 'protect' Russia's national interests. He continued that Russia had long entreated the government of Estonia to act swiftly and severely against the dissident elements within its borders which were doing so much harm to the sons and daughters of Russia living there as guests. As the attempts had been less than successful, and the solutions offered by the beleaguered Estonians hardly workable, the government of the Russian Federation had no option but to take matters into its own hands. Once the dissident elements had been eliminated, the announcer concluded, Russia would be ready to negotiate a withdrawal. He warned

Nato not to overreact and instructed the Estonian armed forces to remain in their barracks or risk annihilation.

The West could hardly believe that Russia had invaded Estonia. The press corps was aghast. The news came as a major psychological blow to the generations that had been nurtured on peace, stability and diplomacy, always under-pinned by an American big stick. Internal unrest and political upheaval were a normal price to pay for the maintenance of free speech and the incorporation, or otherwise, of minority groups and views into ostensibly democratic systems. Real war in one's own back yard, as opposed to policing actions to sort out Balkan warlords and those of similar ilk, was some-thing that nations of the Second and Third Worlds became involved in. The collective European experience was that real war happened only in Asia, South America, Africa and the Middle East, but not in Europe. The armies of the West fought wars, certainly, but not in northern Europe, and only around the world in pursuit of 'just causes'. The generation of pensioners nodded sagely. At last their children might perhaps understand how they had felt as children and young men and women under the threat of Nazi jackboots. Could it be true that the sixty years of peace in Europe were no more than an aberrant blip in world history, and that war and rumour of war were indeed the normal state?

The Russian steamroller left its start lines at exactly mid-night. The leading divisions were used in a pincer attack around Lake Peipus, thrusting due west towards the capital Tallinn and south-east to seal the border with Latvia.

By first light on 26 April all serious resistance in Estonia ended. The main cities of Tallinn and Tartu were both taken. In Tallinn there was some heavy fighting. The remaining pockets of armed resistance in the city comprised a loose collection of police, small regular army units and hundreds of youths armed with Molotov cocktails, the occasional Kalash-nikov and a great deal of nationalistic fervour. The units were brutally eliminated by the Siberian assault teams who did not seem to have the words 'prisoners', 'surrender' or 'mercy' in their vocabulary.

While Nato's Reaction Force was under way, Russia declared that its 'police action' was over and that it would look to ensure that a 'responsible' regime, more sympathetic to Russia's interests, was installed to govern Estonia. Once this had been achieved, Russia said, her forces would withdraw. Additionally she warned Nato that a significant presence in the other two Baltic states would be viewed as an act of deliberate provocation. To reinforce her position of military strength and to remind both Latvia and Lithuania of their vulnerability, two tank corps were moved from the Belarus/Poland border, one each to the Belarus/Lithuania and Russia/Latvia borders.

For Nato, having been outmanoeuvred once, the question of sitting idly by while Russian troops sat menacingly on the borders of a further two vulnerable states was not an option. As the NRF passed through the Kattegatt and Skaggerak on the 25th, Nato felt confident enough to deploy a sizable advance force by air to Riga. The first real lines in the sand were to be drawn. This was done without the full approval of the Latvian government, which, having seen what had happened in Tallinn, with rumours of rape, pillage and mass executions rife but unsubstantiated, preferred appeasement to direct action.

Typhoons to Denmark – The First Air Battle

The Nato troops that landed in Riga consisted of elements of the UK's 24th and 5th Air-Mobile Brigades (the former flown in directly from their reserve positions in Poland), a light armoured reconnaissance squadron and advance units of the American 82nd Airborne. Nato's nervousness about the vulnerability to Russian fighters of such a large gathering of transport aircraft was reflected in the size of the defensive fighter force that was assigned to protect the air landing operation. The first air battle of the war took place high over the Baltic Sea, just off the coast of Latvia, as the first Russian CAP flew to take up station on combat air patrol. Squadron Leader Glen 'Thomas' Hardy, who led the sortie, said afterwards:

The Eurofighter Typhoon, on its eventual introduction to squadron service in 2003, was a fine, agile and beautiful machine, incomparably better than its predecessors. But its value had been degraded by two decades of delay. It was not vastly superior to the new F-18E/F Hornet nor the new Su-32 Flanker – but superior it was. And in air war terms any difference in performance was the difference between killing and being killed; there was no middle ground for air combat. All air combats since 1982 involving the West versus others had ended in cricket scores. There was no attrition, no sense of fairness, no even losses. One was either massacred or did the massacring, that much we already knew.

The Typhoon was not stealthy in the purest American sense of the word and was inferior to the F-22 Raptor which was replacing the F-15C Eagles. It was, however, less than half the price and, since much of the 'sensing' of enemy aircraft was now done by passive rather than active means, and because none of the potential enemy aircraft was any more stealthy than Typhoon, pure stealth was something of an expensive and desirable but not essential luxury. And the Typhoon was multi-role. The Raptor was pure air superiority; a two-seat bomber version was still under consideration. Once the sky had been swept clear of enemy aircraft it no longer had a role. It was an interesting point for debate in the fighter bars: one Raptor or three EFAs, whose side would you want to be on? To the pragmatist, in anything that involved air-to-ground missions, which was what the future seemed to hold in terms of out-of-area operations, rather than defeating hordes of enemy fighters, there was no choice. And even when it came to the latter in the Baltic, the Typhoon was to prove itself more than up to the task. But in the late 1990s hard choices had to be made. The army had turned to air power, recognising its dominance over the traditional battlefield, and had procured eighty WAH-64 Longbow Apache attack helicopters, but had to trade in a few hundred tanks and armoured personnel carriers to obtain them. The RAF was justifiably proud of its Typhoons. The Typhoon could switch from air defence to reconnaissance and ground attack with a mouthwatering array of guided and unguided weapons for missions at all altitudes.

Admittedly the practical aspects of being all things to all men were difficult at first. Both the Americans and Canadians had tried dual roles for their F-4s and F-18s respectively during the 1980s without much success. The conclusion was that excelling in both the fighter and bomber roles could not be done. However, the advent of the F-15E Strike Eagle changed this 'given' as the F-15Es and the US Navy F-18Ds and Fs proved it was possible, with two seats, to be world-beaters at both. With the advent of EFA the advanced technology incorporated was aimed at reducing pilot work-load. The philosophy behind the cockpit displays and ergo-nomics was to ease the assimilation of information. What the RAF was perhaps a little slow in realising was that to fulfil both roles to the maximum capability of the aircraft two seats were required. The USAF had its F-15Es, the USN Hornet Fs, the USMC Hornet Ds, the French Air Force two-seat Rafales, and the Swedish Air Force had one-third of its Gripens produced as two-seaters for the mission commanders and their deputies. The first two-seat Typhoons would not roll off the production line until 2007, and only then because British Aerospace had correctly anticipated the trend and had had the design and configuration of the Typhoon 2 (or Tempest, as it was later known) ready for some time. The collapse of the procurement of a long-range replacement for the now venerable but very capable Tornado GR4 on cost grounds had led the RAF in 2004 to lay firm plans for an elegant solution. It would become a two-aircraft-type force. The Tornado GR4s would be replaced by Typhoon 2s with conformal fuel tanks, giving the RAF a total fleet of 340 Typhoons and 100 JSFs.

The move towards two seats was driven, like most Western war-fighting equipment problems, by information. The pro-blem with the advanced sensor suite was that although the information displays were extremely pilot-friendly the stum-bling-block, or more accurately bottleneck, was assimilation of the mass of incoming information by one brain. The best efforts of the boffins were unable to produce a computer or system that could analyse, prioritise, and most importantly gauge when to feed vital information to the pilot, as well as another human in the back could. This became glaringly obvious in computer link-up and simulated missions where there was always a dynamic and rapidly changing air-to-air or air-to-ground environment, often conducted at night and in bad weather, under fire with the unexpected happening at regular intervals.

We deployed as two four-ships from Leuchars, Scotland, late on the evening of 19 April to Karup in Denmark as the first part of Nato's Reaction Force (RF) Air. We had heard about Russia moving into Estonia on the news a couple of days before. I didn't think that this would be something we might go to war over. At 1700 hours on the 18th the boss of the squadron instigated the emergency recall procedure for those away on leave or doing courses and called the whole of 111 Squadron (the Tremblers) into number 22 Hardened Aircraft Shelter (HAS). He told us we had a job of work to do and only twenty-four hours to get ready. The other two operational EFA squadrons were also given orders to move to bases in eastern Germany. The air defence of UK plc would be left to the EFA training unit and the last two aged Tornado F-3 squadrons.

I'd done the same thing as a sprog Flying Officer on the old F-3 back in '91 when we deployed to Saudi. This looked like being the same thing: a show of force to deter any further aggression. Then we weren't allowed up into bandit country; this time I had the niggling feeling that the quantum leap in capability between our Typhoons and the F-3 might nudge our masters into being slightly more aggressive with their fighter assets. I didn't realise at the time just how aggressive they were going to be.

We arrived at Karup and put the aircraft to bed in the HASs. Our hundred or so ground crew arrived packed into four Herc Js along with ground power sets and the first part of the 'fly-away pack'. This was an assortment of equipment, spare parts and weapons which included 27mm ammunition for our guns (I was certain we wouldn't need that) and racks of ASRAAMs and AMRAAMs. The poor ground crew had a miserable night. Everything had to be unloaded and stored in double-quick time, in the dark and in the teeth of an ominous and bitter easterly wind. The land around Karup is flat and boring, agricultural browns and dull greens for miles around offering no natural protection. As soon as we were done with the jets the boss told us to get our heads down as we'd be up over the Baltic Sea first thing. The ground crew were not impressed. Normally on arrival at an overseas base there'd be a beer call with the hosts to cement relations. At Karup there were no locals. There was sod all. Good old Nato had kept the base capable of functioning, for just such an emergency, years after the last Saab Draaken fighter had left for Austria. From inside our concrete 'Hard' we were unaware of the frantic night's activity as a seemingly endless stream of Hercs disgorged the rest of our pack and two RAF Regiment squadrons: one an air defence unit (19 Squadron) complete with HVM Starstreaks (if they had to be used in anger then we really would be in the pooh) and the other (66 Squadron) a field squadron for ground defence (and if they had to be used, hopefully we wouldn't be there!).

We were up at 5 a.m., breakfasted and into briefing by 6.30. Arrivals in new theatres usually had hours of briefings on local air traffic procedures, civilian airspace structures and the like. Our briefing was quick and dirty. Our own air traffickers had been brought over from Leuchars and Danish civilian airspace had been suppressed at midnight as we slept. Silent Procedures were in force and were almost identical to those we used at Leuchars. There was a single air corridor established from Karup due east to the island of Bornholm and thereafter we could do pretty much what we liked.

Walking out to the jets in light drizzle, it was quickly clear that the engineers had done a brilliant job – good lads and lasses every one. They looked wiped out at the see-off and in need of some decent rest. They deserved it. Karen, my crew chief, looked awful: no make-up, grimy cheeks, tousled hair. I didn't dare tell her. 'Had a hard night?' I ventured as she strapped me in.

'You could say that, sir.' She managed a smile. 'Jet's in perfect nick. Try not to break her, sir, and do come back in one piece.' Ever the professional, what a hero.

'Thanks,' was all I could muster. 'See you later.' It was

amazing the number of people needed just to get one jet airborne. The supply and movement people (now called 'duvet fluffers' instead of 'blanket stackers') ensured all the right bits got to the right place at the right time. There was a myriad of different types of engineering specialists from airframes (riggers) through engines (sooties) to avionics and electronics (fairies) to the aircraft see-off teams (linies). Most were extremely clever and able, some had university degrees. Also in the background making up parts of the whole were the firemen, the administrators and ops support people providing intelligence and so forth. Any of them failing to do their job to 100 per cent of their ability might mean failure of the mission. For the RAF almost every individual played a critical part. The size of the collective effort was immense, yet the public so often saw just we pilots at the pointy end.

The first trip was to be a rolling six-hour combat air patrol (CAP) over Bornholm. In the old days this meant using up jets and aircrew fatigue at a significant rate with two up, two in transit out and two in transit back the whole time – you needed a whole squadron just to maintain one position. Unfortunately, for the pilots at least, once airborne and at height the Typhoons stayed up for ever and a day even without a tanker. So for the four days we settled into a routine of two three-ships twelve hours on, twelve off. Of the twelve on, two hours were spent in transit to and from the CAP area and six on station, with only a short visit to the tanker to top up. With thirteen pilots in theatre this was easy. The only downsides were sore butts and using pee-tubes.

For the next few days this was how it stayed. Morale improved considerably when the Regiment Field Squadron managed to purchase a dozen barrels of Carlsberg beer during a local area recce. Of Russian aircraft we saw none. We did manage a few practice air combats against the Swedish Gripens. Beyond visual range they were no match for us and dogfighting was so one-sided it reminded me of my F-3 days when we were foolhardy enough to tangle with F-16s. It was nice to be on the other side of the fence. Confidence was high and rising, but with it so was the tension.

Civilian air travel suffered from severe disruption when the

NRF task force commander imposed a two-hundred-mile Total Exclusion Zone (TEZ) around the fleet. This was enforced by carrier-based F-18Es as well as land-based F-22s flying from the UK, Denmark and Germany, and of course ourselves. TG-77 steamed through the Skaggerak and Kattegatt on the 25th, ahead of the amphibious elements of the NRF. The imposition of a two-hundred-mile TEZ around the two carriers meant that for us things became a little more restricted. We couldn't move in the TEZ without the permission of the Anti-Air Commander on board the lead Aegis anti-air cruiser, USS *Port Royal*, who had the apt call sign 'Mother May I'. For any aircraft that entered the TEZ without Mother May I's permission the two Aegis cruisers in TG-77, the USS *Port Royal* and USS *Lake Erie*, were formidable opponents. They were the first to have installed the USN's Linebacker ATBM system using Standard missiles; the SM-2 Block IVA was used for lower-tier defence and, with new guidance and an extra 'killer' stage, the SM-3s had a capability somewhere between the Patriot PAC4 and the Israeli Arrow 2. This meant that if they could hit ballistic missiles they would be particularly deadly to aircraft.

That same day we heard that the Russians had moved down to the border with Latvia and would be in a position to jump within forty-eight hours. There was clearly a race on between the Russians sweeping south and west through Latvia and the TG trying to get enough forces ashore to draw some sort of line in the sand. It soon became clear that Nato was losing the race and the decision was made to fly in the 1st Air-Mobile Brigade direct to Riga. There were already special forces on the ground and the airport was still clear, but time was running short. The brigade would fly direct from RAF bases at Brize Norton and Lyneham and would require both a fighter sweep and an escort. The Tremblers got the first job; to be done with the help of US F-18E/F Super Hornets from the carrier. That at least was a relief. The last thing we wanted to do was ride as outriggers to a small fleet of assorted transports doing 300 knots.

The six of us took off in pairs at thirty-second intervals with the sun at our backs low on the north-eastern horizon. We climbed vertically, the following pairs keeping their spacing using their IRSTSs (Infra-Red Search and Track System) and in no time we were through the layers of stratocumulus clouds and up at 42,000 feet. This was a nice height, the height where the curvature of the earth first became apparent, fighter country. One minute before entry into the TG-77's TEZ, I checked in with Mother May I that we were 'on time, as fragged' (i.e. as tasked). In reality this was unnecessary but it made us all feel a whole lot happier that the PWO(A) on the command at Aegis Area Air Defence Ship had personally approved our presence. We watched the Hornets join from below, having followed their progress on our JTIDS displays from the moment of launch. Over Bornholm we descended to flight level 250 and plugged into the tankers, which were flying a line astern race-track pattern. Again full of gas, we cruised back up to 42K and set off east into the gathering darkness.

I felt a little uneasy at the prospect of flying a sweep so far east followed by a loiter time over Riga while the transports arrived to disgorge the air-mobile brigade. The first sign of trouble came from 'Magic', our AWACs: 'Magic is curtains,' was all he said. This was the code word to let all those on frequency know that he was experiencing jamming on his radars. We later learned that all along the Estonian coast and border the Russians quickly installed a chain of mobile radar jammers. These had been the first units to arrive, hot on the heels of the tank and APC Operational Manoeuvre Groups which occupied the most northerly Baltic state so rapidly. The system called Tuman (Russian – 'Fog') had been in Russian service for several years. For reasons that were fast becoming blindingly (no pun intended) obvious, the Russians had kept it under very tight wraps. The design was optimised for use against both the terrain following radars (TFR) of all-weather fighter-bombers and against the E-3 AWACs-series aircraft. The chain acted as an electronic field that gave false signals to TFR-equipped aircraft, forcing their systems to climb to an altitude where they would become more vulnerable to surface-to-air missiles. The secondary capability was the production of a fog of electronic interference over a wide area that reduced the effective detection range of the AWACs from some 300 km down to 50 km. 'Magic' could see well as far as the coast but not much beyond it.

This was not a good development since it meant that our detection of any potential 'hostiles' would be later than ideal, and we had to consider switching on our own radars, the ECR-90Cs, to sweep the skies. Sending our own ergs across the ether would tell anyone listening that we were on our way. I had a quick chat with 'Lazarus', the lead Hornet, and we decided that they would go in one minute ahead of our six with all systems active, then peel back over Riga. This tactic meant that the 'active' Hornets would certainly act as a beacon and let any Russians know they were there, but our hope was that with attention focused on the Hornets we would be able to jump anything sniffing at them. In the game of three-dimensional chess that is modern air combat, getting into a position of advantage without being seen is the equivalent of starting a game against an opponent who does not have a queen or rooks. As it turned out it worked like a dream. Checkmate followed in four moves.

At 120 miles to the Riga bullseye we picked up the first signs of trouble. The DASS (Defensive Aids Sub System) suite started picking up signals from a Mainstay III Russian AWACs as well as intermittent SU-37 radars in search mode. The ESM listening system had been developed from the German ECR Tornado's ELS. As far as detection went the latter was better even than the F-15 Eagle and as good as the F-22 Raptor's radars in full active mode. German ECRs had had the dubious privilege of being put up the front of all Nato's aircraft packages when available simply because their electronic ears were so good. If fighter opposition was detected they would turn tail; if SAMs showed an unwelcome interest they would be repaid with a HARM up the snout.

I called 'Bandits bearing 050'; Magic responded with 'Picture clear'. No surprise there – the Flankers were probably in the climb just east of Tallinn doing their radar functional checks. I watched the Hornets on the IRSTS bear left on to 050. They knew we weren't known for calling false contacts. A minute later we followed them. At eighty miles the Hornets switched on their radars. The result was spectacular. Within thirty seconds the DASS was picking up multiple SU-37 radar hits in search mode. No doubt the controller in the Mainstay had detected the Hornets and ordered the Flankers to go active. The next five minutes were a time to remember.

Lazarus did the sort: 'I got twelve in three box fours at 50 angels 35, at 55 angels 20 and 60 angels 45 and we're jumping.'* With that the Hornets blew their external fuel tanks off and accelerated ahead of us to Mach 1.3, fanning out into 'wall' formation – four line abreast. We did likewise, the tanks separating cleanly with a 'bub-bub' dull thud from under the jets. The 'sort' came through on the JTIDS link. It looked just like one of the scenarios we'd flown at Red Flag against the Aggressor Squadron. We watched as the back four Flankers turned the long way round on to north, attempting to head out for an unseen right hook. Our rules of engagement were clear. The bottom line was that the Hornets and us always had the right of self-defence. If attacked, and that meant locked up by a hostile radar, we were clear to engage.

I moved the throttles to max dry power and smiled, as even at this speed there was a satisfying kick in the back as the jet responded eagerly. Through the sound barrier, mild buffet, up to 1.3, co-speed with the Hornets, and then back a tad on the throttles. At max dry all of the jets were capable of a Mach 1.42 super-cruise and a couple with particularly well-tweaked engines were capable of 1.45. This was fast. And in a fighter speed is life. If necessary we still had the afterburner to reach Mach 2, but for now thirteen nautical miles a minute was sufficient. According to my JTIDS read-out the Flankers were doing Mach 1.2, which gave us a closing speed of two and a half times the speed of sound, or twenty-five miles a minute. The Hornets would merge with the Flankers, now some fifty miles distant, in just two minutes.

Lazarus again: 'Lazarus is Martha, I repeat Lazarus is Martha. Venom rotate!' This was it. The Hornets had been locked up by the lead Flankers and were turning about in full

---

* Translated, this meant that on his radar he'd picked up twelve Flankers in three groups of four, flying in box four formation at ranges 50, 55 and 60 nautical miles at 35,000, 20,000 and 45,000 feet respectively and the Typhoons were accelerating to engage.

military power. I saw the glow of the afterburners before the
Hornets turned at 5G and started their bug-out on a heading
of 235, descending as they did so. Almost immediately there
was a sequence of more distant twinkles of light. Combat! The
Flankers had launched their Alamo Ms at maximum range.
Our 'bandits' had become 'hostiles'. Master arm switch to live.

'Thomas engaging,' I called. And then to the leader of the
back pair of Typhoons, 'Miss Ellie, you cover the northern
pack.'

'Roger,' she replied. They peeled off left into the gloom. A
year later she would become the first female Typhoon squadron commander.

'Martin, cover the middle four.'

'Roger,' he replied.

'Thomas has the front four.' And to my wingman, 'Gus,
take the right two, I've got the left.'

'Roger.'

Thirty miles, just over one minute to merge. The Flankers
were approaching the AMRAAMs no-escape zone at this
height.

'Gus, gate,' I called, for maximum power. We parked the
throttles in the top left-hand corner. This would give us
around Mach 1.75 by the time a high PK (Probability of Kill)
firing solution was reached. I spoke to my computer, 'Betty'
(for that was her name). 'Radar on, select AMRAAM one.'
With the JTIDS information from the Hornets' radars now
working in memory mode it was time to let the missiles know
where the targets were, even though it would alert the Flankers
to our presence. I clicked the cursor on the front left Flanker
and then moved it and clicked on the back left jet. Twenty-
seven miles. The Hornets disappeared below us at the speed of
heat. The small points of light, which we knew to be the
Flankers' Alamo missiles, followed them down. That was a
relief. The Alamos would run out of steam and fall harmlessly
into the Baltic. Radar off. Twenty-four miles. The radar had
been on for just twelve seconds; the Typhoon's computer told
each missile where its target Flanker was. The missile was now
screaming to be unleashed. The engagement tone changed to
an insistent high pitch and the target box in my HUD flashed

with a '97' to let me know that the optimum time to launch was now.

I pulled the trigger. There was a slight delay which seemed like an eternity before the missile sped off with a 'fwoosh' like a Bonfire Night rocket. The computer jumped the target marker to the second Flanker. The marker flashed as it too entered 'no escape'. 'Betty, select AMRAAM two.' Pull trigger and 'fwoosh' again. On my right I saw three missiles leave Gus's jet target-bound. The couple of milliseconds' delay had been too long for his nerves and the front right Flanker was about to be greeted with two supersonic telegraph poles on the nose. In such situations an air show tail-slide would be of very little use to the Flanker.

With the Flankers clear of the coast, Magic was back in the game. 'Knight zero one, I have eight hostiles on your nose twenty miles, four at angels four two, trailing group four at angels three seven, thirty miles.' That much I knew already. But it was good to have someone feeding the JTIDS God's-eye view of the combat.

Hard left on the stick to 5G, speed bleeding to Mach 1.02. Gus and I peeled outwards and back the way we came. Above us Dennis, leading Knights zero three and four, called 'Engaging,' and we saw four AMRAAMs zip past us going in the opposite direction as fiery darts towards the trailing four Flankers who were still climbing to meet us. The warning panel indicated their radars were in narrow search. Trying to lock us up, no doubt. No need to deploy the Turds (TRD – Towed Radar Decoy) just yet.

'Knight zero five, you have four bandits north-east at seventy angels four zero.' Magic to Miss Ellie.

The JTIDS link with Magic was now feeding good information on the Flankers behind us. Betty was the next input: 'AMRAAM one timed out . . . AMRAAM two timed out.' This told me that the missiles I had fired should have reached their targets. I waited a couple of seconds. Magic: 'Splash one, splash two, splash three Flankers, bull's-eye two seven zero, sixty-seven miles!' Sweet music! Three of the four Gus and I had fired at had disappeared from Magic's radar. Glancing down at the JTIDS, it was clear that the front right Flanker was the only one that had survived our first salvo of rockets. It was possible that Gus's two AMRAAMs which were fired so close together had interfered with each other in their active terminal phase and that the trailing missile had blown up its leader. Whatever, there was one Flanker of our group still alive and he was either very frightened or very angry or both. I looked back over my left shoulder to catch two distant explosions. Again a result I'd hoped for. Magic again: 'Splash one . . . splash two . . . Flankers, bull's-eye two eight zero sixty-nine!' What next? I wondered. Seven still unaccounted for. Magic read my thoughts.

'Knight zero five, four hostiles turning east, sixty miles, angels three zero.' Miss Ellie was going to be denied a fight as the third Flanker four-ship turned away and descended towards the safety of Estonian airspace. They weren't going to risk an uneven fight and the ultimate probability of a cold night in the freezing Baltic Sea.

'Miss Ellie, disengage . . . acknowledge,' I called. No point in risking our assets in what might turn into an extended chase into the unknown.

'Roger, disengaging,' she called. The disappointment in her voice was transparent.

'Dennis, disengage.'

'Roger, disengaging. Following you out.'

'Lazarus turning inbound.' The Hornets were hungry for some action. The JTIDS showed them pass above us, looking for those that had survived the first AMRAAM onslaught.

'Lazarus, you have two hostiles on your nose twenty-two miles angels three four, heading just left of south, one further hostile eighteen miles angels two five and descending heading one three five.'

'Lazarus is Judy on the pair. Engaging.' 'Judy' was the standard fighter code word used to indicate that the fighter, in this case Lazarus, intended to go for an autonomous intercept on the two Flankers that had evaded the AMRAAMs fired at them. He clearly had other ideas about risk and reward. We saw them off to the south as they lit their heaters and accelerated to maximum speed after the shaken and retreating pair. Looking up and left, it wasn't long before we saw two bright flashes as Lazarus and his wingman fired their rockets at the pair. This may have been to distract them so Lazarus could close for a better shot. From the three-dimensional geometry in my head this certainly looked like a max-range shot for a receding target. This pair of Flankers would have seen five of their squadron mates hit by our AMRAAMs and gone into 9G-plus evasive manoeuvres, no doubt pumping out most of their on-board chaff and flares in the process.

'Knight zero one, lone Flanker reversed west, angels twelve, two two miles, bearing one hundred.' This was unexpected. 'Front Right' was clearly more angry than upset and wanted to exact revenge.

'Gus, turnabout,' I ordered. 'Let's go down.' With that I rolled the jet on her back and pulled down towards the lone Flanker. 'Betty, radar on. Betty, deploy Turd. Betty, activate Turd.' Shields up, I thought. The direct voice input (DVI) was brilliant, and unlike the females in my experience she obeyed everything I said, and instantly. Miss Ellie's DVI code was 'George', so no doubt she also thought the same about her electronic 'man'. Time to get back to work. 'Front Right' was some 20,000 feet below us. He was the only contact on my radar screen and his blip was going in and out of memory mode. I didn't really want to take a fifty-fifty shot. It was obvious that he was manoeuvring below in and out of the null zone called the doppler notch, an achievement in itself against the ECR 90, something I had not seen before, and this was also against a background of minimal sea clutter. This man knew his stuff.

Magic interrupted our precipitous plunge. 'Splash one Flanker. Lazarus, your nose two zero miles now single hostile bugging out east.' Good grief – one of the long-shot rockets from the Hornets had found its target. Better to be lucky than good, I thought, perhaps a little unfairly.

Attention back to 'Front Right'. We were now in the completely unfamiliar situation of a six-versus-one. At fifteen miles the IRSTS was getting interested in the Flanker's hot spots against a cold black Baltic Sea below. At twelve miles he faced up. Betty: 'Missile inbound, missile inbound!' The DASS

and Turd had been talking to her. The system knew the
Flanker's radar had taken a snap lock on us and an Alamo
was on its way. We turned north-west to put the missile on the
beam and looked out to see it. To my surprise there were two
telltale flares coming up from the right. 'Front Right' had fired
two Alamos: one with an active seeker head and similar in
design philosophy to the AMRAAM, the other with an
infrared seeker head after my jet pipes or warm leading edges.
Betty knew what she was doing. I checked anyway. On the
DASS display I watched the chaff and flare bundles count
reduce. Betty had dispensed four flares. Two were the older
type which burned brightly immediately on leaving the aircraft. The sea and low cloud were suddenly lit up ahead by the
artificial suns that had just left the aircraft. A couple of
seconds later there was a more steady glow as the third
and fourth flares (a type brand new into service and simply
called 'slow burns') lit with a reduced glow and more steady
build-up to maximum brightness. These had only come into
service some three months previously, and there was even a
civilian specialist from British Aerospace deployed with us at
Karup to help our engineers ensure a smooth software and
hardware integration. The latest versions of Western and
Russian heat-seeking missiles now had sophisticated flare
rejection capabilities which enabled the missiles to ignore
infrared hot spots which were higher than a set threshold
or increased their heat output above a set rate. The super-
flares were designed to mimic closely the heat signature of our
engines, then slowly increase their burn to seduce the incoming
missile away. By the time the threshold limiter cut in it would
be way too late for the missile, having eventually rejected the
flare, to reacquire or have the legs to hit the original target.

Throttles idle. I watched one of the missiles jink left and
start to move right, across the canopy, to aim behind us.
Relative motion was good. It meant that whatever you were
looking at wasn't going to hit you. It was the infrared Alamo
which had taken the bait. The second missile remained im-
passively on course, static on the canopy. Time to take matters
into my own hands. Maximum dry power. Roll inverted.
'Betty, chaff chaff!' I called to her. The days of all-fingers-

and-thumbs manual override were long gone. Now pull like a bastard ... 7.5G ... grunt ... roll the right way up ... reverse ... 8.9G ... grunt ... look for missile ... nothing ... must've missed. Then I saw him. 'Front right' was co-height eight miles to the east, around 5,000 feet and going in the opposite direction but almost certainly turning towards. Now was the time to test this Typhoon to its limits. I snap-locked him in the helmet-mounted sight. 'Betty, select AS-RAAM.' Even though I was turning for all I was worth he remained in my four o'clock, well off boresight. The seeker head on the ASRAAM had no such doubts. It screamed at me to be let loose. I obliged. Swoosh! The ASRAAM flew out ahead only a short distance before executing what seemed to be an impossible UFO-like 160-degree right turn as it took full lead and accelerated towards the point in space where it had calculated to meet 'Front Right'. He clearly saw it coming and pulled his jet as tightly as it would go. The Flanker was still world leader in terms of pure nose authority, and I watched him pull some 12G which snapped the jet round on to north. The disadvantage of such a manoeuvre was the loss of all flying speed – as demonstrated at air shows. No thought of a return shot at us. He was obviously a little preoccupied. The ASRAAM wasn't distracted. It detonated some thirty feet short of him, ensuring a shower of hot supersonic tungsten mini-bricks splattered through the rear of the jet. It was as though someone had bitten his back end off.

'Clucking bell!' It was Gus, unable to contain his astonishment.

'Knight, say again.' Magic had not understood.

'Magic, Knight disregard.' The front half of the Flanker was flipped backwards by the destructive force behind and started tumbling away and down from the large puff of smoke in the sky that marked the point of the fireball which had destroyed the engines and rear fuselage. I watched the front half fall end over end, leaving a trail of bits falling off through wisps of smoke. Then came the unexpected. The canopy blew off and a micro-second later there was a flash propelling a small black dot away from the stricken remains. The black dot was arrested and then suddenly obscured by the blossoming of a white parachute canopy. 'Front Right' was not only a fighter, he was clearly a survivor too. For the first time the humanity of war struck me. The other jets we'd shot down had been just that, jets. They were impersonal enemy fighting machines trying to shoot me down in mine. But out of this mass of falling wreckage had popped a man. I wondered briefly about the fate of the others. Had they got out? If not, did that make me a killer or a fighter pilot who in five short minutes was two short of becoming an ace?

'Splash one Flanker,' Gus called somewhat belatedly on my behalf, shaking me out of my sudden emotional turmoil.

We climbed leisurely back to 40,000 feet and regrouped. Twenty minutes later the air armada arrived below us. A mass of transports flying a one-minute trail escorted by what must have been a whole carrier air wing of Hornets.

Our job done, we headed home, west towards the lights of Bornholm and eastern Denmark. Nobody spoke, which was standard procedure, but everyone was elated at our success – I could feel the suppressed joy emanating from every cockpit, with the possible exception of Miss Ellie's. We taxied in and shut down. The whole of the ground crew, it seemed, had come out to greet us. I jumped down off the ladder, grin broadening as the rush of all those who had been part of getting the mission airborne clamoured forward to get a first-hand account.

It was Karen, my crew chief, who had won the race. Instinctively I gave her a big hug. She glanced over at the empty weapons pylons that had had rockets on the last time she looked.

'Had a busy day at the office, dear?' she asked with a look of thinly disguised innocence.

'You could say that, but I'm a bit sweaty now.'

'He is a greedy bastard!' It was Gus, barging through the rapidly growing throng, his hand outstretched to congratulate. 'Still, the formation was his train set and I guess he gets to play with it how he likes.' Gus was over the moon. Sky TV interrupted our double handshakes . . .

Postscript

After the war, in 2008, I met 'Front Right' at the Farnborough Air Show. There was a group of us in one of the British Aerospace hospitality tents, sipping vintage champagne, when a short and rather shabby-looking man sporting a large handlebar moustache on his upper lip and carrying a wrapped litre bottle cradled to his chest appeared at the entrance.

'Are you Thomas Hardy?' he asked in perfect English. I nodded. 'How do you,' he said, thrusting out a grasping hairy hand which squashed my fingers. 'I am Colonel Boris Ivanovich Yeremenko, former commander of the 72nd Intercept Squadron, Leningrad Military District.'

Before my mind could work out who he was, Gus, still by my side, said, ' "Front Right" to you, Thomas. He's the one I missed.'

'How do you do . . . er, Colonel,' I stammered.

'Congratulations on your kills. You and your men took away my squadron, my command and my career.' Oh goodness, I thought, he's going to hit me. Then he smiled.

'I'm now a senior executive for Gazprom, earning a damn site more than you. So I came to see who you were, out of curiosity, of course, and to share a vodka. There are no hard feelings.' With that he ripped the flimsy paper off the bottle to reveal a litre of Russia's most expensive Gorbachov 5 Star Elite vodka.

'Would you like a drink?'

We built an opera house that night rather than the usual shed and, as you do, ended up making endless toasts to each other and our air forces as the very best of mates.

The next morning we were all nursing very sore heads . . .

The Race for Latvia and Lithuania

Both sides were acutely aware before the Baltic air combat of the superiority of the training and technology of Nato's

The Baltic War (22nd April – 2nd May 2006)

FINLAND

GULF OF FINLAND

Leningrad

KEY
═══ Borders
─── Major Road Links
─── Major Rivers
⬇ Amphibious
⊠ Mechanised
◯ Armour

Paldiski

Tallinn   Jarve

ESTONIA   Lake
                 Peipus   3rd Shock
                                 Army

                 Tartu

                 26th
                 April   Pskov

BALTIC   LATVIA   RUSSIA
SEA
          Riga
                 30th April
Liepaja   Riga   Ceasefire line
          Airport (West)   2nd May
                              R. Daugava

          Patton's Sprint

⬇ NATO   Daugavpils
Amphibious   Klaipeda
Landings
26/27th April   LITHUANIA

R. Nemunas
                 Kaunas   BELARUS
Kaliningrad Oblast   Vilnius

Kaliningrad
                 28th April
POLAND   Suwalki
                              Minsk
      1GE 2GE 13GE
      ◯   ◯   ⊠   Grodno
      1NL 12US 1BR
      ◯   ⊠   ◯
      NATO 1st Corps

primary air forces over their Russian counterparts. The Baltic fight had merely served to underline this fact. The Russians howled with protest but thereafter avoided engaging Nato jets in air combat; they would let their ground troops do the talking.

So although Nato was effectively handed temporary control of the air over Latvia and Lithuania, the politicians hesitated to take direct action against Russian Army units. The reason for this policy was that the 'occupation' by both sides of Latvia and Lithuania had developed very much into a race. Both sides expressed a desire for a peaceful solution and neither was prepared to formally declare war. Sixty years of European diplomacy had proved that possession was nine-tenths of the law.

In Riga the paratroopers from the 82nd Airborne and UK 2nd Parachute Regiment and Royal Anglian Infantry Regiment, which had arrived courtesy of the air transport armada, established a defensive perimeter to the east of the city covering the most direct axis of any attack on the capital. The only armour and anti-tank weapons they possessed were Hummer Jeeps mounted with TOW missiles and the now aged Scimitars and Spartans of the Kings's Own Hussars, although the latter were retained in reserve to defend Riga airport. This was something of a gamble for Nato. The political arguments for, and political utility of, light reaction forces were well understood. These forces were, however, aware of their own limitations. Their counterparts in the heavy armour units were dismissive of both their fire-power and their mobility. 'Fly light, die early' was one of the more unkind mottoes given to the light reaction forces. Nato would have preferred to have made a landing from the sea directly into Riga harbour. However, even in late April, there was still too much ice to make this a viable proposition, and anyway the Russians were expected to reach Riga before a link-up could be effected between the airborne and amphibious elements of Baltic Forge. And even if they arrived a close second, the mining of the bay might already be complete and it would take Nato a while to clear usable sea lanes.

The Nato plan was, therefore, to put the air-mobile units into

Riga and land the 'heavies' partly at the small port of Liepaja
and partly further south down the coast. There was a single
stretch of the Baltic coastline which had two modern road and
rail links and was the only one that remained free of ice
throughout the year, and so would act as an excellent area
in which to put a major logistic base for prolonged operations.
From this area units were in easy reach of the Lithuania/
Kaliningrad border to seal off any potential moves by Russian
forces moving out of the Oblast, and would also be easily able to
move rapidly to reinforce Riga or east along the new motorway
to Kaunas and Vilnius. The audacious plan by Nato to seize
Riga in force, dig in, and then wait for a link-up with heavier
ground troops arriving from the south and east was not dis-
similar to Montgomery's Arnhem plan of sixty years previously.
The Allies were more confident of success this time.

The Russians repeatedly stated that they had no intention
of engaging in combat with Nato forces and were merely
reacting to the presence of large and capable Nato units in the
Baltic states, on the very edge of their own sphere of influence,
which they considered to be illegal. Their moves into Latvia
and Lithuania were a mirror of what Nato was doing. The
double invasion of Latvia and Lithuania had the air of an
uncertain and tense race. Once the finishing lines had been
drawn the negotiations could begin.

At 0100 on 27 April the two armoured columns of Third
Shock moved across the border, both attempting to gain the
honour of reaching Riga first. Nato responded by beginning
the transfer of its German-dominated second-echelon forces
from eastern Germany to positions on the Poland/Lithuania
border. Twenty-four hours later the two Russian armoured
corps that had been moved the previous week from the
Poland/Belarus border jumped off into Latvia and Lithuania
from the east. Teams of Special Forces Spetznatz troops were
flown in at night by helicopter to seize key crossing points and
road junctions, as well as to act as delaying forces against any
direct move from Nato.

Nato commanders, not wishing to escalate the conflict
unnecessarily, held back from authorising direct attack
against the broad and fast-moving Russian armoured col-

umns that were not in direct contact with her own forces. SAS and US Ranger teams had also been inserted into all the Baltic states to delay and disrupt the Russians. They were particularly successful on the approaches to Riga. The Latvian countryside is not conducive to the rapid movement of large tank columns off-road, and the demolition teams caused several serious delays by blowing vast holes in the small roads and mining stretches of others. When the Russian tanks attempted to bypass the obstacles, many became bogged in the large areas of marsh that were beginning to thaw. They were often forced to wait for the combat engineers to come up and fill in the gaps or remove mines; a process slowed considerably when they came under sniper fire from enemies that seemed to blend in with the terrain. With both Nato and Russia's commanders identifying the same vital points it was inevitable that before any of the main bodies of troops reached these areas there were several fierce combats between the small these units. The clashes between these units were a secret war. Neither side acknowledged the presence of their élite troops in the Baltic. Losses were hushed up and the few prisoners taken by both sides were spirited away for interrogation amid a shroud of secrecy. It was only when a prisoner exchange was agreed one year after the ceasefire that the extent of these small but fierce engagements became public knowledge. At the time, until the battle for Riga, both sides' official positions were ones of brinkmanship: avoiding conflict while taking the maximum amount of land.

It was in the fading light on the 26th that the NRF made its unopposed amphibious landings on the coast. Within twenty-four hours, once the beachhead area was secured from air attack and enough supplies had been landed to sustain an advance, the 'heavies' would be ready to move. One hour before the troops landed Lithuania formally asked Nato to defend her sovereignty and at first light on 28 April the German 1st Panzer Division launched itself north-east up the one main road between Poland and Lithuania. Its mission was to occupy all of Lithuania as rapidly as possible, since it had become clear that the Russians would avoid advancing directly into any American or 'real Nato' resistance.

Panzer Marsch!

The order they had been waiting for crackled loudly over the battalion net: '*Panzer marsch!*' This was it. Nato on the attack.

Oberstleutnant Ernst Hoffman slipped down into the tank commander's seat and slammed the turret hatch above him. 'Driver, forward. Full speed.' His quiet order was almost an apology as the fifty-tonne Leopard 3 leapt out of the hide in a cloud of late summer dust. In part it was a feeling of guilt: his grandfather had travelled this very road in 1941 as part of Von Leeb's Army Group North on its way to Leningrad. At least this time he knew that the Germans had the full backing of Nato both politically and physically. Stacked up behind 1st Panzer along the roads on the plateau that dominates Poland's border with Lithuania were 2nd Panzer 'Die Berlinner', 13th Panzer Grenadier, 1st Dutch Armoured Division and 12th US Mechanised. In reserve, and covering the Kaliningrad front to the west, were the 1st British Armoured Division, which had been pulled out of the front line facing Belarus, and two Polish divisions (though the latter were in a position to do no more than act as a relatively static rearguard).

Visibility was perfect and 10 km ahead Hoffman could see magnified through the periscope the village of Kalvarija. The village spires stood out as black and grey against the yellow rolling hills. This was the battalion's first objective on the road to Kaunas, capital of Lithuania. Left and right of Hoffman's tank came the other thirty Leopards of the battalion. They looked resplendent in their new 'Eastern Europe, Summer' camouflage colours of burgundy green and sand. Not since the summer of 1944 had German tanks looked so good. A battalion of thirty-odd Leopard tanks going full tilt at some 110 km/h was a truly magnificent sight. A cloud of orange dust billowed out behind each tank like a rooster tail.

Behind trundled rather more slowly the forty-plus Marder armoured personnel carriers carrying a battalion of crack Panzer grenadiers.

On either flank he could see but not hear two pairs of Tiger attack helicopters that acted as flank guards as well as reconnaissance. They would play a giant game of leapfrog, one hovering at fifty to a hundred feet while the other bounded forward a kilometre before rearing up like a stallion into the hover to wait for its partner to repeat the process. German Panzer troops would never have advanced like this on exercise – artillery would normally have softened up the objective – but this one was full of friendly Lithuanians.

There was a flash in the village now some eight kilometres distant. This was a disappointment and a surprise. Intelligence had indicated the nearest Russian spearheads still to be many miles away to the north and east. The flash quickly turned into a racing plume of white smoke. Hoffman knew at once what was happening. 'SAM launch! SAM launch!' he yelled into the battalion net. A second missile followed the first three seconds later. The helicopters were not slow to react. The missiles were clearly aimed at the most easterly of the four and, judging by his actions, it was clear that the pilot knew it. The helicopter converted from the hover to a nose-low head-on charge at the missile, which had turned into a weaving orange dot as the boost phase ended and the white smoke disappeared. Travelling at Mach 3, the missile seemed certain to hit the helicopter until the pilot pulled the aircraft into a gut-wrenching turn at no more than twenty-five feet. The blades of the helicopter almost cut into the ground. As the aircraft turned, its rear was covered by three great flashes of fire. Most of the tank commanders watching the duel assumed that the helicopter had had its back end blown off and blessed their own steel-and-ceramic protection. The flashes were caused by the Tiger pumping out decoy flares. These did the trick, and the first missile sailed through the middle of the glowing magnesium before detonating in a rather tinny shower on the other side. The second missile had more time to adjust to the helicopter's evasive manoeuvring, but in trying to take the shortest route to its target at almost zero

feet fused on the ground some 100 metres short. The helicopter righted itself, the drama over. A collective sigh of relief
was audible above the crackle on the net. The pilot and his
gunner, along with the rest of the Leopard battalion, looked
left again towards the village, waiting for the next salvo. They
were not disappointed. The leading platoon of tanks suddenly
disappeared in clouds of thick white and grey smoke. The
defensive systems had detected laser beams being fired at the
tanks and activated the smoke dischargers. This meant either
armour-piercing or HEAT rounds would be impacting in a
couple of seconds or . . . Hoffman saw them, four small winks
of light followed by four tiny puffs of smoke. Anti-tank
missiles, the fast laser beam-riding type! As one the tanks
lurched to a halt, the drivers throwing them into reverse gear.
The lasers designating tank targets for the missiles should not
be able to penetrate the special smoke that rapidly grew into a
wall of ground fog as each tank fired its dischargers. Two
missiles flew unseen over the tanks. The third must have
stoofed into the ground short. The fourth found a target but
only by default. It hit the upper side of the front turret's sloped
armour on the tank of Hoffman's second-in-command, Major
Pfizer, and ricocheted up above the small instant fog bank
which had formed below like some crazy firework. On the
way it had collected Pfizer's right arm just above the elbow.
Pfizer was Germany's first casualty of the war.

Curiously, above the sound of the grumbling Maybach
engines, automatic rifle and machinegun fire could be heard
coming from the village. The classic answer would be to drop
a few rounds of 155mm artillery into the village or perhaps
level it with a devastating salvo from the MLRS rocket-
launchers. This was out of the question. Hoffman knew that
the village's inhabitants would still be there, cowering in their
cellars, no doubt. This really was a major inconvenience of
modern war; only zero civilian casualties would be tolerated.
The village would have to do this the hard way, inch by inch.
Soldiers first, armour covering. The battle group retired two
kilometres to put it out of reach of the small SAMs and anti-
tank guided missiles held by the defenders. Hoffman was
under strict orders not to engage Russian troops in direct

assault but to dig in. This could hardly apply just a few kilometres over the border. Moreover, massive casualties among his soldiers would not be tolerated at home. Hoffman called Brigade-General Mielke, who said he would get back. Two minutes later it was General-Leutnant Netzer, the Corps Commander himself, who came on the battalion net. He told Hoffman that the forces were almost certainly Spetznatz and could be safely eliminated, but needless loss of German lives would be unacceptable.

Pfizer, put in an armoured ambulance which headed for the mobile field hospital, was mortified, not because he had lost part of his arm but because his war was over with the first shots the enemy fired and with them his chance for personal glory was also gone. Presently the grenadier company commanders huddled around the battalion commander's vehicle. This would be a dismounted attack, one company up, two in support. Advance mounted until fired upon. One hour later the tanks of Panzer Battalion 803 nosed nervously to within 500 metres of the village. Any closer and they would be vulnerable to RPG attack. Clearing villages was an all-arms affair; tanks never went first. The 120mm smooth-bore guns sat pointing menacingly at the village, each one aimed at a different area of suspicion. This was called 'overwatch'. The helicopters buzzed cautiously around the outskirts, always watching each other's backs. It was time for the infantry to have a look. The Panzer grenadiers, armoured infantry, who until now had been moving a respectful distance behind their better-protected brethren, dismounted from their armoured personnel carriers and moved towards the line of houses, a mixture of wooden dachas and more austere stone buildings. In one of the boxy, tasteless state-built buildings they found the bodies of five Russians, almost certainly special forces troops. By their sides two of the latest SA-22 man-portable anti-aircraft missiles, as well as an assorted mini-arsenal of everything from Kalashnikovs to Sanddragon anti-tank missiles

Their vehicle, a sparkling new eight-wheeled BTR 90, was found in the street behind the house. A runner sent from the Panzer grenadier company commander doubled back to where Hoffman's tank was idling. The grenadier's green collar flashes were clearly visible as he clambered up the side of the tank to give Hoffman a note scribbled on a piece of card. It read: 'Sorry we were a little late. Enjoy your war.'

Hoffman cursed. The special forces had done the job and melted away. Must've been British SAS or American Rangers. Why did they have to do everything? His fulminating was interrupted by the distinctive hiss of Mielke's voice breaking radio silence.

'Mielke here. What's going on, Hoffman? Why has the advance stalled?'

'We are resuming the advance, Herr General!'

Hoffman pulled out his map and began to check the plan for the next phase of the advance. As he did so a small group of drably dressed civilians approached his tank. They were waving flowers and Lithuanian flags and wearing huge smiles.

'Thank you for coming to liberate us!' called a tall blonde girl who was at the head of the group, and with that she threw a bunch of red roses at Hoffman. Too bemused to react, he watched as they hit him on the arm and came to rest on top of the turret. This was the signal for the rest to rush forward as more and more civilians appeared from doors and alleyways to greet their 'liberators'. Several of the first group began to attempt to climb on to the tank and started throwing confetti and toilet rolls.

'Don't mention it, it's a pleasure. Get off my fucking tank, you peasants,' Hoffman yelled back, maintaining a fixed smile throughout. He remembered his grandfather telling him of the enthusiasm of the Lithuanians and Latvians for the Germans as they raced through the towns and villages on their way to Leningrad. The young men in these two countries had been only too eager to volunteer for service on the eastern front; indeed, they formed two whole SS divisions made up of Baltic men.

Unseen by Hoffman the blonde had by now managed to clamber up on to the back of the tank with the help of her friends. In his headphones Mielke was back on the battalion net and was clearly not satisfied.

'When will you be able to move?'

'In around thirty min . . .' began Hoffman, before he was smothered with an over-affectionate hug and kiss.

'What did you say? Say again! What's going on?' Mielke was like an impatient terrier.

'We're having a little trouble with the locals.'

'What? Are they firing?'

'Not as such, Herr General, they are clogging the streets. They seem to want an impromptu victory parade.'

'Good grief! Let me know when you resume your advance. Mielke out!' It took twenty minutes and a burst of machine-gun fire into the air for the Panzer men to silence the crowd and explain that they had the rest of Lithuania to liberate and were already behind schedule. By the time they nosed into Kaunas the city was already packed with US Marine armour. The prospect of a huge traffic jam was averted by the swift arrival of German military police. Hoffman's perceived tardiness was rewarded by 1st Panzer being turned due east in Kaunas instead of north as was originally planned.

Patton's Sprint

The NRF landings went extraordinarily well, although the concentrated mass of military equipment in the harbours at Klaipeda and Liepaja made worryingly inviting targets for massed Scud or air attack should the Russians decide to escalate the conflict without warning. The first unit to enter the race was the US Marines' 2nd Tank Battalion, commanded by a certain Lieutenant-Colonel David Patton, a distant relative of the famous World War II General George Patton. Patton was very much cast in the mould of the great general, and his audacity enabled Nato to gain much of Lithuania before being halted by the Russian line coming from the other side of the country. Patton ordered the engine governors to be taken off his battalion's M1A1 tanks – they were originally fitted to the powerful gas turbines to prevent excess wear and tear. The top speed of the Abrams was increased from 45 mph to 65 mph. The fifty tanks set off

at full throttle, looking and feeling very much like a modern
version of the 7th Cavalry, down the expressway from
Klaipeda to Kaunas, pennants flying in the wind. They were
flanked on either side of the expressway for the whole of the
route by a continuous rotation of AH-64 Apaches and the
newer Comanche gunships. The 140 miles to Kaunas were
covered in an astonishing four hours. They had expected to
link up with the German 1st Panzer Division coming up from
the south out of Poland, but it was nowhere to be seen until
late afternoon. *En route* they encountered only two small
Spetznatz teams, who were so surprised by the speed and
spectacle of the armoured juggernaut approaching that their
aim with the light anti-tank weapons was thrown such that
not a single tank was damaged. They were rapidly dispatched
by the flying escorts. In fact the only losses the Marines
suffered sounded similar to retirements from a Formula
One grand prix. One Abrams had the military equivalent
of a high-speed blow-out by shedding a track at 60 mph
before careering off through the side barriers and into the
undergrowth. Two others ground to a halt in clouds of smoke
with blown engines, and a fourth had gearbox failure. These
were left on the hard shoulders for the armoured engineers,
who were in hot pursuit of Patton's men, to deal with. There
were other Russian Spetznatz teams who were supposed to
act as blocking and delay forces. They decided, on seeing the
charge of Abrams, that discretion was the better part of
valour and certain death, and only emerged later to harass
the military convoys before the ceasefire came into effect.
Once the Marines had secured Kaunas the northerly charge of
the second-echelon Nato force towards Latvia was handed to
the US 12th Mechanised Division with 13th Panzer Grenadier
in direct support. 1st Dutch Armoured joined 1st Panzer,
relegated to the less glamorous task of setting up blocking
positions along the Nemunas River to the east.

    In the air Russian fighters did not again challenge the Nato
patrols after the Baltic air battle, and they retreated prudently
at the approach of Nato fighters. The latter, however, as well
as the numerous fighter-bombers and reconnaissance aircraft
that flew as far east as twenty miles from the Russian and

Belarus borders, became mere observers of the international injustice unfolding below. They could only look down on the steady progress of the Russian tank, APC and truck columns as they made steady progress west and south-west across Latvia and Lithuania. The minimal infantry forces of these two states were, when they inclined towards token resistance, cleverly dealt with by the advance Russian psyops (Psychological Operations) battalions that accompanied the leading formations. They were given a wide berth on both sides by advance elements and then hailed by the psyops troops, who gave them three options: put up short but ultimately futile resistance as they were virtually surrounded and die; surrender; or depart for Nato lines within two hours. Unsurprisingly, most of them chose the latter option and sprinted towards Nato's advancing forces in whatever transport was available. It was bad luck for some that they were riding so fast towards safety in old Russian equipment because the isolated special force units mistook them on three occasions for advance Russian recce troops and opened fire accordingly.

High above, the Nato fighter-bombers waited in vain for the call from the ground to give them approval to obliterate the convoys that presented such inviting targets below. As the Russians studiously avoided even switching on the tracking radars of the mobile SAMs accompanying the tanks, the fighter-bombers and SEAD aircraft were not even given the excuse of acting in self-defence. There was, however, one significant action that did take place, and this was on the eastern side of Riga.

The Battle of Riga Airport

The Russians were well aware that Nato's 'light' forces lacked real mobility and significant integral heavy fire-power once they were in place. Even the élite 82nd remained without main battle tanks. Although it would have been easy to have assigned heavy armour to support the 82nd and the British units in Riga, there simply weren't enough transport aircraft

to do the job. The delivery of a single M1A1 Abrams tank by
air required a C-17 to make a minimum eight-hour round
trip, not including loading and unloading time. With the
Abrams weighing in at 52 tons there was only 25 tons of
spare freight capacity left. Alternate loads of up to six Apache
gunships, a dozen Hummers or a full company of infantry
with all their support were far more cost-effective. The tanks
would all have to come by sea. As soon as Russian reconnaissance drones had established the size and strength of
Riga's defences, Russia determined to test Nato's resolve.
The delaying actions fought by the special forces in Latvia
were not enough to stop the leading tank companies of Third
Shock getting to Riga before relief arrived from the south.
Unfortunately the sister tank battalion that drove north-east
had not emulated Patton's sprint. The 52nd and 54th Motor
Rifle Divisions dug in opposite the line of troops on the
eastern side of Riga. Meanwhile 1st and 2nd Guards Tank
Divisions, probably the best units Russia had, swept around
Riga to the south before swinging north-west in order to
encircle the city completely and overrun the airport before
Nato had time to react. This was to be, special forces aside,
the only act of deliberate ground combat initiated by the
Russians. Their motives in ordering a localised escalation
were threefold. Firstly, they realised that the dash by the
US Marines to Kaunas and the rapid progress of 12th US
Mechanised and 13th German Mechanised meant that Nato
would win the race for Lithuania and be in a position to make
deep penetrations into Latvia. Secondly, a serious attack now
might cause Nato commanders to halt these forces and
change their direction of attack. Thirdly, they had to be sure
that their decision to avoid general conflict, based on their
assessments of the relative combat power of the Nato forces
opposing their best troops, and the political mettle to use
them, was justified. If the best troops Moscow could offer
were to fail then they would at least have the satisfaction of
knowing that their tendency towards caution was wise. Thus
it was decided to go for a limited assault on Riga airport. This
single limited attack would have serious repercussions for the
conduct of the war that was to come in the Middle East,

although they were hardly realised at the time, and anyway, both sides were 'up for it' in terms of a quick fight.

'Hunting, Shooting and Fishing in Riga'

The following extract is taken from the book written after the war by Major Charles H. J. Davies, who commanded the 3rd King's Own Hussar (3 KOH) Reconnaissance Squadron Detachment during the defence of Riga airport.

I was not overly impressed with the mission we had been given. At the time I was certain that airfield defence was something that was supposed to be done by the RAF Regiment. However, since the RAF Regiment had had their armour taken away by past 'rationalisations' and were reduced to infantry in Land Rovers with a few mortars, the planners of the operation to take Riga had decided to add weight to the RAF Regiment's No. 67 Field Squadron, and 3 KOH was accordingly assigned. It was for me an unhappy marriage of convenience because, as there was another RAF Regiment squadron, No. 22 Starstreak HVM (replacing Rapier) which had the job of point defence, I came under the direct command of an RAF Regiment wing commander. In military circles the rules of command were clear: whoever brings the most 'men and stuff' gets to captain the team, and eight Scimitars and four Spartans with Trigat missiles were not enough.

After unloading the vehicles from the C-17s I hurried to his first in-theatre 'O Group' being held in the corner of one of the airport engineering hangars by the wing commander. Following a brief introduction, the wing commander, who had the face and build of a prize fighter, informed me that I should refer to him as 'sir' or 'boss': I took an instant dislike to the man and resolved to call him 'Wingco'. When he unveiled his master plan for the defence of Riga airport, through a poorly disguised broad Northern accent, I had cause to wonder idly how it was that such men ever reached the officer ranks, let alone relatively senior command. Although I must confess I did have a pretty dim view of the RAF officer corps at the time. I thought they all wore white socks, shirts with kit-kat pockets and no double cuffs, called everybody 'mate' (the latter was confirmed by a couple of Harrier pilots on my staff college course) and answered every question on military matters with the phrase 'air power'.

I would much rather have been put out on the east side of Riga, where the rest of the army was. Surely that was where the battle would be fought and the medals won (how wrong can one be?). And although I approved of Wingco's plan to put the Trigat Spartans out covering the southern approaches to the airport, I was less certain of the wisdom of concealing the Scimitars along the edge of a small wood overlooking the runway itself – less of a light armoured reserve and more a case of hiding in case we got shot at was my view. My gloom was compounded when at the end of the briefing Wingco announced that he would co-locate his tactical HQ in 'your wood, Charles' and as a PS had the temerity to whisper that I might consider getting my hair trimmed. I confess I was apoplectic but remained silent and managed a smile in return, inwardly pleased that such working-class 'oiks' would never be allowed to sully the carpets of the Guards and Cavalry Club.

With the Spartans and Scimitars dug in to hull-down positions, the next day I received the unwelcome news that the new Junior Minister for the Armed Forces would be making a daring and hush-hush visit to Riga to add political weight to the boldness of Nato's action in Latvia.

At dawn the following morning there he was in full combat gear, having leapt, with small entourage and selected members of the press, out of the first C-130J to land at Riga in the cold morning rain. He was whisked by Land Rover straight to the Tac HQ for breakfast with the men. There was a feeling of pervading unease as Intelligence had just called the Wingco to inform him that Russian troops had been spotted only fifteen miles to the south by the reconnaissance helicopters. The senior commanders were confident that, as they had done the previous evening on the east side of the city when they encountered the Allied line, the Russians would halt and dig in. The Russians had done this across the country as the two sets of forces completed the race for land; nevertheless, it would be a nervous wait for confirmation. And there in the midst of this situation was the short man with the limp handshake on a VIP visit, fully kitted out in combat gear, trying to out-Tarzan the original 'Tarzan Heseltine' himself. The unreality of the situation beggared belief. I then watched in horror while the end of my career flashed before my eyes as the minister insisted on standing in line with the men for a standard breakfast, which included, as every meal did where it was possible to set up a field kitchen, chips, beans and curry. The junior minister, left of centre, single and a little camp, tried to engage the disinterested cooks in some light-hearted banter. 'Have you considered trying healthy alternatives such as baked potato, yoghurt or muesli?' The duty chef, Corporal Jones, taken aback by what he considered to be a plainly stupid question, forgot himself and answered truthfully, 'We tried serving a meal without chips and there was nearly a fucking riot . . . er . . . sir.' Trying to cover the embarrassing language, the senior catering NCO, Staff Sergeant Broad, only made matters worse by adding quickly, 'That's right, sir. In this man's army that sort of food is reserved for communists and pooftas.' The pall of silence that descended over this canteen cameo was suddenly interrupted by the sound of heavy-calibre machinegun fire to the south, answered by the dull thuds of high-calibre tank guns. On cue the field telephone jumped into life with a shrill ring and I picked it up. All eyes looked to me expectantly; those with some sixth sense were already picking up their personal weapons.

'Stand to!' I yelled. 'Russian tanks have just driven straight over the outer perimeter posts. Our boys thought that they simply hadn't seen them so fired warning machinegun fire at the tanks, which replied by firing back. Flight Lieutenant Ponsonby says his company position is about to be overrun.'

The warning sirens were now wailing across the airfield to signal a general alert. Peering through my binoculars, I could see the AH-64s' blades turning as they prepared to take off. Elsewhere men and women were running for slit trenches and bunkers. Out of nowhere a pair of Russian fighter-bombers appeared, going at high speed and very low level. As they crossed the middle of the airfield each disgorged a line of eight black dots which slowed as small parachutes arrested their descent. There was a ripple of sixteen explosions as the bombs detonated. The first stick fell harmlessly adjacent to the runway, throwing up huge spouts of earth. The other stick walked its way on to the flight line, and as the blast pressure waves hit me I saw one of the Apaches engulfed in flame and the distant figure of a crewman on fire running, falling and rolling, in a vain attempt to put out the flames – horrible.

I jumped into the turret of my Scimitar, the *Moodkee Wallah*, and touched the blade of the sabre I'd had screwed to the back of the turret, as I always did, for luck. My driver had already started the engine and was awaiting orders. I saw that Wingco had grabbed the minister and thrown him into the HQ's machinegun trench. Two more bombers appeared thirty seconds after the first pair. The Starstreak HVMs were ready for them this time and I watched transfixed as the missiles sped towards the attackers. One of the bombers had attracted shots from two positions and began to turn away, jettisoning his bombs as he did so, scattering them in a wild pattern across the northern end of the airport. I lost sight of him as he disappeared behind the airport buildings, speeding off to the north-east, missiles still chasing.

From the south I could hear the sound of my Spartans firing their anti-tank missiles from their concealed positions. They would be lucky to get one tank each if the Russians had closed the range before being spotted. Main gun tank rounds would hardly notice their armour as it passed through to explode inside. I was at a loss as to what to do with the Scimitars. The best we could do was a futile charge in the hope of getting in among the infantry carriers. Our 30mm Rardens would bounce off the tanks' armour. I shouted to Wingco for instructions. He shouted back to sit tight. We sat tight.

Five minutes later our short wait was rewarded. From the south four Havoc gunships nosed their way up to the perimeter fence flying at around ten feet above the ground. They were preceded by the growl of their rotary cannons, probably engaging the defending Starstreaks, otherwise they would certainly not have been as far as they were now. They were moving at a fast running pace and were only a thousand metres or so away, so I decided that we should let them have it with everything we had. The rearmost Havoc was the nearest. I fired a short burst with the cannon, *Pom pom pom pom pom.* The other Scimitars opened up with me. To my delight at least two of the shells hit home and the helicopter simply dropped to the ground with a crunch, coming to rest in the ditch that ran next to the perimeter fence. I switched to the second Havoc and gave him a short burst. This time the results were more spectacular. We must have hit a fuel cell because the rear of the helicopter disappeared in a ball of fire before it rolled right and broke in two before smashing itself into the ground.

Above the din Wingco yelled, 'Good shooting, Charles. All that time spent on clay pigeons and grouse wasn't wasted, then!' Damn cheek! The other two Havocs were, however, on to us by now. The leader pushed forward to accelerate, skimming the blades of grass as he did so and turning menacingly to square up to us like a giant bug-eyed beetle. I caught sight of Wingco behind the GPMG firing like a man possessed. The minister, who I later learned had once been in the TA, was feeding the belts of ammunition and seemed to be having the time of his life.

Sergeant Rossovski, the Havoc gunner from 22nd Assault Helicopter Regiment, continues the narrative from the other side:

We were surprised when we received orders for the attack on Riga and were not a little worried. The advance by Third Shock down the coast had been pretty fast. There wasn't much formal resistance to speak of but the leading columns were occasionally inconvenienced by enemy special forces or partisans. By the time we arrived on the scene they had almost always melted away, although we did lose one Havoc to a Stinger missile shot which hit the engine exhaust and took the rotors off.

On arriving at Riga we were ordered to stay well out of range of the Nato lines that were dug in around the east and south of the city. Our RPVs, however, found a gap in the hastily established lines to the south-west of the city on the approach to the airfield itself. As we landed for a refuel we already guessed what was coming as it was impossible to miss two whole tank divisions setting off to sweep around the south of Riga then up and into the airport. The defenders would not have had more than one hour's notice, and it was only this much because our fighters carried out an aggressive feint out over the sea approaching the mass of Nato ships off the coast from the north. While the US Navy and land-based fighters were busy reacting to that threat, eight twin-seat SU-37 Flanker fighter-bombers sprinted in at ultra-low level for a raid on Riga airport. When they were fifteen minutes out we got the call to move.

We approached the airfield as an eight with great caution. Four up front and four around 2 km behind. Our first job was to silence the dangerous Starstreak batteries that were positioned 5 km south and west of the airport. Although our reconnaissance had pinpointed each position and we had them clearly marked on our maps they were damnably difficult to see unless you were on top of them. This would be a game of cat-and-mouse. Our own missiles had a maximum range of 8 km and we knew the Starstreaks were deadly out to 7 km, dangerous out to 9 km, and possibly still effective at 12 km, even at targets like us that were essentially on the deck.

We crossed the line on our maps that marked the edge of the Starstreak MEZ (Missile Engagement Zone) with trepidation, expecting at any moment to be flung into violent missile avoidance manoeuvres. As each pair crept forward not much above walking height the second pair would remain on overwatch, hovering at around 20–30 metres above and behind a farmhouse or similar building. From these overwatch positions they would be ready to call the launch of a missile and either engage or duck as they saw best.

On our right horizon we could see the tank companies moving forward to overrun the airport's southern perimeter defences.

The battle was joined and very soon there were columns of black smoke from burning targets, whether the enemy's or ours we could not tell. As we scanned the ground looking in vain for our designated targets, help in finding them came from an unexpected quarter. A pair of Flankers screamed in very low and fast to drop their bombs on the airfield. A second pair followed closely, and it was then that the Starstreaks revealed their positions. There were flashes of igniting missile motors around 4 km to our front followed by white smoke plumes as the Starstreaks accelerated off after their targets. Both of the rear pair of Flankers were hit, their funeral pyres billowing up, the impacts unseen, several kilometres beyond the airport. This was our chance. While the missile crews were concentrating on the attacking bombers we would be able to sprint in and deliver a telling blow. Without a word it was clear that all four Havocs had realised the same thing, and in we went at top speed, flying around the edges of buildings and tree lines to cover our approach. At 2km range we could make out four fire units. My pilot popped up to 20 metres to enable me to let off a whole rocket pod at one of the units, which would serve at least to keep their heads down. As we closed to 1,200 metres it was clear that they had spotted the danger and two of the batteries attempted visual engagements. By the time the missiles were launched we were inside minimum range and watched both missiles rush unguided well over our heads. To our right rear, however, one of our comrades' machines was not so lucky and took the full force of three darts through the front of his cab at a height of no more than 10 metres. The Havoc simply disintegrated. It was a Pyrrhic victory for the SAMs. We were on to them. I selected the trusty rotary cannon and in seconds it was all over – the menacing Starstreak fire units were reduced to aluminium and electronic trash.

With our primary targets destroyed we were able to attack the airfield. Our orders were to destroy as much hardware as possible. The only threat to us now, or so we thought, would be hand-held Stingers and Javelins from any troops actually on the airfield. As we swung north to the southern boundary fence we passed over six of our own tanks, burning after being hit by ATGMs. Further on, in camouflaged pits, were the hulks of four English APCs and around them a further three disabled tanks of our own. Around the positions were strewn the dark shapes of wounded or dead attackers and defenders. This had been the scene of very recent fierce fighting. (This was where the RAF Regiment company had been overrun.) We then passed what remained of the leading assault company and soon were up to the southern perimeter fence. There before us was an array of juicy targets on the flight line, including three transport aircraft and beyond them Apache gunships, one of which was burning; the two others had rotors turning ready for take-off.

It was as we hesitated for that split second that all went wrong. There was a muffled call on the radio, and glancing behind we saw the numbers two and three hit the ground; both were taking hits from unseen cannon. We didn't want to hang around and my pilot dipped the nose, and as soon as we had enough flying speed stood the Havoc on her side and turned to get out. As we turned I spotted a row of gun flashes coming form the edge of the wood that lies on the western edge of the airport. We straightened up to engage at around 700 metres' range. As we did so there were several loud bangs and a patter of smaller clicks as the cannon and machinegun fire struck us. A large hole with fracture lines appeared in the armoured glass above my right shoulder where a cannon shell had entered. This was too hot a reception for my pilot, who cranked the Havoc left again and tried to get out of the withering hail of fire. I managed only to fire the gun in the general direction of the tree line before we were away, the Havoc still juddering from hits as we went. By the time we were 500 metres clear of the airfield the cockpit started to fill with fumes. Looking over my shoulder, I saw we were on fire and braced myself as my pilot shouted that we were ditching.

We hit the ground slightly nose up and rumbled painfully to a halt. I undid my straps and tumbled into the slushy field of mud and old snow. Looking back up at the helicopter, I saw that in the rear cockpit my pilot was slumped forward, unmoving. The Havoc was a mess with holes all over it, looking more like a colander than a flying machine. It was a wonder we made it as far as we did. I thanked the makers of the armoured hull for my survival, then cursed them as I tried to hack through the thick glass of the rear cockpit to free my trapped pilot. Remembering the escape handle, I pulled it and the canopy unlocked. My pilot was not in good shape. He had been hit and had a gaping wound in his chest. Blood was oozing everywhere through his flak jacket and flight overalls. He wheezed uncomfortably as I pulled him gently to the ground. For us, in the shadow of our smouldering and wrecked chariot, the war was over.

Major Davies finishes off his narrative:

The lead Havoc straightened up and I could see its cannon firing back although the gunner's aim was all over the place as first the ground to our front was ripped up then the branches over our heads. As he was the only target now in sight we were all blazing away at him. The Havoc turned to depart and began to pour smoke as it absorbed multiple hits. This one was not going down and we continued firing until he was outside maximum range. I levered myself up through the turret, propped on my elbows for a better view, and was greeted with the sight of Wingco jeering and still firing like something out of a war comic. 'Got him! Got him! We got him! Take that, Ivan! Did you see that, Minister?' Minister was not paying attention to the shouting Wingco. He was on his back in the slit trench, dead. A 23mm shell had effectively scalped him. The top of his head was missing and from my turret I could see bits of his exposed brain poking through the mass of blood. In between retching at the sight I wondered what the papers would say. The final blast of cannon fire had also caught one of the Scimitars, raking the turret and giving the tank commander, Lieutenant Mark Boden, severe stomach wounds from which he would die three days later.

It was then that our own jets appeared, or rather their missiles. We watched as HARMs were fired at the Russian mobile SAMs before swarms of F-18 Hornets dived down on the still-unseen tanks that were approaching the southern perimeter. We decided to stay put, not wishing to present ourselves as potential fratricide victims. They came in at steep angles one after the other, covering the advancing armour in cluster bombs and CRV-7 rockets. In the twenty minutes that followed there must have been at least thirty Nato jets that were called on to the hesitating Russian tanks. Wingco jumped out of his trench, having accepted apparently matter-of-factly that a junior minister of HM Government was dead. He ran a few yards so that he could see what was going on beyond the tree line.

'D'you see that, Charles?' he repeated several times. 'Ayr paar,' he said, mimicking my accent. 'That's ayr paar, that is.' Air power indeed. I knew then that if we won he'd be unbearable . . .

The leading division of Third Shock took a pounding from the US Navy Hornets that had finally had their patience rewarded. They were joined by three AH-64 Apaches that managed to get airborne after the initial Flanker raid. By the end of the afternoon the Russian advance had reached its high-water mark. Nato lost five jets, shot down by the accompanying SAMs and Tunguska 35mm self-propelled AA guns before they were neutralised. One hundred and thirty knocked-out tanks and various armoured vehicles were enough to convince the Russians to discontinue their assault. At 1700 the Russian High Command and all state television and radio stations in Moscow broadcast on all channels calling for a ceasefire and an end to hostilities. Nato, whose control of the area was only through air power until the link-up forces arrived from the beachhead, readily agreed. By midday the following day, apart from a few minor skirmishes between Russian and American reconnaissance troops, peace had broken out. The lines in the sand had finally been drawn across the Baltic states.

Peace in the Baltic

Russia had played her hand and felt that Nato would far rather negotiate than allow its soldiers to lose their lives in this barren corner of northern Europe. Now that Nato had dug in in strength in the Baltic, Russia could be satisfied that she had fulfilled her part of the deal agreed with the Islamic Alliance. Although she could not have known then that her poor performance at Riga would be decisive in Nato's future decision-making with respect to events elsewhere. Russia's next aim would be to ensure that the negotiations for her own withdrawal were protracted while at the same time ensuring that the majority of the forces moved into the Baltic states and Poland would be forced to remain so that Nato's bargaining strength would be neither threatened nor undermined. Nato was indeed not keen on a 1991-style offensive against a far more capable opponent. Nato's interim objective of physically halting the Russian attempt at rapid occupation of the Baltic states had been achieved with little loss of life and no loss of face. Nato's planners and her political masters were certain, as Russia and the Islamic Alliance had hoped they would be, that softly spoken diplomacy backed by a proven superior military big stick and the threat of massive economic sanctions would be enough of a combination to convince Russia to withdraw peacefully – even if that took a year of diplomacy.

As the fighting halted and both sides apparently dug in for the summer, the Islamic Alliance watched closely. The final result exceeded all expectations. Not only were Nato's main forces pinned down in a state of siege for at least the summer, but the confidence of American foreign policy ensured that these forces were added to. The Republican President insisted that ultimately a military solution to the crisis would not be ruled out. This would lend weight and the authority of military power to the forthcoming negotiations, whose aim must be both Russian withdrawal and a clear signal that such local imperialism would not be tolerated in future.

Under US leadership the most powerful Nato nations began a build-up of forces and logistic bases for a possible military campaign in the short term. In the longer term the stockpiling and posturing would lay the ground for a new iron curtain, albeit several hundred miles east of the original one, but Nato was not prepared to risk again the territorial integrity of its members, especially Poland, as long as Russia remained belligerent.

The spring and early summer saw the US and Nato plunge into feverish planning for a secret build-up of forces, equipment and supplies for a Gulf War-style campaign to liberate Latvia and Estonia, should peace talks fail. The Germans even hinted that the plan ought to include an option for the forcible reoccupation of the Kaliningrad Oblast – to be carried out by non-German forces. As the summer wore on the prospect of all-out war, in spite of the continued build-up, seemed remote. The Kremlin and Islamic Alliance planners were ecstatic. By late June Nato had the best of its air forces, heavy armour and mechanised units focused at the wrong end of Europe. By the time Nato was forced to start looking seriously in the direction of Israel's neighbours, it would be, so the Islamic Alliance hoped, too late to be able to contribute much. They had, however, underestimated Nato's tenacity, unity and new sense of purpose when it came to fighting an extended 'real' war.

Chapter Seven – The Beginnings

Marseilles – The First Shot Is Fired

On 12 July, as part of the call by Saladin to 'train and exercise the soldiers of Islam to the full for the coming battle', the Algerian armed forces were put on full alert. All branches of the services adopted a war posture. The military contingency plans, drawn up so that Algeria could demonstrate her military prowess in times of tension, kicked into gear in the form of a series of air, land and naval exercises. Unfortunately, so the story went at the time, an over-zealous young Algerian officer, commander of a battery of three Scud 3 launchers, decided to take the small matter of realism a little too far. He, like many Algerians, held a seething hatred for France. On the one hand it was because of her colonial past and what he viewed as France's rape of Algeria over many years. And on the other he was one of many voices that accused France of propping up the military regime that had denied the people of Algeria the Islamic government that they had to wait more than a decade for. In the years of murder, terror and counter-attack, hardly a family was left untouched. His brother and sister had been killed by what he assumed to be 'government troops'. The troops were on a mission to the more remote mountain villages to flush out suspects and punish those who supported 'Islamic terrorists'. At the time he was just thirteen and was out with his goats when the soldiers struck. Up until the moment before he found his siblings bleeding all over the floor of their kitchen/living area from machete blows, he had been too young to have an opinion. For ten years thereafter he had a burning desire for revenge. It consumed his life, motivated him and gave him a sense of destiny. And he had worked and waited patiently for his moment to come.

He joined the infantry soon after the revolution, then transferred on commissioning to the Rocket Forces. Now he alone had control over a missile. The missile looked much the same as any other Algerian Scud, painted in the mottled yellows and browns with distinctive splashes of green that were the camouflage of the Algerian armed forces. He was trusted. He had the launch keys. He would show France how much the loss of his brother and sister meant to him. More practically he was able to justify his action historically: France had for years supplied Israel with the means to make war against Islam; she had illegally tried to interfere in the Algerian Revolution; she had sold the Israeli Air Force a hundred Dassault Mirage III fighter-bombers. France had oppressed and downtrodden her former colonial state for nearly half a century and, to the decent Muslim mind, represented all the perceived excess and Western moral decay which any true Muslim abhorred. Finally, and more practically, she was well in range for an accurate Scud 3 shot.

To the astonishment of the missile crew, the firing guard was lifted, the keys inserted and the firing pulse sent. It took a mere forty-five seconds to complete the action. Not one of the crew dared say a word. This young officer had been brutal with them in the past and his authority was unquestioned. The Scud worked as advertised and crashed off the rails, clouds of white smoke marking the path of the brightly burning rocket motor. The missile, tipped with nerve agent Sarin, arced high over the Mediterranean and slammed, seven minutes later, into Marseilles' traditional early-morning port marketplace. One hundred and eighty French citizens were killed and at least three hundred injured. Some of the death throes, as bodies twitched and struggled against the nerve gas, were captured on amateur video and broadcast around the world. The scenes were pure carnage. The West rocked with shock and the outrage of its own people, not Arabs or Slavs or Jews but rich Westerners, and hundreds of them, bleeding, burnt and shredded. There was scarlet blood in every scene shown – on the walls of buildings, in pools on the street, in trails where people had crawled, and pumping out of gaping wounds where many lay beyond the help of the emergency services until it had been confirmed that the Sarin had dispersed. The implications of that single strike sickened Europe. If France could be hit no one was safe. France, ever independent, declared her right to self-defence and threatened Algeria with 'being erased as a nation' if such an atrocity were to be repeated. In the meantime, with the UN Security Council deadlocked, thanks to Russia and China, France gained approval from the USA, Britain and other European allies to make an 'appropriate response'.

Subsequent evidence has emerged since the war which would seem to suggest that the firing of the Scud was no accident. The young Algerian officer had, in fact, served as Saladin's aide-de-camp from his taking of office until February 2006. Saladin, it seemed, had personally selected him from a host of other young candidates who worked in and around his outer offices. The Algerian was, Saladin decided, the most trustworthy, reliable and angry. A few telephone calls and the electronic transfer of money to a couple of private accounts in Algiers ensured that the young officer was given a personal crash training course in Scud operations and a 'no questions asked' policy as regards his methods of command of his own Scud battery. The plan worked perfectly, and as soon as his mission was complete the young officer was 'removed from command' for public consumption but secretly flown to Tehran to a hero's welcome.

'An Appropriate Response'

One week later, on 19 July, the aircraft carrier *Charles de Gaulle* sailed from Toulon and took up station 150 miles off the coast of Algeria. The carrier's Rafales were joined by eighty French Air Force jets, thanks to the efforts of the entire French air-to-air refuelling fleet, in two days and nights of continuous air strikes. The initial strikes were made by French Air Force Mirage 2000s carrying Apache stand-off missiles. The 2000s were able to carry one each and launched at one o'clock and four o'clock in the morning. The Apache itself had a range of some 200 miles, a terminal accuracy of around 10 meters and a 450-kilogram high-explosive warhead. The Mirage 2000s did not have to fly far south over the Mediterranean to reach their launch points for the targets in Algeria. The two waves flown were sufficient to expend fully half of the number of Apaches bought by the French. The Algerian Air Force's fighter aircraft and radar installations were the primary targets. Very few were in hardened shelters and the majority, lined up in the open or under canvas protected by revetted walls, were turned from national assets into twisted smoking heaps highlighted by a circular area of black soot on the beige concrete. At dawn the carrier aircraft and those that arrived via tankers were forced to search for new targets. In those forty-eight hours the Algerian Air Force and air defence command were reduced to useless bits of metal and broken buildings. Most of the aircraft were destroyed on the ground during that first night wave. The planners were ecstatic; it was a repeat of the Israeli victory in 1967. The final wave of attacks on the morning of the third day were, however, to prove France's undoing.

The ageing Mirage 2000D two-seaters were the bomber version of the more glamorous Mirage 2000. They had recently converted from the light bombing role precision attack, one carrying a laser-designating pod to mark targets for wingmen carrying laser-guided bombs. They were tasked with destroying the Algerian Air Defence Command Headquarters building in the centre of Algiers. Each of the wingmen carried two 2000lb laser-guided bombs which were to be released at a predetermined point and then guided on to the target by the lead Mirage carrying a laser designator.

This trio of Mirages was led by Capitaine Marc Deschamps. He and his back-seater Albert Foch were shortly to become the most infamous aviators in modern French history. At 0650 hours on this bright blue July morning this was the last thing on their minds as they sat at 35,000 feet in the quiet humming cockpit. All had gone well in the week they'd had to train to use the laser tracker and combined infrared low-light television display. There was very little that could go wrong. From the tanker they headed south, some two minutes behind an eight-ship of navy Rafales from the *Charles de Gaulle*. As soon as the African coast was in sight, Deschamps craned his neck and squinted to check that the other escorts were all in the right place. They were there – four Rafales flying loose escort above and behind at 42,000 feet, accompanied by a Falcon 400 executive jet, which was used to monitor all Algerian radio traffic. Flying shotgun and rather closer than he liked were three Mirage 2000 fighters. Deschamps knew they wouldn't be needed; the Algerian Air Force was a dead animal. The very worst was that a couple of rogue MiG-21s or MiG-23s that had not been destroyed might try to have a suicidal pop at them just to challenge French mastery of Algerian skies. Nevertheless, thought Deschamps, they were welcome to come along for the show.

'I got a good picture,' muttered Foch, who'd had his eyes glued to the TV picture once the coast had come into sight. 'No moisture or cloud to mess things up. I only had to make a couple of minor manual adjustments to the contrast and brightness. They really are going to enjoy these pictures back in Paris this evening. This is a perfect day for bombing.'

The three bombers and their entourage coasted in some fifty miles east of Algiers and executed a hard turn to starboard for the run to Algiers. '0653,' said Deschamps. 'Seven minutes to bomb strike time.'

'OK,' agreed Foch. 'Let's see . . . zoom . . . track . . . autotrack . . . lock. Yep, that all looks fine.' Foch still hadn't looked out of the cockpit. Like most back-seaters the world over, he had been given a new toy to play with and play with it he would. He had found a small barn on the outskirts of one of the many coastal villages and was testing all the tracking functions. His running commentary on what he was up to served, he thought, to give his pilot confidence. Deschamps was mildly irritated by the endless droning coming from behind. The 2000D assignment was his first experience of flying with another person in the cockpit. He had spent his whole career in single-seaters until this tour of duty, and found it very difficult sometimes with another person in his cockpit.

'Will you stop wittering? I only want to know if the damned thing isn't working. Got that?'

'*Oui, mon brave.*' Foch was stung and resentful. This wasn't a good start to the target run. Three minutes later Foch had picked up the eastern outskirts of Algiers. All remained quiet on the electronic warning gear. It was as if all Algeria's radars had been switched off.

'Picture clear,' came the monotonous call from the Falcon. Foch moved the tracker to the right along the coast to the northernmost pier of the harbour. So that there would be no mistakes, this unique feature was used as a master reference datum. Its position relative to the headquarters building was already in the computer, so that once it had been tracked and locked a single button push would move the whole picture and tracking cross to the target building.

'Offset identified, marked . . . and tracked,' said Foch slowly and as mechanically as he could. 'Now . . . press and . . . gotcha! Target identified.'

'Excellent,' agreed Deschamps. 'Two minutes to weapons release . . . now . . . Melons.' He transmitted the code word which both told the bomb carriers that they had the target marked and allowed them to make their switches live. Deschamps's relaxed demeanour was interrupted by a shout from behind. Foch was off intercom and shouting to him, his oxygen mask dangling by his chin.

'Marc, I've just zoomed in to max to check the final aiming point on the building and its about two hundred feet off to the right, on the northern end of the building.' Foch was beginning to sound a little uncertain. Deschamps was almost overcome with the ridiculousness of the situation. His back-seater was shouting at him because they both knew that every switch they made and everything they said was recorded on to digital tape and would be analysed at length later during the debrief. Deschamps hated this further intrusion in his cockpit; a spy in the cab as well as a navigator. He flicked off his oxygen mask and yelled back.

'Well, move the bloody thing, then. This won't look good on TV if you're tracking the wrong part of the building when the ventilation shaft we're supposed to be aiming at is clearly visible on the left end of the picture, will it?'

'Hmm.'

'What? What is it now?' Deschamps was rapidly rising through irritated to apoplectic.

'Well, we haven't done much manual override practice, but I'll give it a go.'

'This is no time to be learning on the job. If you can't hack it we'll just revert to bombing the north end of the building and blame it on the planners.'

'OK, taking manual now.' Foch was back on intercom. 'Deselecting autotrack, coming left with the cross . . . whoa! . . . It's fucking sensitive!'

'Happy,' transmitted Deschamps. This was a plain lie; it was supposed to confirm to the bombers that the aiming point had been refined and was being tracked. Thirty seconds to bomb release, one minute to bomb strike time.

'Have you got it?' he asked Foch tersely.

'Yes, yes, at last, sorry about that. It's a very sensitive system. I just needed a couple of seconds to adjust to the rate the tracking box moves with the tiniest adjustment on the hand controller, but I'm happy now. Let's see, fifteen seconds to release, tracking box bang on the ventilation shaft.'

'Excellent, well done.' Deschamps was torn between sarcasm, relief and an inclination to offer congratulations.

'Bombs away,' came the call from the bombers. Foch and Deschamps glanced over at the bombers to watch as the four bombs separated cleanly from numbers two and three. The trio then began a lazy right turn northward to safety. All the while Foch was heads-in, confirming that the tracking was still good and counting down on his stopwatch the seconds to bomb strike.

'Twenty seconds, tracking good . . . ten seconds . . . five, four, three, two, one . . . hmm . . . any second now . . . no impact.'

'Bomb strikes observed!' came the excited call from the number two.

'Not on the building I was aiming at,' observed Foch matter-of-factly, still focused on the headquarters building on his TV picture. Deschamps remained uncharacteristically quiet and pulled the jet around to the left to observe the growing pillar of smoke and rubble for himself.

'Good grief, the bombs have gone way long, well over the top. What on earth has happened? You did have the right building, didn't you?'

'*Merde*,' was all Foch could muster. Deschamps became silent again, awaiting the inevitable. 'I forgot to switch the laser on. Shit, shit, shit.' They both knew that when laser bombs did not guide the small fins by which they were guided acted like wings. That meant that a precision-guided bomb that was going to miss would miss by at least an order of magnitude more than its dumb counterpart. Indeed, years earlier the RAF had reverted to using dumb weapons released in a high-angle dive for precision attack in Bosnia because the miss distances were so much smaller than those of 'unguided' guided weapons. The bad press from inadvertent civilian casualties – 'collateral damage' was the military euphemism – was so great that using precision weapons with 95 per cent reliability was considered too great a risk. Foch and Deschamps flew home via the tanker in silence and to a firm place in French history. Recrimination was pointless. They both prayed that they hadn't hit a marketplace or something, as the RAF had done at Falujah during the Gulf War for exactly the same reason.

As it turned out they hadn't hit a marketplace. They'd done much worse. All four bombs went ballistic, their wings ensuring that they would miss by a long way. And miss they did. A shabby high-rise apartment block took the full force of 8,000 lb of high explosive and kinetic energy. The blast, over-pressure and cross-fragmentation of four large bombs amounted to a destructive synergy much boasted about in the brochures. The building was hit at the base and then at even intervals up its east-facing side. It crumbled to a heap of screaming rubble and dust as if demolished by engineers. The decrepit state of such a tall building was an indicator of the number of people living in squalor inside. Over two thousand were killed; many more were injured as the debris cascaded out from the stricken building in a tidal wave of masonry, sweeping aside many of the flimsy structures which counted as dwellings and shops in this run-down area of the capital.

TV crews raced to the scene and took pictures of broken, bleeding and burned people. It was the children – not the dead ones, but the ones crying helplessly, some with their limbs at odd angles, others naked with torn flesh, screaming next to parents who in their lifelessness would not respond – who provoked the most intense reaction. The world watched its television screens horrified as the news broke. The triumphant pictures of clean military conflict and the efficient destruction of an enemy – destroyed machines, not people – were quickly forgotten as the French armed forces fell from the moral high ground. Western feeling changed from self-justification and jingoism to disgust at the 'mistake'.

France, as enigmatic as ever, stood relatively unrepentant. Such things happen in war; it was unfortunate. The French military was heavily criticised by its peers. But France was independent, had always been, and would always remain so.

Israel Mobilises

In Jerusalem the Scud that hit Marseilles was viewed as no accident. Recovered Mossad and Shin Bet files reveal that the Israeli intelligence agencies had made the connection between Saladin's former ADC and the Marseilles Scud shot. Israeli agents in Marseilles captured, tortured and shot a pair of Iranians they had been tracking for some months. In their dockyard flat Mossad apparently found videos and sensing equipment in the aftermath of the attack giving a full read-out on the effects of the Sarin attack. As far as Israel was concerned this was proof that the attack was a test and not an accident. It showed that the Scuds possessed by the Islamic Alliance had both the accuracy and the technology to enable the lethal dispersion of a chemical agent.

As well as the evidence of preparation and readiness for war that was shown by the Marseilles Scud, Mossad networks throughout Islamic Alliance capitals were reporting back clear signals of the beginnings of covert mobilisation. On reviewing the evidence, the Israeli war cabinet decided that it had no option but to go for full but discreet mobilisation. The order was sent out on 19 July, the day the French bombing campaign began.

Israel, certain now that an attack in some form or other was imminent, and confident that she had the military might to withstand any conventional assault, started to call up her reservists. The process had been under way for forty-eight hours before it was officially announced. The news that evening from Algiers only served to give the call-up an extra edge. As far as Israel was concerned the venting of any subsequent collective anger by the Islamic Alliance could only be directed *en masse* against Israel herself as an ally of the Americans, the British, the French and all other traditional enemies of Islam. The government stated that Israel was determined that if war was to come she would take appropriate action at a time that she viewed as most opportune, even if it meant striking first. She would not be caught on the defensive as in 1973, when she bowed to political pressure from the US to act only in retaliation because if she struck first, regardless of the realities of the situation, she would be seen as the aggressor and would lose much world sympathy. By 2006, given the arsenals of her potential enemies, Israel had learned from Yom Kippur in 1973 that political niceties and world opinion were an irrelevance if the survival of the nation was at stake. This policy would be adhered to until the final battle.

Israeli soldiers and settlers in the West Bank and northern Israel had been in a state of tense siege for almost a year before the Israeli invasion of Sinai. With the official announcement of mobilisation on 21 July Israel withdrew all her negotiators from the West Bank and Gaza peace talks. In both parts of the occupied Palestinian state Israeli soldiers, as soon as their numbers had swelled sufficiently, were able to move more permanently into the most dangerous Hamas and Hezbollah-controlled areas. Their reinforced presence gave them more confidence to conduct mass arrests and carry out the occasional summary execution – only when the suspect attempted to flee or resisted arrest, of course.

Islamic Alliance Announces General Mobilisation

The outrage across the world caused by the carnage in Algiers, as well as the 'surprise' announcement of mobilisation by Israel, created for Saladin exactly the opportunity that he had been trying to engineer. Even the West was surprised by the Israeli decision to mobilise, and the UN Security Council accused Israel, in diplomatic terms, of overreacting. Saladin was delighted. His original plan had been to call for mobilisation in response to the expected French reaction and attack Israel as the most convenient focus of all things Western. He would have called for revenge on an arrogant West that, as he saw things, had awarded itself the divine right of judgement over international crimes and punishments; the latter it was willing and able to mete out as it saw fit without fear of response. The number of casualties in Algiers, as well as the spectacular colour coverage on television, the Net and in newspapers, had exceeded all Saladin's expectations.

Now that Israel had so clearly bitten the bullet and had made a poor attempt to conceal her mobilisation, Saladin's plans were able to proceed apace. He had no need for a campaign of exhortation and a call to arms. The Islamic Alliance nations were also ready for a fight. All spring and early summer Israel had been brutally repressing any demonstrations in the West Bank and Gaza, as well as continuing to deny the Palestinians anything more than the minimum amount of water for mere existence. Meanwhile Turkey was again threatening to close the sluices that now controlled the flow of the Tigris and Euphrates.

The Israeli mobilisation enabled the Islamic Alliance to abandon all pretence of pursuit of a diplomatic solution to the growing crisis and to lay the blame at Israel's door. In the weeks that followed, the full mobilisation of the armed forces of Egypt, Libya, Saudi Arabia, Jordan, Iraq, Iran and Syria took place.

Turkey Mobilises – Nato Plans

On 23 July the ruling Turkish military government declared its outright support for the Israeli cause. The Turkish Army, already half a million men strong, mobilised and inside a week had swelled to over one million in number, although some units were of dubious fighting quality. Turkey declared its airbases open to Nato aircraft and within three days the first squadrons began arriving. The Turkish Army began to deploy its vast forces on its southern border facing the Lebanon, Syria and Iraq. The Islamic Alliance nations had, like the Israelis the previous October, begun extensive covert preparations for full mobilisation. Saladin was satisfied that the Russians had been successful in tying down the best of Nato's heavy divisions in the Baltic. But the battle of Riga, or more accurately the disastrous failure of Russia's best units in that battle, actually gave Nato an exact gauge of both Russia's intentions and the real limitations of further Russian expansion attempts. Nato, her divisions combat-ready and well provisioned, was able to begin to make contingency plans for a move for the bulk of her best units from the Baltic to the Middle East in case the threat to Turkey became a real one.

In the Middle East the tension rose daily. By the middle of the last week in July the flurry of diplomats jetting between capitals had become unrelenting. Both the US's and Nato's senior commanders had privately concluded that war was inevitable. The preparation for war across the Islamic Alliance was unmistakable. That the best of Nato's heavy units were in the Baltic was not a major concern. The Russian attack on Riga took on a new significance. It had served to demonstrate the real quality difference between the Russians and Nato troops and their respective air forces, and Russia was well aware that she risked losing large parts of her army if she provoked a stronger response from a prickly and alert Nato.

Nato commanders watched as the Syrians built up their forces along the border with Turkey. They became more alarmed with the build-ups on either side of Kuwait, where 15,000 US soldiers were stationed, and the Saudi and Iranian threats to Qatar and Abu Dhabi, each of which had garrisons of 5,000 US soldiers.

Turkey, although she had the largest and arguably the most powerful army in the region, requested that Nato troops be sent in to augment her own forces which were facing a clear and threatening build-up across her southern border. In Nato headquarters at SHAPE in Belgium the generals were reluctant. There was no sign of any immediate offensive into Turkey, and even if there had been the terrain that marked the southern border of Turkey was such that it offered great advantages to the defender. Nato, however, reassured by the crushing nature of its victory at Riga, began to rotate the best heavy units and many of the Reaction Force air units out of the Baltic region. They were replaced with lower-grade units that were deemed adequate to act as a holding force should Russia be tempted to move west again.

Chapter Eight – Exercises in War

Exercise Holy Wind

With mobilisation complete, Saladin now put the next stage of his plan into action. The single future scenario that the West had planned and endlessly war-gamed was the closure of the Strait of Hormuz by Iran. Through this narrow strip of water that separates the Persian Gulf and the Gulf of Oman and the Indian Ocean passed nearly a quarter of the world's oil supplies. The Strait is less than forty miles across at the point between the northern tip of Oman and Qeshm Island, due south of Bandar Abbass. The scenario had become an increasingly complex one over the years. Originally, before the Saudi Revolution, all the West would have to do was act with force against Iran alone; now things were a little different. The three states that had remained free of revolution and retained family plutocracies as their forms of government – Kuwait, Bahrain and Qatar – were no more than island garrisons in a sea of hostile neighbours. The US Fifth Fleet still had its headquarters in Bahrain, but the Pentagon was becoming increasingly reluctant to base any more than a handful of aircraft in any one of the states.

The key change to the strategic geography of the region was the revolution in the United Arab Emirates (UAE). With the UAE firmly in the Islamic camp the western end of the Strait of Hormuz was bordered on both sides by countries potentially hostile to the West. The amount of oil exported by the three small states was not overly significant; however, the US had signed mutual co-operation pacts with all three countries. This meant that the US would be obliged to defend them if they were attacked. The closure of Hormuz would effectively deny sea access to reinforcements headed for the region, as well as effectively cutting off what was a reduced but still essential friendly oil supply. And of course, for the US and the West, there were the bigger issues of violations of international law through armed aggression that could not be allowed to go unpunished on principle; especially when the West had vested interests in the region and the US was the *de facto* world policeman.

Most importantly, the US and the UK had significant army and marine garrisons in each of the three states. These could not be allowed to be cut off and left marooned, which was what the closure of Hormuz would achieve. Of course, they could be and were supplied by air, but this, apart from being expensive, used valuable air transport assets that were needed elsewhere. The US military was forced to lease civil transport 747 jumbos to augment Military Airlift Command. Also, the air bridge was vulnerable in that from Oman, where the nearest friendly seaports were, the transport aircraft had to be escorted through hostile airspace with the whole gamut of fighters, EW and SEAD aircraft and tankers. And reinforcing the garrisons by air would only in turn exacerbate the resupply problem.

The problem for the airbases, ports and garrison areas in the three states was a severe one. Every inch of these areas could be hit by artillery fire from Saudi Arabia or Iraq, or was a matter of minutes away from a hostile air attack. It was little wonder therefore that the US Air Force generals became increasingly nervous about letting their valuable and potentially war-winning assets sit vulnerably on the ground at the desert and island airbases. This meant that the nearest bases for land-based air power were in Oman. The only alternative options for the US and her allies to project power into the region were the use of the newly commissioned arsenal ships with their massive complement of cruise missiles (the project had been rapidly restored after the Second Korean War), long-range bombers, or carrier-based air power. Again, although, given the circumstances, somewhat reluctantly, the advocates of naval aviation and carrier visionaries were able to congratulate themselves on their foresight.

The Islamic Alliance was able to close Hormuz almost by

stealth. The Iranians had conducted regular large-scale exercises every two years to the growing discomfort of the US and the West. They normally involved around a quarter of a million troops, as well as virtually the entire Iranian Navy and as much of the air force as could be packed on to the four major bases surrounding Bandar Abbass. In the ten years before the war the Iranian Navy had more than doubled in size to some 50,000 men, somewhat larger than the once mighty Royal Navy. The most significant development in her capability to threaten Western warships and the supertankers was the purchase of a further five Kilo-class diesel attack submarines. This gave her a working fleet of eight. In addition she had achieved a massive expansion of her mine-laying capability as well as producing an impressive array of locally manufactured mines. Both the submarines and the advanced mine capability were acquired from Russia. The West had scoffed at initial Iranian attempts to become serious submariners, rudely observing that the boats' captains were disinclined to submerge for fear of sinking. It was true that the learning curve with the first three Kilo boats had been steeper than the Iranian Navy had expected. Poor serviceability and a naïve approach to the problems presented dogged the first five years of operation of the Kilos.

By 2003, however, the Iranians had, through sheer persistence, become confident enough to expand the fleet. Iran was rightly extremely proud of her achievements in underwater warfare. The only other nations in the Islamic Alliance that had successfully pursued the building of a submarine force were Egypt and Pakistan. There were other significant improvements to the Iranian Navy up to 2006. She had purchased three Chinese frigates, giving her a total of six, a further twenty Houdong-class fast-attack missile craft, giving forty in all and, multiple shore batteries of C-802 SSM Silkworm missiles and locally produced cruise missiles. To protect her main naval base at Bandar Abbass and her whole Persian Gulf effort, Iran had also purchased several batteries of the S-300 Russian Patriot SAM equivalent, to complement her batteries of 80–100-mile-range SA-5 SAMs and Improved Hawk SAMs. The Iranians' purchasing pattern was similar to that of many nations that turned to Russia for equipment, and enabled the latter to overtake both France and the UK in volume of military exports, while purchases from China ensured that this country's military export market remained buoyant.

Exercise Holy Wind began on 29 July. The forces involved were on a scale never before seen in the region. The combined navies of Saudi Arabia, the UAE, Iran and Pakistan were able to muster twelve submarines – the six Pakistani submarines were a mixture of French Agosta and Daphne classes, both of which carried Harpoon SSMs – twenty frigates and almost fifty missile attack craft. On the ground two major exercises were conducted. The first involved for the first time ever ground and air forces from both Iraq and Saudi Arabia, and was centred across the border to the west of Kuwait where the US-led Coalition had concentrated its attack to retake Kuwait fifteen years previously. The second was a joint Saudi and UAE operation along the border with Qatar. The official theme running through both land and air exercises was ostensibly to practise countering Western aggression from out of Kuwait and Qatar.

In the region at the time, the US 5th Fleet had a force that was powerful but not overwhelmingly so. The USS *Carl Vinson* (CVN-70) was the only carrier actually in the Persian Gulf. She was supported by two guided missile cruisers, four destroyers, two attack submarines, an amphibious assault ship with the 27th Marine Expeditionary Unit embarked, half a dozen support ships, and, most significantly of all as events would transpire, a single mine countermeasures ship. The Pentagon had watched the build-up of Islamic forces from space with increasing angst. But the major surveillance effort was dedicated to a close watch on the direct ground threats posed to Kuwait and Qatar. A carrier battle group of similar size and composition had been dispatched from the Indian Ocean Fleet but remained a day's sailing distance away by the time the exercises ended on 5 August. This battle group did, however, have one significant addition, and that was the second of the two newly commissioned arsenal ships, the USS *Merrimack*.

The Royal Navy Gulf Patrol, working directly with the 5th Fleet, consisted of a small squadron with a destroyer, two guided missile frigates, two mine-hunters and two mine-clearers. There was little the US and UK forces could do other than watch and listen to the exercises from a distance. On 4 August things turned sour. The Iranians announced that they had successfully deployed in excess of six thousand mines of various types across the Strait and as far as Qatar's and Bahrain's territorial waters. They had been able to do this from a multitude of coastal and inshore patrol vessels as well as from small freighters over the six-day period. The vast mine-laying operation had gone essentially unnoticed as the whole of the West's strategic and operational-level reconnaissance and surveillance efforts were directed at detecting the first signs of intent to use armed force against Kuwait, Qatar and Bahrain. The three small states and their garrisons did indeed live through the first week of August in the grip of invasion fever, and were relieved at the first signs of the exercises winding down without any hostile action. It took a while, however, for the implications of Iran's announcement late on 5 August to sink in. The actual number of mines laid was around three thousand. However, as the Iranians and the West well knew, counter-mine warfare was still as much an art as a science. Seabed mines were particularly difficult to detect and deal with, especially if encased in wood and covered in a fertilised mesh that encouraged the growth of sea flora within a matter of days. The other three thousand 'mines' were simple decoys. These consisted mainly of oil drums filled with varying levels of concrete that caused them to float at various depths. The problem for any hunter or clearer was that every decoy had to be treated as live, and ascertaining the status of every 'mine' detected was a painful and time-consuming process. The other problem with mine warfare was that the US had singularly under-invested in this 'unglamorous' area for more than four decades. The assets available for such a mammoth task were relatively few. The thought of coping with the problem presented made Western naval staffs groan in anticipation.

Iran and her allies had achieved two notable successes.

They had proved that it was possible for them to operate in a joint and combined manner, albeit with nowhere near the slickness and precision of similar US-led exercises. And while the West's attention was diverted, they had effectively closed the Strait of Hormuz and isolated the three states not in the Islamic Alliance and their UK and US garrisons. As for the three isolated Gulf states and their garrisons, the US Pacific Fleet was recalled to San Diego to prepare for a long journey to the Middle East. The only airbases available to the West that were not within artillery range of Islamic forces were those in Turkey, Cyprus, southern Oman and on the remote Indian Ocean island of Diego Garcia. This meant, as Saladin had known for some time, that sea-delivered air power in the form of either carrier air wing strike aircraft or the ubiquitous cruise missiles would assume a much higher importance in a potential war than at any time since the Pacific theatre in World War II.

The Closure of Suez

Saladin's master plan was unfolding with an ease and certainty that startled the West. While the West (and the US in particular) was reeling from this body blow that had them feeling outmanoeuvred, and in intense discussion as to whether the Islamic Alliance 'success' in Hormuz constituted a blatant act of war, Saladin put the boot in. Late on 5 August Egypt announced that she would be closing the Suez Canal to all shipping for seventy-two hours in order to conduct extensive exercises with Libya in the Sinai and Canal area. Saladin considered that the only options available to the West were either to negotiate over Suez or become involved in a 1956-style air/sea/land operation, and the historical precedent did not sit comfortably in the minds of Nato's political leaders. Saladin was well aware that there was an outside chance of Egypt being bullied, threatened, cajoled or browbeaten directly and indirectly by the US into keeping the Canal open, so he decided to ensure that the closure was physical. In the early hours of 6 August the Iranian-registered tanker the *Rafsanjahni Star* radioed an SOS message that she was under attack before all messages ceased. The tanker, a massive 85,000 tons, was passing through the Canal that night. Assault teams in fast rubber boats had fired grappling hooks for purchase before boarding her via scramble nets hauled up her hull sides. At gunpoint, according to the Cairo press at least, the black-clothed raiders had ordered the captain to halt the ship mid-channel at the Suez Canal's narrowest point before ordering the captain and his crew into the lifeboats for the short trip to shore.

Thirty minutes later there was a series of muffled explosions from within the bowels of the ship. When dawn broke there was no sign of the raiders or their rigid inflatables with their huge outboard motors. The ship had settled on the bed of the Canal in four sections, loosely held together where the carefully placed explosives had not quite shredded the double hull; her gantries and upper superstructure were still well above the waterline but she was clearly going nowhere fast. The Suez Canal was well and truly blocked. This clearance project, like that in Hormuz, would be both time-consuming and painful. No one claimed responsibility and Egypt pleaded innocence and ignorance. That it was an inside job, orchestrated from somewhere in Tehran, was not in doubt. The Iranian crew was hastily flown back to their home port of Bandar Abbass before the West's media could get to grips with them.

Saladin was initially well pleased with the previous forty-eight hours' events. He had reasoned that the closure of the Suez Canal meant that serious reinforcement from the West to the isolated garrisons and states was only possible via the Cape of Good Hope. Any attempt at air resupply or reinforcement would now be through hostile airspace and would anyway only provide a fraction of what it was possible to move by sea. And the threat to US and British forces in the Gulf would, Saladin felt, be the focus of any response. He was able to smile with a great deal of satisfaction from his command bunker in Tehran; now he would be able to sit back and enjoy the response of the West – or so he thought.

He had had enough for the moment of frightening the ruling families in Kuwait, Qatar and Bahrain. They could all be dealt with later if things went according to plan. Saladin ordered a trickle transfer of troops and equipment from Saudi Arabia, Iraq and Iran to begin. The destinations of these troops were dispersed locations in north-western Saudi Arabia, Jordan, western Iraq and Syria. While the West was fulminating about the physical closure of the Strait of Hormuz, and the political closure announced a day later in Cairo of the Suez Canal, the Islamic Alliance forces would be able to begin the covert build-up of forces which, Saladin hoped, would be able to ensure Israel's eventual destruction.

The West went into a state of profound shock. Not for the first time in the past decade all the technological and military advantages held by the West were unable to match what the Arab mind could achieve by cunning and guile. The knee-jerk reaction from the Pentagon was what it had always been since the 1991 Gulf War: to advocate a series of punishment air strikes primarily against Iran. The weakness with such a strategy was, however, that no matter how much coercion was achieved by any air or cruise missile strikes, the problem of laid mines and a stricken supertanker were not something either side could undo in a short space of time.

US reconnaissance satellites also picked up the first signs of troop transfers from east to west across the few communication routes in Saudi Arabia, Iraq and Iran. The US had also been watching Egyptian and Libyan moves across the Suez Canal and in Sinai, and concluded that a limited attack against Israel from the west was 'now not beyond the bounds of possibility'. The US President and her closest advisers correctly determined Saladin's ultimate objective of annihilating Israel and decided to act with care and certainty. The looming bigger picture was a descent into the bloodiest conflict the Middle East had ever seen rather than a simple individual reaction to the Suez and Hormuz crises.

At 2200 GMT on 6 August, after consultation in the new four-country Security Council (Russia had been temporarily expelled following the Baltic War), the US broadcast a statement that deplored the Islamic Alliance actions. She called on the Alliance for restraint and an immediate commencement of international mine-clearing operations in the Persian Gulf. The US Congress went into extended session to debate whether or not the activities of the Alliance constituted an act of war. The US gave the 'offending nations' forty-eight hours to agree in full to a multinational clearing of the Strait of Hormuz and Suez and a suspension of all military exercise activity. If full and unconditional agreement to the US plans was not forthcoming within the deadline, then the US (and Nato in the wings) would take all necessary measures to ensure a return to the *status quo ante*.

The following forty-eight hours brought a wall of silence from the Alliance. The transfer of troops from the Gulf to within reach of the Israeli border continued with measured pace. Once the deadline expired the US declared her hand. The US and the major Nato European powers, especially the right-wing governments in the UK, Italy, Spain and Germany, raised the stakes of the game. In a terse statement they declared their full support for Israel and her right to nationhood, adding that any military move against Israel would be construed as an act of war against the greater interests of the free and civilised world. This was an unexpected and worrying development as far as Saladin was concerned. He had planned and prepared for a direct response from the US, but not from the rest of the West. The new Nato, with France chiming in with full support, was not going to allow itself to be outmanoeuvred again. Turkey and Greece also took the unusual step of issuing a joint statement of full co-operation in any Nato action. Indeed, it was the flimsy Syrian threat to Turkey which Nato used to justify the initiation of actual preparations for direct intervention.

All this was music to Israeli ears. Nato had realised that she had to prepare for the worst. And, although all the Islamic Alliance rhetoric was aimed at Israel and America, the surveillance results continued to point to a much larger operation afoot.

Chapter Nine –
A Tale of Two Strategies

The West – Ether and the Up

From the millennium the US had made it clear to the world that she was ushering in a new approach to foreign policy. The message of successive Presidents was that the US would no longer be passive and reactive in her defence against the forces of destabilisation and terror. She would actively seek out the 'troublemakers' at source and would be less constrained than at any time previously in history when considering all options for global action. America had carried this policy through and it was evidenced by her actions in Korea, Serbia, China and Iraq. And America had forces of unparalleled power. The basis of this power was her huge technology advantages in 'Information Warfare' and 'Aerospace Power' – the 'Ether' and the third dimension, 'Up'. The motto of the twenty-first century US war-fighting machine, if it had one, would have been 'Gather, Process, Strike'. RSC41 (Reconnaissance, Surveillance, Command, Control, Communications, Surveillance and Intelligence) comprised the operations of the gathering and processing of information while air power became the primary expression of 'Strike'. Apparently oblivious to the cost, the American military was at least one technological generation ahead of the rest of the world. Her post-millennial strategy had resulted in the building of a further twenty B-2 bombers, each one named after a state capital, at a cost of some $1 billion each, and by 2006 the commissioning of the first two in a series of six arsenal ships. Strategic air attack and cruise missile diplomacy had become the foreign policy gunboats of the new millennium.

And the US had no reason to suppose that her conventional supremacy, especially the dominance of 'Up', would be challenged in any conflict short of nuclear war.

The answer to the problem of keeping the Islamic Alliance and Israel from pressing a mutually assured destruction button was therefore predictable. The US, with Nato in support, would embark on a strategic air campaign with the long-range assets available. The Pentagon's response to a real military threat to Israel had been war-gamed on computers for many years. The air campaign would strike directly and with precision at the enemy's strategic centres of gravity to persuade him to desist. The senior USAF generals were pleased that they would be given the chance to demonstrate where the hub of US global power and reach lay. Some were bullish enough to hope that the conflict could be defused through using air power alone. The USN would be able to contribute, certainly, but only once its carriers and cruise-missile-armed ships had steamed to within range of the target sets. There remained a hope that 'air power alone' would be able to do the job. The unwritten assumption underpinning this neat theory was that the potential enemy would be modern, mechanised and industrialised, and would react to such a campaign as any Western country might. If they were denuded of air defence and left open to attack from the air, the destruction of target sets within the military infrastructure and communications networks would render the antagonists unable to command or resupply/reinforce their forces. This would leave them feeling vulnerable and with no option other than to capitulate. The target sets identified as being crucial to the survival of any state were known as 'centres of gravity'. Colonel John Warden, the real architect of the 1991 Gulf War air campaign, first coined the phrase in 1988. The term 'centre of gravity' was based on Clausewitz's 'hub of all power and movement', describing 'that point where the enemy is most vulnerable and the point where an attack will have the best chance of being decisive'. The centres of gravity included the enemy's command and control structure, key industries and transportation systems.

The Pentagon planned a graduated strategic air campaign

of unprecedented scope and breadth. The initial stages were critical. It was felt that if the right targets were chosen and hit with sufficient accuracy and levels of destruction, then the Islamic Alliance might be stopped in its tracks. Therefore every country in the Alliance would be attacked, except Pakistan, whose commitment was less than full, and would taste at first hand the reach of US air power. Each country would be subjected to selective air attacks – surgical strikes, aimed at causing maximum disruption to the politico-military hierarchies and entities – and, with friendly media encamped in the 'enemy' lands, maximum effort would be given to minimising civilian casualties. Senior USAF generals opined that the amount of air power that would be brought to bear would be so destructive that any 'centre of gravity' theory was largely irrelevant. The real USAF strategy was 'We will attack *everything* in case *something* makes a difference'. This logic did not, however, acknowledge the massive resilience and recovery rate of any human-based system. It was forgotten that Germany had to be completely crushed and Japan 'nuked' before their respective systems finally acknowledged collapse.

The target list for the strategic air campaign was massive, but the parallels with the Rolling Thunder campaign in the late 1960s, when American air power had failed in Vietnam, were discussed with some discomfort in the Pentagon's underground planning rooms.

The American military saw a window of opportunity that they intended to seize with both hands. A strategic air campaign gave them free rein to attack all those parts of Islam that were considered dangerous to the future of the West. The targeteers nearly wet themselves in anticipation. Air power had the ability to reach out and destroy those factories and institutions that held potential terror for the West, from overt nuclear research facilities to every mildly suspicious pharmaceutical manufacturer. The target folders, prepared a decade before, were dusted off. The purely military aims of the campaign were to cause an expectation of real and lasting damage to the military and industrial bases of targeted nations, as well as cutting off the deployed military forces from both their supply bases and command centres. The US government, by taking such a strong and unprecedented step against a conventional threat, hoped to persuade the Islamic Alliance that any subsequent use of weapons of mass destruction would incur even more severe damage in each country. At the same time the campaign would be an attempt to convince Israel that US and Nato air power would bring about a swift conclusion to the conflict without the need for Israel to use nuclear missiles.

The desired end state was to use air power alone to coerce the Alliance countries into negotiation and withdrawal. The US Army remained sceptical of the 'air power alone' theory, which it privately described as 'half-assed', and referred back to T.R. Ferenbach's famous quote: 'You may fly over a land forever, you may bomb it, atomise it, pulverise it and wipe it clean of life – but if you desire to defend it, protect it and keep it for civilisation you must do this on the ground, the way the Roman legions did, by putting your young men into the mud.'

The more cautious and pragmatic voices of the US and Nato's armies and navies pointed out that air power alone had never 'won' any war. The historical evidence was clear. For air power to have any real menace or lasting effect it had to be either through the (unthinkable) use of nuclear weapons or be backed by the threat of intervention by sizable ground forces which would require the navy to transport them and to protect their major supply lines. Reluctantly, therefore, Nato began to implement one of its 'least likely' contingency plans and agreed to begin send ground forces to Turkey.

The lure of a clinical solution as promised by the air power apologists was too great for the politicians to ignore. The clinching argument for the campaign was that the offensive forces used represented the absolute minimum risk to the lives of the US and Nato forces involved. The stealth bombers were virtually invulnerable to enemy fire, and the cruise missiles were unmanned and difficult to shoot down. The politicians were appalled by events in Israel and the Middle East and were prepared to try any avenue that might avert a large-scale war. The campaign plans were drawn up and the Spirits, Nighthawks and Tomahawks (B-2s, F-117s and cruise missiles) would be unleashed without warning – or almost without warning. Saladin had long been a student of US foreign policy and had noted that the single definitive precursor to every attack by the US and her allies over the previous decade was an exodus of embassy staff. As soon as this happened throughout the Alliance countries on 25 and 26 August, Saladin set in motion his own counter-plans.

The East – Tankers, Body-bags and CNN

Saladin's counter-strategy was based on his own studies of post World War II wars and intimate knowledge of the real vulnerabilities of the West's air power and media-driven societies. Saladin knew that he would be unable to achieve his aims through any conventional war with the West. The strategy was devised to exploit the weaknesses of the West's political and military systems. The Islamic Alliance simply had to gain enough time to annihilate Israel before suing for peace in the face of the West's inevitable eventual theatre military superiority. The major threat to the Islamic plans was Western air power. In its element it was decisive, pervasive, dominant and ubiquitous. Where possible this would have to be disrupted at source rather than at point of bomb release – and Saladin had identified the pivot of Western air power as its large air-to-air refuelling fleet.

Saladin also knew that Western civilisations demanded, or at least had expectations, that any war should be short, decisive, morally just, within international law and entail few body-bags. He had to ensure that none of these criteria was met. The first two would be achieved through direct military action, the latter three through the media.

The defining moment for the US, and therefore the West, in the use of military force came not from Iran, Iraq or even Vietnam, but from Mogadishu in 1993. The scene of ugly deaths and the dismemberment of a Black Hawk helicopter crew shown on worldwide television was sufficient not only to change the whole US policy towards Somalia (she withdrew and Somalia reverted to warlordism) but also shaped the approach of the whole US military towards war. Future US foreign policy would be conducted on the bedrock of technological advantage that enabled it to dominate the information war and the air. To the US and the West, war was about technology and military might. To the Islamic and Eastern mind (and the Israeli for that matter) war was a struggle of willpower, endurance and resolve. The West was also obsessed with winning the media war.

What increasingly occupied the minds of editors vying for audiences and readership were the more controversial aspects of any military operation, i.e. when they went wrong and 'innocent civilians' were killed. This would unleash a moral outrage whose combined effects were called the 'CNN Effect'. The potential power of the West's media was far greater than any military weapon possessed by the East. The first doubts about any campaign were sown by graphic footage of dead and dying 'friendly' soldiers or blown-apart 'enemy' civilians. Capable of turning public opinion overnight, the direct and indirect power of the free media were more constraining than anything the Islamic Alliance would be able to call on. As soon as the 'civilised' public – in the UK led by Sky News and the *Sun* newspaper – even hinted that it was less than wholly satisfied by friendly military conduct, the politicians would put pressure on the senior military commanders. Thus, in the interest of good public relations and 'openness', the campaign on the home front would degenerate into the worst excesses of civilian and military micro-management. The real focus of military decision-making during conflict would become 'the highest levels' – the euphemism for Prime Minister or President. The democracies of the West, as concerned with popularity, image and re-election as much as executing sound policy, would begin to suffer increasingly from 'POP' (Public Opinion Paralysis). The need to 'be in control' so obsessed the West's leaders that a senior White House aide once boasted that 'Sergeant Smith won't be able to have a fart without direct approval in triplicate from the Pentagon'.

The more it appeared to the West's public that they were about to become mired in a situation that bore similarities to

Vietnam, Afghanistan, Somalia and Kosovo, to name only a handful of muddled, irritating, politically damaging, protracted and difficult-to-understand affairs, rather than a Gulf 1991 or Korea 2003 scenario, the more likely the stomach for a real fight would waver.

Operation Western Shield

The US by now had a very firm grip on the leadership of Nato. The nations of the West had decided that they should not only be ready to deter and directly counter any attacks by the Islamic Alliance, but that in taking such a strong and united line they might avert the looming war – Israel's intensified preparations had not gone unnoticed – and use the combined threat of economic and military muscle to restore world order. Nato feared that Alliance attacks in one form or another might result from their support for the Israeli cause. It was almost inevitable that force would be needed to clear a safe passage through the Hormuz minefields. The first step, rapidly agreed by Nato's Military Council, was to prepare and move as many air units as could be spared from Nato's northern and central regions and away from the Baltic front to the southern flank. France, Italy and Spain were particularly willing, given the direct threat posed to them by North African nations, which had been demonstrated so clearly in Marseilles.

During the three weeks that followed, the airbases from Cape Trafalgar through southern France and Corsica, Sardinia, Sicily and Italy, Greece, Crete and Cyprus, to the whole of southern Turkey up to the Iranian border, saw a huge gathering of Nato's most potent conventional weapon – its air power. The collection of fighters, fighter-bombers, electronic warfare aircraft, SAM-hunters, AWACs and tankers, as well as a myriad of other support aircraft, was both awesome and threatening. The British and German units concentrated their deployments on Cyprus, Crete and Turkey, both countries willing to share the risk and reward of being the most likely to see action. Nato's leaders were in no doubt that this was the irresistible force. There was a hope at SHAPE near Mons in Belgium that when Saladin saw the size and resolve of a united Nato he would back down honourably.

There was, however, a nagging doubt. Any meaningful projection of Nato air power into North Africa or more probably Egypt, Syria, Iran and Iraq in a campaign of coercion would require the extensive use of tanker aircraft. Tankers could not be hidden in concrete shelters like the smaller fighter-bombers and were therefore much more vulnerable to terrorist attack and even the most inaccurate of Scud hits. Nato planners were aware of this, and the tanker and AWAC bases were accorded the highest priority in the allocation of robust airfield defence units, as well as Patriot SAM batteries (even though the latter were not proof against a determined Scud barrage). This was not, however, the only move by Nato. The lack of airbases within easy reach of Nato's southern area prompted SACEUR to order the US 2nd Fleet from the Atlantic to join the two carrier-strong battle groups of the US 6th Fleet in the Mediterranean. Additionally, one of the two carriers that had been in the Baltic was detached to join the gathering fleets in the Mediterranean. The second of the US's arsenal ships, the USS *Monitor*, was nearing the end of sea trials off Newport. All non-essential finishing work was abandoned and she sailed within seventy-two hours to join the 2nd Fleet as it prepared to enter the Strait of Gibraltar. The plan was that the rest of Europe's carriers, lightweight compared to their American counterparts but each with a couple of squadrons embarked, would join up with US units in Naples and thereafter proceed where required. The UK ordered HMS *Illustrious* to sail from her stand-by position in the western Baltic and HMS *Ark Royal* from Devonport to sail for the Mediterranean. Already in the Mediterranean were the Spanish carrier *Principe de Asturias*, the French carrier *Charles de Gaulle* (the most powerful of the European carriers with its sixty Rafale Ns – the two new British carriers, *Eagle* and *Hermes*, were still not complete and were subject to seemingly endless delay and wrangling between the MoD and the Treasury), and the Italian *Giuseppe Garibaldi*.

The moves by the US and Nato's air and naval units alone would, a decade beforehand, have been seen as an expensive overreaction. In 2006, however, with the experiences of Korea, China and the Baltic as supporting evidence, the doctrine gurus concluded that the proportionate and graduated use of force was not necessarily a valid concept in the new world (dis)order. Nato's natural disposition, given the full backing of nationalistic and pro-military governments, was now one of unstated belligerence, confidence, perceived superiority and a less appeasing attitude than at any time in its history. That this new doctrine was the real result of the 'CNN Effect' and the subsequent zero friendly casualty tolerance was unofficially acknowledged. If one used overwhelming and decisive force against an enemy then the conflict would almost invariably be shorter, and friendly casualties much fewer.

It was still an unfortunate surprise for Saladin and his military advisers to learn that Nato was preparing to spoil their plans and appeared to be serious about the use of ground forces. It would take time for the build-up of troops to be in a position to attack Israel, but he had hoped that Nato would stop short of sending virtually its entire air armada to the Middle East, let alone armoured divisions to Turkey. It was now that Saladin had reason to curse the Russians and their abortive attempt to take Riga airport. It had become clear as the days passed that the Russians had achieved the opposite of the intended effect of pinning down Nato's best troops thousands of miles away. Nato felt that her second-line troops, backed with sufficient air power, were more than a match for the best Russian troops on the Baltic front. Moreover, the build-up of reserve formations and the stockpiling of supplies in northern Europe had continued throughout the early summer. This had served to furnish a credible force whose primary aim was to underpin the diplomatic shuffles but was also actually capable of wresting the Baltic states back by force. By early August Nato was certain that Russia had no further designs or desire to re-engage militarily, and the transfer of ground troops and their stockpiles of ammunition and equipment from the cool

Baltic to Turkey's border with Syria and Iraq began in earnest.

The operation was massive and called for the movement of twelve Nato divisions, by air, land and sea, which would join twelve Turkish armoured and mechanised divisions. The non-Turkish Nato forces comprised: UK 1st Armoured; Spain's 1st Mech Division with an attached mountain brigade; France's 3rd Armoured Division and 1st Mech Division; Italy's 2nd Mech Division; Germany's 4th Panzer and 9th Panzer-grenadier Divisions; the US's 7th Armoured Corps of 2nd and 4th Armoured, 17th Mech and 26th Infantry Divisions and the 1st US Marine Division. Such a move of half a million combat troops and matériel was larger than that of 1991 and perhaps needs a little more explanation at this stage. The detractors of the plan cried foul and argued that it was an impossible task. Getting so many troops and their equipment to the Baltics and Poland had been no mean feat, and that was via a much shorter, better-developed transport infrastructure with multiple resupply lines. This bold move had everything against it, with choke points across the Bosporus and few good roads leading across the rugged terrain of southern Turkey. The unsung heroes of the operation would, if it succeeded, be the logisticians.

The Tungsten Lady, like Saladin, also had a vision of how the new world order should unfold, and her opportunity to shape it had come sooner than expected. She had long believed that the world should be run by the forces of democracy and stability (the US and her allies and anyone else who agreed with their outlook) without threat to the West's life-blood of oil and without threat to the existence of individual smaller nations. The US and the West had built up six months' worth of strategic oil and petroleum reserves for just such a situation, so the halting of all oil flowing out of the Middle East was of little immediate concern to the West. The Tungsten Lady had known all along that there would come a time in the twenty-first century when the US and the West would have to deal with nations or alliances that threatened these principles of world order, though she had not expected the confrontation to come as rapidly and as soon as now seemed likely. The Islamic Alliance was attempting, in her view, to cross all three boundaries, and had to be stopped. The Second Age of Revolution, by which the period of 2001 to 2006 is now known, and the emergence of Saladin had given the Islamic nations the ability and solidity to challenge the West. As a by-product the number of available bases for the West's primary instrument of foreign policy enforcement, air power, had been drastically reduced.

The closing of Hormuz in particular, and the subsequent Egyptian and Saudi mining of the Red Sea and closure of Suez, had pushed secure basing for aircraft even further away from potential target areas in the Middle East. Fully 75 per cent of the West's air assets would be unable to reach the most likely targets without air-to-air refuelling. And although this problem was not as critical as it might have been a decade earlier, thanks to the entry into service of long-range stand-off weapons such as Storm Shadow, Apache and SLAM, the conduct of air-to-surface war had not changed significantly when it came to mass. These smart weapons and their larger sisters, the cruise missiles, required excellent and timely intelligence to be employed effectively. While they could be pre-programmed to hit fixed sites and installations, the problem of using them in real time against a fluid enemy had not been fully solved. The US was able to use her new Data Link 20 to feed secure real-time targeting information from the strategic reconnaissance drones Global Hawk and Dark Star. The rest of Nato, however, was still converting to Link 16, which had become entry level standard for any nation that wanted to work in concert with US forces and take advantage of information the US chose to feed them via the link. Also, the specialist stand-off weapons were both expensive and relatively few in number. Thus the reality of an extended conflict meant that even with control of the skies at least 80 per cent of air-to-ground sorties would be conducted by fighter-bombers. These carried short-range weapons that required flight to within a few miles of any target if they were smart weapons and direct overflight if using dumb bombs. And the latter still dominated the West's weapons inventories.

The President and the Pentagon planners knew that this
was the real nub of the basing issue: for all the high tech in the
world, air power would only be decisive in a large-scale
conflict if sufficient weapons could be brought to bear on
targets that mattered. This could only be achieved on the scale
that it seemed would be required by fighter-bombers with
short-range weapons. The fighter-bombers could only reach
such targets either by an extensive use of air-to-air refuelling
tankers or by being launched from aircraft carriers close
inshore. Hence the vital importance in the plans being made
by both sides of tanker aircraft and carriers. Even then it was
clear that there would be a huge shortfall. Saladin had laid
plans to deal with both.

The US and her allies set a second deadline, this time for the
beginning of a strategic air campaign, of 1 September 2006.
This was determined as much by the time it would take to
have sufficient air units and adequate supplies in-theatre to
conduct a meaningful campaign as by anything else. The US
had twelve carriers supporting ten active battle groups. This
was around four short of what they required to meet the
simultaneous crises. In early August the US had two carriers in
dry dock, one in the Baltic, three in the Mediterranean, two in
the Arabian Sea, one off the Philippines, and three from the
Pacific Fleet near San Diego. An enhanced US Pacific Ocean
Carrier Strikefleet was ordered to assemble in San Diego to
prepare to sail to the Middle East. This would be the largest
assembled since World War II and included four carriers, with
one being rushed out of dry dock. The plan was that this
group would then join the pair from the Indian Ocean Fleet in
the Arabian Sea to become the most potent physical expression of naval air power and power projection seen since
Midway. However, it was the lack of 'in-range' air power
that precipitated the US President's decision to go for the
'Army Option', much to the delight of army, naval and
marine chiefs.

The President, the Pentagon and Nato's Military Council
agreed that the primary aims of 'Operation Western Shield',
as it would be known, were to guarantee the territorial
integrity of Turkey. This would have the effect of drawing

Islamic Alliance forces away from positions that threatened the 35,000 garrison troops in the Gulf. The forces of Western Shield would also act as a deterrent to more overt threats to Israel, and if deterrence failed they could act as peace enforcers through direct military action against errant states. The hidden agenda was also easily read. A sizable ground offensive carried out against Syria, Iraq, Iran and possibly also Saudi Arabia and Egypt by combined Nato and Turkish forces (with additional help from Israel to be expected) would rid the world of the 'threat' of what the President described as 'tinpot fanatical religious dictatorships hiding behind the respectability of greater Islam and the Sha'ria'. The Tungsten Lady saw the armed forces of the West as a 'force for good' that would eventually, as the US had done in Japan post-World War II, establish free and democratic regimes throughout the world. The defeat of the Islamic Alliance would be a first step in achieving this cherished dream. No sooner was the ink dry on the initial plans for this first step in ultimate global policemanship than it began to go off the rails.

Chapter Ten – The War in Sinai

Prelude to Sinai

From his command bunker in Tel Aviv, Major-General Moshe Levi, Chief of Staff of the Israeli Defence Forces, watched the build-up with both confidence and detached disbelief. In 1973 he had been second-in-command of a company of M-60 tanks and had seen these patterns before. Then Israel had hesitated to take any pre-emptive action against the build-up by the Egyptians, who were then on the other side of the Suez Canal, and it had nearly cost Israel her nationhood. She had become less sensitive to world opinion since then, and less reliant on foreign, especially American, imports of military hardware to sustain her forces. In 1973, even when it was obvious that the combined Arab forces would attack on both fronts, the air force was refused permission to strike a fearful blow, as it had done in 1967, on the morning of the combined Arab attack which was eventually launched just after lunch.

There were significant differences now. In the east, on the borders with Syria, Jordan and Lebanon, all was quiet. It was clear that although the Islamic Alliance armies in the east had mobilised, and even though there were increasing signs of a build-up by Iraqi, Saudi and Iranian forces in Jordan and Syria, these forces remained dispersed and clearly uncoordinated. Intelligence had indicated that it would take them at least two weeks if not three to be in position for an assault on Israel. And even when they were ready the nations involved would almost certainly face a US-led strategic air campaign. Although Levi, like his counterparts in Tehran and Washington, had serious doubts about the effectiveness of any strategic campaign, and was well aware of the shortfall of longer-

range tactical air power that was in the same class as the F-15I
Thunders. The Israeli view was that, in spite of the US and
Nato's prompt action, there would be little the West could
physically do to arrest a concerted attack on Israel before the
end of August. Saladin planned to steal a march on the West
by neutralising much of the potential air power available.
Additionally Turkey, despite her unfailing loyalty to Israel,
would not be persuaded to launch a supporting attack into
Syria and Iraq before the Nato heavies were both in place and
committed to action. Moreover, Turkey, ever opportunist,
was intent on using the 'preparation phase' to carry out her
own form of ethnic cleansing among the Kurds in southern
and eastern Turkey and northern Iraq. The West was forced
to turn a blind eye to Turkey's activities. Nato's military
planners knew that the major threat to the tenuous supply
lines of any sizable force in southern Turkey would come
from the various Kurdish independence factions. The Turkish
action was also an attack on the roots of Saladin, himself a
Kurd; his village was razed to the ground.

It was obvious to the Israeli High Command that a fer-
ocious assault on Israel was the Islamic intent; a simultaneous
attack from both sides of the country – a repeat of 1973 but
with significantly larger and more capable forces. The Algerian attack on Marseilles was taken by the Knesset military
committee as a clear sign of belligerent intent by the Islamic
Alliance. Israel was not going to sit and wait for VX nerve-
tipped Scuds to start arriving in her cities before she took
action. To Levi, and the rest of the military committee for that
matter, the solution was obvious. Strike west first at the
Egyptians and Libyans while on exercise, or just post-exer-
cise, using combined armour and air power in a blitzkrieg
campaign. Push them into the Suez Canal and beyond, then
turn to bolster defences in the east and prepare for major
thrusts on Damascus and Amman. Such a heavy blow in the
Sinai would, if powerful and destructive enough, possibly
persuade the rest of the Islamic Alliance that any conventional
assault on fortress Israel would be foolhardy. In military
history the great commanders had arisen from relative ob-
scurity as those who had the vision to see the windows of

opportunity and take them. For Levi, his time had come. He turned from his musing over the intelligence map on the wall and looked round at his expectant staff.

'OK, gentlemen and ladies, Operation Sword of David will commence forty-eight hours from now.'

The main exercises took place west of the passes between the high Sinai northern plateau and the Suez Canal and on the western side of the Canal. They were small (involving three Egyptian and one Libyan divisions) when compared to the total size of the mobilised forces that were mustering west of the Nile. The satellite reconnaissance pictures also revealed that the Egyptians had mobilised their entire pontoon bridging fleet. In the forty-eight hours following the closure of the Suez Canal the Egyptians and Libyans had successfully managed to get three armoured and three mechanised brigades across from Egypt proper into Sinai over some twenty bridges. These forces joined the exercising divisions in the Sinai. Once the forty-eight hours was up, Egypt promptly dismantled the twenty bridges used and held them ready for what Israeli Intelligence assumed would be further rapid deployment across the Canal. This was an impressive statement of capability, and Israel was sufficiently worried by the speed and weight of movement across the only natural barrier between her and her potential enemies to the west to consider multiple air strikes on the temporary bridges. She was dissuaded from taking pre-emptive action after the US received direct assurances from the Egyptian Prime Minister that there was no hostile intent whatever towards Israel. This was of course a bare-faced lie, but the Israelis accepted the assurance in the full knowledge that knocking out pontoon bridges was a difficult, costly and unrewarding exercise for air power. In 1973 waves of Israeli aircraft had flown the SAM and ZSU gauntlet in an attempt to stem the flow across the bridges. Every time a bridge was hit, however, the engineers simply cast off the damaged sections and replaced them with new ones. No single bridge was out of action for more than four hours.

It was an inescapable fact, however, that the pattern of deployment was, with the exception of the forces in Sinai,

virtually identical to that of 1973. The evidence was overwhelming. The Egyptians and Libyans had shown themselves
prepared to close the Suez Canal. They had done it once
without too much protest from the UN and could easily do it
again. The four Egyptian and one Libyan divisions in the Sinai
were not strong enough to hope to attack Israel and expect
any measure of success. Behind the Suez Canal, however, lay a
formidable force.

The Egyptians were no longer considered low-grade cannon fodder with second-class equipment – although the
smaller Libyan forces still fell into this category according
to Israeli intelligence documents. Ever since the Russians had
been thrown out of Egypt in the mid-1970s, Egypt had
carefully cultivated a close military relationship with the
USA. The packages that followed included the very best in
terms of training and training advisery teams, as well as top-
notch equipment. By 2006 the Egyptian Army, 300,000
strong, boasted no fewer than four armoured divisions, eight
mechanised infantry divisions, four powerful Republican
Guard divisions, and several independent brigades. The Republican Guard divisions were formed by the Revolutionary
Government initially, like Hitler's SS, to act as a private police
force. The commanders of these 'élite' units argued successfully for priority treatment in terms of men and equipment.
The resulting formations were also similar to the German SS
divisions in that they were larger than their regular sisters,
received the most and the best equipment, and had two
artillery brigades each (equipped with self-propelled 155-
mm M-109A2s) as opposed to the normal one. The reorga-
nisation of the army following the revolution saw all eight
hundred M1A1 Abrams tanks assigned to the Revolutionary
Guard armoured brigades, and these were easily a match for
the Israeli Merkava 3s. The other armoured units had all but
discarded their Russian equipment; only the mechanised
divisions were equipped with Russian T-62s. The remainder
shared around 1,750 American M60A3s between them. The
Egyptian Air Force had also seen a quantum leap in its
lethality thanks to two decades of closer ties with the US.
The last MiG-21s were retired in 2002 and by 2006 the EAF

had two hundred F-16s (mostly Cs) and seventy-five Mirages (thirty Mirage 2000s). Of all Israel's neighbours it was Egypt which was therefore the most formidable on paper, and the Israeli General Staff was well aware of this. The nightmare scenario for Israel was to be forced to fight a war simultaneously on both her borders against what was becoming a far more capable opponent. This had happened in 1973 and, although Israel triumphed, the memory still sent shudders through the halls of power.

The Israeli General Staff knew that the Egyptians' use of their bridging equipment had been measured. If they again threw pontoon bridges across the Canal they would be able to move a great deal more equipment, men and material across to the east bank in a very short space of time. Israel might have as little as one week's notice of an attack out of Sinai. Once formed up on the east bank of the Canal, it was certain that any forces would move east rapidly – along the superb network of military roads constructed by Israel between 1967 and 1973 – to deploy into jump-off positions for the inevitable attack on Israel. Such an attack would certainly be co-ordinated with an assault from out of Jordan, Syria and Saudi Arabia. This scenario was not one the Israeli High Command was prepared to allow to develop.

On 10 August, just three days after the closure of the Suez Canal, Egypt announced that on 13 August she would be carrying out a further series of exercises, this time lasting seventy-two hours. The Israeli High Command and government convened an emergency meeting of the National Military Council in closed session. After thirteen hours of heated discussion through into the early hours of 11 August, it was the military and Cabinet hawks who emerged victorious. The Prime Minister and his war cabinet were persuaded by the conclusion that war with some or all of Israel's neighbours was inevitable within the next few weeks or months, if not imminent in the following days. The IDF therefore planned to mount a spoiling operation into the Sinai. This would be a rapid attack of speed and manoeuvre with the Israeli armour concentrated with attack helicopters to keep the enemy off balance. The armour's main thrusts would enable it to get in

behind the key positions and destroy the lines of communication and supply, before delivering a coup de grâce on
what were expected to be rapidly retreating Egyptian and
Libyan units in Sinai. The primary aim of this attack would be
to capture the Sinai and secure the east bank of the Suez Canal
before Egypt and Libya could bring significant forces to bear.
The Israelis would then dig in so that any attack the Egyptians
were considering would have to be made through a costly
assault across a major, well-defended water barrier – the least-
favoured type of attack practised in staff colleges the world
over. The secondary aim was initially to deliver a knockout
blow to the Egyptian and Libyan forces east of Suez and then,
if the opportunity arose, to push on to the west bank of the
Canal and repeat the destruction wrought in 1973. In any
event, the desired end state of the campaign christened 'Sword
of David' was, if not to eliminate the threat in the west from
Egypt and Libya, to make it doubly difficult for any ground
assault to commence. If this was not entirely achieved the
Israelis would at least have the consolation of inflicting
significant casualties on the enemy and would gain a significant amount of land – the whole of the Sinai Peninsula – for
defence in depth, strategic manoeuvre and post-conflict negotiations.

The justification for the assault seemed all the more assured
when Egypt amended the announcement of the second set of
exercises to extend the timescale to seven days and the scope
to up to eight divisions across the whole of the Sinai Peninsula. Curiously, in what looked like anticipation of the Israeli
strike, the activity across the Canal was already at fever pitch
by 9 August. Israeli strategic reconnaissance confirmed that
additional units were pouring east across the Canal and
forming up on the east bank. If Israel needed proof of Egypt's
intent, surely this was it.

The attack was originally set to begin at dawn on 12 August
2006. However, at midnight on the 11th/12th forward commanders were beginning to receive reports that Egypt's military engineers had indeed successfully constructed no fewer
than twenty-seven pontoon bridges across the Canal and were
operating around half that number of ferries. The more

Egyptian units got to the east bank the less the chances of an Israeli lightning victory were. High Command began to hesitate while intelligence reports were confirmed. The men in the front line anticipated the bringing forward of the date and time of the attack to try to catch the Egyptians before they had any real cohesion. The time to attack was now. The tank commanders cared not a jot for the political niceties. They were delighted that the army had been given a mission for which it was purpose built – heavy armour assault. The revised order for the Israeli attack came through at 0600 on the 12th. Men like Brigadier Gabriel Yosef, commanding the 7th Armoured Brigade, were disappointed. The assault would begin at dawn on the 13th. During the next eighteen hours he managed only two hours of snatched sleep as his brigade completed frantic preparations for the attack. The proactive strategy was much more to his liking. In an offensive mode the Israelis would retain the initiative, attacking at the times and places of their choosing. The further incentive for a rapid campaign of destruction was that if it was powerful enough the Islamic Alliance might think twice about an attack against Israel's eastern border. In any event the more powerful units of the Israeli Army would have time to redeploy to face the threat from the east, with their rear and flanks secure, and might even be in a position to launch a second spoiling campaign. This bold strategy was far preferable to having to defend a broad front with little or no room for retreat, pressed in by enemies on both sides. This was what had happened in 1973, and Israel was not going to make the same mistake again. As far as Gabriel Yosef and the majority of the Israeli Defence Forces were concerned, world opinion could go hang. 'World opinion' did not have its very survival at stake. Israel did.

There are only four axes of advance across the Sinai: in the north is the long, straight coast road from El Arish to El-Qantara. This is separated from the next east–west axis, the road to Redifim and Ismalia, by twenty-five to forty miles of sand dunes and the Jebel El-Maghara. Running fifteen miles parallel to the latter, and separated by the towering jebels of Yelleq and El-Hallal, is the Bir Hasanah and Suez City route.

Finally, to the south there is a highway of dubious quality running from the southern tip of Israel at Aqaba which links up with the Bir Hasanah highway just east of the Mitla Pass. SIGINT and satellite reconnaissance indicated that rather than continuing east as expected to form up near the Israeli border, the enemy units had halted and were digging in in strong defensive positions. Part of the Israeli plan, and one of the keys to its success, was the presumption that the swift Israeli armoured assault would catch the majority of the enemy units in transit, do enough damage to initiate a panic, and the rest would be a turkey-shoot. Indeed, the IAF would be able to excel at blasting the inevitable traffic jams that any mass movement of armies entails. This job would be all the easier if the Egyptians were caught in transit to jump-off positions, since the formidable Egyptian Air Defence Command would not have its layered SAM umbrella in place if the Israelis struck swiftly enough.

Levi was, for the first time in his life, clouded with doubt. Had they misread the enemy intent? Surely not, because with every minute that passed another dozen vehicles headed east over the Canal. But the Egyptians were digging in and, as their dispositions became more clear with time, it looked to Levi like a well-prepared defence in depth. All along the main access routes into Sinai, Israeli troops were ready to launch. Any further delay now or reversal of the decision might, in the longer term, leave Israel less prepared in the future, and she might also pass up the chance of dealing decisively with a significant portion of her hostile neighbours's military potential. Levi was also well aware that the direction of the Egyptian/Libyan troop movements could be reversed in a matter of hours. If too many enemy divisions were allowed unfettered transport to the east bank of the Canal their sheer numbers might lessen the blow of the intended Israeli lightning strike.

In Levi's command bunker they watched the easterly movement of the forces into Sinai. There was a growing sense of unease, however, as the impression in Levi's HQ grew that the Egyptians were waiting for them. Levi decided that the growing evidence of the Egyptian's digging in merited consideration by the Prime Minister himself, and by midday on the 12th the war cabinet had reconvened to study the evidence and weigh up the pros and cons of continuing with an assault on the 13th. A six-hour debate ensued, and it was decided, on balance, that Israel still had to take the initiative. The timing of the assault was again delayed from its original start time of dawn on the 13th to begin with air and artillery attacks at midnight on the 13th followed by the ground assault at dawn on the 14th.

Operation Sword of David – The Seven-Day War

In the minutes before dawn on 14 August, Brigadier Gabriel Yosef stood up in the turret of his command tank and from the small hillock surveyed the desert ahead in the growing dawn through his binoculars. The Merkava 3 was arguably still the best all-round tank in the world. He, at the tender age of thirty-eight, was in command of some hundred of the monsters. The legendary Israeli 7th Armoured would soon be on the move again. He could hardly wait, confident in the ability of his men and machines to sweep aside all opposition that the Egyptians and Libyans might be able to muster against them.

The Merkava 3 was uniquely Israeli, born in battle, developed through hard-won action. The heavy tank was still the queen of the desert, no matter what the helicopter boys thought. The past three decades had seen the world of heavy tank design try to get the balance right between mobility, firepower and protection. The M1 Abrams was an attempt to be a world-beater in all three areas. The German Leopards 2 and 3 had developed from a fast and relatively lightly armoured fighting vehicle into one where extra armour was being continually added to give it the protection somewhere near that enjoyed by the Abrams and the British Challenger 2. The Israelis had considered buying Leopards but the official report had concluded that they were great machines as long as you didn't fire at them with anything. In contrast to the rest of the world, the Israeli tank designers had come down firmly on the side of protection. The resulting Merkava 3 with its appliqué and reactive armour and with the crew situated behind the engine was easily the most survivable tank of the early twenty-first century. Such protection gave rise to huge confidence among the tank men. They felt unstoppable, and were eager to take part in what promised, at last, to be some decisive military action after the years of messy border wars, bus bombs, occupation and terror. There was the added advantage that, except for Gaza on the right flank, there would be no fighting in built-up areas. The Israelis had been hurt in 1982 in southern Lebanon fighting in the small towns and villages where they were vulnerable to ambush from RPG-7 rockets fired at point-blank range. The open desert was their element, and, combined with artillery and attack helicopters, they intended to be a hot knife through butter.

Yosef mused on the developments of the past three weeks which had brought him and his brigade to within minutes of action. Military Intelligence had a clear picture of the Egyptian and Libyan force deployments. There was only a light covering force of infantry supported by occasional tanks along the border with Israel. However, he and his men were aware of substantial forces arrayed behind the thin picket line just across the border. Indeed, there were indications that the Egyptians and Libyans had significant armoured forces arrayed in Sinai. If that was the case there was nothing so invigorating as a good tank battle to sort the men from the boys. Just a week previously Egypt had announced the closure of the Suez Canal for forty-eight hours as part of an unprecedented joint exercise with the bulk of the Libyan Army and Air Force. Forces unknown had then physically blocked it with the supertanker. The other three major partners in the Islamic Alliance, Iran, Iraq and Saudi Arabia, were not an immediate concern for Israel. While they were occupied on the brink of war with the West over the control of the Persian Gulf and the reopening of the Straits of Hormuz, and while the transfer of men and equipment continued from east to west, they would not be in a position to threaten Israel. And Turkey's timely mobilisation and the first of Nato's reinforcements would fully occupy the attention of Syria. Yosef was, like most senior unit commanders, furious about the uncertainty and the delay. The units assigned for the attack had reached a peak of readiness. It would now be difficult to maintain that peak in the face of rumour and counter-rumour. Worse, the delay greatly increased the chances of the Egyptians divining the exact nature and scale of the forthcoming Israeli operation, and would enable them to throw even more forces across the Suez Canal and give increased preparation time for those units digging in. Now the waiting was nearly over.

Just before midnight the previous evening Yosef had sat with his six battalion commanders and the artillery and air fire control officers in the M577 command vehicle going over the attack plans for this morning. The 7th Armoured's initial mission, acting as an independent brigade, was to protect the right flank of Saul Division's attack down the Redifim road and the left flank of the Magen Division's attack on El Arish. The first line of resistance had been identified as running from El Arish to the Jebel El Halal. The expected opposition along this line consisted of two Egyptian mechanised divisions separated by a Libyan infantry division. All officers expressed discontent at the delay but were excited at the prospect of action. Yosef had only a tightly knotted stomach and a certainty that however carefully the plans had been laid they would have to be adapted after the first contact with the enemy. His men had yet to taste the fog and friction that separate real war from exercises. The winner would be he who appreciated the changing situation and reacted the quickest. Under their command was, for the first time in Israel's history, a whole generation of soldiers without high-tempo combat experience. The sound of jets passing overhead unseen in the black sky brought smiles to their faces. The F-16s and F-4E2000s had begun pounding identified defensive positions to prepare the way for the morning attack. Yosef warned his men not to expect too much from the air power passing overhead. Air power always looked impressive. To the accompaniment of bombs and air-to-ground missiles exploding only fifteen miles to the west, causing the horizon to light up orange and red, Yosef went on to explain that it sounded good too. He had, however, been on the receiving end of Israeli air power in 1982, and had had cause to be thankful then that for all the high explosive and columns of smoke that accompanied air bombardment it was rarely as impressive in terms of actual results – men and material neutralised – especially against an enemy that was dug in. For air power to be effective against such positions it required mass, something only the US possessed, and the persistence of repeated attacks – regardless of the pilots' genuine but misleading claims about damage inflicted.

The horizon to the front of the brigade was clear except for a couple of columns of thin grey smoke. At five minutes to go Yosef gave the simple order: 'Seventh Brigade start engines.' A cacophony of a hundred diesel engines roaring into life followed. With two minutes to go the driver and gunner confirmed that all the Merkava's systems were up and functioning well. The sun peeped above the eastern horizon, casting long shadows to the west and giving the flat country ahead an unreal low red tinge. The second hand on Yosef's Tag Heuer ticked down to 0500. He stood up in his turret, glanced left and right at the mighty force under his command, and brought his arm up and then rapidly down, pointing east. The Merkavas set off at a careful pace across the desert. No one wanted to throw a track or become bogged in soft sand just past the start line and miss out on the prospect of an exciting few days in the history of the glorious 7th. Overhead, noses dipped menacingly towards the ground as though sniffing out prey, swept eight AH-64 Apaches. They headed west, looking full of purpose and a self-assurance that gave the tank men who were watching confidence. They would see and make contact with any resistance first. Each had eight Hellfire missiles and two full pods of rockets under the wing-stub pylons, for dealing with armoured and non-armoured targets respectively, as well as a 30mm cannon.

All the doubts that had preceded this moment vanished from Yosef's mind. How could anybody stop such a force? Leading a hundred tanks, each kicking up its own cloud of dust, gave Yosef an excess of the 'feel good factor'. He was certain that whatever lay ahead his men and machines would cope, and within the week, if not sooner, he assumed, they would be on the banks of the Suez Canal. His men would cope, but the attempt to get there would indeed be a new experience for the Israeli Army.

The Sinai Desert: A Soldier's View

The night was black and cold – dry desert cold that makes the bones ache. Was this the moment in his life that Ijaz had been waiting for? Tonight he was sure his men would be given orders to unleash the massive attack on an uncomprehending Israel. Death, destruction and revenge on Zion would surely follow. Major Ijaz Al Kindi, commander of C Company, 3rd Brigade, of the Libyan 'Lion' Infantry Division, pulled a cigarette from the crumpled packet in his breast pocket. He lit it with his 1991 Pennsylvania original Zippo without a cupped hand, in defiance of the desert breeze. He had come a long way since his capture during the war for the liberation of Kuwait. As a mercenary, or foreign adviser to the Iraqi Army, he had been fêted on his release. He thought back to those heady days. It was then that he had first tasted Western cigarettes, an unexpected gift tossed into a group of dishevelled and frightened PoWs by a sympathetic Scots Guardsman. The aristocratic officer had given him the Zippo after his interview; he said he was trying to give up. Ijaz had never worked out how the white soldiers all looked so healthy and without exception slightly overweight in a climate that must be so alien to them.

His company had been without fresh food for two days. However, although the water had also stopped arriving they had been able to send a truck with jerry cans back to the wadi to draw supplies. The logistic effort to organise such an exercise on a massive scale at short notice was huge, and it was no surprise to anyone that it hadn't been completely organised. In fact his unit's part in the 'exercise' had been a simple march east to the border with Israel. They had been ordered to dig in just east of the El Arish wadi, which was one of the very few green areas in the arid Sinai Peninsula. The sacrifices and discomfort would surely be worth it in the end. Worse for Ijaz, the supply of Moroccan cigarettes had stopped as soon as the commander had informed them that this was no longer an exercise. He was now down to his last two packets and was trying to cut down to just one cigarette an hour, which was difficult. They had also been issued with live ammunition and spare gas masks, but no further orders. He couldn't help thinking that his men were far closer to Israel than they needed to be for a military exercise. The unit should have stayed in Libya, near the border at El Alamein would have been perfect, protecting the Scud battalions there perhaps. Here in the eastern Sinai they were blindingly obvious targets. His discomfort deepened as he mused on the possibility that they had been deliberately misinformed by higher headquarters, put there to attract attacks. His left knee started to shake uncontrollably; even now the fear of a certain, pointless, miserable, agonising death filled his dreams and his moments of empty thoughts. Last night the air had been filled with the unmistakable sounds of tank engines being gunned to the rear. He assumed that the armour was being manoeuvred into position ready for an attack. Only much later would he realise what was going on.

His infantry company had a platoon of aged T-80s assigned to them and a platoon from the 56th Engineers. He didn't like the tank men very much, strutting around in the sun in their black overalls, barking alternate orders and insults to the infantrymen to dig 'proper' tank pits for the forty-five-ton monsters. The sides of the emplacement were never quite high enough or straight enough or thick enough to satisfy the armoured egos. A full week they had sweated, before the lieutenant, who boasted three wives and an apartment on Gaddafi Avenue in Tripoli, declared himself satisfied. He wore a stainless-steel crescent moon on a chain around his neck. His gold teeth and arrogant self-assurance were enough to ensure instant servility, envy and dislike in those he chose to give orders to. He had said the evening before the first bombs came that this assignment was only temporary for him; his uncle was in the process of getting him a platoon of T-100s in the Guards Tank Brigade, currently on truck transports *en route* between Cairo and Gaza. That would be where the war was won, the lieutenant had declared, not here by the peasantry, the 'cannon fodder', as he called them, in the middle of nowhere, miles from the real front line. The last time Ijaz had seen the lieutenant alive was when he'd contemptuously hoicked a ball of thick green spittle in the direction of the section huddled around an inadequate fire before retiring to his airbed under the warm engines of the tank.

Ijaz awoke from his doze at the sound of jets high overhead. It was just after midnight. This must be it, he thought; at last the offensive to eliminate Israel would be under way. In theory they should've received orders to move and join in the offensive last night. Maybe this was being left to the Egyptian mechanised units north and south of their position. This conundrum was solved for him when the number-two tank exploded in a shower of white-metal sparks, at first turning the night into day, then everything into black as the fireball subsided and his eyes failed to keep pace with the rapidly changing light conditions. The blast wave had kept them all pinned to the desert floor; the hot air whipped their thin blankets and blew the red talc-like sand into their eyes and nostrils. Ijaz recovered sufficiently to look up again at the number-two tank, which was fizzing, grumbling and spitting as its ammunition exploded inside, giving its intestines a grudging and destructive internal fireworks display. The number-three tank was the next hit. Its turret, sheared off whole, was flung into the desert sky, toppling end over end as it went. Then there were shouts. Ijaz recognised the lieutenant's voice, shrieking and screaming like a traumatised child. The voice became muffled as its owner slid unseen into his tank. The diesel engine splattered unhurriedly into life, its exhaust fumes adding to the stench of cordite and another, more nauseating, sweeter smell, which Ijaz did not then recognise. The T-80 lurched two feet back up the pit where it had nestled so securely before stalling in a graunching of gears. The voice was now squeaking in a mixture of anger, fear and rage. Ijaz began to pray quietly to Allah; he wished noise didn't carry so well in the desert air. It was then that the lieutenant's tank was hit. The first bomb landed fifty yards to the north, the second, a blink of an eye later, went straight through the front glacis plate where the driver was sitting. Neither detonated. The lead tank seemed to pause, as if unsure how to react to the intrusion of 2,000 lb of metal fragments and high explosive. It then split at the seams, jets of furious white and purple fire issuing through the weaker points where the tank's shell had given way in an effect like that of a firecracker inside a crustacean. Out of the turret hatch Ijaz saw a black figure emerge, climbing through the issuing inferno which looked like a jet engine on full afterburner. The figure jumped to the ground, ran twenty yards and collapsed in a smouldering heap. The noise of the jets died away as quickly as it had come. Ijaz counted slowly to a thousand before he dared to move. He then got up and called over the machinegun section. Gingerly they crawled to where Ijaz was. Together the three men moved at a slow crouch towards the body, wary lest the three metallic pyres had further nasty surprises. The body was on its side. Ijaz turned it over, a chunk of charred boiler suit and something sticky coming away in his hand as he did so, exposing a pure white upper arm of bone. The machinegun loader shone a dim torch into the face, which was in shadow. There was no face, only a black and brown skull with spots of white. The teeth were fixed together in a grim smile, held there by the fusing of upper and lower golden molars. Ijaz then noticed the sweet smell again. He checked the rising vomit in his throat and turned away in disgust. The lieutenant was probably dead before he got out of the tank, Ijaz concluded; the nerve endings and muscles had continued to carry out the brain's instructions until they were burned away. Ijaz threw his blanket over the shrivelled cadaver and motioned to his men. In the morning they would bury him, only temporarily, of course.

No one slept for the rest of that night. Ijaz swore at his radio operator, who was unable to reach any higher command net. They listened to the sound of jets overhead all night, unseen and menacing. The sound of distant thunder rumbled on and on to the north and east as the jets found their targets. Occasionally the horizons glowed brightly and suddenly with high explosive and then faded more slowly. The desert night disappeared as quickly as it had come. The sun rose steeply and with it the temperature. Ijaz looked over at the tanks. Once so menacing and full of military might when the men had retired to their blankets last night. Now a platoon of 135 tons of useless steel. The number-three tank was turretless and clearly wrecked. The other two looked fine from this distance, except for blackening around the edges and at the seams where the internal agonies of their destruction had split the sides. Thin wisps of acrid smoke rose from both.

Ijaz decided to make a personal inspection of the tanks, after breakfast, of course, and after another bout of swearing at the hapless and apparently incompetent radio man. He lit up his first cigarette of the day. There wasn't a better start to the day than a breakfast of gritty, hot, sweet coffee and a couple of stale cigarettes. They had just got the fire going when the infantry company commander appeared. They had hardly seen him during the four days. He yelled at them to stand to. They were at war now and the Zionist assault would begin today following the softening-up air attack last night. How did he know all this? Ijaz wondered. Weren't we supposed to be attacking the Israelis? What was going on? The machinegun group jumped down into their pit. Salim was only a boy of sixteen but he was a good gunner. Abdul was married with three children. A piano teacher by profession. Now his deft fingers were used to feed the belts of ammunition smoothly into the gun. He had been positively plump when he joined up a month ago. Now he was dried out and thin. More of a raisin than a prune. With his weight had gone his interest, his joviality and his enthusiasm for everything. He wanted to go home.

Ijaz jumped into his pit. It was no more than six feet long, two feet wide and four feet deep. The end two feet had a step so that a man with an anti-aircraft missile had room to stand up, pivot round and fire. Ijaz's pit was grandly called the 'surface-to-air missile position'. To him it remained a pit; a coffin-sized one at that. Ijaz's missile man, Hussein, had three

missiles. They were old SA-14 Gremlins of Russian origin. Ijaz
wondered at their effectiveness against modern fighter-bombers. He had had two hours of instruction from the divisional
'expert' before the expert had to move on to the next SAM
position-holder. Only fire at receding targets. Do not fire
unless the heat signature is strong enough – the light will come
on to tell you this. Launch angle must be a minimum of 15
degrees above the horizon. The missiles will not catch targets
doing in excess of 1,000 km/h or above 3,000 metres altitude.
Ijaz could feel the warmth of the sun begin to tingle happily on
his left cheek as he gazed east towards the rising hills of the
Negev central plateau. It was then that he saw them. Black
dots emerging out of a hidden gully to the east. The images
shimmered, distorted by the heat rising off the desert floor.
The sound of distant high-bass hammering reached their
positions to confirm his worst fears.

'Locusts, a plague of locusts!' was all he could yell before
diving into the slit trench. Eight AH-64 Apache helicopters
nosed their way menacingly forward. Death for many was
only a couple of minutes away.

Collecting his thoughts, Ijaz lay in the bottom of the trench,
trying unsuccessfully to strap his tin helmet on. In a couple of
minutes the gunships would be upon them, spraying death
and destruction. Ijaz and his men were not equipped to deal
with armoured gunships. The choices were obvious. They
could sit there and die, or they could run. Surrender did not
occur to him. In an instant his mind was made up. The first
green bushes of the wadi were only 800 metres to the east. If
they could reach those . . .

'Abdul, Salim, Hussein, let's go! Come on! Get out of here!'
Salim, the boy, looked at him querulously, and apparently
without fear, turning round from his position behind the
machinegun. His voice was level and controlled against the
growing clamour of approaching helicopter blades.

'Are you going to give up without fighting the evil Zio-
nists?' Ijaz couldn't believe such a stupid question. How was it
that teenagers all felt themselves to be immortal? He had no
time to explain. Abdul and Hussein had understood instantly
what was going on. Hussein dropped the surface-to-air mis-

sile unceremoniously into the bottom of the trench and Abdul
let go of the links of machinegun ammunition he was cradling.

'In the face of such superior enemy forces I intend to make a
tactical withdrawal,' Ijaz explained. Salim was furious as he
reached down to pick up the missile.

'You are cowards. You are running away. I will report you
to the authorities for this treachery as soon as this is over.'

'To do that, my little friend' – Ijaz lowered his voice to a
condescending father-to-son tone – 'you will have to get out
of this alive. May God be with you.'

With that Ijaz and the other two were up and out of the
trench, sprinting for all they were worth to the safety promised by the green vegetation of the wadi. The other men of
the company were not slow to follow and soon there were
sixty of them running across the desert scrub. They had
covered just two hundred metres when there was the unmistakable thwacking that signifies high-velocity cannon shells
passing overhead and near by. The Apaches had opened up
on the rabble running for cover. The 30mm shells crashed and
cracked as they ricocheted off the rocks and stones that lay
strewn in abundance. Ijaz and his companions hit the deck
and instinctively belly-crawled behind the nearest large
boulder. To the left and right of them men were still running.
Ijaz winced as he saw a group of a dozen only twenty-five
metres away scythed down in the angry hail spitting from the
gunships. Soon there was no one left running. The short
silence that followed was broken by the screams of men
coming to terms with their newly shattered bodies as they
floundered in the dirt in pain and tried to stop their lives
spilling out on to the desert floor.

Ijaz, his breath recovered but his chest still stinging and raw
from the effort of his first extended sprint for over two
decades, ventured a peek out from behind the boulder. He
looked back at the company trenches and saw the lone figure
of Salim standing in the trench with the SAM at his shoulder.
He saw Salim fire the SAM at one of the approaching Apaches. The missile left the tube at high speed and dived
straight into the ground a hundred metres ahead of Salim's
exposed position before skipping vertically upwards in an

uncontrolled spiral and then dropping like a used firework.
Salim had had no training on the SAMs, so it was little
wonder that he hadn't elevated the launcher sufficiently.
Two of the gunships took an immediate interest in this first
distraction of their destructive efforts and lined up on Salim's
trench. Unperturbed, Ijaz watched Salim fire the machinegun
at the approaching helicopters, which were now more than a
little curious. Salim disappeared in a cloud of dust kicked up
by a short burst of cannon fire from the nearest Apache. Ijaz
admired his spirit and determined to recommend him for a
medal after the war – posthumously, of course.

Salim's lone attack on the Apaches temporarily halted the
hail of fire that was being rained on the now much-reduced
company, who were either hit or cowering. As one they rose
again and resumed their sprint for the wadi. Ijaz and his men
were saved by two small groups of men who tried to surrender. One group was massacred, apparently without mercy, as
they stood waving their arms and dirty rags and bits of
clothing they hoped would be seen as flags of truce. In the
heat of the battle the Apaches probably didn't even realise
that they were trying to surrender. The second group, however, had more luck, probably because they had deployed a
large white sheet. Where they got that from Ijaz could scarcely
imagine, but he didn't care anyway as they reached the edge of
the wadi with the Apaches hovering menacingly yet uncertain
of what to do near the men trying to surrender. The distraction was enough and Ijaz, Abdul and Hussein sprinted grate-
fully through the increasing amounts of vegetation before
diving head first down the wadi sides and out of sight of the
helicopters.

They hid, panting, cut and bruised, beside one of the many
varieties of thorny bushes on the wadi's eastern slopes. The
Apaches were hesitant to fly over the wadi as it would be an
easy place in which to conceal a deadly anti-air ambush, either
with a mass of shoulder-fired SAMs or small arms and AAA
fire. For fifteen long minutes Ijaz and his men hid, their faces
pressed to the sandy soil, and listened to the Apaches roving
north and south along what had been the divisional defensive
position. The combined clattering of their blades was inter-

rupted by bursts of gunfire, from heroes like Salim no doubt, thought Ijaz, which were responded to in kind by the heavier hammering of the Apache's cannons or the 'swoosh-bangs' of air-to-ground rockets being fired. Finally, and mercifully for the dozen men who were all that was left of 'C' Company, they either lost interest or ran out of ammunition and were last heard disappearing north towards El Arish.

Ijaz called his remaining colleagues to his position. To a man they looked dishevelled and beaten up. Only four of them had retained their weapons. Ijaz had regained his composure and authority as company commander and re-iterated his intent to live to fight another day. They would, he stated, cross the El Arish road and the wadi and aim to regroup some seven miles to the west on the road to the airbase at Libni. There, he was sure, they would find some Egyptian or fellow Libyan units they could join.

Four hours later they had covered the distance. The sun was vertically above them and its unmerciful beating on their backs had reduced them all to stooping figures dampened by their own sweat. The road was empty when they reached it. High above they could hear but not see the sound of military jets carving sonic booms through the sky. Six or so miles to the south was Libni airbase. Ijaz could see columns of thick black smoke rising through the shimmering heat haze. There also was the sound of heavy gunfire and the rumble that indicated the movement of massed armoured vehicles coming from that direction, and Ijaz was not inclined to walk straight into the enemy. Suddenly, from the north, coming out of El Arish, appeared a small column of vehicles apparently trying to break the speed limit. As they approached Ijaz saw that the lead Jeep, a wide-bodied American-made Hummer, was proudly sporting the green, white and red Egyptian tricolour. This emboldened him to step out into the middle of the road and wave the convoy down. The Jeep screeched to a halt inches from Ijaz, who stood unmoving. An angry Egyptian major jumped out brandishing a new AKM assault rifle in Ijaz's general direction. Ijaz noticed the deep green collar flashes with 'Revolutionary Guard' etched in contrasting white

Arabic script. What on earth were they doing here? Ijaz had heard that they were being kept well in reserve.

'What the fuck do you think you're up to?' asked the short major without ceremony. 'We nearly ran you over.'

'We're trying to rejoin remnants of our unit, Third Brigade, Libyan Lion Division. We were in the wadi this morning.' The major's attitude changed.

'I hear you took quite a beating. Anyhow, we've already picked up a couple of your men a few kilometres north. We're short of infantry support so get your men into the second of our three support trucks, and fast – there should be enough room. The Israelis have reached El Arish but we're not caving in this time.' Without further ado he jumped back into the Hummer, which sped off southbound. Behind the lead Jeep came six French-made 4 × 4 Panhard P4Rs, two mounting flat-folded radars and the other four carrying four Crotale missile boxes each. Ijaz realised, as the second lorry pulled up, that this was one of the mobile SAM batteries that the Guards had 'acquired' from the air defence forces for their own protection. After travelling south for just a kilometre or so, the lorry swung off west, following the other vehicles along a poorly marked dirt track. Through the flapping canvas Ijaz could see that they were heading for the southern end of a range of low hills. The driver crashed down through the gears, gunning the engine, his shouts urging the lorry to keep up with those in front as the ground rose steadily. None of them wanted to be caught like this out in the open.

Just under twenty minutes later they had reached the summit. On it was a destroyed early-warning radar. Ijaz surmised that it had taken a hit from an Israeli anti-radiation missile the night before when the first Israeli jets had appeared overhead. There was a great deal of shouting as the short major stood like an imperious traffic cop, directing each vehicle into position as they arrived. Ijaz jumped down with the other men and watched the lorry trundle off down the western slope to a less exposed position. The major, traffic direction over, beckoned to Ijaz and told him to take charge of the platoon-sized collection of stray

Libyans. The battery men would need help camouflaging the vehicles and digging trenches. And there was Salim, getting off the last truck. Somehow he had survived. The major, efficient and businesslike, jabbed his finger at the map he was holding. Ijaz would have to have a chat with Salim later, just to clear up the misunderstanding. He was sure Salim would understand.

'This is Hill 1191.' The major was jabbing insistently, demanding full attention. Ijaz was impressed; the man reminded him of the British officers he'd met as a PoW – he was clearly a professional.

'Our mission is to provide low-altitude air defence for the First Guards Division. The Division will be putting in a counter-attack to the south-east, across the northern end of the Libni airbase.' He looked up and pointed in the general direction. For the first time Ijaz noticed below the spectacular view of the desert plain they had just crossed, stretching bright yellow to the east before merging with the greens of the wadi just below the horizon.

'Now that you are temporarily under my command I shall exercise full authority over you and your men. Is that clear?' Ijaz nodded dumbly. 'Should we come under direct attack you will command the warning force and rearguard, here just below the summit on the eastern side, while we move to a safer position from our location in the dead ground to the west. Your men will be able to get all the weapons, picks and shovels they require from the first truck. Let me know when they have finished their work and are ready.' Ijaz was surprised at the man's confidence, and considered a protest about there being nothing between their exposed position on the hill and the advancing Israeli hordes. He also wondered why the Crotales were being placed below the heights on the western side of 1191 when in order to fire at anything attacking from the east they ought to be sighted where Ijaz and his men would be, on the eastern side overlooking the whole of the plain. Ijaz thought better of venturing an opinion. The man clearly knew what he was up to.

The major did not wait for any response anyway, turned on his heel and left to supervise the exact sighting of the radar and missile Panhards. The Crotale is a very capable system it can engage targets at between less than 50 feet and 10,000 feet, out to a maximum range of 10 kilometres. Its most worrying feature for opposing aircrews is its ability to acquire, track and engage targets almost entirely passively via an integrated TV tracker. This means that aircraft would be unaware that they were under attack unless they spotted the missile launch and that the battery site would have to be 'hard-killed' by iron bombs as anti-radar missiles would have nothing to lock on to, giving them no opportunity for a 'soft-kill'.

As the afternoon drew on, the men on Hill 1191 settled down to wait. The sounds of distant battle to the south grew uncomfortably closer. Little was seen of the IAF. Then, at just after 1600, Ijaz spotted a growing dust cloud several miles to the south which seemed to be heading north-west. He shivered. Israeli armour!

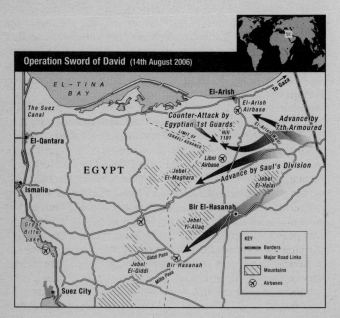

Operation Sword of David (14th August 2006)

EL – TINA BAY

The Suez Canal

El-Arish

El-Arish Airbase

To Gaza

Counter-Attack by Egyptian 1st Guards

Advance by 7th Armoured

El-Qantara

LIMIT OF ISRAELI ADVANCE

Hill 1191

El-Arish Wadi

EGYPT

Libni Airbase

Jebel El-Maghara

Advance by Saul's Division

Jebel El-Halal

Ismalia

Bir El-Hasanah

Great Bitter Lake

Jebel Yi-Allaq

Giddi Pass

Jebel El-Giddi

Bir Hasanah

Mitla Pass

KEY

▬▬▬ Borders

——— Major Road Links

▨ Mountains

⊗ Airbases

Suez City

The Battle of Hill 1191

At 1300 Yosef called a halt. He had reason to be well pleased with the morning's advance, although there were more worrying developments elsewhere. The three battalions that made up his brigade had lost only four tanks: two to mechanical breakdowns and two more bogged down in patches of very soft sand. The 3rd Battalion had been dispatched to the north of the El Arish wadi to secure the road junction south of the airbase. It was originally planned that Magen's Division would take this but Magen's men had become embroiled in heavy fighting on the eastern outskirts of El Arish and for the airbase itself. The 7th Armoured had not seen a single enemy soldier with any fight left. They had passed groups of dazed Libyans, sitting aimlessly in the desert, ignored their attempts to surrender – no time for prisoners – and pressed on west past blown-up foxholes and occasional bodies that, although not long dead, were already attracting swarms of flies. Above, Israeli jets thundered in both directions; to the Canal, Yosef hoped, or at least against the columns of reserves that must be presenting temptingly dense target arrays as they crossed the desert. In that, he would later find out, he was wrong. The IAF had no intention of committing itself to the deep battle through what would be fierce SAM and Triple-A fire unless the situation was dire. And with the army on the offensive desperate measures were not yet called for.

To the 7th's left, Saul's Division had made excellent progress down the Redifim road. The Division had crashed through the Egyptian 17th Mechanised which was anchored on the northern end of the Jebel El-Halal. The old T-62s and converted T-55s that the Egyptian mechanised units possessed were no match for the Merkava/Apache combination in what was pure tank country. The armoured infantry units accompanying the lead tanks only had to dismount from their M113 personnel carriers to round up prisoners. By mid-afternoon they were within striking distance of the El Arish–Bir el Hasana road where the first line of significant resistance was dug in. Indeed, on the right flank, adjacent to the 7th

Armoured Brigade, a large battle group had fought its way on to and captured the Libni airbase – long since rendered useless as such, thanks mainly to artillery fire. The Israeli high command realised that El Arish was proving to be a significant stumbling-block, controlling as it did the route to the whole of the coastal plain. The Egyptian defenders in and around El Arish had prepared the defensive position well and had had time to lay significant quantities of anti-tank mines covered by well-concealed and mutually supporting ATGM and HMG fire positions. MBTs were deployed in hull-down fire positions or held in reserve in the streets of the town itself. Magan's initial attempt to outflank El Arish to the south cost him twenty-one tanks and was aborted as the full extent of the minefields became known. The units defending El Arish were the 18th Mechanised and 2nd Armoured Divisions, the latter equipped with upgraded US M-60 tanks. El Arish also marked the beginning of the Egyptian SAM and AAA umbrella.

Decades of fear about the proven capability of the IAF had ensured that the Egyptians had a formidable array of surface-to-air artillery. Their arsenal included over 2,000 guns ranging between 20 and 100 mm in calibre organised into 100 AD artillery battalions, including systems with Skyguard radars; over 500 strategic SAMs of the SA-2 and SA-3 variety; 4 batteries of Patriot, 12 batteries each of US Improved Hawk and Chaparral; and 14 batteries each of Crotale and SA-6/11. In addition to this the army deployed around 3,000 hand-held SAMs, 40 SA-9s and 1,600 AD guns, including 120 ZSU 23/4 Gundishes, and 350 57mm guns.

The sheer size of the AD forces, even discounting those that remained deployed to protect national strategic assets in Egypt, would have been daunting for any air force to face. The IAF could not hope to play a significant role in supporting the ground forces until it had carried out a measure of serious destruction against the AD forces without sustaining much damage itself. It was true that in 1973 the IAF had been deadly when it caught Egyptian units outside the SAM umbrella, and that the SAM threat was most effectively removed by the armoured counter-thrusts across the Suez

Canal. What made life more difficult for the IAF was that with the exception of the strategic SAMs and larger-calibre AA guns, just about everything in the inventory was mobile. Also, the mix of Russian and more capable Western equipment compounded the problems faced and, on paper at least, showed an improvement in quality of an order of magnitude between 1973 and 2006.

Any IAF jet or IDF helicopter that ventured to within 25 kms of El Arish would have to be extremely careful, especially when loitering to try to pinpoint targets within the town itself or dug in on the outskirts. For the first day at least the IAF confined itself to testing the robustness and density of the layered SAM/AAA umbrella. Throughout the day the IAF was only able to nibble at the outer layers of what was likened to a Spanish onion of ground-based air defence. The IAF still had nightmares about 1973, when it suffered heavily at the hands of both Syrian and Egyptian SAMs. In 1982 the situation was very different. Through exhaustive reconnaissance, planning surprise and the use of artillery, the IAF managed to destroy the Syrian SAM defences in the Bekka Valley in a morning. This time the IAF recognised that it was back to a 1973 scenario whereby the location of the majority of enemy SAMs remained a movable feast and as such it would be foolhardy to press beyond what was required by the army. Thus packages of fifteen to twenty aircraft at a time were sent against single batteries within hours of their positions being uncovered and confirmed. Even this was difficult where engagement zones from other SAMs and AAA overlapped the designated target. Those batteries providing cross-cover had to be soft-killed with HARMs and other ARMs while the bombers closed to ensure hard kills, preferably with Mavericks, which afforded them some stand-off capability, glide bombs or, against the less capable SAMs, even iron and cluster bombs.

It was to be expected that the Israelis would opt to outflank El Arish well to the south by a push west to south of Hill 1191 before swinging north through the dunes to cut the road that led west out of the town. This would, it was hoped, not only cause the defenders in El Arish to fall into disarray or capitulate, but also enable the army to destroy a significant number of the dangerous mobile SAMs and guns that were preventing the IAF from bringing all its power to bear. At 1500 Levi made up his mind and called Yosef direct. He was aware of the dangers of purely armoured thrusts into the unknown and assigned the 7th Armoured two battalions of infantry, borrowed from Saul's Division, and gave him first call on the eight AH-64 Apaches to support the push to the sea. Yosef replied that the 7th Armoured would be ready to move by 1600. Levi finished by sounding a single note of caution; that the 1st Egyptian Republican Guard Division had last been seen along the road to El Arish before nightfall the previous evening. As they stood that afternoon, the division was 'unlocated'. At this Yosef exploded.

'What do you mean "unlocated"? How can we lose a whole fucking oversized Egyptian division?'

Levi was quick to calm his fears.

'I know, I know, and you'll be reminding me next that they've got Abrams. Well, currently we've got all of Magen's RPVs and half of Saul's looking for them. I should have a good answer within a couple of hours. Also, in case you're worried, I have the personal assurance of the IAF Chief that two flights of the F-15I Thunders at Nevatim are loaded and ready to pile in should you get into trouble.'

Slightly mollified and not wanting to push things too far with his superior, Yosef replied, 'OK, I'll try to stay out of too much trouble.'

'Give me a call once you're on the beach,' said Levi encouragingly.

'OK, I'll do that, sir. Out.' With that Yosef turned to study his maps. The nagging doubt and unwelcome news about the Egyptian Guard would not, however, go away.

At 1600 Yosef was back in his turret, scanning the horizon with his field glasses. The line of advance was flanked on either side by rising hills. Out to the left was the north-eastern end of the Jebel Libni, and to the right, rising high above the plateau, Hill 1191. Yosef ordered the advance, and the 130 machines that now made up his enhanced brigade set off across a two-mile frontage; the Merkavas and four of the

Apaches in the lead (the other four were at cockpit readiness) and the M113s carrying the infantry a respectful distance behind. With the desert now at its driest at this time of day, Yosef knew that their movement, thanks to the clouds of choking dust, would make them visible for miles. He watched with satisfaction as several rounds of 155mm artillery landed on the summit and forward slopes of Hill 1191. There was, he knew, an abandoned radar station there and, although they had no reports of any other activity on the hill, it would be an obvious place for any Egyptians in the area to place artillery or forward air observers. The top of the hill disappeared in clouds of smoke and dirt thrown up by the impacting artillery rounds – that should keep their heads down.

The advance went well until they were abreast of the southern end of Hill 1191. The Apaches were understandably not keen to be the first to go over the top and into the unknown. Four RPVs had been lost to the west of 1191 in the past three hours, so whatever was there certainly had a significant air defence capability. As the first tanks of the reconnaissance platoon crested the small saddle, Yosef's tank was a good mile behind, along with the main body. From the valley beyond all hell broke loose. There was the unmistakable sound of 120mm gunfire, and as quickly as they had disappeared over the crest the first platoon of four was attempting to reverse back to safety, discharging their smoke canisters as they did so. One Merkava was hit and destroyed out of sight below the crest, two more as they reached the most exposed position on top of the crest itself, one seething as the fire-suppression systems cut in to attempt to contain the growing explosion from within. The fourth took two glancing blows on its right side as it backed to safety, one ripping the track off and the second shearing off the front drive sprocket and first road wheel. It reversed, slewing rapidly to the right as it did so with no traction on one side, before sliding to a halt below and at a right angle to the crest.

Yosef called a halt as the commander of the fourth tank bailed out of his smoking and crippled machine and ran to his own, easily identifiable with his personal light blue Tribe of Benjamin pennant fluttering atop the main radio antenna.

Yosef waited patiently as his Second-in-Command's Merkava sped forward to pick up what appeared to be the lone survivor. He leaned forward to listen to the animated young lieutenant, still out of breath but with the adrenalin pumping through his speech after his shocking initiation in battle.

'There's about twenty or thirty of them in hull-down positions about three clicks from the crest. We had no chance. They must be M-1s or M-60s to have hit us from that range.' Yosef silently cursed the Americans who had given Israel's enemies their best equipment.

'OK, thanks. Get back and see if your men are OK, then wait for the engineers to recover your tank.'

Yosef knew that what was to come would be a test of will, training and morale. He had no option but to go over the crest after minimal preparation with all guns blazing. The two sides in this tank battle were equally well motivated and, if the enemy did indeed have M-1s, were equally equipped. He called the battalion commanders and discussed the situation with them. They agreed that positive and decisive action was their only option. The artillery observers were dispatched to the crest with their periscopes to bring down artillery fire on the Egyptian positions. There were three batteries of M-109 self-propelled guns available from Saul's and Magen's Divisions. That should give the Egyptians something to think about. The discussion was, however, cut short as the air was split with the cracking of incoming artillery. Yosef recognised the sound; he had heard it many times while on patrol in northern Israel and southern Lebanon – Katyushas, rocket artillery. He closed the hatch as the pressure waves from the first blasts hit the tank. Through his periscope he watched as the artillery observers' carrier was hit as it attempted to weave wildly through the rain of molten steel. The light aluminium armour burned fiercely like matchwood. Although his brigade was tightly bunched they would be fine unless suffering a direct hit. While rocket barrages were the most intense, frightening and destructive of all types of artillery barrage, they were also the shortest and there would be a lull while the equipment was reloaded.

Yosef was aware of the disadvantage Israel had in this

particular type of artillery vis-à-vis her neighbours. With respect to Egypt and Libya alone, Israel, mortars aside, could field over 1,600 conventional artillery (mostly superior self-propelled) pieces to 2,200 (mostly of the inferior towed variety) but a mere 100 MRL types compared to nearly 1,000. The Islamic predilection for rocket artillery owed its origins to the desire to acquire a system that would out-range the vastly superior Israeli self-propelled artillery and the sophisticated counter-battery radar and computers which, like all modern Western systems, were able to put down deadly counter-fire within seconds. Egypt had not been slow to take full advantage of the Russian 'export to anybody with cash' arms bazaar of the early years of the millennium, especially as the US had refused to sell Egypt MLRS. The most expensive purchase was three batteries of the Splav 300-mm BM 9A52 Smerch. Each battery had four 8×8 MAZ-543A launch vehicles and each vehicle twelve tubes. The different Smerch variants had maximum ranges of between 70 and 100 km, which was well in excess of anything the Israelis or for that matter the West possessed. The rounds landing among Yosef's brigade could be coming from as far away as the lateral road just east of the Suez Canal. There was another thought that caused Yosef to wonder. Israeli Intelligence had indicated that the Egyptians had acquired a significant number of 9M55K1 top-attack rounds. These were 15kg sub-munitions that deployed from the mother round (thirty per tube) and descended on a mini-parachute. An infrared seeker searched for suitable targets during the descent and on detection of a suitable heat source within a hundred metres fired a shaped charge jet of white-hot liquid metal at the top of the target. Yosef had just reached the 'surely not' stage of analysis when calls started coming in on the brigade net. Within ten minutes the attack was over. As the dust settled Yosef listened to his commanders' reports in silence. Nearly forty tanks were hit, some taking as many as four rounds through the engine decking. Six Merkavas were destroyed either by explosions or subsequent uncontained fires. This was not a good start to the battle. But even before the dust settled things were about to get worse.

Yosef sensed an explosion to his right and instinctively
dropped to the floor of the turret. The brigade net burst into
life with shouts of 'Contact front engaging!' The Egyptians
had used the rocket barrage to enable them to take the
offensive against the stunned Israelis. Now, from hull-down
positions along the two-kilometre crest, Egyptian M-1
Abrams were firing at will at the still-stationary Merkavas.
The balance of fire-power was critical in this, the first major
tank battle of the war. Yosef called the Apaches to engage and
put a request in for air support via Saul's divisional HQ. The
Egyptians had no fewer than thirty machines in good firing
positions on the southern end of the crest within seconds of
the first Merkava being hit. Following the frantic initial
exchanges the Egyptians then delivered another punch, which
sent the Israelis reeling. Over the northern side of the crest
poured a stream of Abrams, too many to count but at least
another thirty, Yosef thought, all of them going at top speed
and firing as they approached. The Americans had taught
them well.

The Merkavas fired at the approaching mass for all they
were worth. The individual excellence of Israeli tank gunnery
was balanced by the Abrams' superior fire control, the fact
that they presented fast-moving targets and that their armour
was such that they required two or three direct hits to be
stopped. Yosef was no longer Brigade Commander but just
another tank fighting for survival in this furious battle.

'Target right ten, 1,500 metres . . . fire!' The target took a
hit on the front glacis but came on. 'Same target, 1,450 metres
. . . fire!' The Merkava rocked as it absorbed the recoil of the
120mm smooth-bore; another hit, this time on the turret
front. Still no apparent reaction from the Abrams. 'I have
it!' Yosef used his override to take control of the gun from his
gunner. He took a couple of seconds longer than normal and,
using the 14 × magnification, aimed carefully at the small gap
between hull and turret. The computer read 1,350 metres.
'Fire!' This time the result was spectacular. The 120mm
tungsten dart split the Abrams in two. The turret flew off
in a huge explosion as if levered by a mighty wrench and
back-flipped twice before coming to rest 50 metres behind

what was now a smoking hulk. 'Move, move, move!' yelled
Yosef to the driver. It would be suicidal to remain stationary
in an exposed position. The driver gunned the Teledyne
Continental V-12 diesel to the rev limiter and the tank into
reverse. The sudden demand of 900 hp made the transmission
roar, but the tank responded by leaping back. Yosef fired the
60mm turret mortar as they reversed; six rounds of smoke at a
fixed 1,500 metres range. He noted with satisfaction that
others were doing the same, and smoke rounds began to form
a rapidly growing black wall and obscure the enemy tanks in
the best positions on the crest. They were the biggest danger to
the existence of the 7th; with attention focused on the rapidly
advancing Abrams, those on the crest in overwatch positions
had been able to fire at will and pick their targets virtually
unhindered. Through his sight Yosef saw multiple small red
dots, travelling noticeably slower than the dots of small
brilliant-white fire that were tank gun rounds, disappear
through the dust and smoke towards the crest. The Apaches
had at last found their targets and were firing Hellfire missiles
at the Abrams. Also the TOWs mounted in the infantry
vehicles to the rear were now finding targets among the lead
Abrams. As the first four disappeared into clouds of belching
black smoke and fierce ammunition fires, each one mortally
wounded, Yosef realised the critical moment in this battle had
come.

He spoke tersely on the Brigade net: 'Seventh Armoured
advance!' Without waiting for a direct command his driver
crashed the Teledyne into low gear and stood on the pedal.
They raced forward, headlong into the Abrams, which had
now slowed perceptibly. Glancing left and right, Yosef noted
that he still had a good number of 'runners'. The two
armoured forces merged into a wild mêlée with main guns,
smoke-launchers and machineguns chattering in the din.
Tanks optimised for combat at ranges of three to four kilometres were now wheeling round each other in a deadly
metallic dance through growing clouds of choking oily and
cordite-filled smoke which reduced visibility to tens of metres
at times and engagement ranges to the same.

An Abrams appeared to the front of Yosef's tank, two

hundred metres range, going left to right at full speed. The
gunner had seen him too, and within seconds the barrel was
traversing right, holding its position as the tank and turret
dipped and bucked across the uneven terrain. Wham! The
gunner fired. Almost simultaneously there was an explosion
of white metal sparks on the rear of the Abrams as the
tungsten dart wrecked the engine. The Abrams skidded to
a halt and was enveloped in black smoke issuing from its rear.
At just under a hundred metres range Yosef watched the crew
bailing out. The gunner was in no mood for compromise and
felled the three figures that emerged with a long burst that
sprayed the Abrams and the ground in front of it.

'Left, target left!' It was the driver. Yosef and his gunner
had been distracted by a second of compassion for the
Egyptians who lay motionless by the Abrams. He looked left
and saw what the gunner was yelling at. Another Abrams had
appeared only fifty metres away at 90 degrees and on a
collision course. The Merkava sprinted forward as the driver
changed rapidly up through the gears. Yosef swung the turret
to bear and the gunner squeezed off a snap shot at what was
less than thirty metres. The Abrams had jinked as if in pursuit,
intent on ramming, and fired at the same instant. Yosef's shell
smashed into the front left of the Abrams' turret; the Abrams'
shot went through the rear end of the Merkava and into the
ammunition storage. From below him Yosef knew they were
in trouble as he felt a heat blast and heard a thunderous bang
accompanied by yelps from the loader and gunner. The
collision was now inevitable, and he shouted 'Brace! Brace!'
as the two armoured monsters crashed together with an angry
roar and a crunch of snapping and twisting metal. Yosef
blacked out.

2nd Tactical Air Defence Battery (Crotale)

Ijaz had no time to enjoy the spectacle of the advancing Israeli
armour. Within seconds of alerting the major on the field
telephone he heard the high-pitched whine of incoming artil-

lery shells. No time or need to give orders to his new command; they would all have heard the approach of death. To a man every one of them curled like foetuses into the bottom of their hastily dug foxholes in another attempt, at least their third that day, to make themselves as small as possible. Ijaz accepted his fate with stoicism. His life was not in his own hands any more. As the first shells hammered and shook the ground around him, or fused in low airburst mode, sending out showers of deadly splinters over the forward slopes, he began to pray. The noise was fantastic and Ijaz was jarred, concussed and deafened by two 155mm shells that landed within metres of his earthen womb. The barrage lasted only four minutes, but to Ijaz it might have been a thousand years in hell. When it stopped they all lay there quiet and motionless. Those that had survived could scarcely believe it, and hesitated to raise their heads lest they fall victim to one final shell.

Ijaz slowly checked himself over, making sure first of all that his limbs and manhood were intact. His heart jumped as he felt a warm trickle of blood on his neck and collar. He was relieved when he gingerly probed his neck to find that the blood was coming from his ears. He was also disappointed and ashamed that he had wet himself. Ijaz was just considering that it could have been much worse when he noticed Abdul. Abdul the piano teacher was in the same foxhole. He held out his hands in supplication towards Ijaz, his eyes appealing. 'Help me,' he pleaded softly. Ijaz forced himself to look down at Abdul's outstretched arms. His left hand was missing. A bloody stump with splintered brilliant-white clean bone protruded from under the sleeve of his dirty combat jacket. His right hand was a crazy mixture of black burns and flash-dried dark red blood, the fingers a tangled mess. His piano-playing days were over. Ijaz ripped his field dressing off and bound the hands of his comrade.

'You'll be fine,' he lied. 'They have surgeons in Cairo that work miracles these days.' Abdul was in deep shock but no pain. Ijaz sat him in the corner of the foxhole and injected him with morphine. Abdul simply stared ahead with great sadness and waited for drug-induced sleep to overtake him. Then, above the silence that lay as a blanket on the hillside, and above the ringing in his ears, Ijaz could hear the sound of tanks, many tanks, the grumbling diesels growing louder as they drew nearer. The war was still going on. Ijaz ventured a glance out of his trench, fully expecting to be rewarded with a high-explosive tank round or burst of machinegun fire for his curiosity. What he saw gave him mixed emotions. The tanks were still some way off, at least five kilometres, but it looked to Ijaz as if the whole Israeli Army was coming his way. He called the major with a recommendation to abandon the position while they still had a chance to escape. The major thanked him for his report and added matter-of-factly that if Ijaz appeared on the western side of the hill where the battery was before he had permission then he would shoot him personally. For Ijaz the sense of impending doom returned. This was hell and he didn't much care for it.

He watched dejectedly as the Israeli advance came ever closer. The tanks and APCs were in a regular battle formation as if on exercise. He called the major again as four of the leading tanks approached the saddle that linked 1191 with the north-eastern end of the Jebel El-Maghara. The major sounded a little more agitated. No wonder, thought Ijaz, we're about to be surrounded. The major again disappointed by not ordering a withdrawal and thanked Ijaz for his report before hanging up.

Then, to Ijaz's surprise and delight, as the first four tanks crossed the saddle they came under a hail of fire from friendly forces unseen to Ijaz, hidden by the summit, one of them brewing up almost immediately and two others quickly following. The visual spectacle was accompanied by a delayed soundtrack as the cracks of high-velocity tank gunfire and exploding rounds washed over the hill together.

Then the hair stood up on the back of Ijaz's neck as his nervous system detected more incoming artillery before his senses were able to transmit the fact to his brain. He ducked back into the trench, again coiled up against the rain of death as the crescendo grew from a low whine to a deaf-ening howl. As the first rockets impacted the plain, which was filled with Israeli armour, it was with some relief he realised that this barrage was not aimed at him personally or his men. He watched the advancing horde disappear under the rain of rockets and sub-munitions. From his grandstand position he saw vehicle after vehicle hit by the heavy artillery fire. And then better was to come. As the Israelis halted uncertainly, the sound of advancing armour grew from his right. Then the Egyptian Abrams appeared on the crest and then as another thirty or so swept down to meet the Israelis head on. The ensuing tank battle was more like a knife fight in a telephone box. The close-range clash of armour reminded him of scenes of Kursk he'd read about as a boy rather than the perfect environment for long-range gunnery he had expected.

For ten minutes it was exciting as tank after tank on both sides was hit or disabled. Then his heart sank. The Apache gunships that had ruined his day earlier were back. The fire-power of the helicopters was what turned this initial engagement in the Israelis favour. Standing off at some eight kilometres' distance, each Apache carried sixteen Hellfire missiles. Soon it was clear that of the fifty or so Egyptian tanks that had faced up to the Israelis barely half a dozen were left. He knew then that whether the major was going to shoot him or not it would not be long before the remaining Israelis on the plain below him, although they were down to about half their original strength, would take the offensive. And he and his men were not going to hang around for that.

Of the Abrams that had lined the crest, only five withdrew undamaged and out of sight. Within minutes the Israelis resumed their advance, the Apaches again hovering menacingly. As the Apaches approached to within two kilometres and the nearest tanks started their uphill climb to Ijaz's position, a mere 1,500 metres away, Ijaz now had no hesitation and ordered his remaining men to leave the trenches and sprint over the summit to where the Crotales were waiting. The Israelis, whether they saw the two dozen men scrambling up over the summit of 1191 and disappearing down the other side or not, decided not to bother engaging what were mere infantry – and retreating infantry at that. His chest heaving, Ijaz led his men down the north-western slope. There before him was the major, again brandishing his AKM menacingly. Ijaz half expected to be felled by a well-aimed burst from this man with a mission. The major was not surprised to see his 'infantry protection' appear. He too had watched the Abrams' deadly duel with the Merkavas and Apaches.

'Get into these trenches here!' he barked, waving at a row of trenches to his left. 'You'll find some anti-tank weapons, the latest RPGs. If you don't attempt to halt the advance I'll have my machinegunner help you.' Sixty metres off to the right was a machinegun crew crouched ready behind their weapon. Ijaz's heart sank as the gunner looked up at him and nodded in an 'I've got your number, mate' fashion. It was Salim. Ijaz realised then that he'd not seen the little hero for some time. He jumped down into the nearest trench and looked at the assortment of weapons. There were six RPGs, three each of two new types, neither of which he recognised. He picked up and examined one that had a large box-shaped warhead rather than the normal cone. The major was still watching.

'That one is the FRPG, it's filled with fuel air explosive. Deadly if you can hit anything with it. Flies like a bitch, though, and difficult beyond fifty metres.' Ijaz nodded silently and glanced at the other type of RPG, knowing that the major would continue his instruction without being asked. He was that sort of person. The major did not disappoint.

'And that one with the elongated cone has a double-charged shaped warhead. The first sets off any reactive armour being carried and the second punches through the gap. A brilliant weapon.' Ijaz was inclined not to agree. Any weapon that meant you had to be within a few hundred or tens of metres of enemy tanks to fire it did not qualify as 'brilliant' in his mind.

There was a shout from an unseen voice emanating from just inside the door of the nearest missile vehicle.

'Major! We've got a report on the radio says that a flight of enemy aircraft just passed over the coast road heading south at very low level. They were too low and fast for the battery there to engage. They'll be with us in around two minutes!'

The major disappeared. Ijaz remembered Abdul and crawled over to where he had left him propped up in the trench. He had slumped forward, his good hand holding the mangled stump. Ijaz lifted his head and began to repeat his empty reassurances. Abdul was smiling, his eyes wide open. But he was dead. Ijaz could feel the sorrow and the urge to weep welling up from within. As his eyes filled with tears there was a loud shout. In one of the trenches on the northern end of the position there was a young Egyptian lieutenant with a pair of binoculars. He had seen the approaching jets. He stopped shouting and reached down into his trench, re-emerging with a small metal pole. It was a pointing stick which enabled passive acquisition. He pointed the stick at the group of aircraft. Ijaz could still make out only one aircraft, and even then all he could see was occasional glimpses of its shadows on the desert floor. There was a chorus of metallic clunking and high-pitched whines as the four missile vehicles responded in unison to the stick's beckoning and pointed at the onrushing jets. As each used their TV trackers to acquire individual aircraft, the missile-launcher motors made tiny adjustments as a firing solution was calculated.

Claw Formation

Major Tal was promoted after leading the successful raid on the Tehran parade in 1995. At the age of thirty-three he considered himself the luckiest man in the world to be in command of his own F-15I squadron. He led his eight-ship, split into two fours, 'Claw' and 'Talon' formations, against the Republican Guard Division during the battle of Hill 1191.

We got orders to launch on a CAS target just after three in the afternoon. We had been assigned to direct support of the 7th Armoured Brigade. Reconnaissance drones, those that weren't picked off (we later learned most of them were downed by British-made Javelins that had been acquired by the Egyptians), managed to get some good instant recce pictures. They had found a mass of Egyptian armour that had moved off the coast road and headed south-east behind the jebels in an attempt to hit the flank of the Saul's Division drive.

Just as we got airborne one of the crew chiefs who'd been listening in at the CP came out to tell us that the 7th had become engaged in a heavy tank battle around Hill 1191. Although they had taken significant losses they were about to push over the saddle and on to the coast. First, however, they needed to clear the area behind 1191 where they suspected (and we knew) that reserves of Egyptian armour lay waiting.

We flew out of Nevatim and turned north-west. Within seven minutes we were coasting out over the sparkling Med to the north of Ashqelon. The eight of us flew just north of west for a further fifty miles. At wave-top height we would be just below the radar horizon of anything that was sweeping our area. Our plan was to go in behind Hill 1191, attacking on a heading of south-east so that we could make a supersonic exit straight back towards safety. Also, if anyone was hit anything other than catastrophically, he'd be able to bale out over our own lines. We were aware that the rest of the air force was engaged in taking out the first layers of the enemy SAM belt. This was why we decided to attack from the rear and not from behind the heads of our own troops. We still did not know the strength of the SAMs to the south of 1191.

We saw nothing over the sea except for a few very surprised-looking fishermen, who looked up anxiously as we swept by, level with the topsails of their small fishing boats. Then it was time to turn in. A single RPV, one of the high-fliers that had avoided destruction, had sent pictures via our data links to my back-seater. The pictures gave us a God's-eye view of the target as well as the exact position of the enemy armour just five minutes previously. My back-seater remarked that there was so much enemy armour still behind 1191 that we could hardly miss with our twelve CBU cans. We opted to stay ultra-low and picked out a line of eight tanks that would fall within the footprint of our weapons. As my back-seater punched in the new release point I concentrated on searching the skies ahead. The radar warning gear was all quiet so we switched the display to air-to-ground mode and left it at stand-by. An 'S' turn left and right twenty miles before coast-in would give us the right line up from the coast all the way to weapons release. We would much rather have fired Mavericks from a few clicks' distance or come in at medium altitude but both options would have exposed us to SA-11s and I-Hawks. The amount of triple-A we felt would be minimal. At ultra-low altitude the biggest enemy was the ground, which had a probability of kill of 1. Triple-A looked frightening but rarely, unless hit full on by a hail from an updated ZSU 23/4 Gundish or 57mm S-60, did it do much serious damage.

At fourteen miles to the coast the warning gear gave a single squeak. We knew that there might be a temporary radar situated on the Bardawil sand bar out to our right, but now we were under two minutes to the coast, doing 580 knots, on the deck, and around four minutes from weapons release. We swept in over the mud, sand, salt flats and marsh that mark the eastern end of the Bardawil, which was our initial point. Switches live, radar on. Here comes the road in two miles. Good grief, look at that lot. What's that just beyond the road? Tanks and APCs well out to the right. Climb a little to avoid the telephone wires, lattice water tank on the left. Bang on track. Nav kit looks good. Hey, those are French-made SAMs. We're on top of them. Hi, guys! They look a little surprised. Look left at number two. He's so low he's got a dust rooster trail kicking up behind him as his jet sits on the pressure wave between itself and the desert floor.

Back-seater has the target area identified. Looks like there's about thirteen tanks in the weapons footprint, which causes him to exclaim in eager anticipation. Thirty seconds to run, just under five miles, switches checked live. Some tanks only visible because they're moving and kicking up dust. No chance from this sort of attack of telling friend from foe until you've done a couple of slow passes directly over the top. Flash off to the left. Large plume of smoke. SAM! SAM! Launched from the hillside. No intel of SAMs up there. Flare, flare! Hard left, turn towards. The jet feels sluggish. Punch emergency jettison. A dozen rapid thuds. Missile coming towards, heading slightly to left. Have sighted second missile fired from hill. Break right, pull 9 Gs. Grunt, don't black out. Straighten. Chaff, chaff! Look left, explosion behind. Second missile passes overhead.

Aim for crest and row of burning tanks. Up over small hillock. Upside down. Crash! We've been hit. Feels like a huge hand has taken a swipe at the tail as the jet jumps bodily in space. Right aircraft. Check systems. Fire caption warbling, neither engine looks good. Glance in mirror to see plume of black-and-white smoke. Another warning tone. Hydraulic system warning captions both red. I guess we're about to lose control. Over crest and on to plain beyond, which is crammed with burning tanks, dust and smoke, in a gentle climb. Hydraulics read zero. Climb to 5,000 feet and slow to 360 knots, engines losing interest. Head for safe lane. Stick inputs making less difference. Stick hardens and now requires all my strength to do anything. Certain were over Israeli lines. It's time to go. Eject, eject! Bang! My head is crushed forward into my groin. Sharp pain in my back. Feel like I'm tumbling through space. Arrested by opening of parachute. Seat falls away. Look for somewhere to land. Remember drills. Crash into ground in an uncontrolled heap. My back-seater lands only thirty metres away. An APC full of infantry approaches. Thank God they're Israelis. We should be back at base in a couple of hours.

Hill 1191 – Conclusion

The first Crotales were fired when the Israeli aircraft were only about five kilometres away. The noise was surprising, but there was a discernible pop a fraction of a second before the missile was launched as the end of the canisters, which kept the missiles sealed from extreme temperatures and protected from pervasive sand dust, was blown off. By the time the second Crotale was fired, Ijaz was braced. Suddenly it was as if the idea had caught on. In seconds there were eight missiles in the air, two from each launch vehicle. The Israeli aircraft seemed intent on their targets off to the south-west. Then as one they became aware of the menace coming from their left.

This was fantastic. Ijaz had never seen anything like it. His sorrow evaporated to be replaced by a child-like wonder at the spectacle of war. The first four F-15s turned together as if in a formation dance. Brightly coloured flares popped out from behind them. Ijaz watched the nearest. He had turned and was heading directly for their position. He pulled up still some distance away and Ijaz froze. A cluster of bombs departed from the jet. He had seen them, no doubt, and was set to kill the whole battery. Ijaz was about to dive back into his trench when the jet banked over hard right and away south. The bombs were clearly going to fall well short. There was a huge explosion behind the jet; Ijaz could now see it was an F-15. The second missile passed over the F-15, which had bunted forward and was now nosing along the desert floor again. Ijaz jumped as two more missiles were fired from the nearest TEL. They reached the F-15 just as he was climbing over a small hill. One impacted the top of the hill but the second got him squarely between the jet pipes, shredding his tail-end and turning the yellow-and-pink sand trail into one of dark smoke and vapour. Ijaz watched him climb steadily, although it was clear the F-15 was mortally wounded, limping through the air. Ijaz heard a great cheer from inside the Crotale TEL as the crew ejected and the F-15 plummeted vertically, trailing fire, before smacking into the desert floor in an angry fireball.

Ijaz watched the other F-15s (there were at least six) carry out evasive manoeuvres against the Crotales. One other was hit. Half of his right-side flying wing and tailplane were blown off by a near-miss. Amazingly the F-15 continued to fly, trailing more small bits as it did so, and soon disappeared out of sight to the east. Another was not so lucky and ploughed straight into the ground on the far side of the valley, a burning furrow of high-octane fuel marking its demise. Of the other five only two got their CBUs off anywhere near the tanks, which disappeared in a mass of small explosions and smoke under the hail of destructive bomblets.

As the last of the F-15s disappeared the major was up and about, shouting orders. He was delighted. Now the Crotale SAMs would have to move. There would be an air strike or artillery all over the back of 1191 now that their position had been revealed. Anti-air assets, the major knew, always jumped to the top of any target list once they were identified. There was also a more pressing need. In the valley below, to the south, the first Merkavas had appeared and were but distant dots. Soon they would be able to engage the Crotale battery directly. Ijaz was about to get his men to run for the nearest transport of any form but the major had read his mind.

'You will wait at least until we are out of tank gun range. Then you can follow. The reload vehicles are now empty. You and your men will be able to squeeze into them *after* you have beaten off the first Israeli attack. My new machinegunner has the keys.' He gestured in an exaggerated manner to Salim, who waved back. With that he was gone. The 4 × 4 vehicles were very agile on this loose terrain, their wide-grooved tyres giving them extra grip. The two Jeeps and four TELs sped off down the hill on what was barely discernible as a track.

When the major was no more than five hundred metres distant Ijaz stood and shouted to Salim.

'Salim! Salim! Come on, let's get out of here.' Salim regarded him for a moment, then slowly trained the gun above his head. Ijaz continued, 'Salim, you don't want to die here, pointlessly on a stupid hill in Sinai. Come on . . .' He didn't finish the sentence. A burst of tracer rounds thumped the air above him. Salim had clearly gone mad. He gingerly lifted his hands above the trench. Salim did not fire. That was some progress. Ijaz could see that he was grinning. In the valley below another long-range tank battle had begun as more Merkavas poured over the crest. Ijaz flinched as he saw four Apaches nose their way above the crest line and then push forward to behind the leading tanks. The first thing they saw was the major's Crotales. In seconds a salvo of Hellfire missiles had left the rails of the Apaches, and not much later the mini-convoy of six hammered as it moved at top speed. The Hellfires ripped through the thin armour of each vehicle. Two exploded instantly, with debris being flung high into the air. The other four continued moving although they were aflame, as if the drivers and vehicles had not for a few moments understood that they had suffered catastrophic damage.

But the Apaches had stayed still for too long, perhaps

enjoying the kill. One of them exploded too. Ijaz looked for the killers and saw that it was a group of Abrams he had not noticed until now further off to the south. He watched as a second Abrams fired its main gun not a second after the first and the round sped as a white orange ball in a shallow arc and smashed a second Apache to bits.

Ijaz had had enough. He had just determined to leave the trench and risk Salim's revenge when the sound of tank engines near by reached his ears over the din of the battle raging below. He had forgotten about the Merkavas that had begun the slow ascent some time ago. He looked back up to the top of the hill. There, 150 metres away, were two Merkavas and a swarm of khaki and light-green-clad infantry. A burst of tracer from Salim either felled several of them or sent them to ground, for suddenly all that was visible were the two tanks which had halted and were searching the ground ahead uncertainly. Ijaz's nerve returned. He reached down into the trench and picked up one of the fat fuel-explosive RPGs. Very slowly he lifted it above the trench and dared to look himself. He could hear bursts from Salim's machinegun. The tanks were both trying to pinpoint the machinegun position and were spraying the area with their own machineguns. Ijaz erected the very crude sight on the RPG. Taking aim at the nearest tank, he squeezed the trigger. The projectile fired cleanly and in the right direction. It struck the ground twenty metres short of the tank in a huge sticky explosion like a paint bomb, and the jelly ignited a fraction of a second later. Ijaz ducked back to the bottom of the trench. There was another fat RPG. From off to his left there were two explosions. When he looked again the nearest tank was pouring smoke, probably hit by an RPG from another position, but also Salim's machinegun position had disappeared, no doubt hit by a high-explosive shell. Ijaz did exactly as he had done fifteen seconds previously, but this time aimed for the top of the tank. The projectile slammed into the lower side of the turret. Again its contents hesitated and then ignited. Either the armour or the seals had been pierced – it didn't matter which to Ijaz – as the tank fizzed and rumbled inside as an internal fire took hold in seconds. This was the signal for the accompanying infantry to retreat back over the hill. Ijaz, now more courageous than ever, gave them a whole magazine from his AK-47 to help them on their way.

He ran over to Salim's gun position. He found Salim twenty metres from the gun. He was a mess. His face was black and burned and his lower jaw had been blown off. His upper and lower body didn't seem to fit together, and Ijaz could not look at the mess and blood long enough to work out what the explosion had done. The body moved and gurgled. Salim was still alive. Ijaz, full of compassion, had no hesitation. Salim had won his place in heaven. Ijaz reloaded his AK-47 and fired half a magazine into the blackened torso, splitting open the head and almost cutting the body in two. It was the humane thing to do.

Ijaz grabbed the keys from the breast pocket of what had been Salim and jumped into the reload vehicle. The handful of men followed him, and they sped off north away from the battle, determined to live to fight another day.

Sinai Aftermath

The Battle of Hill 1191 proved to be a turning point in the overall battle for the Sinai. The Israelis were able to push through to the coast behind El Arish, although the mighty 7th Armoured was reduced to one-third of its original strength. Also, this was not before most of the defenders had extracted themselves from the town as the left flank of the Israeli drive north to the sea was menaced by the arrival of at least one Guards division. What 1191 had proved to both sides was that highly motivated and well-trained Egyptian troops, using the very best of American equipment, were almost a match for the once invincible Israeli Army. The two Egyptian Republican Guard divisions that were committed to battle fought with skill, determination and bravery as they were committed in turn against Israeli armoured units that had sliced through the less well-armed mechanised and Libyan divisions.

Senior Israeli military figures had been complaining for

some time about the standard of the recruits they were receiving for training, and now their worst fears were being realised. The qualitative gap between the new generation of Arabs and Israelis in terms of pure fighting mettle had narrowed considerably. The first seeds of the decline in the Israeli Army were seen in the mid-1990s with desertions by serving soldiers at an all-time high. There had been instances of not only mutiny but also whole units abandoning their positions without a shot being fired when under attack from guerrilla groups in South Lebanon. The young Israelis followed the West in their desire for individual fulfilment, leading to increased drug abuse and more social legitimacy being given to both the alternatives to military service and to reserve duty. The combat formations suffered the most. The majority of those called up applied for posts that would earn them a skill, a technical qualification or a trade that would be useful when their time of conscription was over. The other bonus of such trades was that they were normally placed well away from any fighting. Few volunteered for thankless service as line infantry and the prospect of facing angry demonstrators with hidden snipers in Gaza or the West Bank. Fewer still relished the more frightening prospect of occupation duty in the north with very active Islamic 'terrorists' taking a regular toll of young Israeli lives, regardless of the number of reprisal sorties flown by the IAF. Concern for self had replaced the themes of collective responsibility, working and even sacrifice for the common good that had characterised the first fifty years of Israeli history.

The result was that General Levi did not feel confident about sprinting to the Suez Canal even with the forces at his disposal. Although in ninety-six hours (between 14 and 17 August) of fighting the army had made considerable gains across the Sinai, they had done so at no little cost. The units that had fought against the Egyptian Guard had suffered up to 50 per cent losses, the others no more than 25 per cent, but there was still a host of Egyptian and Libyan units dug into strong blocking positions with flanks secured by the towering jebels of central Sinai. For the remaining three days of the war Israeli forces probed warily. Assaulting on narrow fronts, probably through minefields against good defensive positions, was not an enticing prospect. Levi knew that in the north, on the coastal approach, there were at least two more Republican Guard divisions, and he had already seen enough of these and their quality to force a bloody head-to-head in order to attempt to outflank the whole Sinai defensive positions. The Israelis had fought well against an enemy that had improved out of all proportion and had inflicted losses on him in a ratio of around three to one. This was not enough. If this had been the only front then Levi would have considered pushing through for a decisive outcome. He knew, however, that most of these same units would be called on at some stage in the not too distant future to fight against the combined forces of Syria, Saudi Arabia and Jordan, possibly as well as units from both Iraq and Iran. He could not afford to exhaust the Israeli Army. Also, he considered that even though the Israelis had achieved a less than overwhelming victory, as they were used to, the offensive had served its purpose in putting the enemy in the west on the defensive and inflicting significant casualties on him and some of his best units. He was confident that minimal Israeli forces could now be deployed in the west in anticipation of a holding action against the weakened Egyptians and Libyans, while the bulk of the army moved to face the inevitable threat from the east. There had also been the nasty incidents of the bombings in Cairo and Tripoli.

Less than Decisive

The Israeli Air Force had not exactly covered itself in glory during the seven-day conflict. The air force argued that its primary concern had to be gaining control of the skies. The sheer size, mix and depth of the so-called Air Denial Umbrella that was defined by the various SAM and AAA engagement zones was such that it would take a great deal of time and effort for the IAF to destroy sufficient parts. Only when it was clear that enough damage had been done to the air defences,

Above: One of Deschamps and Foch wingmen just airborne out of southern France in their Mirage 2000D, armed with Laser Guided Bombs on the way to Algiers. (20 July 2006)

Right: USS Dwight D. Eisenhower heads north through the Suez Canal, the last NATO ship to do so, two weeks before it was closed. (21 July 2006)

Right: A unique shot of an Egyptian 2S6 Tunguska engaging and shooting down an Israeli reconnaissance drone west of El Arish. (14 August 2006)

Left: Evening prayers. An Israeli soldier of the 7th Armoured Brigade bows his head in silent prayer beside his Merkava tank on the eve of Operation Word of David (13 August 2006)

Below: 'A Plague of Locusts' Israeli Longbow Apaches stalk Egyptian armour using pop-up tactics in the Sinai. (14 August 2006)

...t: Egyptian Crotale of the 2nd Tactical Air Defence *...*ery engages Israeli fighter-bombers west of Hill 1191. *...*August 2006)

...w: Egyptian Revolutionary Guard M1 Abrams *...*ares to counter attack Israeli thrusts around Hill 1191. *...*August 2006)

Above: Israeli Arrow 2 launching from the Mount Carmel site (Peled's 4th Battery). (21 August 2006)

Above right: Hurried preparations by the 13th Patriot Battery on deployment to defend Ramat David Air Base. (15 August 2006)

Right: An Israeli F-16 armed with four HARMs awaits its pilot prior to a night SEAD mission over northern Saudi Arabia. (21 August 2006)

Above: B-2 'Spirit of St Louis' returns at dawn to Diego Garcia after its raid on Bandar Abbas. (27 August 2006)

Left: The resumption of the strategic campaign, a Tomahawk cruise missile launched from DDG 52 Barry, an Arleigh Burke Class destroyer. (31 August 2006)

Above: 'Force Multiplier'. A US F-16 takes fuel off a KC-135 tanker over the eastern Mediterranean. (31 August 2006)

Right: The very capable Russian-supplied S-300 SAM launched at NATO aircraft over eastern Syria. (1 September 2006)

Below: A US B-52G high over Kent, England en-route to Syria armed with clusters of ALCMs. (31 August 2006)

Lt. Mordecai Jakob poses by a Hamas propaganda poster during leave. (September 2005)

US Army Bradley IFVs entrained in Stuttgart prior to transit to the Polish border. (March 2006)

let alone the EAF and its F-16s (none of which had been encountered, incidentally), would the IAF be free enough to be able to bring significant ordnance to bear against the emplaced and dug-in infantry, tanks, anti-tank missile positions and artillery that formed the Egyptian and Libyan defences. The two low-level attacks that had been attempted in direct support of the army had not been overly successful. As far as the public was concerned, no matter what the IAF spokeswoman said in her soothing tones, the IAF had not performed quite as had been anticipated, and the Cairo and Tripoli incidents left everyone in doubt about the prestige and honesty of the air force.

The West was extremely surprised that Israel had chosen to start an aggressive shooting war without direct provocation, and viewed the Sinai action as all the more untimely and unseemly in the light of the West's clear and unavowed support for and commitment to Israel's survival. The West watched Israel's less than spectacular advance through the Sinai with some satisfaction. It was hoped that Israel, having seen the relative performance of her own troops against the Egyptians at its worst since 1948, would be more inclined to accept a peace settlement. Saladin, however, was not interested in peace at any price with Israel, and attempted to politically isolate her further from the international community and cause her most ardent supporters and apologists to hesitate. His plan was simple, based on deception and Europe's predisposition to believe anything its media stated while being suspicious of any statement of innocence emanating from Israel. The West's media were invited to cover the fighting on the Arab home front during the Seven Day War. Television ratings had always soared during the previous decade when the US and her allies had had occasion to attack Iraq. There was something perversely satisfying about watching journalists encamped with the enemy flinch and panic as the weapons of their own countrymen hammered into the palaces, headquarters and chemical and biological weapons production plants in Baghdad, all the while accompanied by endless flak of all calibres and the occasional salvo of SAMs. The prospect of more of such footage proved too tempting to miss, especially for those news networks that missed most of the France/Algeria spat. Also, the Israelis had bombed Amman, Damascus and Beirut during previous wars, so the form book was good.

Although the IAF, concerned only with control of the air, had no plans to bomb either Cairo or Tripoli, Saladin was not going to let the world's media be disappointed. They had come to watch the Israelis attack the cities and that was what they would get. The aim of the air raids was to martyr or maim around a thousand Muslims with CNN, Sky and NTV watching the horror unfold live on prime-time television. The psychology and the power of the media were well understood in the East. They were exploited later throughout the war by the Islamic Alliance, who invited television correspondents into all capital cities and provided them with escort and protection transport and allowed them both freedom of movement and zero reporting restrictions.

It was just after midday on 17 August that Cairo and Tripoli came under attack from 'a number of Israeli jets'. Naturally, CNN, the BBC and all other world networks were in attendance. Out of the blue skies over both cities appeared F-15s and F-16s with Israeli markings which proceeded to dive-bomb what CNN called 'suspected terrorist headquarters' in full view of the world's cameras. In Cairo the central mosque was hit and over four hundred worshippers were killed or wounded. Egyptian SA-11 Gadfly missiles managed to shoot down an F-16 (the pilot ejected but was clubbed to death on landing in a poor suburb by furious citizens) and there for all to see across the world on part of a wing was the Israeli Air Force roundel – a white star of David on a blue background. In Tripoli a school was bombed; some eighty children were killed or maimed. The pilots, who had all scored direct hits on their intended targets, returned to their remote top-secret base in northern Sudan. Soon after landing the two F-15s that had come from Saudi Arabia and the remaining F-16 (of Egyptian origin) were repainted and returned by other pilots flown in at night. The three pilots who had survived the mission disappeared from the base soon after landing. It was rumoured that one of Saladin's personal aides presented them with the Order of Mohammed, the highest award for bravery in the Islamic Alliance's new military structure, before shooting them in the back of the head as they knelt for prayer. Whatever really happened to them, their whereabouts remain unknown to this day and their mission, as far as Saladin and his top half-dozen closest advisers were concerned, was a spectacular success.

Israel became isolated when the world woke up to television pictures of jets with Israeli markings bombing both Cairo and Tripoli. The journalists of the West watched the bombing raids unfold, at first with some excitement, especially at the downing of an F-16 which was caught clearly by a triumphant Sky News. This then turned to horror as the cameras raced with the first medical teams to the respective scenes of carnage in both cities. Israel denied everything. An indignant reporter from the BBC was the first to find the piece of F-16 wing with the Israeli Air Force roundel. It was clear that the planes were Israeli; the BBC could prove to the world that they were Israeli. The Israelis were the killers of innocent civilians and schoolchildren; the whole world could see that.

The world turned as one against Israel in disgust. Nato, and in particular the US, felt betrayed. The only people apart from the Israelis, whose protests of innocence fell on deaf ears, who knew who the real perpetrators were, namely the Islamic leadership and the Pentagon, each had their own good reasons for keeping silent. The Pentagon was keen to exert pressure on the Israelis to eventually become part of Nato's top-secret plans to assault the countries at the core of the Islamic Alliance. This meant that Israel should be dissuaded by whatever means from launching what Washington called hastily prepared and limited-effect spoiling raids. The Israeli war machine would be far more effective working in concert with Nato when the time came. Unfortunately the time would never come. As the fighting ground to a halt in the Sinai and both sides dug in to lick their wounds the war took on a new but not unexpected dimension. Saladin had had to modify his master plan slightly with the Israeli attack on the Sinai, but was delighted at the performance of the Egyptian and to a lesser extent Libyan troops. The world waited for the Alliance response to Sinai, but more especially to the 'outrages' of Cairo and Tripoli. Saladin did not disappoint and announced a 'Rain of Death' on Israel. The real war was about to begin.

Chapter Eleven – Scuds,
Arrows and Strategic Air Power

The First Shower

Lieutenant Mordecai Jakob had been with the 4th Israeli Air Force Arrow 2 battery for a mere three months. On graduation from officer school in mid-2005 he was sent to the Missile School at White Sands, New Mexico, to learn his trade on what was probably the best Anti-Tactical Ballistic Missile (ATBM) in the world. The new Arrow 2 ATBM, the product of a $2 billion investment by the USA following the failure and cancellation of her own THAAD (Theater High Altitude Area Defence) system, had gone into full production two years previously. It was due to both supplement older Patriot systems and complement the Patriot PAC4s. The Arrows were part of a defensive shield planned by Israel after the 1991 Gulf War. The shield had taken a large slice of defence spending, and technical hitches in the missile development meant that the system was some four years late into service. The system revolved around four Ofeq 5 (Ofeq is Hebrew for Horizon) surveillance satellites, a Citron Tree fire-control radar and Green Pine fire-control system. The 250kg Ofeq satellites were put into retrograde east–west orbits. Their high-resolution cameras, backed up by infrared sensors, gave Israel near real-time coverage of most of Iran, Iraq, Syria, Jordan, northern Saudi Arabia and the whole of North Africa. From three hundred miles up the IR systems were fine-tuned to detect the very distinct signature of a Scud or similar ballistic missile in terms of flash of heat at launch. On detection the launch data were fed directly to the Citron Tree fire-control systems of every Arrow battery. These systems, each of which was able to track up to twenty incoming missiles, were linked such that in automatic mode the computers decided which battery would give an optimum launch against which incoming missile or missiles for an intercept point some sixty miles out from the battery. The Israelis had four out of a planned eight batteries in service and they were very effective. In the ATBM role the Israelis had Patriot PAC4 SAMs. The PAC4 was a further development of the PAC3 that had emerged from the 1991 Gulf War to fulfil the ABM role.

On mobilisation of the Israeli Defence Force, the final two weeks of Jakob's course had been condensed into two eighteen-hour days. He was put on the first flight back to Ben Gurion with orders to report to Ramat David airbase, which lay on the Megiddo Plain some fifteen kilometres west of Nazareth. From Ramat David, where he was issued with two brand-new sets of combat fatigues and full NBC protective gear as well as his personal Uzi submachine-gun, he was helicoptered west along with seven others in an ancient and overloaded Iroquois to the eastern slopes of Mount Carmel. Carmel was the position for the 4th Battery which had been the last to form and was commanded and manned by reservists. Jakob jumped out of the Iroquois as it waited impatiently to disgorge its small load, the rotors making the low thudding that was unique to the Iroquois. In spite of his apprehension he could not help but admire the scene that met his eyes. Carmel rises to 546 feet, and from its summit the view is magnificent. To the west and south the golden coastline stretches away towards Tel Aviv; the coastal expressway and the sea lie ten kilometres due west; to the north and north-west is the busy port of Haifa and its bay, which loops up north to Acre and Lebanon. To the east and north-east rise the Galilean Hills and beyond them the Golan Heights. Due east beyond Ramat David is Nazareth, and beyond that the land falls away out of sight and into the Sea of Galilee. This would indeed be a lovely place in which to spend a war. His mind wandered back to his fiancée Cecilia. He had seen her just once in the past four months when she had flown out to visit him in New Mexico for a weekend of passion and sexual release rather than romance. She was now back in Tel Aviv, continuing to work as a trainee doctor in the infectious and tropical diseases clinic. They were both saving to buy their own place before getting married. After all this was over he would bring her up here to admire the view – with a blanket, of course.

He surveyed the battery position. The Green Pine fire-control radar (FCR) sat smugly just to the east of the summit. It was considerably larger than the Patriot FCRs, and like all phased-array radars looked like a large black chocolate bar on its side atop a flat loader packed with electronics which had had its wheels raised and was anchored with six extended folding legs. Around a hundred metres away, and parked in a large tailor-made earth berm, was what was to become his office, the Citron Tree fire-control system. This was the nerve centre of the Arrow 2, and it was inside the relatively spacious air-conditioned cabins that man and computers worked together to sort the incoming missiles. The scars in the ground still showed where the ground had been dug to enable the mass of direct-link cabling between radar, fire-control and missile positions. His battery was assigned to defend against missiles coming in over the Golan Heights aimed principally at Haifa, Israel's primary port. He looked further down the slopes and was able to make out four of the battery's eight twin launchers; the distinctive tubes that housed the missiles resembled ordinary lengths of sand-coloured oil piping with reinforcing bands at regular intervals along their length. The battery second-in-command (2ic) nodded to each of the new arrivals and without ceremony ushered them into a bare Portakabin that served as a rest room, makeshift briefing room and, when it was raining, as a smoking room. He was pleased that the last time the new boys had worked on the system was in the full-up war mode at Holloman a mere forty-eight hours previously.

'You will find your assigned work stations here identical to the simulator, except of course for the wind and dust and flies on top of this holy hill.' He was right, and the new arrivals, the final complement for the 4th Battery, felt immediately at home. That afternoon and evening they went over and over the battle drills and throught multiple computer-generated attack scenarios until the 2ic was satisfied that they all knew exactly what they were about. At 2300 they fell into their beds, mentally and physically exhausted.

The following day, 21 August, the battery commander, Lieutenant Colonel Peled, made his first appearance. He welcomed Jakob with a firm handshake that entailed grabbing the ends of his fingers and crushing them before Jakob could get a grip. Peled seemed ancient to Jakob. Although he had just turned fifty, he had long snowy-white hair, fierce and steel-blue eyes and a cracked face that had spent many years squinting in bright sunlight. Jakob had heard of Peled's legendary drinking exploits at Holloman the year before. After remarking about his ridiculously short US Marine-style haircut, Peled offered the newcomers a glass of chilled dry white wine. He had two passions – wine and missiles, not necessarily in that order. Peled took the new arrivals on a lightning tour of the battery site. He seemed extremely pleased with this opportunity of command, and Jakob thought he was remarkably relaxed considering that the Islamic Alliance had formally declared war on Israel a week ago and that the jihad was spreading throughout western Europe. Many were surprised that at his age he should be given such a chance, especially when he was nearly sent home after a bar-room brawl in New Mexico that ended up with two German officers being hospitalised. It turned out, as Peled went into transmit and expected his junior captive audience to receive, that he had served as a teenager in 1973 on Hawk missiles. His battery was the highest scoring in all Israel, with eight confirmed kills of Egyptian MiGs. After missing out on promotion past major, he was forcibly retired in 1990, at the age of thirty-five, and started his own wine business. He was recalled to active duty when Iraq invaded Kuwait in August 1991 and was senior liaison officer to one of the Patriot batteries assigned to defend Tel Aviv. Retired again at the end of 1992 he remained restless, but the army could not keep him out and he served three months out of every year as one of their most active reservists. His social ineptitude, which had cost him promotion, did nothing to dim the admiration of his regular peers who rose through the ranks. It was no surprise to any that this rough diamond was chosen to be the first non-regular army student on the Arrow course, or that he was given command of the first reservist battery. In 2005 Israel realised she needed fighters, and Peled's pedigree was good.

The Jeeps tumbled down the dirt track to the lower slopes, where there was an infantry company and Improved Hawk battery deployed to defend the Arrow 2 site. Peled introduced his new charges to the Hawk and infantry commanders and then indulged in a round of disdainful muttering about the claimed capability of the American-made Patriots. The conversation quickly turned to the intentions of Saladin and the Islamic Alliance, especially the apparent failure of the Sinai offensive: the closure of Hormuz, isolation of the Gulf 'garrisons' and the halting of the flow of oil out of the Gulf. They were certain that the US, would ultimately carry out her threat of an air campaign. Peled produced two bottles of white wine, apparently from nowhere, and suggested that they all enjoy a glass together before the sun went down.

Peled raised his glass solemnly. 'Gentlemen, a toast to Israel and a secure future for our children and their children.' The tin field mugs were clinked together. On cue, before the second drink of the afternoon reached Jakob's lips (he guessed it might have been Peled's fourth or fifth of the day), the air-raid sirens began to wail. Seconds later Peled's combat mobile phone rang on his hip. He turned to the assembled group.

'Let's go,' he said quietly. 'War is our business and business is picking up.' As the Jeeps raced back up the hillside to the command bunker, he explained that the satellite surveillance systems that were focused firmly on Iraq and Syria had detected the launch of several weather balloons from previously unremarkable desert sites. This meant only one thing – a Scud attack was imminent. The helium weather balloons, which, if detected, gave around five to ten minutes' warning of a possible launch, were used to make atmospheric and upper wind measurements which were fed back to the launch computer to enable the Scud to be fired on an optimum trajectory.

As they reached the summit of Carmel, Jakob glimpsed the
sun just disappearing as a red orb below the western horizon
before they sprinted to their battle stations. Jakob stood
behind his oppo, who was 'on shift'. The display was bright
and full of colour like any normal personal computer display.
All the information fed into the fire-control computers was
converted from raw radar data; the difference between a
computer-generated simulation, the real thing and a computer
game was zero. Jakob took his electronic gas mask out of its
bag and clipped it on to his belt. He had just plugged in his
lightweight headset when he heard the man in front, whose
name he didn't know, call, 'I've got six tracks, launch location
middle Iraq, probably near Al Habbaniyah, twenty miles west
of Baghdad.' He moved the mouse over the small symbols.
The computer had already given each one a letter and a three-
digit number – these were A001 to A006. 'Recommended
ABM launch in seven minutes, first intercept point Tiberias,
recommend Alert 4 and NBC 5.'

'Alert 4 and NBC 5 it is.' Peled turned the recommendation
into an order. The battery tannoys repeated the instruction.
Alert 4 meant that there was a confirmed hostile attack and
the incoming missiles would be landing within the Arrow 2's
engagement area footprint (Alert 5 was the highest level and
indicated that the incoming missiles might be aimed at the
battery itself). NBC 5 forced all personnel to don their
electronic gas masks and operate hoods up with the control
cabins fully sealed with over-pressure confirmed in anticipation of a nuclear, biological or chemical attack. The over-
pressure ensured that air only flowed out of the sealed cabins,
even if they suffered minor shrapnel damage, thus ensuring
their occupants maximum protection from chemical or biological attack.

Travelling in excess of Mach 4, the Scuds would take
around fourteen minutes at a range of 450–500 nautical
miles (1,000 km) from launch to impact. The Arrow 2
accelerated rapidly to Mach 4.5 after launch and was capable
of intercepting targets at ranges between 16 and 48 km at
altitudes of up to 40 km. The Arrow 2 was designated a
middle-tier weapon, meaning that it was able to hit the

incoming missiles well before they neared the impact point. Upper-tier weapons that had not been fully developed were the Brilliant Pebbles space-based missile defence system – the core of President Reagan's SDI Star Wars programme – and more recently the Airborne Laser (ABL) mounted in the nose of a 747 jumbo to knock down missiles as they entered the boost phase shortly after launch. Patriot PAC3 and PAC4 were lower-tier weapons, capable of point defence within a ninety-degree arc out to around 25 km from launch but down to altitudes as low as 1 km. The technical difficulty of hitting an incoming missile with an ABM such as the Arrow was on a par with getting one bullet to hit another at a passing speed of around Mach 9.

'Request auto engage,' said the operator.

'Request denied,' came back Peled from his commander's station. 'Let me know as soon as the computer has completed a ballistic analysis and given a ninety-five per cent confidence level of the ten-kilometre impact area.'

'Roger.' The operator put a box around the six trajectories on his screen and left-clicked, then selected 'impact zone' from the menu. Immediately six large circles appeared, with a Scud impact marker at the centre of each. These were the 95 per cent confidence zones. As the seconds ticked by and the trajectories were analysed by the Ofeq and Green Pine systems, the radii of each impact zone slowly reduced.

'Optimum launch in two minutes,' said the still-anonymous operator. 'OK ten-kilometre impact zone for Alpha 001, 002 and 003 is Ramat David, and for 004 through 006 it's . . . Nazareth. Permission to engage.'

'Denied,' replied Peled, sounding like a courtroom judge. 'Hold fire on all launchers.' Peled had made his decision. The ABM defence of both Ramat David and Nazareth was assigned to the Patriot battery just west of Ramat David. Nazareth was just inside the MEZ of the PAC4s.

'Eight new tracks identified. Launch position near Al Hasakah in north-east Syria.'

'OK, same procedure as before. Ten-kilometre ninety-five per cent as soon as you have it.' It appeared that for Peled the attack was some kind of chess game. Jakob took the opportunity to look outside through the cabin's periscope. It was completely dark now. He zoomed east towards Ramat David and Nazareth, where he knew that families would now be running to basement shelters and fumbling with gas masks. Suddenly in the foreground there were three bursts of brilliant light as the first PAC4s were fired in anger at the incoming Scuds. The telltale orange flare of the rocket motors was clearly visible as the three missiles accelerated vertically, and then their trajectory flattened as they sped out towards Nazareth to what would be maximum-range intercept points. Twelve seconds later the sounds of the Patriot launches, what always seemed to be an excessively loud bang, reached the cabins. Another three Patriots were then fired, these three maintaining a near-vertical trajectory. Before the sound of those launches reached Carmel, Jakob saw, much lower than he'd expected, two spectacular showers of sparks over Nazareth, off to the right; looking south-east there was one explosion that blossomed with red fire as one of the Scuds hit the airbase at Meggido. The first Scud to impact Israel hit the administrative area of the base, demolishing some emergency sleeping quarters that were occupied by F-16 technicians. Three were killed and another seven wounded, two seriously. The latter were medevacked by helicopter to a burns unit in Tel Aviv. Off to the right, as the launch bangs reached the cabins, there were three explosions high above Ramat David as the PAC4s found their targets. A shower of falling, burning debris followed, some of it still supersonic, indicating that it was one thing to hit a Scud, another to completely destroy it.

As the first of these bits were impacting the fields beyond the airbase, Jakob noticed the telltale blue-and-white hot glow of military jet afterburners lighting up on the runway. There were four F-16s actually on the runway and, in the lit-up scene, Jakob could make out another four waiting in position and yet more emerging from the HAS sites. He smiled with pride. The airforce had always been ready to strike back if Israel was attacked. She was not going to stand and receive punches without reply as she had done fifteen years earlier. This time there was no fragile coalition to hold together – the US and Nato were already making moves in support of Israel.

Jakob was in no doubt that the IAF would avenge the deaths of Israeli civilians. He was just beginning to speculate on possible targets for the jets when the voice of the anonymous controller pulled him back into the cabin.

'A007 through 009, ninety-five per cent is Haifa dock area, 010 through 012, ninety-five per cent is . . . Ramat David, and 013 and 014, ninety-five per cent is . . . 4th Battery position, Mount Carmel.' A shudder of fear ran through all those present. It was an odd feeling that out there somewhere there was someone, hundreds of miles away, who was trying to kill you. Peled was becoming more enigmatic than ever. The atmosphere reminded Jakob of those scenarios he'd seen in tense dramas based in submarines, where all eyes and ears were on the captain, each mind willing him to act but none daring to speak. It was 4th Battery's captain who broke the tension.

'Very clever,' was all Peled said initially. Then, 'You are clear to engage 007, 008, 009, 013 and 014' – an audible and collective sigh of relief went up in the cabin.

'Roger, clear engage 007, 008, 009, 013 and 014,' repeated the anonymous controller, no emotion in his voice.

'And we can expect a mini-shower from the south-east any minute now,' said Peled.

'Affirm,' said the controller. 'I have six more tracks coming out of northern Saudi on the pipeline road.' Good grief, thought Jakob, Peled must be psychic. Apparently reading their thoughts, Peled continued, 'Gentlemen, this score of missiles is merely a probe by what has become a clever and wily enemy. He will seek to test the defences of different areas from different angles with different combinations of Scuds to see which combination gives him the maximum chance of penetrating our defences. It will take him a little while to analyse these attacks, a process that will be helped enormously by CNN and Sky World. Then, and only then, will we see either a massed barrage or the beginning of chemical, biological or, dare I say it, nuclear attack.'

The controller moved his mouse, left-clicked and announced, 'Launching at seven, eight and nine.' From outside there were three almighty crashes as the first Arrow 2s were thrown out of their snug casings which had protected them

from the elements and roared into life, off to seek the Scuds
aimed at the military dock area of Haifa's harbour. Seconds
later two more launches followed, aimed at the pair of Scuds
inbound on 4th Battery's position. Peering through the periscope, Jakob was temporarily blinded by the crescendo of
light that flooded the upper slopes of Carmel as the Arrows'
boost motors cut in only fifty feet above the ground to begin
the missiles' acceleration to nearly Mach 5.

'Alpha 015 through 017, ninety-five per cent is Ramat
David, and 018 to 020 is Meggido.' The controller was still
sorting the missiles, but learning fast what Peled's remit was.
'Confirm zero engagement of 015 to 020.'

'That is correct, well done,' replied Peled. The rules of
engagement (RoE) for the Arrow 2s were held on a need-to-
know basis. In 4th Battery only Peled and the 2ic knew
precisely which rules for the firing of the precious Arrow
2s had been laid down by the political and military authorities
'at the highest level'. The controllers, and for that matter the
enemy, were left to work them out. The anonymous controller
had correctly guessed that 4th Battery's mission was to
protect itself and Haifa, as dictated by the Prime Minister.
It was a fair guess therefore that 1st Battery was covering
Jerusalem, 2nd Battery Tel Aviv and 3rd Battery Ramon and
Area 657 high on the Negev Plateau where Israel's nuclear
arsenal sat embedded in silos drilled into the bedrock. In the
next six minutes the controller identified a further seventy-five
Scud launches, none of which would fall within the 4th's area
of responsibility. There was one anomaly in the attack. The
anonymous controller picked up a single missile, A039, fired
from somewhere on the Iran/Iraq border. The 95 per cent
impact area was calculated as fifty miles west of Tel Aviv, way
out to sea. This missile was assumed to be one that had lost its
trajectory, and was ignored as it splashed innocuously into
the sea as predicted.

From remote desert sites in southern Egypt, eastern Libya,
Jordan, Syria and Iraq began the rain of Scuds on Israel,
although, as Peled had correctly assessed, these first hundred
were merely a testing of the defences. The major targets were
the seven Israeli Air Force bases – in the south was Ovda,

north of the Negev Desert heights was Ramon and the nuclear
silos, east and west of Beer Sheba lay Hatserim and Nevatim,
south of Tel Aviv were Hatzor and Palmahim, and finally in
the north on the Meggido Plain south-east of Haifa was
Ramat David – and the port facilities at Haifa and the Arrow
2 battery positions. The Islamic Alliance had chosen this
initial target set for several reasons. The airbases were well
defended with Patriot PAC4s. It was Nevatim, home of the
Israeli F-15I Thunder squadrons, that received the most
attention. If any one of the F-15I Thunder hardened shelters
could be hit the $80 million aircraft – the most valuable and
most capable in the air force inventory – inside would be
destroyed or badly damaged enough to preclude any role
being played by it in the coming conflict. Also, by attacking
almost exclusively the Israeli military, something that would
be seen as retaliation for Israel's clear aggression across the
Sinai, the Alliance would be able to maintain the moral high
ground. This was especially true if the response by Israel was
anything other than proportionate. And if it was disproportionate, and the Alliance intended to ensure this, then it would
be dealer's choice for the next level of escalation of the
conflict. The relatively few missiles aimed into the Arrow 2
MEZs were simply to test the still-unknown capability of the
Arrow 2 system. Once this was established the Alliance would
be able to adjust its Scud attack strategy for maximum
military and political benefit.

Jakob was back at the periscope. Two more Patriots left the
rails at Ramat David and swung rapidly north to intercept
012 and 013. Jakob wondered why a third had not been
launched at 014. After a short pause a further three Patriots
crashed off south-east in an attempt to intercept Scuds 015 to
017. There was then a glow at the top edge of the periscope's
field of view as the Arrow 2s hit the Scuds incoming at Haifa
and Carmel. The controller ran a rapid analysis of the intercepts. The screen now had multiple traces which were the
radar returns of falling bits of Scud missile and Arrow 2
debris. On a raw radar display, and even to the latest software
of the Patriot PAC4s, any one of these pieces of supersonic
junk might represent an unscathed Scud. The Israeli radar and

computer engineers had leapt ahead of the best US research in their ability to sort live Scuds from bits of broken-up Scuds. It soon became clear that this problem was still very much unsolved when it seemed to Jakob, observing events through the periscope, that 13th Patriot Battery, two miles west of Ramat David, appeared to launch all of its missiles as one. No fewer than eight Patriots left the rails with what sounded like a stuttering thunderclap. Indeed, down at the 13th things weren't going so well.

There were two problems that faced the IDF commanders. The first was, as both sides knew, that the Alliance had probably been able to manufacture more cheap Scuds, possibly as much as four times as many as the Israelis had ready-to-fire Patriots and Arrows. Therefore, even if every one of the 400 ATBMs hit an incoming Scuds there would be no defence against the estimated 700 to 1,200 Scuds which would follow through the defensive vacuum. While the Patriot PAC4s were able to hit incoming scuds they were occasionally unable to actually break up the warheads. The PAC4s, travelling at Mach 3, were trying to destroy incoming Scuds travelling at Mach 4 – the passing speed was some Mach 7. It had proven very difficult to develop fusing sensitive enough to allow detonation at the right time, given intercept angle, with enough blastfrag warhead to destroy incoming missiles on the smaller Patriots. Worse still were the near-misses which caused the Scuds to 'wobble' on their trajectories, then break up in a cartwheeling motion into three or four major components, looking to all the world's anti-missile radars like an advanced ICBM which has just split off its four or five separate warheads. Both the Patriot operators involved in manual engagements and those systems operating in fully automatic had to be able to discern, in seconds, the difference between a MIRV attack (Multiple Independent Re-entry – sub-warheads separating from a 'mother' missile during re-entry) and multiple 'killed' Scud fragments. On the PAC4 the software was still not perfect. The 13th at Ramat David had suffered a launch failure in the A014 intercept. Compounding the problem was the fact that A014's trajectory was right on the extreme left-hand edge of the 13th's MEZ. The controller had attempted to use a short cut and go via full automatic for a quick-launch solution on the fast-approaching 014. Unfortunately, the short cut disabled the discrimination software and the system launched eight Patriot missiles at 014 and the largest falling supersonic pieces of 012 and 013 – an expensive error.

Commanders like Peled were well aware of the numbers game in the missile/anti-missile scenario and were instructed to be rigorous in their interpretation of the RoE and selective in their engagements. This meant waiting, often until the optimum launch point was past, to be certain that the incoming missile was going to hit something significant. Israel could not afford to waste missiles, as resupply was only really possible direct from the USA by air – and with Nato attempting to shift its weight from north to south all air transport, even commandeered civilian aircraft, was at a premium.

The cabin's field telephone rang and was answered by a clerk. He listened, then walked briskly to Peled, who went to the phone, picked it up and without preamble said, 'I'm sorry, Josh, I cannot help you at the moment, you know the score.' And put the phone back down again. 'Fucking idiot,' he then added to no one in particular. Jakob learned later that it was the commander of the 13th begging Peled to cover Ramat David after the inadvertent launch of so many of his missiles. The commander of the 13th was sacked the next day. The initial shower of Scuds was over inside one hour after the first launch. All the airbases targeted had taken at least three hits each, but the damage caused was relatively small, with only three aircraft damaged to varying degrees and one destroyed outright. Not a single Scud impacted in the zones defended by the four Arrow 2 batteries intact.

The IAF response to this first attack was measured. Throughout that night until dawn the following morning IAF F-16s and F-15s flew just under three hundred sorties against what were described as 'strategic targets' in Egypt, Jordan, Syria, north-western Saudi Arabia and western Iraq. Israel was aware that to ensure the support of the US and her allies she had to go some way towards regaining the moral high ground. Not surprisingly perhaps, the fighter forces in

Syria, Jordan, Iraq and Egypt were held on the ground, and
the defence of these countries was left to the SAM units that
ringed the major cities and airbases – although even these
units were suspiciously quiet and most remained passive. Of
the 293 sorties, 125 were fighter sweep or escort, 60 were in
electronic support, jamming and SEAD, and the remainder of
around 100 were, other than a handful of tanker and ELINT/
SIGINT sorties, actual bombing missions.

In the traditional manner of air campaigns of any kind the
IAF was keen to gain command of the skies above not only
Israel but also to a large extent over its neighbours, so that it
would be able to roam at will in future. The Islamic air forces
were aware of their marked inferiority to the IAF, especially in
terms of training and, with the exception of the Saudis and
Egyptians, in terms of equipment. This gap in capability was
even more marked at night. Night-time air combat was still
something that only very few nations could claim to excel at.

The targets hit that night included: the electricity substations that served Damascus and Amman; the Syrian and
Egyptian Air Force headquarters; the two strategic SA-12
sites that ringed Damascus; the major air force bases at Da'ra
in southern Syria, El Jafr in Jordan, H3 in Iraq, Al Salihiyah
just over the Suez Canal in Egypt, and Tabuk in northern
Saudi Arabia. The IAF scored major successes against the
electrical stations and managed to plunge both Damascus and
Amman into complete darkness. Some success was claimed
against the SA-12 sites, but the levels of damage could not be
confirmed, and the attack on the airbases returned some very
indifferent results; indeed, against Tabuk the attack was
tantamount to a failure.

In 1967 the IAF was able to destroy most of her neighbours'
air forces on the ground before they got airborne. This was
before the whole of the Middle East embarked on a massive
shelter-building programme, mostly completed by Western
contractors, which turned the airbases into concrete-rein-
forced bastions. The events of 1967 ensured that the IAF
would never again be allowed the luxury of rocketing and
strafing lines of aircraft unprotected in the open. It was true
that in the 1991 Gulf War and the 2002 Second Korean War

the hardened airbases were of little value against the might of the USAF, USN and their allies. It was also true that such systematic destruction required overwhelming superiority in numbers as well as technology, and numbers were something the IAF did not have. On average, B-2 statistics aside, it took two sorties by any dedicated fighter-bomber to ensure the destruction of a single HAS. And on this night even the much-vaunted IAF was unable to overturn the historical trend, managing to destroy or significantly damage twenty-two HASs, and inflicting no damage whatever on Tabuk, for the loss of seven aircraft. The losses were three F-16s to SAMs or AAA fire and one unknown, and another F16 that probably flew into the ground in the target area on the SA-12 site raid. The other three were two F-16s and an F-15 lost just north of Tabuk in air combat with the Saudi Air Force.

The Saudis, thanks to two decades of the very best of intense British and American training, had no intention of hiding their fighters in shelters and allowing the IAF free rein over Saudi airspace. As soon as the first Scuds were airborne and heading for Israel, the ISAF (Islamic as opposed to Royal Saudi Air Force) launched an AWACs early-warning aircraft from Ha'il, set up a standing CAP of four F-15C north-west of Tabuk, and put the remaining two squadrons of F-15Cs based at Tabuk on five minutes' readiness. This was in anticipation of an Israeli counter-strike against Tabuk. At 0230 the AWACs picked up a large formation of thirty Israeli aircraft heading south down the Sinai Peninsula. The commander correctly anticipated that this force would turn east to launch a raid on Tabuk, and as the Israelis coasted in from the Red Sea a total of twenty-four Saudi F-15s rose to meet them. In the BVR tangle that ensued between the Israeli F-15s and the Saudi Eagles the Israelis had the advantage of AMRAAM missiles over the Saudis' AIM-7F Sparrow missiles but were disadvantaged in numbers, with only half as many dedicated fighters as the Saudis had airborne. Also, the Saudis had the advantage of being virtually above their home base whereas the Israelis were some distance from home and not exactly 'fat for gas'. The other eighteen in the IAF package were comprised of twelve F-16s fitted out in the bomber role and six F-

16 HARM shooters in the SEAD role. The Israelis managed to down seven Saudi F-15s but lost two of their own and a HARM shooter before the mission commander decided against pressing the attack. The Saudi AWAC had taken away any element of surprise the Israelis had hoped to enjoy to enable them to attack and dispose of the expected base defence CAP before the Saudis responded. He was aware from his intelligence briefings that there were at least a further twelve F-15s at Tabuk waiting as a second line of defence and did not want to risk losing half the package. This would be entirely possible if the Saudi superior numbers caught them on the egress running for home with little or no fuel to spare.

When dawn broke on 22 August both sides had reason to be pleased with their night's work. For the Israelis the Arrow 2 had been an outstanding success, and this would be a worry for the Islamic Alliance campaign planners. It seemed that an impregnable shield defended the four critical areas of Israel – Jerusalem, Tel Aviv, Haifa and the Negev nuclear site. One major problem was the ratio of aircraft losses for the night. Wild claims from both sides apart, the true figures of losses to all causes, as both sides knew – aware that this was the true measure of success or failure – amounted to ten IAF aircraft lost compared with twenty-three Islamic aircraft. This was a ratio that the IAF, more used to cricket-score results, would find unsustainable in any long campaign.

The Israeli High Command was also concerned about the relative lack of success of the Patriot PAC4s. Although they had outperformed the Patriots deployed in the 1991 Gulf War by an order of magnitude, they were still having difficulty coping with multiple missiles on the edge of their MEZs. Israel considered every aircraft it possessed as worth its weight in gold since they were all, with the exception of the sixty pure-fighter F-15Cs, capable of fulfilling any offensive role that was required of them. Israeli air power was very flexible and capable of inflicting lasting damage to any opponent under the right circumstances. It hurt the IAF deeply that one $80 million F-15I had fallen victim to a Scud which cost around $750,000 to produce. If the Islamic Alliance stepped up its attacks on the airbases, and if only a handful of Scuds found targets, the Israelis would have to consider denuding the defences of the major cities. This would be an important political as well as military decision in that the Israelis would be accepting the possibility of heavy civilian casualties by moving Arrow 2 batteries to protect the one set of conventional assets that was capable of striking deep into Islamic territory.

None of the Scuds fired that first night had anything other than conventional high-explosive warheads. Shin Bet, the ultra-secret arm of the Israeli Secret Service, had confirmed two years earlier that all of Israel's neighbours had acquired the technology to fill the Scud warheads with chemical agents such as Sarin or VX or, much worse, biological weapons. Despite a decade of denials we now know that the IDF had begun to produce its own chemical stockpiles in 1994, and production was stepped up in 1998. The Israeli delivery mechanisms were, however, through either artillery or, again, the IAF. The Israelis were able to conclude from the first night of Scud attacks that the Islamic Alliance was not prepared to escalate to the use of chemical or biological weapons. This was, the report to the Prime Minister stated, because Israel had made it abundantly clear that she was willing and able to respond in kind or (with nuclear weapons) worse against Islamic city populations that were, in contrast to their Israeli counterparts, essentially unprotected.

In the Israeli press there was an outcry not only against the Islamic Alliance but also against the IAF for not doing more to hit the Scuds at source. The IAF took the criticism on the chin but remained convinced that 'Scud-hunting' was a low-pay-off activity. During late 1944 and early 1945, total air supremacy coupled with accurate knowledge of where the German V-1 and V-2 launch sites were had not enabled the Allies to significantly reduce the number of launches against London and subsequently Antwerp. In the 1991 Gulf War the Israelis knew more than most that 'Scud-hunting' was more of a political than a military success. For every Scud that was destroyed at least one dummy Scud, and two sanction-busting articulated trucks carrying anything from petroleum to fruit and veg, were also destroyed, and the number of sorties required, and the sheer effort, were out of all proportion to the physical results achieved. Individual trucks, which is what the Scuds were mounted on, were easy to hide, especially in anything larger than a Bedouin camp, difficult to distinguish in anything other than ideal conditions with the best electro-optical sensors, and hard to hit. During the Gulf War the pressure to keep the Israelis out of the conflict meant that at any one time up to 25 per cent of attack missions by F-15s, F-16s and A-10s were dedicated to the mobile missile chase. The detractors of the anti-Scud effort claimed that the air campaign consumed a disproportionate share of aerial resources to no good end and failed to destroy a single mobile Scud launcher. The proponents pointed out that the political aim of the Scud hunt was achieved and that the campaign had realised what was described as 'virtual attrition'. Although Iraq possessed between 500 and 600 Scuds, only 88 were fired. The Iraqis spent much time avoiding the hunters; they were denied the use of fixed sites; it was dangerous for mobile missiles to move; and the firing bracket was limited to short periods at dawn or dusk (thermal crossover) and under cover of poor weather or heavy cloud cover.

The IAF, however, probably correctly, concluded that looking for Scuds simply wasn't worth their while, especially as the damage caused by any individual Scud was minimal, although the occasional one or two got lucky. The IAF response would be to hit their Scud-firing enemies elsewhere, where it would hurt them more.

Back on Mount Carmel during the day of the 22nd there was an uneasy calm. Neither side seemed inclined to prosecute their different campaigns during the daylight hours, which were spent in frenzied analysis and planning for the night to come. The day was punctuated by calls for peace and negotiation from New York, but these were studiously ignored by both sides. As night fell everyone tensed up for action. The IAF stood ready to respond to attacks but was not going to be drawn in to a battle of attrition. Peled told his men to expect a slightly different pattern of launches. He was still convinced that this was merely a period of testing the defences, and tried to get through to the IDF's commander-in-chief to tell him that he knew exactly what the 'Arabs' were up to. He got no further than the outer office before being politely told by a regular major, who was the chief's military assistant, that the best brains in Israel were working on the enemy strategy and he might be better off concentrating on doing his own job rather than getting into everybody else's office.

'What the Arabs were up to' became more clear that evening. At exactly midnight the second barrage of Scuds was launched. The main targets were Tel Aviv and the Ramon Nuclear Area and Haifa (all defended by Arrow 2s) as well as several smaller towns. The hardest blows fell against the towns of Nazareth, Ashqelon and Be'er Sheva, which were hit by five, three and four Scuds respectively. In Nazareth twenty-three civilians were killed and many more injured. In the other two towns only a handful of people were killed or injured. Tel Aviv and Ramon were both attacked simultaneously by more than a dozen missiles launched from different launch sites in Egypt, Saudi Arabia and Syria, giving the Arrow 2 systems a serious test of their capabilities. Peled's 4th Battery defending Haifa had to cope with an attempted saturation attack of eighteen Scuds in as many minutes. The Arrow 2s again coped admirably. Only one missile hit Ramon intact, damaging an administrative building, one hit the northern suburbs of Tel Aviv, and two, much to Peled's irritation, hit a ship-loading facility in Haifa docks – doing no damage but killing eight workers. The airbase at Nevatim, home of the F-15Is, was also attacked by sixteen Scuds in a frantic ten-minute period. Seven Scuds impacted one of the squadron areas with remarkable accuracy, destroying three shelters and digging two huge holes in the taxiways. Most of the IAF was already airborne as this onslaught hit. Again that night, as far as the analysts could tell, there were no biological or chemical weapons used. Again there were two missiles whose origins were more likely to be Iran than Iraq which sailed high over Jerusalem and Tel Aviv before splashing down harmlessly into the sea between fifty and a hundred miles off the coast. These were, like the first lone long-ranger the previous night, assumed to be failures by Iran with its new long-range Shahab-4 MRBMs. The Israeli assessment, which turned out to be correct, was that the first two nights of Scud launches were an attempt to assess the real strengths and weaknesses of the Arrow 2 systems that were defending Israel's most sensitive areas.

The IAF had also adopted its strategy to suit the evolving situation. Historically, on the outbreak of hostilities, the IAF would engage in round-the-clock missions as the ground and air situations dictated. In this opening phase of the war there were no 'situations'. However, the IAF had been stung at Tabuk and, despite the success of blacking out Damascus and Amman, was less than happy with the results achieved against the SAM sites and other airbases. There was also the curiosity of the lack of serious resistance by the Islamic SAM operators, and still little sign of movement by the Islamic ground forces, which were still dispersed. The IAF realised that in order to do lasting damage to any single airbase or SAM complex it would have to adopt an approach similar to that used by the USAF – the packages sent against any single target would have to be significantly larger than anything the Israelis had previously attempted. The major problem, along with the inflexibility of large packages of in excess of fifty aircraft, was that the planning and co-ordination of such missions took an inordinate amount of time. All such Nato and US packages were planned twenty-four hours in advance. Thus the daylight hours of the 22nd saw the best pilots and navigators of the IAF fighter-bomber squadrons engaged in enforced inactivity in flying terms but furiously poring over maps, target photographs and package flow diagrams.

The scramble, at 2330 that night, was therefore an ordered and premeditated move, and saw three large packages, two in excess of 80 aircraft and a third of 110, form up and proceed to single targets. The three target airfields were: Queen Alaya, ten miles south of Amman in Jordan; Al Manzilah, fifteen miles south-east of Port Said in Egypt; and, to teach the RSAF a thing or two about air power, the package of 110 was sent against Tabuk. The Israeli High Command insisted on the destruction of enemy aircraft, since they had good intelligence to indicate that if the Scuds were unable to get through then any subsequent biological or chemical attack might be conducted by fighter-bombers armed with large spray tanks. Any single penetration, presumably at ultra-low level, might have devastating effects on a population centre. The first two airfields suffered very heavy damage with the runways blown apart on each and more than half of the HASs destroyed for the loss of a single F-4E2000. Tabuk was wrecked but not before a show of defiance by the RSAF. The IAF fighter sweep, more than three times the size of that sent the previous night, shot down eleven RSAF F-15s for the loss of two of its own. A further five F-15s were hit on the ground or were written off trying to land on runways and taxiways full of holes. The I-Hawk and Crotale SAM batteries at Tabuk managed to down a further three F-16s as they attacked the airfield but were rendered inoperative by some forty HARM shots which the escorting SEAD F-16s used to blast a hole in the air defences for the main bomber package. On returning to base the Israeli jets were met by a nasty surprise as at 0230 another barrage of forty Scuds in total was fired at the main IAF bases. This shower claimed, directly or indirectly, a further three IAF jets. This had been a far more successful night for the Israelis. The aircraft kill-to-loss ratio was up where it needed to be for a longer-term decisive result. For the authorities on the ground in the cities and towns the analysis of Scud debris still showed no traces of known chemical or biological agents.

Lull before the Storm

The next day, 24 August, the Islamic Alliance Military Council declared a unilateral ceasefire. For the Alliance planners the forty-eight hours of experimentation had given them all the answers they needed. The Israelis, cautiously triumphant at their successes so far, considered that they had more than held their own. They concluded that the levels of destruction wrought by IAF fighter-bombers had exceeded the expectations of the enemy, and therefore he would be forced to rethink any future plans for attacking Israel without air superiority. The Israeli government, keen to regain some moral high ground, remained content to play a reactive role to the Alliance attacks. The counter-attacks by the IAF, as long as they did not incur excessive collateral damage in terms of civilians killed, must be perceived as 'just'. In addition, the longer the enemy sustained any missile-based offensive against Israel, and specifically against her major population centres, however unsuccessfully, the more support for the Israeli cause would grow both in America and Europe. The IDF recommended immediate acceptance of a ceasefire, to be mediated by the UN. This would, above all, allow them time to replenish and increase stocks of Patriot and Arrow 2 missiles (around a quarter of all ATBM stocks had been fired in those first two nights). Also, although the overall total aircraft kill-to-loss ratio of the second night had been much better than the first at 47:9, this was still just below what the IAF demanded if the struggle became one of attrition. On 24 August a temporary peace settled over the region. Neither side was in much doubt that the peace would be temporary. The Israelis were left wondering at the relative inactivity of their neighbours' air defences. Only those targets directly attacked had responded in any way, and it was wondered what benefit the Islamic Alliance was gaining by employing only 10 per cent of the known SAM and AAA assets available to them. The perception was that the Alliance still had to find some way of neutralising both the Israeli Air Force and the Arrow 2 batteries before a resumption of any offensive action. The Scud attacks on the airbases had been less destructive than anticipated, although the local successes that were achieved seriously worried the IAF commanders, and the performance of the Arrow 2 had exceeded their most pessimistic estimates with a successful launch-to-kill percentage in excess of 90.

Nato Wades In

Nato considered that the 'failure' of the Scud barrages had stalled any offensive plans Saladin might have laid. In the past a less belligerent and more divided Nato might have given the Islamic Alliance the benefit of any doubt and called a temporary halt to the extensive deployments that were taking place across the Mediterranean. There were, however, other indicators and developments that caused Nato to take the opposite view. And the deadline of 1 September for the beginning of a strategic air campaign was fast approaching. This could only be averted, Nato insisted, by the cessation of all preparations for hostilities against Israel and full co-operation in clearing Hormuz of mines. The first indicator was that the build-up of troops in Syria, Jordan, northern Iraq and north-western Saudi Arabia continued unabated. Strategic reconnaissance had also picked up signs that several Pakistani formations were making the long trek west. Additionally, satellite reconnaissance and secret reporting revealed that Algerian, Moroccan and Sudanese troops were arriving, albeit painfully slowly by Nato standards, on the west bank of Suez. This turn of events merely confirmed the Israeli analysis that the Egyptians were a spent force and that an influx of low-grade fanatics showed that the Alliance, on Israel's western front, was already scraping the barrel.

The second negative indicator was the activities of the Russians. Russia was secretly determined not to let Nato and the US threaten the Alliance with air power unchecked. As soon as Nato preparations for the move into Turkey were confirmed, Russia began to dispatch several SAM regiments into Iran. These were not any old units. The Russians had further developed the formidable S-300 into an even more capable SAM designated the S-400. The S-400 had never been exported and was capable of detecting targets, including, it was claimed, stealth aircraft, and engaging them at all altitudes out to phenomenal ranges of 400-plus kilometres. This development was a major concern to Nato's air campaign planners, who were still less than confident of countering the S-300s. The final indicator was more pernicious and potentially explosive than all the others put together. Saladin, far from backing down and adopting a more conciliatory tone towards Israel and the West, launched into a campaign of powerful rhetoric against the West and Israel. He threatened death from the skies and plague and pestilence on the West, in a clear reference to biological and chemical weapons, for its

unequivocal support for Israel. He reminded the West and
Israel that the Alliance had both the will and the means to rain
down on cities the very worst weapons of warfare. In remote
locations in Syria, Iran and Iraq, the West's satellite surveillance picked up clear indicators of intensified testing of
chemical weapons. In the past the Islamic nations had gone
to great lengths to conceal the testing of such weapons; now it
seemed they were hardly bothering. Even the most casual
satellite reconnaissance analyst could not fail to notice the
extent of the preparations.

The response in the West and in Israel was predictable.
Israel stated that she would not hesitate to use all means at her
disposal to destroy the aggressor states as soon as she felt an
attack was imminent. Nato, having noted Israel's willingness
and preference for pre-emptive strikes, now had a tough call
to make. The indicators were unambiguous. The Alliance was
preparing to use chemical weapons and worse against Israel.
Israel was not only able to respond in kind, she had made it
clear that the use of weapons of mass destruction would
trigger a nuclear response. Nato wanted to avoid a Middle
East meltdown but it was not yet ready with its conventional
'big stick' to dissuade the Alliance from any further action
against Israel. She was still some weeks away from being in a
position to prosecute an 'overland rescue' operation to the
Gulf or react 'from the sea' via the might of the USN and
Marines thanks to the closure of Hormuz.

Nato's offensive timetable had began to slip. The planners
at SHAPE had realised that twelve Nato and twelve Turkish
divisions would not be enough to guarantee a swift and
decisive victory if launched into the Alliance heartland. The
sheer size of the enemy and the distances involved had caused
a double problem and a major rethink. Arrayed against Nato
and Turkey's close to one million troops would be, from Iran,
Iraq and Syria alone, potentially two to three million men in
upwards of sixty divisions and around 1,200 combat aircraft.
More than half of these troops were deployed in positions
from which they could move against Israel. There were many
low-grade reservists, recently mobilised. However, each country also had, as Egypt had demonstrated, a core of well-

trained (some battle-hardened) and well-equipped veterans who would put up serious resistance. Nato decided that at least ten further divisions would be required, and the rationale behind such a move was solid enough. The planners had concluded that more than one thrust axis would be required to keep the enemy off balance and that given the vast areas of ground to be covered the initial plan fell short in pure numbers terms. Fresh forces would be essential in ensuring rapid exploitation following breakthrough at decisive points. Also, with serious resistance to be bypassed, further troops would be required to act as covering forces and flank guards. The final deciding factor was that the more troops Nato could push through any one axis the greater the local superiority would be. This overwhelming use of force had historically served to reduce casualties rather than increase them. There was much wringing of hands and sucking of teeth in Nato's political capital cities, but the logic was irrefutable and every government was keen to avoid charges of reticence and lack of commitment. This was especially the case if such decisions were later to be seen to have increased the size of the casualty list against clear top-level military advice. Thus, after a full forty-eight hours in conference, the North Atlantic Council managed to squeeze an additional ten divisions out of its members for the Turkish front.

The second echelon for what would become Operation Western Strike (naturally following Western Shield) comprised the US 5th Armoured Corps of two mechanised, one airborne and one air assault division, the French Light Armoured Division and Rapid Action Force Division (Foreign Legion and paratroopers), the Spanish Light Armoured Division, the Italian Folgore Armoured Division, the German 3rd Panzer Division, and most surprisingly perhaps two Greek divisions, one armoured and one mechanised. As far as Nato was concerned the build-up in the east had now become a maximum effort with virtually every soldier that could be spared preparing to move to the region. But Nato chiefs were aware that this mighty show of force would take another two months to assemble and organise into any serious coherent fighting formation. The politicians hoped that this unparalleled show of resolve would add weight to the next action they were planning and transmit in no uncertain terms the gravity with which Nato viewed the situation.

The problems with gathering and preparing for such a large operation were not unknown. The wars in the Gulf in 1991 and Korea in 2002 had shown that 'preparation' of the battlefield was an essential element of any offensive campaign against dug-in enemies, and this could only be carried out by the intensive use of air power. In 1991 this phase had lasted six weeks, and in 2002, against a much larger enemy force, in more difficult terrain, more than double that. Nato chiefs considered that anywhere between six and ten weeks of preparation would be required, depending on the level of resistance put up by Alliance air defence assets, and anyway it would be at least that long before the ground troops were in place and ready to begin an assault. Also, the build-up of tactical air power would not be complete much before mid- to late October. The airbases receiving the air armadas in Oman, Turkey and Cyprus still had much work to be done. This involved a crash expansion programme which was known as the 'Dollar Hose' – spray the desert with dollars and instant airbases and dispersal areas spring up. This process required time, as did the emplacement of supporting infrastructure and the prepositioning of stocks of munitions and aviation fuel. The preparations for the more direct second phase of the planned air campaign would also not be complete until the four carriers of the US Pacific Fleet were in-theatre, and they were still a couple of days away from departing San Diego. The US decided the Scud attacks had rendered the 1st September deadline irrelevant. The strategic air campaign would now begin on the 27th. The US felt an unprecedented show of force, bombing across the Islamic crescent might bring the world to its senses.

The First Raids

The *Spirit of St Louis*, B2-007, dropped her pair of tankers off overhead Diego Garcia, where they would land to refuel. She had flown north-east in the black night over the east coast of Oman at 45,000 feet and was now on her bombing run into Bandar Abbas, major port city and headquarters of the Iranian Navy. The electronic warfare equipment was showing all quiet. As the Iranian air defence surveillance radars painted the airspace each one had its signal processed and individually identified. The co-pilot/WSO (Weapon Systems Officer) grunted with satisfaction that the stealth design of the B-2 was clearly working – there were no alarms or increased activity from target-tracking radars. The radar operators remained ignorant of their presence as the radar energy was either deflected away from its source or absorbed by the 'gold plating', as the RAM coating was called. Below they could occasionally see the lights from Bandar through the thin veils of stratus cloud. The WSO checked the JTIDS screen, which gave them a data-linked real-time air picture. There was just a pair of Iranian F-14s flying racetracks at 30,000 feet about twenty miles inland. They posed no danger. At the press of a soft key the WSO confirmed that the auto global positioning system was feeding the integrated navigation systems with a three-dimensional position which was within the minimum thirty-foot confidence level. It was. Bombing had never been less of a challenge. Select weapons. Twenty seconds to run, bomb doors open. Three, two, one – bombs away, sixteen light thuds at half-second intervals. Bomb doors closed. The sixteen JDAMs fell silently towards the city. Each had its own GPS inside. The micro-computers worked frantically towards their own destruction, comparing the bomb position in three-dimensional space with the expected position and position relative to the target. The tail fins twitched slightly to guide the bombs back on course. The first four were aimed at the main power station just north of Bandar Abbas. Just three bombs, precisely aimed, could take out an oil-fired power station for a minimum of three months – the fourth would eliminate the stand-by generator, just to make sure. The next six 2,002lb bombs separated, going in pairs for the electricity distribution substations. The next pair were aimed at an innocuous building which had looked on the intelligence photographs like any other office block. This had been identified as the new location of the central telephone exchange. Copying what Iraq had done in 1991, the Iranians had moved the internal organs of the old exchange as soon as hostilities looked likely. In 1991 the F-117s had scored direct hits with precision weapons on empty buildings in Baghdad – great TV pictures, no military result. Thanks to the CIA and MI6, the USAF were wise to this move. The final four were aimed at the main road and rail bridges on the only route out of Bandar Abbas, north over the mountains towards Kerman. The *Spirit of St Louis* swung into a slow left-hand half-circle so its crew could enjoy the fruits of their labour. Some forty seconds later a series of bright twinkling sparks could be seen among the lights. Almost simultaneously the lights went out, as if switched off by some giant hand. Bandar Abbas was without power and cut off except by sea from the rest of the world. 'Good,' was all the pilot said. He set course for Diego Garcia.

The mission conducted by B2-007 *Spirit of St Louis* was typical of the twenty-five other missions flown by the available B-2s that fateful night. B-2s flying from as far afield as Guam, the Azores and the UK spearheaded the campaign's first wave. This also included F-117s flying from Turkey, Italy, Greece, Spain, Cyprus and Bahrain, and cruise-missile-carrying B-52s flying from the US, the UK and Diego Garcia, as well as cruise missile launches from submarines and guided missile cruisers in the Mediterranean and Arabian Seas. The target sets chosen in every country from Morocco to Iran were the power stations, electricity substations and other elements of the national power grids. The Western air power theorists had been waiting many decades for an opportunity to do just this. There was a school of thought that persisted with the theory that had the US Army Air Force and RAF's Bomber Command in World War II targeted German power sources alone, and continuously, this would have had a far greater and more immediate effect on German military and industrial production than was actually achieved by the combination of precision daylight and night fire-storm methods. The attraction of the electricity grid attack was that not only would the military and industrial users be affected, but that every citizen in every country would feel the direct result of the action and know that American air and cruise missile power (along with a couple of dozen British Royal Navy missiles) were able to reach into every home in every land.

The Pentagon war room watched events unfold via live links from the Space shuttles *Discovery* and *Columbia*. There were scenes of cheering and 'high fives' as they watched the swathe of darkness fall across the Islamic crescent from Rabat to Tehran in forty-five short minutes. From space it seemed as though the evidence of human habitation across North Africa and the Middle East, normally orange-yellow urban hot spots, had been snuffed out. There were even cries in the early hours of the morning of 'It'll all be over by lunch-time, not Christmas' as optimism soared on the expectation of Saladin seeing 'reason' and capitulating to the inevitable.

But even as the late-edition headlines were being written for the West's newspapers, the first of many disturbing and uncomfortable reports began to filter out of the target areas. As dawn spread from east to west and the West's media were politely escorted to survey the damage inflicted by their military brethren, reports of high numbers of civilian casualties began to filter out as soon as stand-by power supplies were activated. It seemed that Saladin had either known exactly what was going to be attacked and had done for some time or had made an educated, some would say inspired, guess at the most likely targets for the first wave of attacks. His tactic had been simple. The Islamic Military Council had ensured that crowds of human shields were driven to the most sensitive military sites as the diplomats and their families departed. The organisation required for such a move was minimal. In each country a few fleets of military trucks each led by a 4 × 4 equipped with a loudspeaker were all that had been required. The people were exhorted to join their menfolk in the front line against the satanic tyranny of the United States and Israel. Throughout the late evening, as the message spread by word of mouth, whole families took their own vehicles and joined the rush to camp out for the night in the name of self-defence. The Western media correspondents were kept in their hotels, for their own safety, so that hardly

a word of the martyrdom to come leaked out of the Alliance
to anyone that mattered or would be able to do anything in
time.

The sight that greeted the correspondents of CNN, Reuters,
AP, Sky and the BBC on the morning of the 27th was truly a
gruesome one. Each team of reporters travelled under a very
heavily armed guard and no access was denied. The road to
the Bandar Abbas power station was jammed with people
seeking their relatives, who had departed the previous night
chanting anti-American slogans and burning flags. At the
power station itself all hell had broken loose. Amid the rubble
of what were formerly the pump-house and control room was
strewn the bodies and bits of bodies of those that were near
enough to take the full force of the blast as the buildings had
disintegrated when the bombs had hit. The gravel and grey
stone desert as well as the concrete hard-standing were stained
with blood that turned darker as it dried in the rising sun.
Loose and torn pieces of clothing, predominantly black but
punctuated by brighter colours worn under the women's
yashmaks or by the children, fluttered where they had been
caught in the early morning breeze or moved gently along by
succeeding gusts. In the background fleets of green-and-white
ambulances queued to take the wounded for treatment. At
Bandar Abbas it was reported that at least 150 people had lost
their lives. The media on-site had no hesitation in flashing
pictures of what they saw around the world. If there was any
doubt about the amount of carnage, or second thoughts by
sensitive or censored Western editors, the Islamic World
Television Service ensured that the people of the West could
judge for themselves through their own broadcast, before it
was disabled, repeated live across the Internet. This was
Algiers all over again, and the scenes were repeated in every
country attacked.

In the Pentagon the Chief of Staff watched events unfold
with increasing disbelief. The mood of optimism and pure
military triumph was replaced by one of guilt and 'blood on
our hands' mixed with outrage that Saladin could be so
cynical about the lives of his own people. All the Chief could
say was, 'This wasn't part of my fucking script.' The West had

fought on and off for sixty years in limited wars. In each subsequent war the taking and holding of the moral high ground had been increasingly important, as important as any actual outcome of the conflicts themselves. The net effect of this moral awareness was an increase in the value of life. The life of the non-combatant had become increasingly sacred, especially to the media and critics of government. And by the millennium the life of each soldier, or more accurately airman, was equally precious. The West's military consciousness had evolved to understand that war was conducted via machines. The man in the street demanded justification for every casualty. The first night of strategic air campaign had demonstrated that the people of the West were not prepared to accept the deaths of civilians used as human shields to protect even the most vital of enemy military installations. The West was tied by its own morality. The President personally suspended the air campaign in order to 'review the options'.

Chapter Twelve –
Asymmetric Responses

Jihad!

All eyes turned to Saladin for a response. He did not disappoint. He called for a jihad (holy war) against the USA – the great Satan – by all true believers around the world, and against all those who supported her cause and that of the real enemy, 'Zionism'. In his speech, transmitted all over the world, he described the previous night's air assault as a blatant, unprovoked and cowardly act of aggression that would not go unanswered. Saladin warned the people of the West that they were now at war with the East. His forces had until now exercised discipline and restraint and respected the ideals of non-combatant immunity. That time was now over. The West's military had carried out an attack without respect for the lives of his people, and the people of the West could expect attack in kind. This was total war. Saladin accepted that the East did not have the might of air power, but it had many other means at its disposal and it would not hesitate to use them.

The call for a total war, the use of all means towards the end, sent shudders through the offices, bunkers, living rooms and streets of the West. The effect of the first night of the air campaign and Saladin's speech achieved very different responses on both sides of the cultural divide. The Europeans in particular felt a wave of fear and doom on realising that Islam could touch its very population centres. The foreboding was a feeling lost since 1939, when Hitler, having taken Poland, stood poised while a nervous world waited to see where he would jump next. At last the generation of the twenty-first

century were able to understand how their forefathers had felt
sixty years previously. The comfort zone of sixty years of
peace and the American umbrella vanished in an instant.
Across Europe a decade of dithering about the development
and procurement of a serious anti-ballistic missile system was
brought into sharp focus as incumbent governments were
harangued by all sides. By the evening of the 27th the cities in
western Europe sat in fear and trepidation awaiting the
unleashing of a rain of long-range ballistic missiles tipped
with biological and chemical weapons against which, as with
Hitler's V-2 rockets, there was no defence. That first night in
London and Paris and all across Europe panic buying emptied
the supermarkets in a matter of hours. The London Underground and the Métro ground to a halt as every station
platform was crammed with people from all walks of society
who had rapidly adopted a 'Blitz' mentality.

Across Europe the "Exiles of Islam", as Saladin called
them, knew that their time had come. All Islam was imbued
with fury and outrage at the air attacks that had killed and
maimed so many innocent civilians. The streets of every city
from southern Spain across France and the UK to Hamburg,
Frankfurt and Munich in Germany, where there were significant minority Muslim populations, were filled with
crowds of angry demonstrators armed with bricks and petrol
bombs. In the UK the Territorial Army, mobilised in May
during the Baltic War, was called in to aid a harassed police
force as darkness fell and rioters began looting. Worse,
several policemen were killed or wounded as shots from
unseen handguns were fired into their defensive lines. The
West had not seen such mass, concerted and well-organised
civil disobedience in living memory. The following day it
became increasingly apparent that this was part of a campaign that had been planned for some time. Indeed it had.
Saladin's speech was the signal that many had been waiting
for. The previous nine months of his tenure as head of the
Islamic Alliance had not been spent in idle protest. The open
borders of Europe had made it very easy for small cells of
activists to be put in place and supplied and equipped for the
coming struggle. The night of the 27th/28th saw no hail of

missiles. The West's flat response to Saladin's implied threat of a mass missile attack was to assure him that any such attack would be replied to with nuclear weapons. However, as the demonstrators melted away or were forcibly dispersed, the explosions started. Car and truck bombs, all packed with Semtex or similar plastic explosives, ripped apart city centres from Bradford and Birmingham to Toulouse, Marseilles and Milan. For the politicians in the West this was a distressing development, and curfews were imposed and national states of emergency declared across Europe. For the military, however, there was worse in store on the 28th.

The War of the Airbases

Royal Air Force Brize Norton, Oxfordshire, England

Corporal Josephine Pollock normally ran the registry of 216 Squadron. She had served nine years and had just extended her service to fifteen on promotion. She enjoyed her job and her prospects were bright. Brize Norton was the hub of the RAF's jet transport and tanker fleets. Tonight she, along with many other clerks, cooks, engineers and other trades, formed part of the station's Augmentation Force (AF). The onerous burden of regular guard duty had long been a source of discontent in the ranks. During the decade of post-Cold War peace and downsizing the plain fact was that there were not enough RAF policemen or RAF Regiment soldiers to adequately guard the main operating bases. Tonight was the first night of Corporal Pollock's second week in the past four on AF duty. Previously the AF was confined to waiting in a crewroom to respond to intruder alerts and practice attacks. Since the Baltic War the AF had doubled in size, and now half of the time was spent in concrete or sandbagged sangars dotted about at remote locations along the airfield perimeter wire. Most of the RAF Regiment had deployed abroad in the past month as tension with the Islamic Alliance had risen and there was an urgent requirement for enhanced ground defence of the fighter and fighter-bomber operating bases in Cyprus,

Italy and Turkey. The UK was regarded as a relatively secure location.

Corporal Pollock was in charge of Location 3C, a round green concrete turret with gun slits, on the north-western fence, not far from the main road to Carterton. She preferred the positions on the southern side of the base, where the new day/nightscopes could be used to enjoy the Cotswold wildlife to stave off sleep and boredom. It was 0430. In the pre-dawn light came the sound of a mechanical digger grinding its way in low gear along the road. It appeared as any other industrial digger, mostly bright yellow and showing signs of wear and tear. Behind it an articulated box-type Volvo lorry, probably with an extremely frustrated driver, she assumed, if he'd been stuck behind the digger all the way through the lanes from Filkins and the Swindon road, and behind the lorry three cars. Her attention was just beginning to wander from the procession and back to rabbit-, fox- and badger-spotting with the 'scope when the sound of grinding gears and a change in engine tone were followed by the digger's headlights suddenly brightening in her peripheral vision. The digger had swung off the road and was heading directly for the green concrete turret.

'Stand to!' she said softly at first, then with increasing agitation and volume to her colleagues, two of whom were slumped in sleeping bags on the floor. 'Stand to, stand to, stand to!' The digger was only fifty metres away and closing fast. To her utter astonishment the artic was following. The intruder alerts they had practised had been nothing like this – all shadowy figures sneaking around until challenged using the correct procedures. Pollock reverted to the drill they had so often used.

'Royal Air Force. Halt or I fire!' With the digger at forty metres and the wide steel bucket raised menacingly, her accomplice, Leading Aircraftsman Edwards, was at her side. The other two were fumbling for their weapons. Pollock felt silly, the situation unreal. She knew the driver could neither hear nor see her over the din of his charge. In accordance with the correct procedure she repeated the challenge at record speed, more to herself than anyone else, then screamed, 'Let 'em have it!' With the digger at thirty metres they couldn't miss. She squeezed the trigger of her SA-80 rifle. Edwards let rip; the bullets clanged against the bucket and front engine and were sent spinning off whining as they ricocheted at crazy angles. Pollock's rifle clicked. Fuck, fuck, fuck! she thought. Safety catch still on! You dizzy tart. She thumbed the safety catch but by this time the digger was almost upon them. 'Get out! Get out!' she yelled, and dived with the others for the door, badly grazing her chin and jarring her whole skull as she hit the concrete outside. She rolled over twice, as taught, then looked up at the digger to her left and the artic beyond that, the taste of her own blood filling her mouth.

There was an almighty crash as the digger demolished 3C, stalled and began to reverse to finish the job. The artic went straight through the double fencing and barbed-wire rolls in between and halted on the other side. The back door swung open. Just a few metres away in the cab of the digger, the driver was silhouetted against the lightening eastern sky. Pollock raised her rifle and squeezed off four shots in rapid succession. The driver slumped forward. Good shooting, Pollock! she thought, her mind mimicking the words of her RAF Regiment instructors. Nice tight group of rounds in mid-upper torso.

Out of the back of the artic jumped several figures, each one hooded like the digger driver. She took brief aim and fired into the group. Two of them fell instantly, the others diving for cover and returning fire wildly. Realising how exposed they were in the open, she sprinted to behind the cover of the digger's large rear wheels. There was no sign of Edwards, and the other two were still lying flat and exposed, cowering with their arms pointlessly covering their helmeted heads.

'Get into cover, you wankers!' she yelled as bullets twanged off the other side of the digger.

'I'll cover you!' she shouted, again feeling mildly detached and idiotic at sounding and acting like a war film cliché. She leaned around the side of the digger's rear and fired half a dozen shots at the now unseen group of assailants. To her astonishment there came a voice from the cab. The driver was hanging out of the cab looking at her, half in appeal and half in questioning surprise to be greeted by a female face.

'What the fook did you do that for?' he asked quietly in a
thick Brummy accent, his life slipping away. Before Pollock
could reply there was a fusillade of shots from her right,
coming from the direction of the road. She ducked and turned
to see that the three cars had stopped and the drivers were
firing submachine-guns. Her next sensation before passing
out was her legs buckling under her as she dropped her SA-80
and looked up at the sky.

The attackers were surprised by the resistance offered by
the personnel of 3C but soon regrouped and jumped into the
hired Mondeos that sped through the gap in the wire once the
firefight was over. The dozen men crammed in, weapons
bristling out of open windows, and the cars raced towards
the target of the attack, the large flight line, fanning out as
they went. When they were within fifty metres the cars halted
and the men spread out. In the background the station alert
siren was wailing and the Tannoy was blaring, 'I say again,
Intruder Alert, Intruder Alert, I say again . . .' Before them
stood a part of the collection of aircraft that was the key to the
reach of Western air power – the tankers.

There were fourteen aircraft on the hard-standings that
morning: six Airbus tankers, three C-17 transports, two
Tristars, two C-130JK Hercules, and a guest American C-
17. Ten minutes later nine of the big jets were ruined and the
other five damaged. Four of the tankers exploded specta-
cularly on receiving direct hits from RPGs, their thousands
of litres of aviation fuel igniting and ripping apart the flimsy
skins. Part of the Quick Reaction Platoon of the AF arrived
on the scene in two ancient Bedford trucks, inadvisably
driving directly towards the attackers' firing positions. Both
were raked with heavy machine-gun fire and halted
abruptly, one ablaze, before the attackers decided that the
time had come to withdraw. They jumped back into the cars
and raced to the hole in the wire. As they approached a third
AF truck was driving full tilt to the gap to block the
attackers' escape, not suspecting that they had been prudent
enough to leave four men there to guard it. The third
Bedford was hit full in the face by an RPG fired at no
more than fifty metres.

It was this explosion which brought Corporal Pollock temporarily back to her senses. Her legs seemed useless but they still had feeling, and there was a warm wet sensation. She realised that she had been hit in both legs below the knees and was bleeding profusely. She had the presence of mind to rip open her field dressing and tie tight tourniquets just above her knees. The sound of shouting above high-revving engines from the wire drew her attention. The Birmingham accents were arguing about whether or not to leave the bodies of their fallen comrades. Pollock eased her way around the back of the digger using her arms, the SA-80 dragged by its sling. The three saloons were now nosing out, the leader dragging barbed-wire coils with him. Pollock did not hesitate. She clipped on a fresh magazine of 5.56mm rounds and set the regulator to semi-automatic. As the first Mondeo passed abeam she opened fire, without any apparent effect. The second and third were side by side, and this time she remembered to aim slightly low and emptied half a magazine into the shiny metallic painted side of the nearest car. The first vehicle was away off down the road but the second was still well in range but receding rapidly. She emptied the rest of her bullets into the rear of the car, noting with satisfaction the rear windscreen shattering as the bullets impacted, but it did not slow.

There were more shouts and shots now coming from the hole in the fence as the remains of the AF that had survived the RPG impact began arriving. She started to feel dizzy and faint again as the effort exerted and the loss of blood forced her system into survival shutdown.

Postscript

Corporal Josephine Pollock was awarded the Victoria Cross for this action, which she survived, fully recovering the use of her legs. She is now married to a Royal Navy officer, has twin daughters and lives in Didcot. A postwar inquiry found that she had single-handedly felled no fewer than fifteen members of the Islamic Action Brigade (Birmingham) out of twenty-five who had comprised the attacking group. Leading Aircrafts-

man Ian Edwards was awarded a posthumous Military Cross.
He stayed defiantly at his post and his body was found under
the rubble of 3C. The Station Commander at Brize Norton
and his Senior Base Defence Adviser were sacked.

The attack on Brize Norton was not an isolated incident but
one of a series of carefully co-ordinated raids that took place
between 0400 and 0800 GMT on 28 August. Saladin and his
military strategists had identified one of the key vulnerabilities
of the pervasive and dominant force that was Western air
power – the air-to-air refuelling tankers. The West's air force
generals had long described them as 'force-multipliers'. The
other major force-multipliers of Western air power were the
AWACs that could control, direct and survey over thousands
of miles of airspace, the Joint STARS which did the same over
land, and Rivet Joint, which was capable of intercepting and
decoding vast amounts of radio traffic. The tankers were
indeed the key to the reach and weapon-carrying capacity of
Nato's fighter and fighter-bomber fleets. Through air-to-air
refuelling, fighters were able to stay on combat air patrol
almost indefinitely, or at least as long as there was sufficient
engine oil and the pilots were not overcome by fatigue. The
fighter-bombers were able to more than double their range and
their payloads if tankers were available. The major drawback
with the tankers and the other adapted civilian passenger jets
was that they were large, vulnerable targets that could not hide
in HASs, so would always be parked in the open. This left them
exposed to any form of attack from single bullets through
mortars to RPGs and ATGMs. Also, for anything more than
first-line servicing, they were forced to return to their home
bases where the technical expertise to find and fix problems was
clustered. Saladin had watched the build-up of ground protection around the forward fighter bases, and although a handful
of tankers were positioned on each of these bases where space
permitted, the majority were dispersed on larger bases in what
were assumed to be more secure rear areas. The Alliance
planners calculated that Nato would underestimate the capability of the Islamic forces to conduct such a rapid, hard-
hitting and well-coordinated campaign. The senior officers
were still not fully tuned in to the broader possibilities of

asymmetric attack, nor the determination with which such assaults would be carried out. To their cost they were still looking skyward for Scud attacks and ensuring that the safety of the fighing air assets was given the highest priority when the big jet bases were struck.

Brize Norton was among the hardest hit but the insurgents also scored significant successes across the West. In Aviano, Italy, two AWACs and four tankers were destroyed; in Incirlick, Turkey, one Rivet Joint, one JSTARS and three tankers were destroyed; in Istres, near Marseilles in France, seven tankers were hit; at Mildenhall, Fairford and Lyneham in the UK a total of twenty-three large jets including transports were hit; and so the list went on. The most successful raid in Europe was carried out against Frankfurt Main airbase. A large cell of sixty insurgents cut through the base fencing in three different places and drove unopposed in their four-wheel-drive Jeeps direct to within five hundred metres of the flight line. The targets were thirty fat air-to-air refuelling tankers, several of which were fully fuelled up. Within fifteen minutes, using Milan and TOW anti-tank missiles from longer ranges, then RPGs and high-calibre automatic weapons from close in, a significant portion of the USAF's tanker assets were burning, twisted shells. The pall of smoke from several million kilograms of aviation kerosene was visible from twenty miles away. Not all of the attacks were, however, successful, and on several bases, notably Cologne in Germany and Hill and Dill AFBs in the US, the attackers were spotted and engaged before doing too much damage. The insurgents suffered overall up to 75 per cent casualties with all but a handful of the rest being captured. For them it was the supreme sacrifice, a sacrifice that gladdened the heart of Saladin and made the commanders and politicians wince with pain as each report came through. America was, however, stunned by the most spectacular attack ever carried out on US soil.

Offut Air Force Base, Lincoln, Nebraska

On the four flight lines stood eighty-five of the USAF's KC-135 tanker fleet. At 1035 the navy blue Hummer Jeep of the

1177th Security Squadron pulled alongside the first line of thirty aircraft. Routine security check. Airman Second Class Mirza jumped down from the cab holding up the collar of his black jacket against his right cheek. Wet drizzle like this was rarely seen in his birthplace in Karachi, Pakistan, but today it made Mirza's black eyes flash with a smile. Twenty years of careful preparation were about to come to fruition. Twenty years to the day since Mirza and his twin brother were chosen as sleepers. Twenty years since the brotherhood had sworn revenge for Operation El Dorado Canyon.

Mirza looked up at the huge grey aircraft, sitting out patiently in the rain like a bored seagull waiting for the squall line to pass. This aircraft, tail number OT 356, the 'Spiro Agnew', had only four hours left in one piece – Mirza would see to that. He walked round to the sheltered side of the truck and opened the passenger door. He reached down into the footwell and pulled a can of Coca-Cola out of the icebox. His grin broadened as he reached into two of the six cigarette cartons on the seat, pulling out one packet of Marlboro Lights and one of Marlboro Reds. These icons dominated the world. Empty packets, discoloured and faded by sun and rain, blew unconcerned from Brazil to Borneo, spoiling as they went. Empty cans bounced along dirty streets and were kicked by skeletal children down shantytown steps in the shabby sprawling suburbs of the Third World metropolises. Now these symbols of America, packed with substances more dangerous to health and teeth than tar, nicotine, caffeine and sugar, were about to bring a shock to the greatest civilisation the earth had ever known. Mirza looked at the coded diagram on the passenger seat. This was to be an exploding jet. He replaced the Coke can, opened the glove box and unscrewed the top of a small jar of clear liquid. He took a small paintbrush out of his upper-left pocket, dipped it in the jar and then dabbed a small amount of the liquid on to one side of each of the cigarette packets.

His mind wandered for a moment as he did so. The liquid was glue – windproof, waterproof, heat-proof, you-name-it-proof. It had been developed to hold together a probe for the surface of Saturn. The micro-explosive in the cigarette packets packed the same punch as an old USAF 500lb Mark 82 iron bomb. It was also developed for use in space and was planned to be used for exploratory surface blasting on Jupiter's moon Europa in the search for extraterrestrial life. NASA had long maintained that the expensive exploration of space would benefit the whole of mankind, and pointed to all manner of things from aluminium foil to 'intelligent' computers as 'proof' that this was so. Mirza smiled again. His mankind were certainly going to benefit from these latest inventions, he thought, but not in the way NASA had in mind.

He positioned himself next to the left main undercarriage leg. The massive fat Goodyear was almost as tall as he was. With two easy and confident underarm actions, borne of endless practice, he successively threw the packets up into the wheel slot so that they sat side by side on the underside of the wing. Only the thinnest metal skins on the whole aircraft now separated the ME-006 explosive and the aviation fuel in cell 'L-13 lower'.

That was easy. One down, or as good as, and twenty-nine to go. He glanced across to the next line and through the drizzle could make out PFC Young working down his line. He got back into the Hummer and drove the hundred yards to the wing of the next aircraft in the line. 'Dan Quayle' awaited its fate patiently in the driving rain. Mirza took a can of Coke and shoved it into his jacket pocket. The 'Coke' aeroplanes were going to be far easier to prime. He unlocked the lower door with the master key and in seconds was up in the cockpit. He put the Coke can down by the captain's window on the left side. Now he had to be careful. Making sure that the can was wedged firmly into the cup holder, he pulled the ring-pull carefully until it clicked, then pushed it back so that it looked closed. This would arm the mini-binary weapon by allowing the two harmless gases in the cylinder inside to mix. All that was now required was a second pull to excite the propellant that would discharge the deadly mixture into the confined space. Mirza jumped down from the mini-ladder, locked up and headed back for the giant Jeep. One of each type done, twenty-eight to go.

Two hours later Mirza's work on the aircraft was done. He drove back to the security squadron headquarters, parked the

Hummer and dropped off the keys as he had done countless times before. He informed the duty controller that he was popping to Burger King for lunch, as he always did, but this time he drove out of the main gate for the last time. He had struck the first blow, his father's honour was satisfied.

At 0230 hours Mountain Time there was a small puff of black smoke accompanied by a crack as the ME-006 exploded and ripped into the first fuel cell. The logarithmic chain of subsequent ignitions was so rapid that a mere two seconds later 'Spiro Agnew' had disintegrated. The emergency crews were alerted to move those checking over the 'untouched' aircraft. The binary chemical Coke cans killed twenty-two maintenance personnel.

Once the attacks were over the final toll of aircraft losses was approaching 230 destroyed or damaged beyond repair, and a similar number left requiring various degrees of viable repairs. The number of tankers hit represented fully half of the West's available tanker assets. For the air force commanders, 28 August 1999 was a black day, but things would get worse.

San Diego – The Second Pearl Harbor

In what was subsequently called 'The Second Pearl Harbor', four Pacific Fleet aircraft carriers were sunk with most of their aircraft by a clever Russian trap sprung in sight of San Diego. As the escorts were engaged in defeating a submarine-launched missile attack, the carriers, heading away from the threat for safety, were hit by super-fast midget submarines launched from a converted Typhoon. Unfortunately there was more to come, and this was by more conventional means.

Chaos off Naples

Since the decision to move the bulk of Nato's ground and air units to the eastern Mediterranean had been made, the major ports across Europe had seen only frenzied preparations. From Bremen, Rotterdam and Southampton to Brest, Lisbon, Marseilles, Naples, Patras and Piraeus, the collective bustle and activity were unprecedented. Much of the heavy gear, as well as ammunition and spares stockpiles for tanks and aircraft, would have to be transported by sea. It was imperative that the sea lines of communication were secured before any offensive action was undertaken. Nato's naval commanders saw the main threat to their dominance of the sea as coming from two areas. Firstly submarines; the Islamic Alliance countries in the Mediterranean were able to muster a motley collection of a dozen ex-Russian Kilo, Foxtrot and Romeo boats. Four of the Egyptian boats had been adapted to carry Harpoon missiles, but at least Nato knew how to defeat these. In addition, any Russian submarines in the Mediterranean would be tracked, if not hounded, by all available assets, and in the third week of August there were two of them, both Akula IIs and neither in particularly threatening positions, nor being particularly covert. Not one of the Islamic submarines dared to leave port, and none would have got very far since each port was blockaded at a respectful distance by the very best USN attack submarines. The second threat, as evidenced by the Iranian achievement in closing Hormuz, was from mines, especially in the Strait of Gibraltar. By late August Nato had deployed the whole of its mine warfare fleet, half to the Med and the other half in transit to Hormuz via the Cape of Good Hope. By the middle of the night on the 28th/29th, when full details of the disaster in San Diego were emerging, every single non-Nato ship became a suspect – anything that was large enough to house and launch even a couple of midget submarines was liable to be intercepted and searched.

Nato's immediate reaction to the Russian attack on the Pacific Fleet suddenly changed the rules. There was little practically that Nato and the US could do against Russia. The three Akula IIs in the Pacific that had launched the missile attack had 'disappeared' while the massive Typhoon sat undetected on the seabed awaiting an opportunity to escape. Nato could declare war on Russia; what might be achieved by such a move was less than certain. The only option was the declaration that any Russian forces suspected of acting in concert with those of the Islamic Alliance would be considered 'enemy' and would be engaged as such.

Commander Ivan Feydorov had, like so many in this war, waited an eternity for this moment. He was thirty-seven years old and the youngest submarine commander in the Russian Navy. His boat, the *Vladivostok*, was sitting in the middle of the American Sixth Fleet Mediterranean carrier battle group, a mere forty miles off the Italian coast south-west of Naples. Sweeping the near horizon through the periscope, Feydorov was able to name every one of the dazzling light grey ships in his sights. He was going to help wreck their day. Had he been more fluent in English he might have enjoyed the pun. As it was his heart leapt in anticipation. He swallowed and ran his tongue round the dry roof of his mouth. He managed a smile, the smile of a man who had accepted the inevitability of death this day and yet had no regrets. He knew that on every bridge the minute he 'appeared' there would be at least two pairs of binoculars trained on his periscope as it cut its own way through the deep blue water, leaving a bright white trail of spume and spray as it did so. Feydorov knew they had tracked him from the moment he had come through the Strait of Gibraltar.

He had really enjoyed the journey down from Archangel. They had set off together in the midst of one of the spring's last howling snowstorms. The American satellites in geostationary polar orbit would transmit their images when the weather cleared up. The images would show that an ice-breaker, the nuclear-powered *Dvina*, two Akula IIs, three Severodvinsks and a Typhoon were missing. In fact three Akula IIs were gone. The Americans would not notice the difference. The Russians had perfected the art of physical and infrared camouflage. This was a skill that had been born out of necessity. The Americans had been looking at all of Russia from space with complete impunity for the past quarter of a decade. The Russians had also launched satellites into orbits almost identical to those of the American military satellites. Although their imagery technology trailed that of the USA by three to five years, the Russians learned enough from their own coverage to realise what worked and what didn't when it came to misleading bored photo analysts and the computer scanners which were replacing them.

Feydorov's elder brother was commanding the other 'missing' Akula II. He had by far the harder task – to remain directly below the icebreaker until past the Greenland–Iceland–UK gap and into the eastern Atlantic. Before they set sail for the Med, the Russians had to be certain of their equipment. This was achieved through a simple and oft-practised ruse. As tension rose in the Baltic, Nato carried out one of its large annual air/land/sea exercises in the Minches – a shallow stretch of water separating the northern Scottish mainland and the Hebridean islands of Harris and Lewis. Feydorov and his masters knew that this was a Nato dress rehearsal for amphibious landings in Latvia and possibly Estonia as part of the military plan underpinning the peace process, and also knew that Nato would expect the mission of the lone subs to be to monitor the exercise. Feydorov's first transmission went out when his ESM suite confirmed that there were no Nato ships within fifty nautical miles. It was a simple message on the international distress frequency requesting assistance for a critically ill crewman. The Royal Air Force was the first to respond to the message. Two Nimrod Mk 3s, brand new into squadron service, were scrambled from RAF Kinloss on the Moray coast. These were closely followed by a Canadian P3 Orion and an American Orion. Once the transmission was complete, the Akula IIs went into hiding and twelve hours of hide-and-seek followed with Nato ASW frigates and helicopters doing their damnedest to find the Akula II and its 'ill' crewman. If this gathering of Nato navies was unable to find them, then the Naples plan, assuming Nato reacted as expected, should also work. Satisfied that they had not been found, Feydorov finally surfaced in the middle of the 'Blue Forces', much to the consternation of the force commander, and announced that help was no longer required. The Russians were still world masters in underwater stealth, and the very latest radar-absorbent anechoic tiles on the Akula IIs were now

proved to be world-beaters. And while Feydorov was playing
games with Nato his brother's boat, the *Tomsk*, had left the
Dvina and married up with a factory fishing ship that had
been going about her normal business off Brixham in Devon.
While Nato watched Feydorov in *Vladivostok* and his comrade in *Kurgan* transit unstealthily from Scotland to the
Med, *Tomsk*, below her factory ship, the *Olga Korbut*,
proceeded unheeded forty-eight hours ahead. Once through
the Strait of Gibraltar the *Olga Korbut* went about its
normal business off Marseilles while the *Tomsk* remained
hidden off eastern Sardinia.

When the signal came on the 28th the *Vladivostok* and
Kurgan disappeared. They knew that the whole of Nato
would soon be in lukewarm if not hot pursuit given events
in San Diego. *Kurgan* led a whole host of Nato ASW ships,
planes and submarines in a game of now-you-see-me-now-
you-don't to the west of Malta. *Vladivostok* did the same in
the Tyrrhenian Sea, where the greater part of Nato's naval
power was gathered.

It was first light on the 29th when Feydorov's periscope
finally broke the surface amid the Sixth Fleet. With all sensors
active, the *Vladivostok* had been able to locate and electro-
nically identify every ship within twenty miles. A short coded
burst of this information was sent to *Tomsk* to prime her
weapons computers. The Nato captains breathed a sigh of
relief and dispatched a pair of Merlins and a pair of Sea Kings
to sink the 'threat'. As they did so the *Tomsk* sprung the trap
unseen and unsuspected on the western side of the fleet. At the
centre of some forty escorting cruisers, frigates and destroyers
were the main prizes – the three carriers *Carl Vinson, Dwight
D. Eisenhower* and *Abraham Lincoln* and the arsenal ship
Merrimack. Standard Nato practice was to put a ring of steel
around the capital ships, but by the time the commanders
realised that there was another Akula II present it was too
late. In eight short minutes *Tomsk* fired four salvos of four
'65s', so called because they were 65 cm in diameter rather
than the standard 53 cm. The 65s were advanced turbine
wake-homeing torpedoes, each with a 500kg warhead, a
maximum speed of 50 knots and a range of 50 km. The four

capital ships all lay within 25 km of *Tomsk*, and it was at 0609, just fifteen minutes after the launch of the first 65, that the last struck home unerringly against the *Merrimack*. The *Tomsk* dived and escaped. Feydorov ordered the crew of the *Vladivostok* to abandon ship as soon as the first ASW helicopter appeared. Although he did not survive, more than half his crew of sixty-five did. US naval aviation was a shadow of its former self. The *Abraham Lincoln* and *Dwight D. Eisenhower* were hit by three torpedoes apiece. Both were ripped apart internally, but as they began to list badly were able to generate enough steam power to survival-launch some sixty aircraft. The *Carl Vinson*, which had the most warning time of the three, was able to manoeuvre sufficiently and deploy decoys in time such that only one 65 smashed into her stern. She was taken in tow back to Naples later that day.

The consequences of the airbase attacks and the wrecking of the Pacific and Mediterranean Fleet carriers began to sink in by the end of 29 August. The situation was not yet dire for the West or Israel, but it was much worse than it might have been. The damaging and destruction of so much of the USN's air fleet combined with the loss of the tankers, or force-multipliers, would seriously curtail the 'reach' and effectiveness of the West's air power. Against targets at longer ranges this was even more acute, and would result in further reduced mass, or concentration, of force required.

In the late 1990s, in the upper halls of military doctrine, there were whispers about 'asymmetric', 'asynchronous' and even 'ambiguous' war. However, it would take time for the inertia of a military that had been defined by the 1991 Gulf War to first of all accept that it was vulnerable and then to adapt the necessary strategies and force and budget structures to address these problems. Indeed, by 2006 the West, led by the US, was so fixated with the 'Revolution in Military Affairs' which revolved around information warfare, cyber-war and generally staying a couple of technology generations ahead of potential enemies, that addressing some of the fundamental vulnerabilities of the basic tools of the trade was still very much an academic exercise. As the 29th drew to a close, the West had had its first real tastes of asymmetric war and sea war against a capable opponent, and in both cases had been found wanting.

The catastrophic events of the past forty-eight hours finally forced the West to face up to the fact that it was now engaged in a total war – all means employed to achieve an end – not a crisis or a short-term spat. The loss of so many American sailors' lives after decades of virtually zero casualties was the cause of profound shock in a society that had come to view war, or at least intervening in other people's wars, as something that the military did at little or no risk to its men. To the average citizen in the West, war had been something that was fought with military technology, the West always won and death and maiming were something that happened to the unfortunates on the other side. What the sights and sounds of friendly casualties achieved was the united view that any action taken against Russian or Islamic forces was now fully morally justified. Those who had been shouting 'outrage and shame' at the 'collateral damage' caused during the first night of the air campaign were the same people who called for an immediate resumption. The West remained convinced that an extended and punishing strategic air campaign would force the enemy to capitulate and thereafter force a peace and allow the diplomats to impose a settlement based on the threat of further air strikes. This view simply missed the point about the use of air power in war. It echoed views expressed by Hitler during the 1941 Blitz, Harris during the Bomber Command campaign, Ridgeway in Korea, the USAF in Vietnam, and so on. The plain historical truth about 'strategic air campaigns' was that unless backed by offensive ground manoeuvre they achieved little other than distraction or the satisfaction of destroying elements of an enemy structure that had little direct impact on the outcome of the war. At least on this occasion the West had had the foresight to plan a major ground offensive, even though it would be some weeks before the preparations were complete. The US President promised destruction from the air on a scale hitherto unseen against all levels of the Islamic Alliance military structures across the crescent of Islamic countries. On the evening of 29 August the air campaign resumed. In the Mediterranean virtually every available ship, submarine and aircraft was assigned to an active hunt for the *Tomsk* and *Kurgan*. Both were found two days later within an hour of each other, the *Tomsk* off Mallorca and the *Kurgan* north of Tripoli, and unceremoniously sunk.

Martial Law

Such was the charisma and influence of Saladin that his call to all the oppressed minorities across Europe to rise up and join their Muslim brothers in harassing the warmongering preparations of the pro-Zionist powers was met with a response that surprised even him. Virtually every discontented citizen and extremist minority group, and not a few students, took to the streets in support of the Islamic Alliance and protesting against the US's 'bully boy tactics'. What followed in the next few days were waves of indiscriminate attacks on civilians in Italian and French cities and virtual open civil war in southern Germany, where the Islamic minority concentrated their attacks on the large Turkish population. In the UK cities of Bradford, Leicester and Birmingham, right-wing fanatics seized the opportunity to indulge in open attacks on the Muslim populations, who responded in kind, while an overstretched and under-motivated police force looked on. Fear, panic and chaos brought every major city in Italy, France and Germany to a standstill. As the attacks and counter-attacks increased in violence, the Islamic military cells were able to step up their campaign of bombing against railways and major road bridges in an attempt to disrupt the flow of men and material to the Middle East. With the scenes in England looking very much like those of Ulster in the early 1970s, the Conservative government declared a state of emergency and martial law. The rest of Europe followed suit rapidly. All Islamic groups had been pre-supplied with weapons by the Alliance. In Britain, with the army fully committed elsewhere, the cities of Leicester, Birmingham and Bradford fell into civil disorder, and some key points were seized by armed militants. The Territorial Army was mobilised. Warfare on the streets spread rapidly.

The Scud War Resumes

Peled and the men and women of the 4th Battery on Mount Carmel had celebrated the first outbreak of peace with an impromptu party – white wine being the main fare, as supplied by Peled's business. During the following week the fire controllers stared intently at their screens while Peled positioned himself by the data link for eighteen hours a day, waiting for a renewed onslaught. They had watched and waited while events unfolded in the escalating conflict between Russia, Islam and the West. At first there was euphoria and a belief that together Israel and the West would be able to smash the threatening hordes. This turned to dismay and uncertainty as news spread of the attacks on Nato air power's 'critical assets' and the pride of the US Navy was dealt a body blow. CNN and Sky News were on in the background, as they always were, and as they were in offices, command posts and bunkers throughout the world, and that evening all ears listened keenly as the US President reaffirmed her commitment to Israel and to the resumption of the air campaign.

Peled, ever the prophet, said simply, 'That's that, then. Tonight we'll be back in business.' And they were. During the week's suspension of hostilities direct-flight resupply from the US had enabled the number of ready-to-fire missiles at each Arrow 2 battery to be increased by 50 per cent and at most Patriot PAC4 batteries by almost 100 per cent. The workforce at Raytheon had been working round the clock to produce more missiles to replenish the depleted stocks. Also, software engineers in both Israel and New Mexico worked to attempt to overcome the software bugs that had made the PAC4s' performance seem so dismal compared to the 'Silver Bullet' Arrow 2s.

It was only twenty-seven minutes after sunset when the first flash warning came through of multiple Scud launches. This time the attacks were markedly different, much to Peled's consternation. The target spread was fairly even between the IAF airbases and the major cities of Jerusalem, Tel Aviv, Haifa, Eilat, Nazareth and Beersheba and the Negev nuclear site.

'Eight tracks, origins eastern Syria, west Iraq, northern Saudi, and a further four, origins Baghdad, west Iran,' intoned Jakob, taking his first shift in the hot seat.

'Mm-hm,' acknowledged Peled. There was a good feeling in the cabin of calm assurance that all was under control. Jakob found himself sweating profusely nevertheless; even the icy air coming out of the air-conditioning didn't seem to make any difference. Jakob watched the screen and was preparing to assign tracks before announcing the computer's calculation of the 95 per cent probable impact areas when the missiles started to behave other than expected. Jakob checked the trajectories and saw that the missiles were at the end of their boost phases. Some, however, seemed to split into a myriad of tracks while others appeared to be manoeuvring, the 95 per cent circles expanding and contracting as they did so. Jakob, riven with uncertainty and faced with the unexpected, turned to Peled for help. Peled was almost laudatory.

'You see, these Arabs are not half as stupid as some would have us believe. It will be interesting to see how the Patriots cope with this lot.' 'This lot', as he explained in the next minute, while watching with detached interest what appeared to be a computer virus unfolding on the screens, was a combination of several different deception techniques that the more advanced Scud-owning nations had perfected. The missiles that appeared to starburst and multiply into many, many more were designed to carry chemical or biological sub-munitions, each missile capable of carrying more than a hundred potentially lethal 5kg packages. Although, Peled opined, it was more likely that the starbursts were simply a version of space chaff designed to overload the computers, and that any Scud with biological or chemical sub-munitions would need to dispense them much later for any sort of accuracy to be obtained. The others, which divided into between four and eight pieces, were fitted with explosive cutting cord that split the missile at the end of the boost phase. Each of the warhead-sized chunks would be coated inside and out with aluminised Mylar or a similar radar reflector, so that the real warhead remained hidden in a cluster of false targets. As for those that appeared to be manoeuvring, this was achieved by one of several methods. These ranged from simply bending the nose cone or misaligning the fins to adding small metallic wedges to the outer surface that caused the missiles to begin spiralling as they entered the thicker air in the upper atmosphere.

Jakob was visibly impressed. Was there anything this snowy-haired wise man didn't know? During the next fifteen minutes, and then throughout the night as the Scuds came over, Peled did the 'sorts' himself. This took nerves of steel and not a little courage to assess which of the incoming Scuds was of which type, and where the threatening warhead was located among the clusters of electronic dots. It meant waiting until the last ten or fifteen seconds of the optimum engagement bracket against each incoming warhead to be certain of hitting the correct one.

That night 165 Scuds were launched at Israel, an even mix of 'standards', 'starbursts', 'cutters' and 'spirals', as they were nicknamed, as well as another couple of Shahab 4s which, as before, sailed high overhead. Peled, for reasons known only to himself, ordered 4th Battery to engage them and both were brought down. Unfortunately some falling debris from the engagement killed a family of seven on the southern outskirts of Haifa. Commander Air Defence in Tel Aviv was on the line within minutes of the engagement. Everyone in the control cabin could hear the high-pitched, angry shouting coming from Tel Aviv. Jakob dared to enquire politely what Tel Aviv wanted after Peled had simply stood and listened then replaced the receiver without comment.

'The general was just reminding me about our rules of engagement and wanted to know what we thought we were doing engaging the stray missiles.'

'Well, I do think the Iranians are having a little trouble aiming those,' ventured Jakob unhelpfully. Peled allowed himself half a smile.

'I'm sure the Iranians know exactly what they're doing and nothing we have seen in this war so far has convinced me that we are up against the halfwits that our superiors seem to think the enemy are.' He could afford to smile; his judgement of the engagements had been almost without error. The 4th Battery engaged seventeen Scuds whose impact footprints had been against Haifa or Carmel. Of those, thirteen warheads had been correctly identified and hit, as well as three pieces of warhead-sized space junk – Peled was annoyed at himself at wasting three Arrows. A single wildly spiralling missile evaded the intercepting Arrow but impacted the western slopes of Carmel some five hundred metres behind the battery. The three other Arrow battery commanders had also done well, a total of only nine Scuds out of in excess of sixty launched impacting within their defended areas. The Patriots performed far worse in their defence of the airbases. Initial assessments claimed that three-quarters of the Scuds had been successfully intercepted, although this was later rounded down to less than half and was probably closer to a third of the eighty or so that were fired. The Patriot batteries had also fired in excess of 130 missiles at the incoming showers of metal and high explosive compared to just 61 Arrows. The actual effects of the Scud hits on the airbases were less than destructive. Four HASs and two storage bunkers were hit and one lucky missile bored a huge crater into the middle of the runway at Ramat David. Except for routine CAPs, the IAF had remained frustrated on the ground, its crews planning and co-ordinating with Nato forces for the relaunching of the air campaign on the evening of the 30th.

The world waited throughout the early hours of the 30th with bated breath, and again all tuned to CNN for the first news of the results from the Bio and Chemical Warfare assessment teams' analyses. There was nothing, not even a sniff of a suspect chemical or associated compound, much less a trace of known biological agents. It seemed that the Arabs had taken heed of the unambiguous threats of massive retaliation by both Israel and Nato. The 'forces of good' breathed a collective sigh of relief; they were confident of winning a clean war played with their rules. And the Scud attacks weren't that bad; after all, London and Antwerp had both been hit by several thousand V-1s and V-2s in World War II and both were still standing.

The Air Campaign

At dusk on 30 August the Nato air campaign resumed. Even Nato and Israeli air power combined lacked two qualities that had always been held up as prerequisites in any form of war. These were sufficient mass and concentration of force, and neither was helped by the loss of US naval aviation and so many force-multipliers. The sheer size of the target areas from Rabat to Tehran, and the number of targets, were a daunting prospect for the air campaign planners. It soon became apparent that the number of cruise missiles required for a protracted campaign was far in excess of ready stocks. The targets had to be strictly prioritised and were approved at the highest levels. The loss of so many tankers also meant that the number of sorties generated would only be just over half what such a force of combat aircraft would normally be capable of.

Israel insisted that the priority targets for the campaign should be the masses of armour and artillery that were deployed in eastern Syria and Jordan. Nato accepted this, as part of dissuading Israel from launching a pre-emptive strike with her Lance tactical nuclear missiles, but insisted on ensuring control of the air over Syria, Jordan, northern Saudi Arabia and western Iraq first. Once achieved, this would allow the air forces to operate with impunity. Nato's first act, however, was to establish total control of the Mediterranean sea lanes. This was achieved during the hours of darkness. Waves of aircraft launched from Spain, Mallorca, Sardinia, Sicily, Crete and Cyprus to assist the naval forces in destroying 90 per cent of the Islamic collection of frigates, fast attack craft and submarines in port. Six aircraft were lost, two to causes unknown and four to an Egyptian Patriot battery defending Alexandria. During the night the Scud attacks continued as before with similar results. Peled had again defied orders and knocked down two strays. The response from Tel Aviv was apoplectic, and Peled was given a final warning with a threat of dismissal.

The only aircraft that ventured over Iran, Iraq and Syria were stealthy B-2s and F-117s. Their targets, attacking in concert with waves of cruise missiles, were the air defence command headquarters, long-range early-warning radars and communications nodes. Once these were neutralised, Nato considered that, as in previous conflicts, if the enemy was deprived of his capability to command and direct any coherent form of air defence, then the threat against the coming waves of more conventional fighters and fighter-bombers would be considerably reduced. The missions were pronounced a success as the emissions from the air defence radars were reduced to virtually nil by dawn. One hour after sunrise the fighter-bomber armada rose to launch an all-out assault on the myriad of SAMs that were directly protecting the Islamic ground forces. They were in for a nasty surprise. Squadron Leader Hardy later wrote of his experience:

We moved from Karup in Denmark back to Leuchars in late June. On 8 August we were put on forty-eight hours' notice to move, and by the 11th the entire squadron was safely ensconced in Akrotiri, Cyprus. Of course, we were appalled at events prior to our own first involvement on the night of the 30th, when half the squadron was assigned to escorting the push that wrecked Alexandria harbour. But with the success of that night and the attacks on the enemy strategic air defence components, we felt both confident and optimistic about the coming day. My flight of six aircraft was assigned as escort to a package of 120 aircraft that were to conduct a medium-level attack against six Syrian SA-11 and S-300 batteries located in a cluster to the east of the Bekka Valley. These were, as far as intelligence could make out, the most westerly of the deployed SAM systems. In geographic terms we felt that this was the outer layer of the defensive 'onion' that would need to be peeled before we could effectively begin destruction of the army units that lay at the core. We knew that the Russians had exported vast quantities not only of S-300s, the Russian version of the Patriot SAM, to Syria, but were not aware that they had also provided at least two decoy radar emitters for every real radar.

We coasted in from an aquamarine-blue Mediterranean over Jaffna on the Lebanese coast and for a short time were able to enjoy the rolling brown and green hills some 45,000 feet below. The only radars painting our formations were as we expected from the Arrow and Patriot batteries in northern Israel off to our right. Our package was indeed impressive: a total of twelve British Typhoons each carrying four BVRAAMs* and two ASRAAMs, and sixteen US F-15Cs that made up the fighter cover; eight Tornado GR4s each with four ALARM 3s, twenty US F-16CJs each with two Improved HARMs, and eight German ECRs also equipped with Improved HARM as the SEAD package. Their role was to silence the SAM sites while the bombers did their stuff. If they were able to hard-kill any SAM radars that would be a bonus. The bomber force comprised twelve Tornado GR4s each carrying two Storm Shadows, twelve F-15E Strike Eagles and twenty F-16CGs all carrying laser-guided bombs. The GR4s had by far the least dangerous job. They would be able to launch their weapons from the holding orbit over Lebanon once the target positions had been confirmed. The remainder of the package comprised eight tankers that set up their towlines just off the coast, a handful of escort jammers and our very own AWACs, Magic Zero Nine.

In the past such targets could easily be attacked by air- or sea-launched cruise missiles. However, we were aware that the enemy was making the most of lessons learned during fifteen years of attacks on Iraq. The new generations of enemy SAMs were very mobile and only needed to move a few miles to make our job of finding and hitting them doubly difficult. Unlike the older generation of SAMs that Iraq had possessed, the SA-11s

---

* BVRAAM – Beyond Visual Range Air-to-Air Missile. These missiles were extended-range versions of the AMRAAMs. In spite of the impressive performance in the Baltic, the AMRAAMs were still out-ranged by and a little slower than the Russian equivalents. The BVRAAM had been rapidly introduced into squadron service between the Baltic War and deployment to the Middle East and had an effective range out to fifty nautical miles compared to the AMRAAMs' thirty.

and S-300s were able to up sticks and move in a matter of minutes and be fully operational at a new site within half an hour of arrival. The other problem that our intelligence services had confirmed was that the Russians had perfected the development of cheap laptop-sized cruise missile jammers and had supplied them in liberal quantities with every S-300 battery. Even after several had been acquired and tested in the US and counters developed, they were still effective enough to degrade the accuracy of cruise missiles by up to 60 per cent. There was also a rumour that the Russians had used a ground-based laser at Karaganda in Kazakhstan to damage eight of the global positioning satellites. The effect of this was twofold. We heard that the Americans had switched to a US-only coded GPS system and that anyone else who tried to use the system was sent streams of ones and zeros that sent navigation systems either to the meridian at Greenwich or to the North Pole. This made using any weapons system or platform that had an integral GPS very much an inaccurate adventure. Apparently an SAS team, known as the 'Karaganda Six', had eliminated the laser, and Russia was issued with a final final warning.

Hence the job of attacking many targets fell to versions of the good old iron bomb. For packages such as ours the major problem was one of real-time reconnaissance intelligence. We knew where the sites were when we planned the mission but the lead times for putting such comprehensive packages to-gether were such that we knew that it was likely that in between us putting the final touches to a co-ordinated plan and arriving at weapon release point it was probable that the enemy would have moved. We did have a few assets that were supposed to ease this problem. There were the electronic support aircraft whose task was to pinpoint enemy radar emissions through triangulation, and sitting high above Syria were a couple of Dark Stars that would have watched the enemy movements.

Sure enough, as we approached the outer edge of the first SA-11 MEZ, the electronic activity started. There were mul-tiple indications of SA-6, SA-11, S-300 and a couple of unknowns in search mode. On the distant horizon there were small launch flashes followed by the telltale orange-and-white columns of rocket plumes ascending vertically as the enemy launched missiles at targets unseen to us. We were aware that there were other large packages on similar missions out of Turkey and assumed that it was these that were drawing fire.

The package started a lazy orbit on the edge of the MEZ while we waited for confirmation from the Dark Stars of the SAM positions. None came, but our uncertainty disappeared when the JTIDS flashed up information from the Electronic Support Leader. To our surprise the SAM sites remained in the same place. This made life much easier, and the package commander informed Magic that we were pushing on time as planned. Magic acknowledged and confirmed what we already knew, that there was no sign of activity from the Syrian Air Force. The Storm Shadow-equipped GR4s opened the show exactly on time as planned and launched their weapons, four at each site, bade us farewell and turned back for Cyprus.

What we did not know at the time, but found out much later, was that the Russians had also supplied imitator radar repeaters that were identical in their electronic signatures to the real SA-11 and S-300 radars in search mode. Additionally the plastics and wood workshops in the Alliance had been working overtime for the previous six months producing ever more realistic mock-ups of everything from tanks and APCs to entire SAM sites. These models also included individual generators and heating elements to mimic the infrared signature of their real-life counterparts. The mock-ups were so good that to tell the difference one actually had to almost go up and touch them to confirm their identity. At between 20,000 and 40,000 feet this was impossible for us, but we were assured that the Dark Stars with their hyper-spectral optical cameras and high-resolution synthetic aperture radars would not be fooled.

Nevertheless, confident of the accuracy of our information, the package pressed to the launch point for the ALARMs and HARMs against the three SA-11 sites. The attack was planned in two phases. The S-300s were sited several miles behind the SA-11s but their much longer range enabled their MEZs to overlap those of the 11s. The first phase entailed a portion of the HARM shooters firing in direct mode at those systems that had not been taken out by the Storm Shadow sub-munitions. With this complete, around half of the ALARMs would be launched to loiter high above the sites as belt-and-braces protection for the shorter-range F-16CGs as they went in with their LGBs to find and take out individual TELs. This process would be repeated against the S-300s, although it would be a far more dangerous game of cat-and-mouse as the S-300s easily out-ranged the anti-radiation missiles. That was the plan, anyway.

On the ground, unbeknown to us, all six batteries had moved twenty miles west. There was so much activity during the early hours at every known site that it had proved impossible for our surveillance people to assess exactly what was going on in sufficient time, and the Islamic forces had learned much about camouflage and deception in every area of the electromagnetic spectrum. The immediate satellite analysis showed no change, and the operators and analysts of the two Dark Stars had just begun the process of refined analysis of the data transmitted by their high-flying stealthy charges when the data flow suddenly stopped. Again, much later, we learned that the Russian-operated S-400 was, as the Russians had long claimed, able to detect and track stealthy aircraft. This was achieved by using a combination of low-frequency radars and back-scatter techniques. The US, in particular the Department of Defense, discounted the Russian claims even though they had achieved similar results in testing. There was simply too much to lose in terms of face and money invested to admit that the most expensive gold-plated air force bombers were indeed vulnerable. The vertical missile plumes we had seen earlier marked the path of eight S-400s that had been fired at, and downed, the two Dark Stars.

The real SA-11 batteries were directly below us, and the S-300s further west than the original SA-11 sites had been. This put our whole package plum in the centre of the combined MEZs. Later I imagined the battery commanders, licking their lips in anticipation, watching us with high-powered TV trackers below, their radars silent, as we walked into the trap. As far as we were aware the Storm Shadows had done a good job, knocking out around half of the imitation transmitters and reducing a good deal of the mock-ups to splintered wood and melted plastic. By this time the HARM shooters had good fixes on all remaining transmitters, and we enjoyed the spectacle of more than a dozen being launched from F-16CJs and German ECRs. It was then that all hell broke loose.

'Missile launch, missile launch!' It was a German voice. Two hundred pilots and back-seaters dipped their wings in unison to personally assess the source of this call of consternation. There it was, a single plume emanating from an area of stubby trees a couple of hundred metres off the main road in the Bekka below. Not much too worry about, probably an SA-8. We knew there would be SA-8s and Manpads taking hopeful shots from all over the Lebanon and western Syria. Since our lowest jets, the German ECRs, were at 24,000 feet and the ceiling of the SA-8 was around 18,000 feet and the Manpads, much lower, we expected to see the plume rise and then fall away as the missile ran out of steam. Seconds after the first launch there was a cacophony of calls as multiple missile launches were spotted from both sides of the eastern Bekka ridge. My initial reaction was 'What a waste of missiles!' but this soon changed when the DASS lit up with multiple electronic hits and 'Betty', my computer, broke her silence:

'Missile warning, missile warning, Grumble . . . Gadfly,'* she said calmly, no hint of panic in her soothing electronic tone. 'Turd deployed.' I could feel a collective 'Oh shit!' coming from the rest of the package. The next few minutes would be every man for himself. Again, virtually in unison, the entire package banged off external fuel tanks to enable increased manoeuvrability of the jets. We all knew that we were in no position to outrun the SAMs, though we would try nonetheless, and wings dipped as each pilot watched the missiles carefully, trying to pick the one that was aimed personally at their jet. From on high with the F-15s we were able to watch those less fortunate below begin wheeling and diving as the white plumes clawed inexorably towards them. I

---

* Grumble and Gadfly were the NATO code-names for the S-300 (or SA-10) and SA-11 respectively.

saw two F-16s with the presence of mind to counter-attack, roll inverted and dive almost vertically at one of the threatening launch areas, their four HARMs fired direct at the enemy radars before they went into wild defensive jinking.

It was then that things got worse. Betty said, 'Missile warning, missile warning! Groucho. Turd active.' Groucho? I pondered and then realised that there were S-400s in the air as well as everything else. A glance to the east confirmed Betty's assessment. There were more than a dozen missile plumes rising. The S-400s would climb to 80,000 feet or more before coming down on to their targets from above. This, combined with fuselage-mounted thrusters as on the S-300s, made them extremely agile in the terminal phase and difficult to out-turn. Previous generations of missiles up to and including the SA-11s could be defeated by a well-timed 6G break. To beat an S-300 required 7 to 8Gs and the S-400 in excess of 9Gs, our experts had informed us.

It was perhaps only fifteen or twenty seconds from the first missile launch that I watched the rising plumes merge with the wheeling jets below. There were at least six hits marked by orange fireballs that turned rapidly into large black clouds to mark the success of a SAM hit. Several plumes continued through the mêlée below and came up at us. I put the jet into a shallow descending left turn, the notched back from max dry for optimum turning performance, and picked out three missiles that seemed to be heading directly for my formation, which was now spread out in an organised gaggle that would allow individual turning room. The three missiles separated and only one seemed intent on my Typhoon. There was only one thing for it. Betty was putting out chaff. I rolled inverted and pointed directly at the missile. Aileron roll right way up. As time slowed down it occurred to me that we had never practised this sort of thing – you either got it right first time or did not survive. At what must have been 500 to 1,000 metres' distance, with the altimeter winding down rapidly through 30,000 feet, I tried to pull the wings off the jet. Grunting and straining against the onset of grey and blackout, my back was already tensed against an expected calamitous crash as the missile fused and shards of white-hot tungsten scythed

through my office. It never came. Instead the jet was buffeted
as the shock wave from the warhead hit, but the deadly
fragments flew parallel to my vertical course. Level off.
Reverse right. There directly ahead and 30 degrees above
the horizon an S-400 coming down. Push like a bastard!
Minus 4G. Temporary red-out. Back to my senses at
15,000 feet and descending. Instinctive hard right. Another
missile passes from behind to overhead and explodes some
way beyond; the jet quivers in the supersonic blast wave. I see
at least ten other jets doing the same dance of wheeling,
turning and diving. A quick scan across the looming Bekka
reveals the unwelcome sight of yet more columns of white
smoke, every one with a Mach 3 missile steaming at its head,
rising towards us. No sense in going back up now. Betty adds
unhelpfully, 'Chaff 25 per cent. Missile warning Gecko! Guns
warning Tunguska.'* I dive for the deck; the only chance of
escape now is to put a bit of granite between myself and the
short-range guns and missiles. Head west for the sea and
safety. Magic has begun calling Syrian Flankers airborne and
the mission commander is issuing a belated recall order. Over
my shoulder, looking back and up, I see several jets trailing
long plumes of black smoke and losing pieces as they plummet
earthwards mortally wounded. Up in the blue the pilots who
had managed to eject from their stricken aircraft fell as small
black dots which blossomed suddenly into parachutes as they
descended through 10,000 feet and the automatic barostats on
their seats activated. There is a call on our formation chat
frequency from my number three, 'Hobbit', who calls to say he
is ejecting. I never saw him again. No one did. Through olive
and orange groves at 2ft 6ins, sidestep whitewashed villages
and then out over the sea and due west to safety. After landing
I was told that the S-400s had also managed to knock out two
of the tankers on the towline. What a disaster!

And so it was. The Islamic Alliance had spent years studying
and learning Nato's air assault techniques, always searching

* Gecko is the Nato code-name for the SA-8. The Tunguska is a lethal Russian
version of the German Gepard and Roland systems combined into one with short-
range missiles and twin 35mm cannon.

for weaknesses. The Egyptians and Saudis had all been taught first hand. No wonder they were able to give the first wave such a bloody nose. From Hardy's Cyprus package thirty-seven aircraft were shot down. The other three packages and two Israeli equivalents had fared almost as badly in similarly sprung traps. A total of 106 Nato jets and 22 Israeli jets were lost. The silence of the air defences and the patience of the commanders had been richly rewarded. For the second time in a week the air campaign was suspended. With the loss of a total of five Dark Stars, even the operations of the B-2s and F-117s were halted, their invisibility now very much past tense and clouded with uncertainty, while the way ahead was considered. The Islamic Alliance had moved every single SAM between dusk on the 30th and dawn on the 31st. 'Air supremacy' was replaced by 'air denial'. The Alliance had won another round.

The roots of this failure could be traced back to a combination of the information revolution of the 1990s and a complacency about the problems posed by a sizable opponent that was more reactive and flexible than the Iraqis in 1991, and the North Koreans and Serbs in 2002. The West had singularly failed to heed the warning signals. While more and more money was spent on tactical, operational and strategic information-gathering systems the complementary infrastructure required to sift, assimilate and then disseminate to the decision-makers and war-fighters remained woefully inadequate. The generals remained bullish, repeating worn-out phrases such as 'Information is power'. What they failed to see was that the whole system was creaking under a flood of information. Throwing more computers and complex software at the problem actually slowed the whole process down as the information had to pass through an increasing number of interested parties before getting to where it was actually needed in a timely fashion. The revolutionary ideas for a 'military information buffet (much like a cybercafé)', where all information and intelligence was freely and immediately available to all end-users, who would be able to take exactly what they required for their missions when they required it, were rejected on grounds of security.

Of course, sensitive sources, in particular agents on the ground and advanced eavesdropping techniques, had to be protected, but with the mass of information logjamming the intelligence cells, and the officers in those cells jealously guarding the precious information, the baby was thrown out with the bathwater. The generals wanted ever more 'hands on' close control of their assets, not a surprise given the West's aversion to even a single casualty for which they might be held responsible by the media (and later sued). But this centralisation of command, a good thing, also took with it the control of forces to higher levels than ever before. This further eroded lower-level commanders' initiative and freedom of action in getting their mission accomplished in the most efficient manner, especially when confronted with the unexpected.

The CNN effect and information revolution had turned senior commanders into 'control freaks'. The elegant ideal of 'gather, process, strike' remained foundering in 'process' against a large and wily enemy. The academics and military intellectuals had spent two decades perfecting the doctrines of peacemaking, peacekeeping, peace-enforcing and force-packaging for limited wars. Somewhere along the line the idea of preparing to fight a Nato versus Warsaw Pact-sized war had become as unfashionable as it was unthinkable. In the rush to command the high ground in the information war, characterised by an obsessional race to acquire new technology, it seemed that the West had forgotten that war was ultimately about fighting and killing.

Nato air commanders spent the afternoon and evening of 31 August examining their navels. The decision was made to continue the air offensive, but it would have to be a throwback to the 1980s. The air denial exerted by the latest Russian SAMs, and fear of the effectiveness and ubiquity of TFR jammers, were such that there was only one conclusion – low-level daylight attack. The first waves would launch at dawn on 1 September, and again the emphasis would be on establishing air supremacy. The Israelis were only slightly reassured by reconnaissance images that showed that the gathered armies of Islam were still sitting tight in holding areas and that there was no sign of them moving forward to pre-assault jump-off positions. Indeed, the only activity from the deployed forces was among those covering the southern Turkish border, where some serious mine-lying was under way.

Chapter Thirteen –
Weapons of Mass Destruction

———

'I will make them eat bitter food and drink poisoned water, because from the prophets of Jerusalem ungodliness has spread throughout the land.'

Jeremiah, 23, xv

'Your wound is incurable, your injury beyond healing. There is no-one to plead your cause, no remedy for your sore, no healing for you. All your allies have forgotten you; they care nothing for you.'

Jeremiah, 30, xiii–xiv

'Tell this to the nations, proclaim it to Jerusalem. A besieging army is coming from a distant land, raising a war cry against the cities of Judah. They surround her like men guarding a field . . .'

Jeremiah, 4, xvi–xvii

A Hint of Death

The night of the 31st/1st saw the heaviest Scud attacks on Israel of the war so far. Almost 250 Scuds were launched against the cities, towns, airbases and army depots of Israel, and more than a few penetrated the Arrow/Patriot defensive shields. There was not a single town in Israel that did not receive at least one hit in a spread of missile attacks that seemed designed to achieve no more than random terror and incidental damage. At dawn the air campaign got under way again. The reach of the attackers was hampered by both the shortage of tankers and the fact that the missions were being conducted at ultra-low level to avoid the dangerous Russian SAMs, which meant that the radius of action of Nato and Israeli fighter-bombers was effectively halved. The three waves launched all concentrated on nibbling the outer edges of the known SAM umbrellas. Cruise and other stand-off missiles continued to be launched against fixed targets such as airfields and supply depots, which served to keep the Islamic air forces on the ground and disrupt the build-up of stocks to the divisions waiting to attack. The SAM targets were difficult to locate and hit with the first pass. Every system moved position on average every three to four hours to stay ahead of Nato's planning cycle. This meant that even when targets were located, and many of these were decoys, weapons were not released until the second or third pass, and then more often than not in the face of a hail of ground fire. The loss rates for the Israeli and Nato aircraft were 4 per cent on the first wave and 2 per cent on subsequent waves. The return was not brilliant; on average two to three TELs were confirmed destroyed for every aircraft lost. The planners estimated that they would need ten to fourteen days before medium-level ops could resume and the task of direct attack against the gathering ground forces could begin in earnest.

On the evening of the 2nd, CNN in Tel Aviv transmitted the first reports of an unusual outbreak of flu, or at least flu-like symptoms. What was startling was that almost all of the flu victims were those who had been injured by the few Scuds that had penetrated the Israeli shield. A quick cross-check revealed that all across Israel, including on the airbases that had been hit by Scuds, there was a similar pattern of flu outbreaks. By 9 p.m. the civilian and military hospital staff were working frantically to identify the strain. Initial blood checks revealed nothing other than confirming that the new strain was not related to the deadly Sydney 2 or Singapore chicken variants. It was clear that there was a direct link between the flu outbreaks and the Scud attacks, and the Israeli biological warfare monitoring teams were frantically engaged on a reanalysis of their samples. Tests for anthrax, ebola, botulin and bubonic plague were all redone, and again all drew blanks, but as the night ticked by the number of reported cases doubled with each passing hour.

At the Tel Aviv Clinic for Infectious and Tropical Diseases, junior doctor Cecilia Marekov had just begun her late shift in the laboratory with her assistant Lila, when they were rudely interrupted by the arrival of a team of 'special analysts' from New York. They had flown direct on one of the last British Airways Concordes which had been commandeered on the direct orders of the Oval Office. There were six of them, all male and all dressed in full lightweight protective gear and all wearing full breathing gear, looking more like spacemen than anything else, and singularly out of place. Cecilia's gas mask was in her office. She would put it on only when the air-raid sirens wailed, as they had done for the past three days, and take it off when the chemical and biological all-clear was given. The analysts were accompanied by three Israeli military officers, the Health Minister himself, who appeared more embarrassed than apprehensive, and Cecilia's boss, a now dishevelled-looking senior consultant. He had had just twenty minutes at home after a fourteen-hour day and had been picked up halfway through his dinner by a Health Ministry Mercedes. After some curt introductions (pointless, Cecilia thought, since they were all well hidden by their equipment), the Health Minister explained that the men were from the Los Alamos National Laboratories and had been placed on stand-by in New York waiting for just such a development.

The Health Minister asked Cecilia's boss to put his three laboratories and all his staff at the disposal of the masked analysts. He explained that, although no one had yet died of the flu, the men from New York were there to confirm the nature of the virus. Within an hour the first couple of patients who had developed the flu symptoms arrived. They were young airmen who had been badly injured and suffered burns when the first Scud had hit Meggido. In the following hour and a half a further dozen with the most severe symptoms of migraine-strength headaches, high fever and intense muscle pain had been transferred to the clinic's isolation unit.

At 0200 on 3 September the team leader called Cecilia's boss and the senior military officer into the number-two laboratory.

'I think we have an idea what the virus is,' he said simply, his Texan drawl booming through the microphone in his suit, 'and it's not good. The closest match we have is to smallpox, that is essentially a variola virus, but it's been genetically modified so we can't be sure yet until it develops what it is we are dealing with.'

Cecilia's boss went into denial. 'It can't be smallpox. We all know that smallpox was eradicated in 1980 and that the remaining sealed strains of the virus, held in Moscow and at Los Alamos, were destroyed five years ago.'

'I can only say that the great triumph of us and the Russians watching each other destroy our remaining small-pox stocks in 2001 was no more than a sham. A publicity stunt, if you like.'

'Fucking hell!' said the clinic director.

'Indeed,' agreed the Texan. 'It would have been very imprudent for us to have done so and there is no doubt that the Russian military came to the same conclusion. Our governments were, of course, as you remember, only inter-ested in a public relations coup. Politicians, though, in my experience, are only interested in presentation. Sometimes they don't have the real long-term interests of their people at heart.'

'So you defied direct orders and retained secret stores of smallpox?'

'Of course, as did the Russians. As an amateur historian I have never been in any doubt that, as they say, what goes around comes around. Smallpox was, unwittingly perhaps, the main weapon of the Spanish conquest of South America. In a few years it had wiped out ninety per cent of the indigenous populations.'

'I am aware of that.'

'And of course the US government used it as an offensive

weapon against the North American Indians in the nine-teenth century, and we killed tens of thousands of them through "helping" them by sending smallpox-infested blankets. So I'm not at all surprised from an historical perspective, you understand, that it should be smallpox that comes home to roost.'

The director did not understand and could feel his anger rising as the Texan continued.

'The potential power of such a weapon to the Islamic Alliance would have ensured that even the most moral of Russian research scientists, or the government itself, would have been unable to resist the financial temptation offered.'

'What's the worst prognosis? Do we have vaccines?'

'If it is a strain that is directly related we should hold sufficient stocks of vaccine to start a massive and immediate immunisation programme. Historical epidemics have been between thirty and sixty per cent fatal. But as I said, that is the best case.' The Texan finished his matter-of-fact analysis.

The clinic director stared at his hands. 'I'll need to inform the Health Minister.'

'I've already done that,' said the Texan quickly. 'And the Prime Minister and Ma'am President.'

'So what happens next?'

'We have to wait for the pustules to develop. Then scrape a couple and do a full analysis. Only then will we know the full extent of the problem.'

'What's your worst guess?'

'Well, assuming the spores are in the water supply and in the food chain, and have been for the past three days or so, there will hardly be anyone in the whole of Israel who is not affected. No one in the world has been immunised against smallpox since the early eighties. As far as we were concerned smallpox was extinct.'

'Oh shit . . . and that's why you guys have been wearing your space gear the whole time. You've known this all along. We're all infected, aren't we?' The director resisted the urge to launch an assault on the clever American, rip his hood off and let him share the feeling of impending doom and the sudden closeness of death.

'Mm-hm, probably,' agreed the Texan, 'But there are always survivors.'

Air Force One

'Ma'am President?' It was Admiral Lee, who had been aft in the communications zone of the most expensive jumbo ever built. The President was dozing on her lounger but had given her decision-makers complete freedom of access to her inner sanctuary, up in what was normally first class, if they felt the situation merited it.

'Ma'am President!' he insisted, this time a little louder. The President awoke to the sight of the tall blond officer, apparently weighed down with the amount of gold braid on the shoulder tab of his white shirt.

'Ma'am President,' he said softly. The President's personal aide was frowning apprehensively at Lee's shoulder, certain that in spite of the President's order, there was nothing short of full-scale nuclear attack that warranted waking her.

'Yes, Frank, what is it?' The President was now fully alert and swung her slender legs to the floor. Lee politely averted his eyes.

'We just had a message from London . . . England,' he added out of habit. 'Their ears people in Cheltenham . . .' He almost added 'England' again but stalled as the President's crystal-blue eyes locked on to his. 'Er, GCHQ,' he continued, 'have intercepted a "prepare to launch" message from the Israeli Prime Minister to four of the Lance batteries and two of the older Jericho One bunkers. And,' continued Lee hesitantly, 'it looks like the Israeli Army will follow the strikes with a ground assault, probably to take Damascus and Amman.'

'Lance,' replied the President. 'Tactical battlefield nuke, max range a hundred and twenty clicks, warheads around ten kilotons. Jericho One, out to six-fifty clicks, fifty-kiloton neutron warhead. Assessment?'

'That if the flu epidemic is confirmed as a prelude to smallpox, and our team leader in Tel Aviv called to say that he was certain it was, and Israelis start dying, it seems the Israeli Prime Minister has decided to launch a destructive attack on his neighbours. The obvious targets for the weapons alerted are Amman, Damascus and Beirut, which are in Lance range, and the Jerichos probably at the areas where the Islamic divisions are preparing in eastern Syria, western Iraq and northern Saudi.'

'Yup. That's the conclusion I'd draw too. Call the guys in.'

Five minutes later America's major decision-makers were seated around the walnut oval conference table. The televisions showing CNN, Sky, the BBC and Arab World Television were turned off. The heated discussion that followed lasted less than twenty minutes. The fact of a biological attack on Israel would explain why the Scuds had not been raining down on the packed airbases in southern and eastern Turkey as the Pentagon experts had predicted they would. The Islamic Alliance was very cautious about drawing the Americans into the nuclear response the President had clearly promised. The President summed up the feelings around the table.

'We have some unfortunate choices to make. If the Alliance has smallpox-tipped missiles then our European friends' population centres are extremely vulnerable to attack. Saladin has been scrupulous about not attacking either our cities or our forces gathering in the Med and Turkey directly since our navy took such a hammering, and, as Marseilles demonstrated, he could, if he chose to, hit virtually anywhere in central Europe. Chief of Intelligence and Chief Medical Adviser agree that this is unlikely and that the Alliance only has sufficient stocks for what appears now to have been a concentrated attack on Israel. Our only chance of taking out all residual missiles carrying smallpox, and they have been fired from many different locations, would be a massive nuclear strike

across the Islamic Crescent. And even then, the moral
implications of killing, I don't know, twenty-five million
Arabs aside, that would not guarantee that a handful of
missiles would not be fired at our own cities in retribu-
tion. And quite apart from that, given the strength,
organisation and tenacity of Islamic terrorist cells within
our own countries, there is a distinct possibility that our
own cities, yes, even here in America, could have their
water supplies directly poisoned in a very short period of
time. We are left with a choice. Escalate the conflict and
risk massive . . . and we are talking hundreds of millions
of civilian casualties on both sides . . . or . . .' She paused,
searching for the right words.

'Or abandon Israel and her six million inhabitants to her
fate.' It was Admiral Lee who put the stark alternative so
crudely. There was a round of gasps at the table. Unequivocal support for Israel had been the cornerstone that
defined US foreign policy since 1956. Now this was about
to be turned on its head in one short twenty-minute meeting.

'Effectively, yes. We just have to hope that Israel wins. So
we'd be happy for the Israelis to hit the Islamic armies with
nukes, causing casualties of between fifty and two hundred
thousand, depending on the number of missiles fired, density,
prevailing conditions and so forth, and as long as the wind is
blowing away from our forces. But, morally, we are, on the
whole, against nuclear attack on enemy cities. Is that
right?' There were nods of silent assent around the table.
'OK, get me the Israeli Prime Minister on the green phone. I'll
tell him.'

Ten minutes passed while they waited for a connection.
Admiral Lee disappeared aft again to personally harass the
operators and find out why it was taking so long for them to
connect with Tel Aviv. On his return all faces in the conference area turned from their small discussion groups to hear
his words.

'We just had a call from NORAD. The Arabs have
launched a nuclear attack against Israel. Initial assessments
show that it was a high-altitude burst, magnitude unknown,

casualties unknown. All telecom lines to Israel are down at the moment. Request Defcon Five, Ma'am President.'

The President was unsure how she should feel at this latest turn of events. Saladin was always one step ahead. Sooner or later she would have to seize the initiative, and she knew then that the later she left it the bigger the initiative would have to be, and her options were running out fast.

'Make it so, Admiral.'

Mount Carmel

Jakob had heard the first whispers about the use of biological weapons on CNN at around midnight. The Scuds were still coming over, but it was clear that the peak had passed. He couldn't relax in his hour away from the console and thought of Cecilia in Tel Aviv. All mobile phones had been confiscated at the start of the war, and he'd only spoken to her once now since his arrival on Carmel. He decided to watch the nightly firework display as the Patriots were launched from Meggido and Ramat David. He could not shake the feeling of sickness in his stomach. He knew that Israel would turn to her nuclear arsenal the minute a biological attack was confirmed.

'Here they come again.' It was Peled commenting on the approach of another two high-flying 'strays'. Jakob watched their tracks disappear into the sea and imagined them splashing down into the Med. Fifteen minutes later the console operator called Peled over. Jakob turned from his observation periscope to listen.

'There's something new here. I've got four more high-flyers, three up front and one trailing.' Without answering, Peled picked up the telephone to Command in Tel Aviv and requested permission to engage.

'What does it matter what level my stocks of missiles are at?' he shouted into the telephone. Another pause to listen. 'They're at thirty-five per cent, sir.' A shorter pause, and then

Peled was almost pleading. 'They're definitely up to something, just let me take the trailer out.' Another pause. 'Yes, sir . . . no, I won't disobey a direct order, but on your own head be it.' Peled slammed the phone down. He knew that he had overstepped the mark again, and rather than await the inevitable dressing down that would follow as soon as the general was reconnected he lifted the receiver off the hook and placed it gently on the desktop.

'To whom can I speak and give warning? Who will listen to me? Their ears are closed so they cannot hear.'

'Isaiah?' queried Jakob, his recollection of Bible quotes, like that of the rest of secular Israel, somewhat vague.

'No; Jeremiah, chapter six.' Peled grinned at Jakob. 'He'll either build up a head of steam and blow his top at me or he'll calm down a bit and attribute my rudeness to battle stress.'

Suddenly everything happened at once. The console operator started to say, 'The trailer has disapp . . .' but he got no further. In an instant night became day. The intensity of the light coming through the observation positions was enough to illuminate the whole of the inside of the control cabin.

'Fucking hell!' exclaimed Peled. 'A nuke! A fucking nuke! This is it!' He didn't elaborate, nor did he need to. The artificial daylight lasted several seconds before beginning to fade. As it started to fade, the electromagnetic pulse hit Carmel. It was as if an unseen hand had switched off all the power. The control crew, now all on the floor, hands covering heads, winced as the computers, cables and other electronic equipment popped, fizzed and sparked in the throes of electronic death by short circuit. Peled was again the first to speak in the darkness as the glow and sparking died down. 'Grab your personal weapons, gentlemen. From now on I fear we will only be of use to Israel as foot-soldiers.'

The Islamic Alliance had played its trump card. The Shahab 4 had been the last of four launched from the western outskirts of Qom, the Iranian holy city. The preparations for the launch of the Alliance's single nuclear warhead had gone well. There was some consternation when the first couple of Shahabs had been downed by Arrows on the first night, but Saladin's ruse of routinely 'wasting' missiles by firing them without warheads along what would be the nuclear missile's trajectory had worked. The Israeli commanders, Peled excepted, came to the conclusion that the 'stupid Arabs were having technical trouble', and felt they could safely ignore the 'strays'. The final 'stray', however, had a 100-kiloton warhead, and it was detonated at a height of 19.3 miles some 90 miles off the coast west of Haifa. Saladin knew that this scenario, an exoatmospheric burst, was one that only the Americans had wargamed properly, and the consequences were so unthinkable that the Pentagon had refused to 'think' any further about the problem, offering the bland reassurances that stemmed from nuclear deterrence theory. 'The whole point of nuclear weapons is not that we actually use them but in possessing more and better ones than any potential enemy we know he will not contemplate using them against us because he can expect a massive response.' This was the testimony given to the Senate Select Committee for Nuclear Strategy by a senior Pentagon official. The problem with this scenario was that the target was Israel, not the US or Nato, and that the Islamic Alliance had gone beyond contemplation and actually used a weapon.

The brightest Islamic scientists had done their sums well. The most frightening effect of an exo-atmospheric burst was not the nuclear fallout (of which there would be none since the fireball would get nowhere near the ground), nor the heat or blast (mostly dissipated through the upper atmosphere), but the generation of a massive electromagnetic pulse. In a process caused by ionisation, the weapon's gamma rays strip the negatively charged electrons from the atoms and molecules in the upper atmosphere, creating waves of ion pairs. The stripped electrons in turn create many tens of thousands of secondary electrons as they hit the denser upper atmosphere. What forms is a huge pancake-shaped pulse that spreads down to the horizon in all directions. With a burst height of 19 miles the area affected is around 150 miles radius from the point of detonation for a 100-kiloton weapon. The pulse is as powerful as, but more rapid than, those produced by lightning strikes, with the energy being delivered in the form of a strong current, and voltage surge creating chaos and distortion of electromagnetic fields over a wide area. The resultant powerful electrical surges are carried through every metallic object in the affected area, such as steel building frames, radio, television and radar aerials and antennae, electricity cables and vehicles (which include, of course, tanks, ships and aircraft). The transient electrical surges damage or destroy any exposed electrical equipment, and this is where the real power of an exo-atmospheric burst lies. Every item that contributes to the definition of the modern world as 'high tech' is extremely vulnerable. The list is endless but includes anything that has solid-state modern microcircuitry and components, transistors, silicon, semiconductor components, communications links, automated equipment, intercom and alarm systems, computers, and so on. It is possible to 'harden' equipment against such an attack by enclosing the most sensitive items in sealable metal cages, using fibre optics, or by burying cables, but these islands of resistance have to remain 'stand alone'. In an instant a modern high-tech state could be transformed into a Stone Age society without heat, light, water-pumping equipment and transport, and be left with a mountain of useless metallic and electronic artefacts of a suddenly bygone era.

The area of the burst affected virtually the whole of Israel, as well as Amman and much of western Jordan, and the nation was plunged into chaos in the early hours. All homes and hospitals and streets were completely without power as even stand-by generators refused to work. Almost 90 per cent of the Israeli military command, control and communications links went down. The Israeli Army was turned into a mass of rifle-armed militia as many of the sophisticated and compu-ter-driven tanks, artillery pieces, infantry carriers and Lance nuclear missiles were rendered useless. At 2330 the previous evening, as soon as the news of a biological attack was confirmed – albeit still officially only a version of flu – the Israeli Prime Minister had had no hesitation in ordering the army to carry out its long-planned attack east. The generals had held the army at six hours' notice to move. The IAF was also delighted. At last it would be able to follow its own war-fighting agenda and stage a massive strike on the Islamic troop assembly areas, tank and artillery parks and lines of communication. The leading army units were to have jump-off from the start lines at 1000 that day with the ground assault spearheads aiming for Amman and Damascus. In an instant, however, the electromagnetic pulse meant that all the roads leading east were jammed with broken-down vehicles. The IAF was caught preparing to give direct support to the army's assault through the thinly held defences on Israel's border. The timing could not have been worse, with many aircraft exposed outside their shelters doing final checks before launching on what were to have been dawn raids. The IAF lost almost 70 per cent of its strength, but most of the computer-driven back-up that makes a modern air force work, from reloading equipment and fuel trucks to mission-planning and data-gathering assets, were a casualty of the pulse.

In his bunker in Tel Aviv Levi finally understood why the Islamic forces had been held well back from Israel's borders in the staging areas in eastern Syria, eastern Jordan, western Iraq and northern Saudi Arabia.

He turned to his assistant. 'Now they will move to attack.'

Preparations to Invade

Saladin had promised his generals a 'great sign in the sky' to mark the day when they would finally be able to move from their waiting positions and attack Israel. And he had given them just that. The exo-atmospheric burst lit up the night sky and was visible from Cyprus and Alexandria in the west to the Jordanian and Syrian borders with Iraq in the east.

The great movement of men and material from the forces of Islam gathered well to Israel's east began at 0500. It would be at least forty-eight hours and probably double that before all were somewhere near their ordered start positions. The Islamic armies assigned for the direct assault on Israel included no fewer than two million men in the east alone, half of whom were reservists, equipped with a massive nine thousand main battle tanks and similar numbers of infantry fighting vehicles and personnel carriers and artillery pieces. The remaining million, almost exclusively reservists, were deployed in dug-in defensive positions covering the length of Turkey's southern border with the Alliance and guarding possible counter-attack routes out of Kuwait, Qatar and Bahrain. One of the more curious aspects of the war was that throughout the conflict the isolated garrisons in the Gulf states were not attacked and, aware of the vulnerability of their positions, were not inclined to initiate offensive action.

The Alliance forces began to deploy in a wide arc from the Lebanon in the north through south-western Syria and along the length of western Jordan and north-western Saudi Arabia. Spearheading the attacks would be some forty crack armoured, mechanised special forces and guard divisions, followed up by seventy or so lower-grade infantry divisions. The remaining twelve armoured and mechanised divisions were positioned as a strategic reserve to bolster the twenty-five divisions covering Nato and Turkey.

Nato's air power had hardly begun its attempt to gain freedom of action in the airspace over Syria and Jordan but would now be forced to concentrate its attacks on the target-rich columns of assorted armour that were beginning to press towards Israel. However, as if the thousands of SAMs and tens of thousands of anti-aircraft artillery were not enough of a problem, the first cold front of the autumn was sweeping across the Nile Delta, pushing ahead of it cloud and rain that made both flying ops and intelligence-gathering doubly difficult.

In the Sinai, with both sides dug in and reduced to artillery duels, the Israelis had withdrawn much of their battered heavy units in anticipation of a strike east, leaving only the thinnest of covering forces, albeit in good positions. The

Egyptians were far from a spent force, and they were reinforced by a continued build-up of Libyan, Sudanese, Algerian
and Moroccan troops sheltering under the protection of the
multi-layered Egyptian SAM umbrella that still had significant numbers of Patriot and S-300s as its backbone.

Chapter Fourteen –
The Beginning of the End

'Death has climbed in through our windows and has entered our fortresses; it has cut off the children from the streets and the young men from the public squares . . . the dead bodies of men will lie like refuse on the open field, like cut corn behind the reaper, with no-one to gather them.'

Jeremiah, 9, xxi–xxii

'You will destroy yourselves and make yourselves an object of cursing and reproach among all the nations on earth.'

Jeremiah, 44, viii

'The whole land will be ruined, though I will not destroy it completely. Therefore the earth will mourn and the heavens above grow dark.'

Jeremiah, 4, xxvii–xxviii

'Their land will be laid waste, an object of lasting scorn; all who pass by will be appalled and will shake their heads.'

Jeremiah, 18, xvi

Number Two Laboratory

At 1235 Lila, the lab technician, had come running into Cecilia's darkened office with the unwelcome news that one of the two airmen from Meggido had developed a rash. They watched him closely for the next couple of hours, and sure enough the areas affected by the rash began to turn into pustules. A couple of the others were also developing rashes. Things did not look good.

They heard no direct news about what was happening across Israel. The military orderly who was acting as messenger between the laboratory and the Prime Minister's command bunker said that hospitals across the country were becoming packed to overflowing with people who had developed early symptoms of the virus. There also were rumours that the army had opened fire on some angry groups of people who had tried to storm two of Jerusalem's hospitals demanding vaccine. In the course of the orderly's three short trips across the city, the number of people in the streets had more than quadrupled. Some were indeed angry; others, who had resorted to looting, engaged in running gun battles with the security forces, while many more were wailing or mourning. There were also many ordinary citizens, police and army personnel who were being tended by their comrades, struck down where they had been standing by the sudden onset of severe flu symptoms.

As the sunset faded the sound of gunfire increased across the city. The lab porter had persuaded one of the ancient diesel generators to work, which provided dim light in the number two lab. The isolation unit was in complete darkness. Cecilia left an exhausted Lila asleep in her chair and picked up her torch to make the hourly check of the 'first twelve'. As she opened the door she did not need a torch to tell her the state of those inside. The stench hit her as a solid wall and she retched instinctively. The smell was awful, and one she recognised from one of her earliest experiences as a medical student. Rotting flesh. She clicked on the torch and illuminated the hand of the young airman from Meggido. Fully half of the pustules had burst to reveal rotting sores that had spread rapidly up the forearm. The tinges of pink, yellow, green and grey flesh were enough to confirm what her nasal senses already told her – gangrene.

She slammed the door and ran to the dimly lit waiting room where the military orderly was kneeling alone, bowed in silent prayer. He turned at the approach of her hurried footsteps. 'Tell the Prime Minister that the virus is one unknown to us. It appears to be a strain of gangrenous smallpox.' She wondered at the minds and motives of the Russian scientists and geneticists who had managed to create such a disgusting hybrid. She would tell the director, but first she returned to the office to let Lila know.

Lila was moaning softly in her slumber. Cecilia felt her forehead; she had started a high fever. 'What is it, Ces? God, I feel awful,' murmured Lila. Oh no, thought Cecilia, not beautiful blonde young Lila. She had so much of her life left to live, so many things not done. And now, though she did not know it, she was destined to a slow, painful, rotting death. Cecilia collapsed to her knees and wept.

The Assault Begins

Israel remained in virtual news blackout for the following forty-eight hours. Subsequent reports indicated that the number of people suffering from what became known as GSP (gangrenous smallpox) increased to just over half a million by the end of the 5th, with double that amount, including a significant percentage of the armed forces, suffering from initial symptoms. The US had flown in three C-17-loads of smallpox vaccine, which soon proved to be ineffective, the crews unceremoniously dumping their cargo under armed guard on the airport concrete. The guards were necessary to stop American citizens who had flocked to the airport from forcing their way on to the planes. America did not want an epidemic brought back with the C-17s. The third plane was rushed by a large group of desperate escapee hopefuls who were gunned down. Later US aircraft resorted to low-level air drops using cushioned packaging for the emergency medical supplies. The President did not want any more nasty incidents.

Israel spiralled into desperate disorder. The sick and dying were strewn everywhere. Most were simply left where they fell; there was no remedy or hope in sight for them. Those who were still able rampaged through the streets looking for 'clean' tinned food, of which there was little available. The army, dying on its feet, took up prepared defensive positions with which to meet the inevitable Islamic attack. There were only handfuls of tanks and anti-tank weapons still working, and these were concentrated on the most likely approaches into Israel,

Nato's response was to intensify the strategic, but still conventional, bombardment of Islamic Alliance military targets and those civilian targets that directly supported the various war machines. Attacks by manned bombers, B-1s and B-2s, were concentrated on those targets that were not directly defended by the more dangerous Russian-built SAMs. Those that were well defended were left to ship, submarine and B-52-launched cruise missiles. In Syria and northern Iraq the tactical air forces achieved considerable success against the military traffic jams that were building as the Alliance divisions moved west, but these were not without some losses, and did little to delay the movement of such a vast army. In southern Jordan and north-western Saudi Arabia the Islamic divisions suffered hardly any attacks. With the Red Sea closed thanks to Egyptian, Saudi and Sudanese mining efforts, Nato air forces simply lacked the reach. The mood in Naples and Mons was despondent. Air power, so often trumpeted as the hero and saviour in past conflicts, simply lacked the reach and mass now required for it to make any significant difference and become more than an irritating nuisance to the two million soldiers who were moving inexorably to the Israeli border. As the first Islamic tanks rumbled across Israel's border in the early hours of the 6th, Nato commanders concluded that their only option would be to launch their planned attack out of Turkey two to three weeks ahead of schedule. The preparations were stepped up to a frantic pace. The race was on.

Across Israel's north-eastern border the attacking forces met with unexpectedly stiff resistance from the Israeli defenders, who now had nothing to lose. Most progress was made in the south between Eilat and the southern end of the Dead Sea, where Saudi armoured units bypassed the port city and advanced rapidly into the southern Negev. In the west the

Egyptians and their allies began a more measured preparation for the attack to retake Sinai. They first had to break through the multiple lines of dug-in defenders, and there were still some units that had not been affected by the EMP, although the remainder of the best armour was being moved to the Golan front, where Israel had no room for manoeuvre. For Israel time was running out and all seemed lost. She still, however, had one final throw of the dice left in her.

Nuclear Research Site 4 – Dimona

Israel had phased out her Jericho 1 missiles, which had a range of 650 kms, and replaced them with the Jericho 2. The Jericho 2 had more than double the range of its predecessor but was still effectively a sub-strategic weapon. A large proportion of the Jericho 2s were also known as 'Enhanced Radiation Weapons', or more usually 'Neutron Bombs'. The warhead sizes ranged from one to five kilotons, which made the largest about a quarter the size of the Hiroshima weapon, but at least as lethal in terms of immediate radiation damage, which made them ideal for attacking massed groups of armour, infantry and artillery. The later Jericho 2s had more conventional nuclear warheads and were targeted against Islamic cities. The Jericho 2s were deployed on TELs which were stored in underground bunkers, typically between five and ten missiles in any one bunker, and each bunker had three entrance/exits from where the TELs would drive out a short distance to a prepared launch site.

The realisation that the small handful of Jericho 2 bunkers were perhaps more vulnerable than was desired, as were the missiles in the twenty to thirty minutes between bunker exit and launch, led the Israelis to change the deployment and operating strategy for her nuclear missiles with the introduction of the Jericho 3. The Jericho 3 was much more akin to an IRBM, its warheads ranging from 400 kilotons to one megaton, and, with a range in excess of 2,500 km, it was able to reach every inch of territory of those states most hostile to

Israel. Over the ten-year period up to 2005, Israel completed a silo cluster programme high on the Negev plateau which closely mimicked that of the US's Minuteman silos. Each silo was self-contained and housed a single missile and launch station for two operators, which was separated by a safe-type door from sleeping and eating quarters for two further personnel. In times of tension each silo could operate completely sealed and autonomously for up to a month with each crew doing twelve-hour shifts. The silos were essentially reinforced concrete plugs shaped rather like a large mallet driven into the ground handle first with a hollow core. The top of the silo was protected by a sliding cover some twenty feet thick, designed to withstand direct hits from even the best and heaviest conventional penetrator weapons in the world, and from nuclear blast overpressures of up to 3,000 pounds per square inch. The cover of each silo was overlaid with four to five feet of earth, sand and gravel, and when closed made a seamless join with the surrounding countryside. The perfect and carefully choreographed camouflage effectively 'disappeared' the silo from prying eyes. That there was something of great significance in the area was, however, obvious to even the most casual analyst of routine satellite coverage. From space the apparently empty area was surrounded by triple lines of electrified fencing and barbed-wire watchtowers and a complex of buildings for the guard force.

Jericho 3, silo number 32

First Lieutenant Leo Erhardt looked at the television monitor for the third time in less than five minutes. The television was his only view of the outside world. In peacetime he was able to swing the camera and survey the browns, light yellows and oranges of the Negev plateau. He would also watch the sun come up and go down. Leo had almost forgotten the camera's real purpose of monitoring the silo's sliding roof and, as a keen ornithologist, enjoyed zooming in on the occasional bird that settled unconcerned on the most heavily guarded zone in all of Israel. As far as he was concerned the camera was a device that helped keep morale up in what was a mind-numbingly boring and isolated routine. It told them when it was night and day and therefore helped regulate their body clocks as well as showing them the reality of the world outside their concrete cocoon.

Research Site No. 4 was the home to most of Israel's nuclear arsenal. Covering an area several football fields in size of rough high-desert terrain, the Site, as it was called locally, had forty Jericho 3 silos. The silos had been completed in the early millennium and were made to blend in with the surrounding desert. It was some comfort to Leo and his shift-mate Uriah that it would take a direct hit from a nuclear weapon to penetrate their sanctuary. Leo swung the camera to the east and south-east. They had been encased for six days now without a breath of real fresh air. Yesterday a number of tanks, infantry and personnel carriers had arrived. As Leo watched they were digging furiously into the desert with picks, shovels and a single digging arm and bulldozer blade attached to an engineer tank. They seemed to be less than well organised, and Leo had observed several bouts of arm-waving and gesticulating as if those in command could not agree on something. There were a couple of female soldiers too, their slender figures and feminine movements all but hidden under khaki fatigues, Uzi machine-pistols and other combat gear.

Watching them, Leo's mind drifted back to Tel Aviv and his girlfriend Lila. He had last seen her in the summer on a forty-eight-hour pass. Now it seemed they had lost all contact. He had not received a letter for over a month, and the news of the war was not good. There were rumours that the cities had been hit by missiles tipped with cocktails of biological weapons, and that many infectious diseases had broken out. Surely the government was still in control, and of course the Israeli Army and Air Force would eventually stem the tide of invaders, as it always had. He could not bear the thought of Lila suffering either from some sort of horrible infection or at the hands of ill-disciplined enemy soldiers. She was so pretty they would not be able to resist her. He hoped she had found a secure and sanitised area in the clinic where she worked. At least if anything did happen she would have the best medical care in the world. For three days now they had had no news of what was going on in the outside world.

Leo and Uri had guessed that all was not well. Yesterday they had heard the roar of what had sounded like sustained heavy artillery. This in itself was only unusual in that normally they lived a life entirely isolated from the outside world and only ever heard each other, the Jericho 2 self-test mechanisms clicking and the endless whine of the pressurised air-conditioning. They had all heard the artillery and assumed simply that the Israeli Army was in the throes of a bold pre-emptive attack against the Islamic forces that had begun building on Israel's eastern border. The outbreak of a ground offensive would also explain the arrival of what appeared to be a reinforced guard for the Site, now visible through the camera still digging away.

Now just over three days had passed since they had sensed what they were convinced had been a nuclear explosion. Leo pondered the events of that morning. He and Uri had been in the rest area when their oppos on the other shift on duty had buzzed through in the middle of the night, rousing them from their sleep in the stale dry air, their voices a mixture of fear and excitement. For around thirty seconds night had been turned into day outside. Within seconds of their being buzzed the shelter alarms had sounded. The self-testing equipment that endlessly checked the integrity of the Jericho 3 and the whole silo operation systems were reporting that the silo cover had suffered a major short circuit. The drill called for a full test of the release procedure in a 'no satellite' window. The next window, during which no known surveillance or reconnaissance satellites would be looking at their area, with enough time for a full launch drill, was three hours away, just after the start of Leo and Uri's next shift. The oppos tried to report the fault immediately to the command bunker but were unable to get through. They called Leo and Uri through the heavy safe door. This was strictly in breach of regulations, but by consensus the four of them agreed that this was an exceptional situation. Forty minutes passed before a group of soldiers approached the top of the silo.

It was the commander himself, Colonel Sh'ev, his long

blond fringe intruding on to his forehead from under his tightly strapped steel helmet. With him was a small entourage of men, what looked like the majority of the command staff, whose agitation was not concealed by the darkness. Leo and Uri went back to the rest quarters in anticipation of a call through the intercom. And they didn't want to be caught breaching the regulations. The intercom was dead, and the television screen was also blank. Back in the silo proper they joined the other pair and watched on the silo monitor Sh'ev's futile attempts to talk into what was a dead camera and equally lifeless intercom next to the covered access ladder. His head movements suggested that he was shouting, and would have been amusing if they did not all have the growing knot of a sense of doom in their stomachs. They had tried to open the access cover, a miniature version of the massive silo cover, but the motor on that too was apparently broken. Sh'ev gave up in disgust and disappeared complete with entourage.

Sh'ev was no idiot, however, and was back within ten minutes. He looked directly into the silo's camera. He held up a white A4-sized sheet of paper to the camera. On it he had scrawled rapidly in black felt-tip, 'Move the camera left for "yes" and right for "no", understand?' Leo motored the camera left and then back to Sh'ev. Another sheet: 'I am Colonel Benjamin Sh'ev, do you recognise me?' Camera left and back. 'Suspect that high-altitude burst has knocked out all of the silo cover motors on Site 4' – another sheet – 'as well as the radio and telephone links to the command post.' And a last sheet: 'You are authorised to open Comms Channel Omega. Do you understand?' Leo nodded involuntarily before clicking the camera left and back. Sh'ev gave the camera a thumbs-up before producing a final sheet. 'Israel expects', was all it said. With that he disappeared into the darkness with his men.

'Well, this is serious,' said Leo to the other three, assuming the air of a senior officer unnecessarily stating what had become blindingly obvious in the last five minutes. They all knew the implications of Omega. Omega was an ultra-secret fibre-optic communications link. Leo had only seen it working twice in the eighteen months he had been at Site 4. Both times had been on evaluation exercises. They were painful experiences; they had had two stone-faced officers with white 'Evaluator' armbands as their sign of authority and clipboards with assessment sheets as they noted down every nuance of the full launch procedure and various failure drills which were practised. This was done to ensure that each silo crew was reliable and combat-ready. Any single failure on either of their parts induced a severe reprimand from the CO. Two failures and they would be assigned to a pioneer unit, losing not only face and status but also their significant extra pay and leave bonuses to compensate for the supreme importance and very nature of their job. Omega, being fibre-optic-based, was resistant to the electromagnetic pulse that had caused the many systems failures in exposed electrical equipment above the ground. It was a miracle that one of the cameras still worked. The Omega system linked them in directly with the command bunker and with the Prime Minister's war room, known as the Ark, excavated six storeys down under the Ministry of Defence in Tel Aviv.

The Omega had been up and running for almost exactly three days now. Purring in quiet competition with the air-conditioning, it blinked into life every four hours with Sh'ev's face appearing on the digital screen. Sh'ev's first instruction over the Omega was to order the crews of the four silos that still had the camera back-up to run through complete launch drills up to and including opening the massive covers that hid the Jerichos from the world outside. At every silo Sh'ev's worst fears were confirmed. The launch sequence automatically shut down as soon as the launch computers were commanded to open the silo covers. They were all dead. The design bureau had not foreseen such a simultaneous catastrophic failure of a simple part of the mechanics of missile silo operations. In the meantime he had done his best to appraise them of the war situation as he knew it and the progress of the work that was going on atop Site 4. The exo-atmospheric burst had effectively sealed all but four of the Jericho silos. Leo wondered about the mental state of the other crews. They would have had no contact with the outside world for at least the first twenty-four hours after the exo-atmospheric burst. With their cameras down and all contact lost, the standing operating procedure was for them to switch their Omegas on after a period of twenty-four hours. Sh'ev would then have told them all that things were not going quite as well as expected and that work was progressing to fix the electrical problems with the silo motors. What he and Leo's crew knew (through watching what was going on through their camera) was that since the burst only four of the silos were actually being worked on. What Sh'ev also knew was that the motors, their switches and microcircuitry had been completely burned out by the electromagnetic pulse and that Site 4 held only four complete sets of spares and sufficient qualified technicians to work on only one at a time. That there were only four sets held Sh'ev now considered to be short-sighted. However, in the fifteen years he had been involved with Site 4 only one motor had ever failed. The whole assembly had been produced by a subcontractor whose small specialist factory was located in the northern suburbs of Haifa. No doubt both the subcontractor and the military held complete sets of spares. The problem now was getting the spares from one end of Israel to the other. The Ministry had rebuffed Sh'ev's persistent questioning over Omega with the line that they were encountering a little difficulty in doing just this, but declined to elaborate. Sh'ev knew that there was no other way of opening the shelters. He wasn't going to share this pessimistic news with the thirty-six crews who might be entombed for some time.

Now it was mid-morning. Leo panned the camera to the group of men huddled around what appeared to be a small hole in the ground which housed the access to the motors and controlling equipment. They were soft-faced and soft-handed technical types who worked with noses and eyes screwed up, surrounded by a haphazard jumble of wires and assorted testing equipment, each with an assortment of pens, screw-drivers and pincers or small wire-cutters in various pockets. The team had been up there on and off for two days, presumably since the spares were obtained. Leo and Uri had watched them for entertainment. Occasionally they would all stop work and glance apprehensively to the east and south – no doubt looking for the source of the rumble of distant gunfire. What had caught Leo's eye now was that they were all standing up, dusting their hands and knees and looking self-satisfied. As he was musing on this turn of events the Omega buzzed into life. It was Sh'ev. His morale-boosting and disarming smile had disappeared. He was looking very serious. For the first time in the past three days he addressed them formally:

'Silo 32, this is control. Stand by for a message from the Ark.' This simple communication made both Leo and Uri sit bolt upright in their seats.

'Silo 32 ready,' replied Leo in the way they had practised on exercises. Then without any further delay a new yet familiar face appeared on the digital screen.

'It's the fucking Prime Minister himself!' said Uri off-intercom, his astonishment articulating the unreality of the situation of the two of them. On all the exercises, they had never seen anything other than senior military officers of various hues standing in for the political masters.

'I am the Prime Minister,' said the Prime Minister woodenly, apparently reading from a prepared script.

'No fucking kidding!' continued Uri irreverently off-intercom.

'Do you recognise me?' said the Prime Minister, pausing and looking up for a response.

'Yes, sir, I recognise you.' Leo now knew what was happening. He looked up at the line of large portrait photographs on the board above the launch consoles. These were the only men in all Israel who had the authority to order a launch of the Jericho. At the top the same Prime Minister stared back. Leo noted irrelevantly that his shirt was now a different colour but the face was the same. Below him was the Minister of Defence, and below him the chiefs of the army, navy and air force. At the bottom of the board was Colonel Sh'ev, whose name, like all the others with the exception of the Prime Minister's was asterisked. The asterisks were to remind the crew that if ordered to release by anyone other than the Prime Minister they had to go through a protracted fail-safe authen-

tication procedure. It would have meant that both crew
members had to take from their personal safes one of the
sealed envelopes they contained. Inside each envelope was a
slip of paper that stated their individual release code word
unique for that particular day. Only the Prime Minister had
the authority to carry out a direct face-to-face release without
the envelopes. Authority for the release of the Israeli strategic
nuclear arsenal was held at the very highest level.

'I authorise you' – the Prime Minister was back to his script
– 'to prepare to launch. Your target code is Alpha Mike Three
Zero Two, mode low airburst. I repeat. I authorise you to
prepare to launch. Your target code is Alpha Mike Three
Zero Two, mode low airburst.' He looked up again expectantly.

'Roger, I confirm that we are authorised to prepare to
launch on target Alpha Mike Three Zero Two, mode low
airburst,' said Leo. Uri repeated the words exactly.

'Let me know when you are ready.'

'Roger, wilco.' With that they took their keys and with a
glance inserted them into the master control panel, twisting
them to the right as they did so. In the background beyond the
blast wall they could hear the faint whine of the missile
systems spinning up from their dormant state. The computer
screen asked silently for the target code, and when both had
punched in AM302 it confirmed that the target co-ordinates
had been passed to the Jericho's inertial guidance system.
Both men now had their attention firmly fixed on the launch
checklists in front of them. Leo read out the checks slowly and
Uri carried them out, repeating the instructions as he did so.
Within four minutes the computer screen showed all systems
go. On-screen was an outline diagram of the missile, green on
black, and the various major components – rocket motor,
batteries, engine, electronics, coolant, hydraulics, warhead,
radar and guidance systems, each with a representative area
on the electronic diagram. As the checks were completed,
testing the integrity of each component, the on-screen Jericho
filled in bright green in turn. When the final check on the
missile was completed the system checked the silo door. The
hollow green rectangle on the screen that sat above the missile

representing the silo door filled in. The computer blinked. 'Ready to launch.' They would know this already both at the site command bunker where Sh'ev was following proceedings and at the Ark.

'Ark, this is silo 32, we are ready to launch,' said Leo.

'Silo 32, this is the Prime Minister, you are clear to launch, I repeat you are clear to launch.' This was it. Uri glanced at Leo and raised his eyebrows half questioningly.

'Silo 32 is clear to launch. Launching in thirty seconds,' said Leo. He turned to Uri. 'OK, let's do it.'

'Unlock guards,' said Uri, back at his checklist.

'Unlock guards,' repeated Leo. With that they removed the keys from the enabling switches and unlocked their respective yellow-and-black-striped metal guards which covered the launch buttons. Unlocking the guards opened the silo's sliding door. They heard the sound of the door opening above them. A glance at the television monitor confirmed that the technicians' work had been a success.

'Confirm guards unlocked and silo door open,' continued Uri.

'Guards unlocked and silo door open,' confirmed Leo.

'Press launch buttons.' Both buttons had to be pressed within five seconds of one another, otherwise the whole launch sequence would auto-shutdown.

'OK, are you ready?' Leo enquired. Uri nodded dumbly. He had trained for this for years, never really expecting that they would ever get this far.

'On the count of three, then.' Uri spoke into the Omega as if to give the target a last chance.

'Silo 32 is launching in five seconds.' His finger hovered over the launch button. The button was white with a dark blue Star of David engraved on it in an exact representation of the Israeli national flag. This was a clever piece of psychology by the designers, reminding those charged with such awesome responsibility exactly what it was they were fighting for. There was no reply from the Ark and no comment from Sh'ev. Both waited expectantly.

Leo continued: 'Three, two, one, now!' He and Uri jabbed the launch buttons together. Immediately there was an ear-splitting roar as the rocket motor of the Jericho ignited, sending vibrating shock waves all through the control area. On the television monitor the screen was filled for a moment with smoke and fire issuing from below ground as if an angry geyser had just blown. Fractions of a second later there was a bang as the Jericho lifted out of the silo, slowly at first but then accelerating rapidly and with certainty as it climbed out above the Negev.

'Silo 32 launch complete. Launch success,' reported Leo. With that the Prime Minister went off-screen to be replaced by Sh'ev.

'Well done, fellows. You've struck a great blow for the freedom and existence of Israel.'

Leo was completely nonplussed. Forgetting the formality of rank, he spoke directly to Sh'ev. 'Not that it matters now, but are you at liberty to tell us where the target was?'

'Tehran,' said Sh'ev without hesitation. Leo and Uri looked at one another.

'Then may the God of Abraham, Isaac and Jacob forgive us,' said Leo simply.

'What?' said Sh'ev.

'Nothing, it's too late now. Another question. Now that our war is over, when can we come out?'

'We're hoping to launch another inside the next two hours. You will have to sit tight. I will let you know.'

'Don't call us . . .'

'What?'

'Nothing. That's OK. Silo 32 out.'

Target Alpha Mike Three Zero Two

The Jericho 3 launched from Silo 32 had a yield of one megaton. It detonated at 1117, around 4,300 feet above the centre of Tehran. The detonation of such a weapon takes less than one millionth of a second, with the processes of fission and fusion taking around ninety nanoseconds (ninety billionths of a second), with 99 per cent of the weapon's energy being released in the final ten nanoseconds. This is the birth of the fireball; in those first few tiny fractions of a second it is only a few metres across and has a core temperature of millions of degrees. Here the destructive electromagnetic pulse is produced. Thereafter, the primary effects of such a weapon are seen in the form of light, heat and blast.

As the rapidly expanding fireball cools to around 300,000°C, the speed of its expansion slows to supersonic and the superheated weapon debris that was travelling inside the fireball with supersonic speed catches up with the outer edge of the fireball. A wave develops at the outer surface of the fireball that shock-heats the air around it, making it incandescently hot, and applies a devastating pressure that has sufficient force to slap down on everything with crushing force. The shock wave travels outward from the point of detonation like an ever-expanding ring. It is followed by intense winds that reach speeds of thousands of miles per hour and die down slowly as the shock wave travels further and further away from the point of detonation. The detonation at 4,300 feet was what is called a low airburst. These are more devastating than ground bursts or high airbursts because, apart from not wasting energy digging a crater, the original blast wave is reinforced by a faster blast wave which is created by reflection off the ground. This doubles the overpressure, or crushing force, of the original wave at around two kilometres from ground zero.

This textbook description* has taken us to 1117 and ten seconds. Below was the vibrant and thriving city of Tehran which had moments ago been full of bustle and business.

The blinding flash from the weapon caused retinal burns to people as far as 20 km away from ground zero. Within a kilometre of ground zero, everything – animal, vegetable and mineral – simply evaporated, or was vaporised by the extreme heat. The desert floor, where once buildings had stood, fused

* Taken directly from *Open University – Nuclear Weapons, inquiry analysis and debate U235 block II 1985: The Effects of Nuclear Weapons*, Glasstone and Dolan, US DOD and DOE, 1977; *Understanding Nuclear War*, Kosta Tsipis, Simon & Schuster, USA, 1983.

into a brown glass. As far out as 6 km living things simply melted, and soft materials such as plastics, wood, paint and furniture spontaneously combusted. On the outer edges of the circle of death caused by the heat pulse skin and bone welded to bricks and mortar leaving imprinted shadows of those that had stood there. Between 6 and 15 km the heat pulse caused instant second- and third-degree burns on any exposed skin. With their clothes afire, thousands of citizens tried to tear off their burning garments, only to find in horror that chunks of cooked flesh came away in their hands, exposing gleaming white bones. And into this area of instant fire followed the shock wave that caught the fires and rolled them into expanding balls of flame rushing through the streets at hundreds of miles per hour. It was as if the air itself had ignited.

The overpressures carried by the blast wave out to 7 kms were equivalent to a 200-ton giant hammer hitting the side of an average family house. Even at 20 km distance, which the blast wave reached approximately one minute after detonation, the force was still sufficient to smash windows and rip off roofs. Debris carried by the blast wave gave it the effect of a horizontal hail of maiming masonry, glass and metal fragments as buildings disintegrated in its path and were swept away. Those that were not were left with their frames twisted and distorted or leaning away from the blast as if in recoil.

But the destruction was not over. As the shock waves subsided in power the rising fireball and the thousands of instantaneous fires that had been caused by the heat pulse had a massive sucking effect in their demand for both oxygen and cooler air to replace that displaced. One minute after detonation the mushroom cloud of heated air had risen to 30,000 feet. As cooler air rushed in to replace the rising cloud, it provided fresh oxygen for every fire that burned, especially those in the outer areas caused by ruptured chemical, gas and petroleum pipes. The result was a massive back blast with winds rushing to the core at more than hurricane strength which ignited a firestorm, fanned the flames and continued to feed it for some thirty-six hours. With temperatures reaching up to 3,000°C, one of the unique and disgusting side effects of the firestorm was the settling of heavier carbon dioxide, resulting from combustion. The carbon dioxide sank into those places where the initial survivors had sought refuge, such as bunkers, basements, air-raid shelters and subway tunnels. The fortunate were asphyxiated by the poisonous gas. Those caught in sealed areas were dry-roasted like nuts in an oven, as the temperature rose but there was not enough oxygen to support combustion. All living things within the firestorm area perished. Inside the first half-hour Tehran lost perhaps one million killed and as many injured. But the shadow of death would hover for much longer, and Tehran was not alone.

The Die Is Cast

The Boeing 747 E-4B had been airborne from Andrews AFB Washington for six hours. The President's sixth sense had alerted her late the night before to the fact that the war for Israel was drawing to a desperate climax. She had given the National Security Council just over ninety minutes' notice that they were required on board what was the national command post in time of war. There was little surprise shown in the offices of the men and women whose views shaped the policy decisions and actions of the President. The most powerful individuals of the strongest nation the world had ever seen had clambered aboard the jumbo. They had spent much of their time airborne since the first hint of the biological attack emerged. The Vice-President and his identical team took up their stations in the Pentagon war room.

Following the difficult decision to effectively abandon Israel to her fate there was little more the President could do other than reiterate clear warnings to both sides that the use of weapons of mass destruction, if continued, might be considered a threat to the very existence of mankind itself.

It was 0625 Eastern Time, and the jumbo was flying a long and lazy racetrack out over Lake Erie at 39,000 feet. NORAD came on the link. The news was that Israel had fired a single Jericho 3 missile which had detonated over Tehran. Casualties were unknown, but expected to be high. In the aircraft there was absolute silence and disbelief. The world was, it seemed, out of control. Only three hours previously the President had assured the Prime Minister of Israel that the United States was not prepared to see her overrun and had repeated that she would do her utmost to defend Israel's right to exist. What her 'utmost' was was still not entirely clear, and practically the President had to admit to herself that America's course was the opposite. That was her second conversation with the Prime Minister that morning. The first had been harrowing. The full extent of the biological weapons attack on Israel was becoming clear. The final barrage of Scud missiles, the Prime Minister had informed her, contained cocktails of super-anthrax and an unknown strain of bubonic plague that was set to wipe out all but a remnant of Israel. The Prime Minister had warned that Israel was now ready to respond in full measure, unless the US was willing to act decisively to bring an immediate end to all fighting. The Israeli Prime Minister sounded desperate, almost in tears, his voice choked as he felt the life-blood of his nation being squeezed out.

US nuclear forces had been at Defcon Five, their highest readiness state since the firing of the Shahab 4. The President had made it clear to the leaders of the Islamic Alliance, including Saladin himself in his Qom war-fighting bunker, that the United States was seriously considering intervening with her own nuclear weapons against the Islamic Alliance ground forces unless the attack on Israel was called off. Saladin had replied that it was too late. Israel as a nation was dead; most of her people were dying and her nuclear arsenal had not only been neutralised but would soon be overrun. History would not thank her for killing hundreds of thousands, perhaps millions, more people in defence of what would soon be an empty nation. He pointed to the preparations Nato was still making in Turkey and said that he would only consider a halt – to watch Israel die – if Nato stopped its own build-up. Then, and only then, would he be prepared to sit down and discuss the future of the region as an equal partner. The President gave him no immediate

answer but could do no more than sigh as she faced her
advisers.

The United States had played all its cards bar one, the
nuclear one. Air power had singularly failed to coerce the
Islamic Alliance into doing the bidding of the West. The sum
of the strategic air campaign was indeed destruction of
infrastructure, power plants, oil, chemical and military industries across the Islamic crescent. Air power had lacked the
mass, reach and concentration of force to do enough damage
to have an immediate impact on the fighting initiative so
cleverly seized by the enemy.

Yet it was still the West alone which had the power and the
inclination to call a halt to the increasing levels of destruction
being wrought by both sides in the Middle East war. The
problem facing the President and her advisers was that for the
West to intervene decisively in what to the antagonists was a
total war, a war where there was no such thing as a non-
combatant, let alone non-combatant immunity, a war in
which every single death on either side was celebrated and
not mourned by the other, would cause many more deaths.
For the West to act decisively to call a halt, the only way open
appeared to be to increase the death toll by many tens or
possibly a couple of hundred thousand by throwing relatively
small nuclear missiles at the Islamic armies. The regional
conflict had escalated into total war. This was not just
another Arab–Israeli spat that could be brought to a swift
conclusion by superpower threats before the diplomats
stepped in to impose another temporary peace while the
antagonists prepared for the next war. This was, as far as
both Israel and the Islamic Alliance were concerned, the final
battle. This was a total war of annihilation, nation against
nation without compromise, as World War II had been. The
advisers had spent the time between the Israeli Prime Minister's pleading call and the news about the nuclear strike on
Tehran pondering sub-strategic nuclear strikes on the Islamic
armies that were closing in on Israel. Their conclusion was
that between eight and twelve weapons of 10 to 20 kilotons
would suffice to guarantee the end of the massed armies of
Islam. It was the same conclusion that Israel had come to.

Ninety minutes later the news got worse. Israel had fired two more Jerichos in quick succession, and Cheltenham had called to inform the President of launch clearance intercepts for a further two. NORAD had detected the launches within seconds. For fifteen minutes the world waited. NORAD came back on the link. Jericho 3s had hit Baghdad and Mecca. Israel was lashing out with all its might as a beaten man might when death seemed inevitable.

'They must be stopped,' breathed the President quietly. For the first time since the outbreak of hostilities the Israelis were referred to as 'they'. For six decades Israel had always been part of 'us'. Now in a single sentence the President had changed the attitude of a nation. She turned to Admiral John Mather Jr, the senior nuclear adviser, who had just returned from the communications area.

'What will it take, Admiral?' she asked simply.

The admiral understood the full implications of her question immediately. 'Well, ma'am, we would have to hit the Negev with probably four missiles. The Jericho 3 silos were designed and built by the very best people we have and the only way to be sure would be to dig them out.'

'Meaning what, exactly?'

'Meaning, ma'am, that we will have to ground-burst them. The missiles will need to be detonated just above the ground so that the blasts physically destroy the remaining Jericho silos. The downside, of course . . .'

'Is the amount of fallout. Is it not?' The President articulated his hesitation.

'Yes, ma'am.' And anticipating her next question he added, 'And the wind is from the south which means that we can expect the combined plume to cover most of Israel, the Syrian coast and southern Turkey, and I'm afraid there's more bad news.'

'What?'

'One of our satellites just picked up a clearance from Tel Aviv for the northern Jericho 2 bunker. They have been stuck fast inside for a few days but it seems that they're about to get one of the doors open, which would release possibly as many as ten ready-to-fire missiles. The targets will probably be Cairo, Alexandria, Beirut, Damascus, Amman . . .'

'They must be stopped,' the President repeated. 'I don't see that we have any other option.' She turned to the assembled company. 'Ladies and gentlemen, do you see any other options?' She was met by a wall of silence. 'So be it. Admiral, what do we have available?'

'Ma'am, we have an Ohio-class submarine fifty miles off Cap St Vincent, south-western Spain. Two Trident D-5s will do the job.'

'Admiral, make it so. And may God forgive me.'

'Yes, ma'am.'

USS *Wyoming* – SSBN 742 – Cap St Vincent

The USS *Wyoming*, SSBN 742, built by General Dynamics (Electric Boat Division) was part of the Atlantic Fleet based at King's Bay, Georgia. She was commissioned in July 1996 and was the penultimate of eighteen Ohio-class SSBNs to be built. Displacing 18,700 tons, the Ohio class was the largest series of submarines ever built by any Western navy. Each submarine carried twenty-four Trident D-5 missiles and each missile could carry between eight and fourteen real and dummy warheads. The D-5 was the final expression of the Trident programme. The missiles were 45 feet long and weighed up to 130,000 lbs each. The maximum range of the D-5 was in the order of 6,500 nautical miles, and by using DSMAC techniques (Digital Scene Matching Area Correlation) the system was capable of delivering each warhead with a terminal accuracy of around 100 metres. Thirteen minutes after the President had given the order, Captain Martin Standen of the USS *Wyoming* was ready to launch. The complete order was transmitted to the *Wyoming* via NOR-AD, dug deep into Cheyenne Mountain near Colorado Springs, including firing, targeting, warhead yields and release code words, and was received via *Wyoming*'s trailing ELF (Extremely Low Frequency) antenna. Standen had no idea where the targets were, and assumed, as did the rest of the command room, that some 'Ayrabs' were about to cop it. If he had known that the opposite was the case he might have hesitated about the next thirty seconds which would secure his place in history, alongside the crew of the *Enola Gay*.

The launches from numbers one and two tubes within thirty seconds of each other went very smoothly. The tube caps popped and the missiles burst to 50 feet above the water before the rocket motors cut in. The first stages accelerated the missiles to 4 km per second before burning out and being blown away. The second stages fired to accelerate the missiles to injection velocity. Within five minutes both missiles had exhausted their fuel but continued to climb through space up to a height of 1,500 km, hurtling silently on a ballistic trajectory through the vacuum at a speed of nearly 7 km per second before gravity pulled them back down towards their targets. As the dip began the 'buses', both carrying four 475-kiloton warheads and twice as many manoeuvring decoys, released their charges. In the final ten seconds the warheads re-entered the atmosphere. One minute later Israel's attempt at mutually assured destruction was over.

Days of Disaster

Masoud al Masoud was one of the first UN aid workers to reach Tehran from the outside world after the bomb had hit. He was flown in by a Russian Antonov transport aircraft as head of the UN Emergency Assistance Team. He died of leukaemia in 2008, a result of extended exposure to the high levels of radiation and fallout in and around the centre of Tehran after the nuclear attack. Of his team of twelve only three are still alive today. All were volunteers and all knew what their chances of survival were. This is an extract from his story.

I was working for the United Nations in New York on a six-month assignment as junior aide to Iran's Deputy Representative. For a civil servant who had been involved only in Department of Health affairs at home, this was my big chance to step on to the first rung of the ladder of rapid promotion to the top. My wife, Sabine, was delighted. However, as we had just had our third son and our eldest had recently started school we felt it was best that the family remained in Tehran to minimise the disruption that two moves would cause. In any event the pay in New York was at least four times my current salary and I would be able to save for a deposit on a flat of our own as well as return just before the New Year with armfuls of presents for those I loved.

We had a tearful parting at home before the Ministry car came to take me to the airport. This would be the first time we had been apart all our lives, having grown up in neighbouring apartments and been married at seventeen. Sabine was worried about the Israelis after the attack on Tehran the previous autumn. I assured her that she was in God's hands and whatever happened it was God's unchanging nature to ensure that justice was done, in this world or the next. I kissed her on the forehead as we heard the Mercedes pull up in the gravel outside. At the knock on the door she wrapped her black gown around herself to hide the blouse and miniskirt she was wearing underneath and lifted her veil and hood so that my last sight of her was her beautiful brown eyes. The baby was beginning to cry and the little ones wrapped themselves around me for one last hug.

The 747 lifted off from Tehran mid-morning. As it turned back over the city to set course for Amsterdam before going on to New York, I was able to see the whole city below basking in the early summer sun with the whitewashed buildings, minarets and mosques both dazzling and sparkling. It was a city that bustled and bubbled with life. The next time I saw the city it was dead.

I watched with increasing unease as the tensions grew in the Middle East. And after the Israelis bombed Cairo and Tripoli my fears grew. It was with some pride, I confess, that we had fired the nuclear weapon that exploded high over the Mediterranean, aimed not at the people of Israel but indirectly at their military machine. I felt sure that with much of their superior technology rendered useless we would be able to win the struggle against Zionism. Israel had shown her aggressive intentions by the invasion of the Sinai, and now she would learn what it felt like to be on the receiving end.

Two weeks later I was having dinner in the hotel restaurant with my colleagues and we were discussing the progress of the war. It was then that the concierge rushed in shouting about a massed nuclear attack by Israel. We were dumbstruck. Surely there was some mistake. Even the Israelis were not capable of such an extreme act. Nuclear war was always a theme that I regarded academically as some distant future event that was too horrifying to even contemplate seriously. And now it had happened and was suddenly an event that had come screaming out of the future to be one of the very recent past. The dining room was empty in seconds. Every other head had a mobile telephone attached to it. I hated them, and the cacophony of 'Greensleeves', 'Air on a G String' and other melodies that rang out in that tinny manner. Perhaps their brains needed a little warming or they wanted to lose their short-term memories to instantly forget what had just unfolded. As we crowded into the lobby to get to the television set I heard above the din the pretty announcer say 'Tehran'. The whole of my world collapsed. Even the news of the American attack on Israel did nothing to stir me out of my robotic stupor. I knew only that I had to get back to Sabine. I had to see for myself.

Within forty-eight hours I was on a flight to Moscow. From there the Russian Antonov, packed with tons of emergency medical supplies and my assembled team of experts, took seven long, droning hours to reach Tehran. I prayed all the way for my family, hoping against hope that they at least had survived. How could this have happened?

We touched down at what used to be Tehran airport just after midday. The landing was very rough as the pilot skidded and swerved down the runway to avoid the debris that was everywhere. As the rear loading ramp was lowered my heart sank. I knew then that my family had died along with the city. I began to weep uncontrollably. Over the city hung a mixed pall of grey, black and brown smoke. It looked as though a giant hand had swept through the city, rather as a child would knock over his building blocks. All the white had gone and the air was rank with acrid smoke that caught in the throat. We had donned charcoal-lined protective clothing as we began our descent. There were columns of smoke issuing all across the horizon from fires still burning in the city and suburbs. With our rubber gas masks on and hoods up, I ordered the driver of the first of our two white Gaz Jeeps to drive directly off the back of the aircraft and check out the control tower while we unloaded the first boxes of saline drips and bandages.

The airport seemed to be deserted, and as soon as the satellite telephones were set up we began our own journey to the centre of hell. It was curiously easy to tell how far from the centre of the blast we were at any one moment that day purely by the state of the survivors. The people that had survived seemed stupefied, aimless and without hope. It seemed that the dead were much better off – the living were depressed and nauseated, but these were the first clinical signs of a slow and painful death through exposure to radiation.

During the following weeks a pall of death hung over the city. The dust that had been lifted by the blast caused the sun and the moon to turn a dark red colour which left us to work in permanent twilight. We knew that this radioactive dust was deadly. There was actually very little we could do for most of the people. And there was human vomit everywhere. Our own when we saw and smelled those who had survived but had suffered disfiguring burns, some crisped to the bone, when we gagged until we were empty of bile, or at the sight of the beetles and bacteria setting about devouring the flesh of the dead as they started to rot. Within days there was a plague of beetles.

In Tehran there was nothing. No water, no heat, no light, no power, no food, no fuel, no rescue services, no fire-fighters, no roads, no transport, no shelters, no doctors, no nurses, no medicine, no social organisation. Nothing. There was only a mass of hopeless humanity that knew it was dying. The first signs of radiation sickness were the vomiting and diarrhoea. Those still alive with massive doses convulsed as we found them. Most died within the first two days through respiratory failure or severe brain damage. The lesser lethal doses were more pernicious. The radiation damages and destroys the internal structure of the cells of the body. The production of blood cells, especially white, drops. The poisoned blood loses its ability to nourish and repair the body. This in turn meant that wounds suffered did not heal and, with the resistance to infection of any kind lowered, disease was soon rife. The hair of those worst affected started to fall out in lumps within days. This was accompanied by severe and uncontrollable bleeding from the nose, mouth and bowels as lethal damage to the gastrointestinal system manifested itself. And all the while the survivors remained stunned, turned mute, full of fatigue, lethargy and without appetite.

For the rest there was only the certainty of the spectres of cancers, and leukaemias. The pregnant mothers were inconsolable in the knowledge that the unborn and even future generations would suffer deformity, mutation and mental retardation. Many chose death before death could claim them or their unborn. These were the days of disaster . . .

Operation Moses

Peled sat with his feet up on the kitchen table. He was peering thoughtfully into a half-filled glass of his finest, driest white, swilling it around from time to time as if uncertain of its body. He and young Jakob had spent the past seven weeks in the now abandoned farmhouse that adjoined his wine-growing estate. They had just had their first serious argument. Peled had been asleep upstairs, and there was a biting cold wind blowing in from the sea. Jakob had had enough of being cold and decided to light a fire in the old kitchen open fireplace. Peled had screamed at him, demanding to know whether he wanted to die today or not. Signs of life, smoke rising from a chimney, would alert the desperate and hungry for miles around. After stamping the fire out and kicking the contents across the cold tiled floor, Peled had opened a bottle of wine and sat brooding silently in the chair for two hours. Jakob, left to his own thoughts, considered events since the exo-atmospheric burst had turned them from high-tech warriors manning Israel's primary defensive weapons system to less than useful infantry.

In the dawn after the burst a perfunctory check was all that was required to confirm that the 4th Arrow Battery was electrically dead and beyond resurrection. Grabbing their Uzis, they had moved off Carmel and down to join the infantry at the bottom of the hill. The infantry, although they had nothing left to defend, had no orders to do anything else, so they stayed put. A whole day was spent digging the deepest slit trench for miles around. Peled intended to sit out the war in relative comfort.

It was the following morning, the 4th, when the first of the soldiers was struck down by the first symptoms of gangrenous smallpox. Within a further twenty-four hours four soldiers were ill. They were ordered at gunpoint into isolation. When two refused, the company commander took out his revolver and shot them. Peled decided that he was not going to be executed by his own people, and that night he and Jakob stole the only functioning vehicle for miles around, an ancient American Willeys Jeep, and headed for the coast south of Haifa and for Peled's estate. Mid-morning on the 6th Peled and Jakob had seen the Jericho launches, not knowing what they were, but guessing correctly as they admired the four white columns of smoke climb into space and disappear into the deep blue heading east and south. Peled expressed surprise when there were the sounds of distant thunder only minutes after, and had muttered something about Babylon getting its comeuppance, but he refused to be drawn on the subject and engrossed himself in a battered copy of a Christian Bible he had found on the shelf.

The next hour had been filled with terror and an expectation of certain death as the American Tridents had hit the Jericho launch areas. When the mild shock waves had finished rattling the old roof, Peled had ordered Jakob to clear the well-stocked larder of food and, muttering a string of oaths against the Arabs and the Russians, they boarded themselves in the cellar.

They had remained there for a week, living on tinned food and drinking wine from the well-stocked cellar, both of them sweating in fear of the first symptoms of flu, before Peled decided that any fallout would now be less of a radiation hazard. When they emerged there was no dust; the winds had been kind to the coastal plain. Peled had danced with delight on the discovery of an antique valve-driven radio set in one of the bedrooms. This ancient technology would have survived the electromagnetic pulse – not a circuit board in sight. There was enough battery life to get a faint signal from the BBC World Service on short wave.

They listened with incredulity as they managed to piece together the course of events since their 'desertion'. The fading battery, however, only enabled them to listen for between five and ten minutes each day. It seemed that Israel had fired Jerichos at Tehran, Mecca and Baghdad and a further four at the massed Islamic armies – these they knew about. But Peled was beside himself with rage when they heard that it was American Trident strikes that had laid waste much of Israel. When he had finished ranting he turned to Jakob and said: 'Now it has happened it is obvious. This was all promised long ago. All we had to do was think the unthinkable.'

They heard reports that thousands of tons of earth, rock, dirt and debris had been sucked up from the ground-bursts to form mushroom clouds that were highly impregnated with radioactive isotopes. The amount of fallout was horrific, and in the weeks that followed they listened to reports of deadly black or red rain. The clouds from the eleven weapons that detonated in and around Israel swept east across Jordan, Syria, Iraq and Iran. The number of people killed, or dying as a direct result of the strikes, was estimated at certainly tens of millions and possibly as many as two hundred million.

Jakob cried as the BBC voice described the devastation and desolation of Israel through the spread of gangrenous smallpox. There was also mention of disorder, gunfights, mass murders and even a rumour of cannibalism in Israel. The Great Plague, as the BBC voice had called it, was no respecter of borders or politics and had spread rapidly outward. It was halted by the third week in October by a combination of military force ensuring that the whole area was isolated –

anyone attempting to leave was killed – and natural barriers. In the west it was halted at the Nile, in the north on the Turkish border, and in the east and south-east only by the flooding of the Tigris and Euphrates and the vast Saudi Arabian desert. The Russians provided a vaccine, and this was rapidly produced at pharmaceutical plants throughout the world as mankind worked together for the first time to avert its own destruction. The BBC voice said that it was certain that the Great Plague had killed at least as many as the nuclear weapons, if not more.

The BBC voice had died ten days ago now, on 1 November, as the battery had finally expired. The last report they listened to announced that Nato and Turkish armies were to be joined from the north and west by Russian armies that were preparing to move through Syria, Iran and Iraq and down to the Saudi peninsula to restore stability in societies where all law and order had apparently broken down. Through the weeks of their isolation they heard sounds of distant gunfire, but did not see a soul. When the radio died, Jakob wanted to go to Tel Aviv to find Cecilia. Peled told him that if there was no law and order it was probable that any survivors would be roving in armed groups looking, and killing, for food. And anyway, he might as well face up to the fact that finding Cecilia alive was almost certainly going to be a lost cause.

'And we have enough here for another month as well as two hundred bottles of wine.' Peled seemed to relish the prospect. 'They will start looking for survivors soon,' he had confidently predicted. And Jakob knew his judgment well enough now to trust his musings on future events.

On 4 November, a week ago, they had heard the first sounds of the occasional helicopter clattering up and down the valley. Every time they heard one they grabbed their Uzis and rushed outside with Peled's old army field glasses to see if they could identify it from a cover position behind one of the low stone walls. It was the sound of a helicopter growing louder and more insistent as it drew close to the farmhouse which now caused Peled to slam down his glass and grab his gun and binoculars from the table.

They were halfway across the open yard when there was an

ear-splitting crash and explosion accompanied by flying bits of metal and stone. Something had just hit and destroyed the Jeep which they had attempted to conceal at the side of the farmhouse. As Jakob hit the dirt he heard the unmistakable low growl of a 30mm chain gun – the speed of sound finally catching up with the cannon shells. Peled and Jakob scrambled on elbows and knees back inside the farmhouse. From their cowering position they could hear a second helicopter edging its way closer.

'Well done,' said Peled sarcastically. 'That's your sodding fire that's attracted their attention.'

Jakob was considering a reply along the lines of it being inevitable that they would have to attempt to contact the outside world eventually, when above the sound of thudding blades there was a loudhailer voice speaking in clear English.

'Come out with your hands up and leave any weapons inside. If you resist the house will be destroyed. You have one minute.' The message was repeated in broken Hebrew.

'Doesn't look like we have much choice. We've got two hopes – no hope and Bob,' concluded Peled. 'Let's hope they're friendly, though I'm not so sure Israel has any friends left. Come on.' They stepped gingerly out into the chilled sunlight. There was a Blackhawk helicopter nose-on at 100 metres' distance. Beyond it to the left, a further kilometre away, sat an AH-64 Apache. Jakob could almost feel the chain gun tracking them as they walked forward, hands in the air.

'They must be Americans!' shouted Jakob over the double clattering of blades.

'Not necessarily,' grimaced Peled. 'The Egyptians have got those as well.'

'Now listen carefully and you will be rescued,' said the loudhailer. 'Take all your clothes off. This is a necessary precaution. You have one minute. Be warned that we have neither the time nor remit for dissent and resistance. Any funny business and you will be shot.'

'Oh dear,' muttered Peled. 'Ritual humiliation comes before execution.'

'That voice is pure English,' said Jakob. 'They must be good guys.'

Peled shouted his reply, his face hidden as he pulled his fleece warmer over his head. 'Do you know how many Arabs were trained at Sandhurst? Their English is impeccable. And anyway, it could be a recording.'

One minute later they were both naked and shivering, hands instinctively covering their embarrassment and shrinking genitalia. The Blackhawk dipped and came forward, remaining in a very low hover less than 50 metres away, still perfectly head-on so that its markings were obscured. The Apache too dipped and flew rapidly towards them in support, pulling up short 200 metres away.

'That's so he can't miss,' said Peled, remaining pessimistic. Out of the Blackhawk jumped three figures, each fully clad in protective gear. One, apparently the leader, had a revolver, the second a submachine-gun and the third sported a set of bright yellow spray tanks on his back which Peled assumed must be a flame-thrower. 'Good God, what a way to go,' he said. The leader gestured to them to come to the helicopter. Peled's worst fears were confirmed when they were close enough to see through the clear visor of the leader. The helicopter had a dusty black, white and red roundel on the side. A smiling face with black eyes and a Semitic complexion stared back.

'Egyptians,' said Peled. He hadn't planned this to be his last word.

'Gentlemen, this is your lucky day,' said the leader in perfect English. He motioned to the flame-thrower man. 'Turn around, close your eyes and brace yourselves. This might sting.' Jakob had already tensed. The smiling command to brace merely enabled his bowel muscles to relax as the flame-thrower man took aim.

Seconds later they were both engulfed in a cloud of cold, stinging, light yellow dust. Jakob nearly shat himself again in relief. 'Flame-thrower man' had transmogrified into 'decontam man'. He spent fifteen seconds spraying their body hair alone.

'All right, all right, Luigi, that's enough. They'll be clean enough for now.' The leader turned back to Peled's uncomprehending face and in answer to his observation said, 'Not Egyptian, my dear chap, English,' and then continued to forestall Peled's further questions. 'English Royal Air Force, I am a Sikh, born in London, on an exchange tour with the Italian Marines. The cab, I mean helicopter, is one we have, erm, borrowed from the Egyptians. Call me Dan. OK, let's get you into the cab. He motioned to the helicopter. They were made to sit in the doorway as Luigi sprayed the soles of their feet. Dan and the one with the submachine-gun sat in the door while Luigi did their boots before hopping up and turning the spray on his own. They were given vacu-packed undergarments, a coverall and a gas mask to wear. As soon as they were dressed, the helicopter lifted up over the farmhouse and headed west for the sea. Dan gave them headsets to wear with throat microphones. He smiled again. 'No doubt you've got a few questions.'

'How many?' asked Jakob. The Englishman knew what he meant. He had answered the question many times before. Jakob wanted to know how many Israelis had died.

'Difficult to say, but the latest estimates are in the region of five to six million. The papers are full of it. They're calling you survivors "The Remnant". It's from the Bible, I think. We reckon that we've evacuated around a quarter of a million with at least as many more to be pulled out. You know what they've called this?' He didn't wait for an answer. ' "Operation Moses". It's a kind of internationally organised exodus.'

'What did you spray us with?' Peled had regained his enquiring mind.

'Oh, that was just a simple decontam. Wait till you get to the *San Marco*, our mother ship, she's a kind of mini-disaster relief centre with a large helipad. They'll really clean you there. You know about the Great Plague?' Both men nodded. 'The problem is the spores in the soil. All the livestock is dead and rotted. The experts say the land of Israel is desolate. They mean largely uninhabitable in reality. They say that it . . .'

Peled interrupted him. 'Will be at least seventy years before anyone can safely return.'

'Very clever,' said Dan. 'How did you know that?'

'Intuition, my dear boy, intuition,' said Peled in his best Oxford English accent.

'OK, let me surprise you,' said Dan. 'I guess that you two claim descent either from the tribe of Levi or Judah.' He waited triumphantly. Peled felt that the conversation had degenerated into the kind of 'what star sign are you?' scenario he had experienced with small-talking bimbos in the States. Nevertheless Dan clearly felt he was on to something.

'I'm Judah,' said Jakob.

Reluctantly Peled answered, 'And I'm a Levite.' He paused before adding, 'The royal priesthood.'

Dan explained that well over 90 per cent of the survivors they had picked up and processed were from the Israeli tribes of Judah and Levi. There were a few Benjamites and only handfuls of survivors from the other nine tribes. The geneticists, biologists and not a few theologians were having a field day speculating on the apparent immunity. The newspapers had called it 'divine ethnic cleansing'.

'What happens next, I mean after we have been "processed", as you put it?' asked Jakob.

'Well, just about every country in the world has volunteered to take some Jews . . . er, Israelis.' Dan picked up a clipboard and leafed through the pages. 'I'm fairly sure that the batch you two will be assigned to after Cyprus is bound for . . . let me see.' He ran his finger down a list. 'Ah, here it is . . . Babylon!' He broke into a mischievous grin as Peled's eyes widened in alarm. 'Only kidding! New York, New York, so good they named it twice.'

'New York, New York, all the scandal and the vice,' sang Jakob, completing the song and enjoying Dan's joke.

'I love it!' they chimed together, and then burst into a fit of laughter behind their gas masks.

Peled smiled too. He realised then that he had not smiled for a long, long time. Such was the irreverence of youth. Their seconds of joy were irrepressible and contagious. There was always hope for the future. He sang softly, 'Start spreading the news . . . I'm leaving today . . .' He was joined in perfect harmony by a female voice. 'I want to be a part of it . . .'

Jakob sat bolt upright. He knew that voice. Until now he

had ignored the other four figures slumped with fatigue at the front of the helicopter.

'Ces, is that you?' he hardly dared ask.

'Yes, Mordi, it's me,' she said softly.

'Hallelujah!'

Epilogue

Today is 11 November 2009. I have been able to give you only a glimpse of what happened, through the eyes of just a small handful of those who fought. There are thousands more tales yet untold, and there will be time enough for them as well as more sober histories when the archives are unlocked. It is ninety-one years since the end of the 'war that was to end all wars'. And we have seen almost a century of endless war. The Jewish nation is again without a homeland and The Remnant is scattered across the globe. The experts say that the very earliest return will be in 2050.

The populations of Libya, Egypt, Jordan, Syria, Iraq, Iran and Saudi Arabia were devastated by the Great Plague. The USA and Europe have already poured billions of dollars into the reconstruction of those cities and societies in a new Marshall Plan. The figurehead of this massive aid plan is retired US President Bill Clinton. What kind of societies will emerge remains unclear. What is almost certain is that the people and not a handful of families will decide. Unless, of course, Saladin rises from the ashes. Of him, his bunker and his staff there has been no trace.

But we have not seen an end to war, the little wars. Sub-Saharan Africa, like Ulster and parts of the Balkans, rumbles on in the grip of seemingly endless and pointless bloodshed. While there are chieftains and warlords, whether armed with machete or submachine-gun and mobile phone, we will always have war.

The Russian Empire is due to join Nato next year, as a full and equal member. With China fully embracing democracy, and Christianity for that matter, there is talk of the possibility of destroying all weapons of mass destruction, nuclear, chemical and biological, within perhaps twenty years. But things are delicately balanced. The US, Europe and Japan will have a

Star Wars Missile Defence System in place by 2015. And unless Russia can make its economy work by selling plough-shares instead of swords, it seems inevitable that the next generation, or the one after, will see war again as soon as the horrors of 2006 have been dimmed by time.

Roll on the next one.

GLOSSARY

AA	Anti-Aircraft
AAA	Anti-Aircraft Artillery
AAW	Anti-Air Warfare
ABL	Airborne Laser
AD	Air Defence
ADC	Aide de Camp
AF	Air Force
AFB	(US) Air Force Base
AFV	Armoured Fighting Vehicle
AGM	Air-to-Ground Missile
AH-1 Cobra	US-built attack helicopter
AH-64 Apache	US-built attack helicopter
AKM	Updated version of ubiquitous AK-47 Kalashnikov assault rifle
Alamo	Russian air-to-air missile
ALARM	Air-Launched Anti-Radiation (Radar) Missile. UK HARM equivalent
AMRAAM	Advanced Medium-Range Air-to-Air Missile
APC	Armoured Personnel Carrier
ARM	Anti-Radar or Radiation Missile
ARRC	Allied Command Europe Rapid Reaction Corps
ASRAAM	Advanced Short-Range Air-to-Air Missile
ASW	Anti-Submarine Warfare
ATBM	Anti-Tactical Ballistic Missile
ATGM	Anti-Tank Guided Missile
AWACs	Airborne Early Warning and Control Aircraft
Battalion	300–500 soldiers, 3–4 companies
BMP	Russian tracked infantry fighting vehicle

Brigade	3,000–5,000 soldiers in 2–6 regiments or 10+ battalions
BTR	Russian wheeled armoured personnel carrier family
BVRAAM	Beyond Visual Range Air-to-Air Missile
C2	Command and Control
C3	Command, Control and Communications
CAP	Combat Air Patrol
CAS	Close Air Support
CBG	Carrier Battle Group
CBU	Cluster Bomb Unit
CDU	Christian Democratic Union
CH-53	American-built transport helicopter
Company	90–150 soldiers in 3–4 platoons
Corps	20,000–150,000 soldiers in 2–6 divisions
CP	Command Post
CSU	Christian Socialist Union (Bavarian Wing of the CDU)
CV	Aircraft Carrier
CVN	Nuclear Powered Aircraft Carrier
DASS	Defensive Aids Sub System – self-protection suite fitted to Eurofighter Typhoon
Division	10,000–30,000 soldiers in 2–6 brigades
DMZ	Demilitarised Zone
DVI	Direct Voice Input
E-3	AWACs aircraft
EAF	Egyptian Air Force
ECCM	Electronic Counter-Counter-Measures
ECM	Electronic Counter-Measures
ECR	Electronic Combat and Reconnaissance
ECR-90	European Combat Radar installed in Eurofighter Typhoon
EFA	European Fighter Aircraft
ELINT	Electronic intelligence
ELS	Electronic Listening System
ESM	Electronic Support Measures
EMP	Electromagnetic Pulse

EuroFor B	European Force in Bosnia – successor to SFOR
EuroFor G	European Force in Golan
EuroFor K	European Force in Kosovo
EuroFor M	European Force in Montenegro
EuroFor U	European Force in Ulster
EW	Electronic Warfare
F-15I	Thunder – Israeli version of US F-15E Strike Eagle
FAC	Forward Air Controller
FCR	Fire-Control Radar
FFE	Front for Freedom and Equality (Algeria)
FIS	Islamic Salvation Front (Algeria)
FRAAM	Future Air-to-Air Missile
FRPG	Five Rocket Propelled Grenade
GBU	Guided Bomb Unit
Gepard	German twin 35mm AA gun
GPS	Global Positioning System
HARM	High Speed Anti-Radiation Missile
HAS	Hardened Aircraft Shelter
HE	High Explosive
HEAT	High Explosive Anti-Tank
HMG	Heavy Machine Gun
HUD	Head Up Display
HUMINT	Human intelligence
HVM	Starstreak Hyper-Velocity Missile – British SAM
IAF	Israeli Air Force
ICBM	Inter-Continental Ballistic Missile
IDF	Israeli Defence Force
IFV	Infantry Fighting Vehicle
IR	Infra Red
IRBM	Intermediate-Range Ballistic Missile
IRSTS	Infra Red Search and Track System
JDAM	Joint Direct Attack Munition – GPS-guided bomb
JSF	Joint Strike Fighter
JSTARS	Joint Surveillance Target Attack Radar System

JTIDS	Joint Tactical Information Distribution System
K-I	South Korean Main Battle Tank
KLA	Kosovo Liberation Army
LAV	Light Armoured Vehicle – family of wheeled APCs built for US Marines exported to Middle East
LGB	Laser-Guided Bomb
Link	Short for Digital Data Link, normally followed by a number
MAC	Military Airlift Command
Manpads	Man Portable Air Defence System – generic term for hand-held SAMs
MBT	Mai MiG Battle Tank
Mech	Mechanised
MEZ	Missile Engagement Zone
Mig 17/19/21	Obsolete Russian fighters
MIRV	Multiple Independent Targeted Reentry Vehicles
MLRS	Multi-Launch Rocket System
MoD	Ministry of Defence
MRBM	Medium-Range Ballistic Missile
NBC	Nuclear, Biological and Chemical
NKAF	North Korean Air Force
NKPA	North Korean People's Army
NORAD	North American Air Defence (Command)
NRF	Nato Reaction Force
PA	Palestinian Authority
PAC	Patriot Advanced Capability
PDL	Point Defence Laser
PFC	Private First Class
PK	Probability of Kill
PKK	Kurdistan Workers Party
Platoon	20–35 soldiers
POL	Petrol Oil and Lubricants
POP	Public Opinion Paralysis
PoWs	Prisoners of War
PWO(A)	Principal Warfare Officer (Air)
Regiment	800–1,500 soldiers in 3–5 battalions

RoE	Rules of engagement
Roland	German short-range self-propelled SAM
RPG	Rocket-Propelled Grenade
RPV	Remotely Piloted Vehicle, also known as drones
RSAF	Royal, latterly Revolutionary, Saudi Air Force
RSC4I	Reconnaissance, Surveillance. Command, Control, Communications, Computers & Intelligence
S-300	Also known as the SA-10 – Russian equivalent of Patriot SAM
SA-4	old Russian-built SAM
SA-6	old but capable Russian-built SAM
SA-7	hand-held Russian heat-seeking SAM
SA-8	Vehicle-mounted short-range Russian SAM
SA-15/16	Improved versions of SA-7
SACEUR	Supreme Allied Commander Europe
SAM	Surface-to-Air Missile
SEAD	Suppression of Enemy Air Defences
SF	Special Forces
SFOR	Stabilisation Force – Nato force in Bosnia
SHAPE	Supreme Headquarters Allied Powers Europe – Mous, Belgium.
SIGINT	Signals intelligence
SKAF	South Korean Air Force
SLAM	Supersonic Land Attack Missile
Spetnatz	Russian special forces – SAS equivalent
SSGN	Nuclear Powered Guided Missile Submarine
SSM	Surface-to-Surface Missile
SSN	Conventional diesel attack submarine
SSBN	ICBM-carrying nuclear-powered submarine
Storm Shadow	UK-built air-launched stand-off missile
SU-27/SU-32/ SU-35/SU-37	Versions of Russian Flanker fighter aircraft
T-62	Obsolete Russian-built tank

T-72	Russian tank, widely exported
TEL	Transporter Erector Launcher (normally of missiles)
TEZ	Total Exclusion Zone
TFR	Terrain-Following Radar
TG	Task Group
THAADS	Theatre High-Altitude Air Defence System
TLAM	Tomahawk Land Attack Missile
TMD	Theatre Missile Defence
TOW	US-made anti-tank guided missile
TRD	Towed Radar Decoy
TRIGAT	Third-Generation Anti-Tank Missile
Tunguska, 2S6	Russian self-propelled SAM and AA vehicle
UAE	United Arab Emirates
UAV	Unmanned (or Uninhabited) Air Vehicle
UNIFIL	United Nations Force in Lebanon
USAF	United States AirForce
USN	United States Navy
VX	Nerve Gas
WBAG	West Bank Action Group
WEU	Western European Union
WMD	Weapons of Mass Destruction
WSO	Weapons System Officer
WTO	World Trade Organisation
ZSU 23/4	Russian-built self-propelled AA vehicle with 4 × 23mm cannon

Index